CIVIL WARRIORS

DELACORTE PRESS

CIVIL
WARRIORS

THE LEGAL SIEGE ON
THE TOBACCO INDUSTRY

DAN ZEGART

Published by
Delacorte Press
a division of
Random House, Inc.
1540 Broadway
New York, New York 10036

Library of Congress Cataloging in Publication Data
Zegart, Dan.
  Civil Warriors : the legal siege on the tobacco industry / Dan Zegart.
      p.   cm.
    Includes index.
    ISBN 0-385-31935-5
  1. Trials (Products liability)—United States. 2. Products
liability—Tobacco—United States. 3. Tobacco industry—
    Law and legislation—United States. 4. Tobacco—
        Physiological effect. I. Title.
          KF226.Z44 2000
346.7303'8—dc21   99-050139

Manufactured in the United States of America
Published simultaneously in Canada
June 2000
10 9 8 7 6 5 4 3 2 1
BVG

For Arthur,

who knew all the right questions

CONTENTS

FIRST MURDERER: Remember our reward when the deed's done.

SECOND MURDERER: Zounds, he dies! I had forgot the reward.

FIRST MURDERER: Where's thy conscience now?

SECOND MURDERER: O, in the Duke of Gloucester's purse.

WILLIAM SHAKESPEARE

Richard III, Act I, Scene iv

THE LAST TOBACCO TRIAL

RON MOTLEY HARDLY SLEPT THE NIGHT BEFORE THE VERDICT.
He went to bed in his suite on the seventh floor of the Radisson at ten o'clock complaining of a headache and never really dozed off. His bodyguard, a refrigerator-sized black man named Larry, who once provided security for the Saudi royal family, watched television with him and retired to his room.

Larry was there because Motley had received a steady stream of death threats since he'd started suing tobacco companies four years earlier. Another had come a week before.

"We know where you are and you'll be dead by midnight," said a voice on his answering machine back home in South Carolina.

By the spring of 1998, the anti-tobacco side had lost a lot of sleep worrying about stolen information, tapped phones, hidden documents, and death threats. It gave rise to jokes about living in a John Grisham novel, but it wasn't very funny for those on the inside of the experience. Jeffrey Wigand, a tobacco whistle-blower and close friend of Motley's, moved out of Louisville, Kentucky, after being threatened by telephone and having a bullet left in his mailbox. The bullet was an armor-piercing Israeli specialty round, a very nasty addition to the day's bills and letters. A lawyer for another ex–tobacco insider became convinced he was being followed one day in traffic, jumped out of his car at a red light, ran back to the other car, and screamed that if he ever saw the driver again, he'd beat him to a pulp.

Motley wondered whether it was all a continuum. Would an industry that lied and shredded also wiretap and have you followed? Would they put a bullet in your mailbox? Would they beat you up? Ness, Motley, Loadholt, Richardson & Poole, Motley's law firm in Charleston, South Carolina, which had spent $30 million on tobacco cases and so far received not a red cent in return, took no chances. They hired the best bodyguard they could find, and that was Larry.

It made eminent sense to me that if anyone was going to be knocked off, it probably should be Motley. I had traveled with him enough to know he was the wartime consigliere, the chief soldier on the plaintiff's side. Here in Muncie, Indiana, he put his case against the industry before a jury for six long weeks in February and March of 1998. He had spent almost five years building it, fighting to get documents, taking scores of depositions, developing elaborate charts and videos on how tobacco smoke assaults the lung, befriending people like Jeff Wigand, whom Motley flew to Charleston after Wigand lost his home, his job, and his marriage.

And now, having completed the biggest fight of his tobacco life, Motley ached to go to sleep. But he couldn't.

Forty other people from Ness, Motley had also come to Muncie, taking the whole third and seventh floors of the Radisson for offices and sleeping quarters from January into the spring. While Motley tossed and turned upstairs, most of them were at a big, loud party in the Radisson bar, where they got drunker and blearier than they had gotten in a really long time. The men and women who attack giant corporations for a living aren't shy and retiring, and there was a good deal of bright plumage in evidence—pastel suits, paisley ties, and cowboy boots—and an abundance of comely female junior lawyers and aides in form-fitting dresses and short skirts. There was a lot of noise and a lot of laughter. A little later, some of the tobacco lawyers showed up, a quieter, more conservative breed. But in the end, the tobacco crowd and the plaintiff's bunch made merry together, more or less, the steadily drinking tobacco men drooping in their trench coats over the Ness, Motley women.

Motley didn't materialize downstairs until the next afternoon, a full day into the jury's deliberations and long after the party had ended. He strolled into the lobby and sat down in a chair to wait for news. Within minutes he was surrounded by the secretaries and paralegals and junior lawyers who make his entourage one of the more fetching flying circuses outside of the rock 'n' roll world— about which a female reporter in Florida once remarked, "Aren't there any *male* assistants?" Somebody opened a couple of beers and the ladies took turns massaging his neck.

It was a balmy March day in Indiana and by seven o'clock there was still no word from the jury. Someone arranged to have a Suburban come and take what was generally called the Motley Crew— and me—to a steak restaurant.

As we drove across the little city and its gloomy boarded-up downtown, I thought back to the summer of 1994, when I first met Ron Motley, which in retrospect seemed a time of such optimism and simplicity.

The man who answered the door of a New Orleans hotel room had slicked-back black hair and a deep southern accent. He wore a hand-tailored blue silk suit, but his socks didn't match; I later learned he was color blind. His handshake was ice cold, as if all the blood had gone to his face, which was red. He had piercing dark eyes, but a voice like warm bourbon.

We sat down and talked while he munched a waffle at a little glass-topped table near the window, his right leg bouncing up and down like it had electrodes on it.

He became steadily more intoxicated with his story as he explained why he was out to get the tobacco men.

"I'm telling you, you can't find a family in America they haven't touched," he said, veins standing out in his neck.

"That's why we're going to beat 'em."

He sprang up and fluttered through the room, yanking papers out of a briefcase, stepping into the bathroom.

"Eventually," he muttered, peering into the mirror.

Then he darted out and grabbed the phone, charming his way past a colleague's child to learn whether Ness, Motley had won a court decision on a $1.3 billion asbestos lawsuit.

At that time, Motley and others were massing the talent of the biggest personal-injury law firms in the country for an assault on the hitherto impregnable citadel of tobacco. This coalition improved the odds considerably for the plaintiff's side against an industry that by a very conservative estimate had wiped out 7 million

Americans since the Surgeon General first warned that cigarette smoking may be hazardous to your health.

Another set of arithmetic showed that the several dozen firms that joined forces with Motley had already extracted billions of dollars from the asbestos and pharmaceuticals industries, whose products had injured a tiny fraction of the lives laid waste by cigarettes. Yet the tobacco industry had never paid damages to a soul. To the plaintiff's lawyers the cigarette cartel was Mount Everest, or maybe Fort Knox. These two forces seemed destined to meet in some historic conflict.

It began early in 1994 with a damaging series of newspaper and television stories about the cigarette companies' thirty-year search for the perfect nicotine technology, which led to an embarrassing run of congressional hearings during which the heads of the companies swore that they believed their hired scientists were more trustworthy than the world public health establishment. The spectacle amounted to a kind of Stalingrad for the industry, a defining moment that finally and indelibly poisoned the atmosphere for the cigarette makers and spawned monumental lawsuits.

And so began not a civil action but a civil war, a conflagration in the civil justice system encompassing first dozens and then hundreds of lawsuits, in which each side fired darts hoping to score a puncture through which they could suck out the other side's money.

The commander of the infantry was Ron Motley, and between 1994 and 1999, I traveled with him all over the United States—Burlington, Vermont, to Ashdown, Arkansas—and saw him prepare or conduct seven trials in five states and bring three to the point where the tobacco industry agreed to pay a total of $33 billion.

Motley was and is one of the most successful civil trial lawyers in the country, not the richest, but nevertheless a millionaire many times over. Unlike others who homed in like birds of prey on weakened opponents looking to settle, Motley's reputation was for winning verdicts in the courtroom.

For this he paid a price. At fifty-three, much of his life had been lived in hotel suites during trials that often dragged on for months, or on his jet—actually the firm's, but his for all practical purposes—as he swooped in somewhere to take a deposition. It was probably fortunate that Motley lived for the thrill of the hunt. There was precious little else in his world: two grown children, two vast houses in Charleston that he almost never saw, and an embittered ex-wife.

He had a charisma that worked with juries, an apparent lack of guile, devilish humor, and could render complex legal or scientific issues into everyday speech. Maybe the female jurors, like other women, were attracted by good looks that one writer compared to Jean-Paul Belmondo's, though as soon as he opened his mouth you thought of Tommy Lee Jones. When he'd mentioned to an asbestos jury in Houston a few years earlier that he was engaged to be married, the panel burst into applause. "That was not a good moment," admitted a member of the defense team, whose clients were later hit with a massive judgment against them.

In private, Motley was less than admiring of many of his colleagues and opponents. He dismissed another personal injury lawyer's efforts as "full of sound and fury, signifying nothing." He didn't suffer fools at all. One of his assistants was "useless as tits on a bull." He branded a cigarette company lawyer "a frustrated dwarf," and said "they can send that guy against me anytime, I'll eat him for lunch." As befitted someone whose talents were outsized and largely self-taught, he saw no equal among other lawyers.

"The difference between me and them is I know where the courtroom is," he said.

But there was more to Motley than an ego that would compare favorably to those of fighter pilots, brain surgeons, and other single-combat warriors. Even when he played to the cameras, he spoke from the heart. He was loyal to clients and their causes. He felt so bad about losing one asbestos case that he paid for the college education of the victim's daughter, who has spina bifida. His interest in cigarette cases had deep roots: he had watched his mother slowly suffocate from emphysema.

As his family life shrank, his work claimed more and more private territory. He bought golden retrievers and named them Chrysotile and Amosite, after varieties of asbestos, but it was Okie, a wiseguy Labrador, who rode in the back of the jet with him on long trips.

Since 1994, he and his people had traveled like a nomadic tribe from Pascagoula, Mississippi, to Palm Beach, Florida, to Texarkana, Texas, to fight the industry in big cases on behalf of the attorney general of each state, each of which ended in a multibillion-dollar settlement. This lawsuit in Muncie, Indiana, didn't settle, but came as the wave of tobacco suits was breaking. Many in Motley's firm wanted to get out of tobacco litigation.

Motley called it "the floating chessboard." He moved the pieces, tried the cases, kept the other side's king in jeopardy. But there were bigger players than Motley who could at one stroke realign the board and change the game—or end it. They included allies in Washington trying to negotiate an end to virtually all tobacco actions. If they succeeded, Motley would probably never again have the full resources of a big firm behind him to take on the cigarette makers at trial.

Motley supported the proposed armistice, having little choice since his firm had helped broker it.

Enter Cliff Douglas, white-collar guerilla, rebel with a fax machine and sworn enemy of both tobacco and the deal. He had been Motley's valued ally, but broke publicly with him over this.

The motto on Douglas's wall was, "If you think you're too small to be effective, you've never been in bed with a mosquito."

Like Motley, Douglas was an attorney who had dedicated his life to a cause. But unlike Motley, it had not made him rich. It had barely made him middle class.

Douglas ran his own consulting firm, through which he lawyered for anti-tobacco lawsuits, gave speeches, did media work, leaked documents, cultivated whistle-blowers, drafted congressional legislation, and helped launch a federal criminal investigation. No single person had done more to make America hostile to tobacco than Cliff Douglas.

Douglas had no Crew. He was a lone wolf, but one capable of causing a lot of mischief. Respected in both the political capital of Washington and the media capital of New York, his recipe for unleashing a great howling upon the tobacco enterprise and its collaborators was uniquely his own.

Take one nasty-smelling industry document . . . baste with sound bites from sympathetic congressmen . . . toss to waiting newshounds—*voilà*! One very bad day on television for Mr. Butts.

In fact, Douglas had been responsible for tobacco's worst television day ever when he convinced a paranoid young female engineer at a tobacco company to appear on a program explaining how the companies manipulated the modern cigarette to make it more addictive.

Douglas did all this from his lair in Ann Arbor, Michigan, a basement office that contained everything needed to do the Cliff Douglas Show: fax machine, phone, computer, bulletin board stuck with buttons with red diagonal NO PARKING–type stripes on them, and desk.

The only exotic piece of equipment in the room was Douglas. I first realized how exotic when someone told me how he and a couple of Douglas's other friends were walking down the street with Douglas in Washington when a man came flying out of a drugstore with a stolen tape player under his arm.

Two store employees were in hot pursuit, but the robber was fast and they were losing him.

Douglas, a marathoner and varsity sprinter in college, whipped after the man and, in a couple of blocks, caught up to him and cornered him in an alley. The robber had to drop the goods to scale a chain-link fence and escape.

After a stop in the bathroom, he rejoined his friends at a nearby Chinese restaurant for lunch. What his friends didn't know was *why* Douglas went into the bathroom, which he confided later to his journal:

> I cried for the poor guy whom I had just helped to chase down and defeat and all the millions of others who feel compelled to feed themselves by engaging in petty thievery.

This was not an Organization Man, which was why he was so effective, and so poor. But the network of people who informally helped Douglas reached just about everywhere, including Muncie. As we drove toward the steak joint, Douglas called the cell phone of ABC-TV producer Keith Summa, who was in Muncie covering Motley's trial, to find out the latest.

"Having dinner with the boys," reported Summa, who had known Douglas for years, the last three of which he had spent following Motley.

"The boys" were his camera crew and a correspondent from ABC in Chicago. Like other reporters, Summa believed that if anyone could win a cigarette trial, and win it big, it was Ron Motley. If that happened, Summa's story was almost guaranteed a slot on *World News Tonight* with Peter Jennings, and eleven million people would learn of it. If it didn't happen, there would be no story at all. Losing to a tobacco company wasn't news. It was extremely routine.

So with Motley's firm eager to leave cigarette litigation after five punishing years, and the press hungering for a big win against the cigarette companies, it all came down to this jury in Muncie pondering a lawsuit on behalf of a woman who died of lung cancer but never smoked. She was, in fact, a Wesleyan missionary who grew up in a religious household, married a minister, had a missionary for a son, and didn't ever see cigarettes in her home, nor alcohol, nor *dancing on friggin' Sunday*, as Motley would say. But Mildred Wiley had worked for seventeen years in a blue haze of tobacco smoke in a Veterans Administration hospital, and Motley contended it killed her.

No, the tobacco companies said. It could have been radon gas in her basement. Or Wiley may have had pancreatic cancer, not lung cancer. *Cancer is a mystery,* the industry liked to say when faced with yet another dead person in court. We *hear* smoking causes cancer, but if you really examine it, you find *science just doesn't have the answers*. It could be radon or diesel fumes—or cosmic rays, as they argued in another case. And always, eminent scientists took the stand to advocate forcefully for the theory du jour. There were hundreds of them, along with experts of all stripes: pathologists, epidemiologists, oncologists, historians, business ethicists, biochemists, toxicologists, otolaryngologists, thoracic surgeons, dentists, psychiatrists, statisticians, and lawyers, always lawyers, thousands of them, all over the world, running this muscular litigation engine. With more than three million dead customers a year, the pool of potential plaintiffs was so vast that if tobacco began to lose with any consistency, the industry would cease to exist.

THE TRIP FROM THE MUNCIE RADISSON TO THE STEAK house seemed to take forever. Motley's cell phone rang, but it was just a message from his secretary back in Charleston.

"Who Are You" by the Who came on the car radio.

"Turn that up," commanded Motley from the backseat, where he was sandwiched between his girlfriend and a female lawyer, his long legs folded awkwardly before him.

"Goddamn, I'm tired of that phone," said Motley. "I'm going pitch it out the damned window. Office calls me about absolutely nothing, like nobody can do anything without asking me about it."

Who are you? Who ooh, who ooh.
Well, I really want to know . . .

Motley brooded.

As the Suburban bounced past a partly extinguished neon sign near the restaurant, it felt like all the years of suing tobacco had boiled down to the twenty minutes it took us to get here. Perhaps they were crucial minutes for the jury, deliberating in a little room on the other side of town.

I woke up in a Soho doorway
A policeman knew my name . . .

The truth was, Motley was far from confident about the outcome. He had put on an impressive case, the cream of the scientific witnesses, dozens of incriminating internal documents. But a trial is like a filter through which only certain particles of data reach the jurors. Industry lawyers had expertly screened out Motley's strongest scientific evidence, which worried him. And there was another vital piece of information tobacco prevented the jury from hearing: that the federal government, in a separate proceeding, had already determined Mildred Wiley died of lung cancer induced not by radon or diesel fumes or cosmic rays, but by secondhand smoke.

At the steak place, waiters scrambled to prepare a table for ten. We had just sat down and were about to order when a cell phone belonging to one of the junior lawyers rang.

"Jury's back. Judge says we have about forty minutes," she said.

Motley frowned, glanced at his watch.

"Well, fine," he said. "Let's have a drink and an appetizer."

Someone phoned Larry at the hotel, where he was making arrangements to shield the Wiley family from the press mob now assembling at the courtroom, from which it was an easy fifty-yard dash to a row of TV transmission trucks waiting on the street outside, engines running, their white antennae aloft.

Soon all of us at the steak place—Motley, me, two local lawyers and their wives, a paralegal, the junior lawyer, Motley's girlfriend, and a reporter for a financial wire service—were climbing back into the vehicles, driving like mad fools for the courthouse, though not before we'd vacuumed up a round of nachos and beer.

THE TEMPLE OF THE LAW

A LOT OF PEOPLE WERE FOLLOWING MOTLEY'S PERFOR-
mance in Muncie, including a tiny, stooped, east Texas lawyer
named Scott Baldwin, who had known Motley for twenty years.
Motley always referred to Baldwin as a beloved mentor and his
greatest influence. Now seventy, Baldwin had observed Motley's tobacco campaign with growing respect. Of course, he wasn't really
surprised, because he had already seen Motley revolutionize the
profession Baldwin helped invent.

The array of scientific expertise Motley wielded in Muncie was
a long way from the two-foot-long ignition key Baldwin cut from
scrap lumber and wrapped in aluminum foil back in 1964, when
Motley was still in college.

The key fit the ignition from a 1960 Chevrolet Bel Air, which
sat on the plaintiff's table throughout a week-long trial. The leads
from the silver ignition cylinder ran to an auto horn on one side and
a car battery on the other. Baldwin had designed this contraption so
that when the circuit was closed by the removal of the key, there
would be plenty of juice for the horn to just blast everybody out of
the room.

What it all boiled down to was that Baldwin's client, Mrs. Bar-
bara June Muncy, was walking down the street in Kilgore, Texas,
when a 1960 Chevy occupied by a mother and daughter rolled to a
stop in front of Duncan's Variety Store. As is still the custom in

some Texas towns, they parked perpendicular to the curb, with the car's nose pointed at the store.

The ignition under the blue metal dashboard of the Bel Air was part of what GM called its "single-key system," which meant the same key unlocked trunk, doors, and ignition. By design, the key could be removed while the ignition was on.

Or even with the engine running.

The Chevy was still idling as Mrs. Muncy strolled by the Variety Store's display window, and continued running as the daughter yanked the key out of the ignition and got out. Then the mother, whose door was blocked by another car, squeezed across the seat to the driver's side to get out, accidentally stomping the gas pedal. It turned out the car was still in gear, and the sedan shot toward the store like a spring-loaded two-ton fist that punched Mrs. Muncy into the display window.

The window exploded, and Mrs. Muncy's left leg was severed, while the flesh was torn from her right leg, exposing the bone from knee to ankle. She was lucky not to have been beheaded, as had happened many times in accidents involving plate glass windows.

All week in federal court, Baldwin stood in front of this little heap of auto junk on the plaintiff's table and told the jury that General Motors *could* have put some kind of a buzzer or a light or maybe even a horn on the Chevy's ignition as a warning when the key was withdrawn. The company *should* have foreseen that somewhere in the world, someone was going to accidentally hit the gas and out would scream this big dumb metal beast. How hard could it be to put a safety gadget on a car ignition? asked Baldwin in his soft drawl.

Completely unfeasible, said GM's expert witnesses, not to mention a nuisance for the driver, and just fundamentally not in the cards in 1960. They made it sound like GM would have had to create some kind of Manhattan Project to pull it off.

The judge refused to force GM to give Baldwin internal documents about the ignition. Undaunted, Baldwin put on a "human factors engineer," an expert on designing machines according to how humans interact with them. He insisted it was no great trick to make a key that won't come out when the engine is running, or have the key's removal trigger a warning.

GM's lawyer got up to cross-examine. Aren't you misleading the jury about how easy it is to do something like that? he asked as he grabbed the two-foot-long silver key and yanked it out, and Baldwin's auto horn contraption went off and indeed it was joyously and triumphantly deafening. It rang loudly in the jury's ears while they deliberated and rang the defense all the way back to Detroit.

Baldwin's $225,000 verdict was reversed on appeal because the law in the early sixties hadn't caught up with what juries were only just beginning to do—punish manufacturers for killing. Still, the case of *Mrs. Barbara June Muncy* v. *General Motors Corp.* instantly made Scott Baldwin a hero of a nascent specialty known as products liability law, whose practitioners sued companies on behalf of people injured by ordinary consumer goods. They were paid a percentage of the damage award, if any. So by hiring one of them, even the poorest citizen could call a giant company to account, at least in theory. The United States was the only country that had this species.

When they eventually joined forces years later, Baldwin used the *Muncy* case to teach young Motley to use "demonstrative exhibits" like his ignition-rig thingamabob, something few civil lawyers did in the late fifties and early sixties, which was when Baldwin started suing giant companies.

He found no shortage of injured clients. So many mass-produced goods were unsafe, and changes in the law were just beginning to force the manufacturer to pay for its mistakes. After all, the victim's only error was to buy something that turned out to have death in it: a birth control device, a sedative, asbestos pipe wrap. Were the corpses gathered in one place, they would make the rows of crosses for American GIs in French cemeteries look like the graveyard of a small town.

America was indeed a dangerous place in the years before product liability suits became common. In the teeth of unfettered mass production, things went wrong. The early sixties automobile had no seat belts, no recessed door handles, and no padding on its all-metal dashboard. Drivers were impaled on the steering column because manufacturers failed to pad it or design it so the steering wheel didn't snap off, leaving a sharpened spike to be driven into the midsection by the force of collision.

Houses held their share of perils. Some walked through sliding doors made of non-safety glass that shattered into jagged chunks and slashed them, or were electrocuted by poorly insulated appliances.

Working people were assaulted frequently by machinery, like the multi-ton punch press that made an "unintended double-stroke" and bit off a worker's arms as he reached in for the just-pressed metal part. Scott Baldwin won over $700,000 for the man with no arms, a small fortune in the sixties.

Baldwin knew the odds of getting money at that time, even for a grotesque accident, were terrible—so poor, almost no one survived on a steady diet of products cases. And workmen's compensation laws bar lawsuits against employers over workplace accidents. But then, Scotty Baldwin and others began suing the maker of the machine that caused the injury instead of the factory. Slowly, courthouse doors began to open.

In the face of epidemics caused by defective products, Baldwin and his colleagues were bringing grievances the government wouldn't bring. Thousands turned to them after a painful encounter with a poorly designed tractor or crane or propane valve. And there were much darker products, like thalidomide, a sedative that fought morning sickness but also melted the fetus into a monster with flippers and no genitals and fingers coming out of the pelvis.

The white-shoe law firms that represented General Motors and John Deere and Union Carbide were a bit miffed by the persistence of this cheezy little gang of storefront entrepreneurs. By the early sixties, some courts were saying manufacturers should be liable for defects *whether they knew of them or not,* a theory called "strict liability" that would be the law of the land by decade's end. Scott Baldwin could see that it might be possible to carve out a niche just suing big companies.

Money was never the attraction for Baldwin, not that there was any in the beginning. He loved the equality pure brain power gave him in a courtroom—that and having some street smarts. It was a thrill to beat up on lawyers who came from better families, went to better law schools, and were paid real salaries. Baldwin also loved the risk. He and other pioneers sued previously untouchable industries, setting precedents—what lawyers call "making law"—that allowed them to sue more. Many came from modest circumstances. Others were brilliant misfits, like Melvin Belli, a banker's son who hated the idea of grinding away in a safe commercial practice and struck out on his own.

They burrowed deeper and deeper into the fabric of the

companies they were suing. They found ex-employees who told the organizations' secrets. And they pried out internal documents, reasoning that if ignorance was no defense under the new theory of "strict liability," then *knowingly* marketing a hazardous product could spell catastrophe for the defendant.

But Baldwin soon found an astonishing thing. The companies *did* know the product was defective, usually well before it went to market. *They always knew.* Instead of fixing or recalling it, they covered their tracks, issued denials. Not only that, they kept scrupulous records of their misdeeds, which Baldwin and others ferreted out using their power of discovery, in which both sides are supposed to share relevant evidence. If a manufacturer knowingly put people at risk, the jury could order "punitive damages" to punish and deter.

And yet the public saw the product lawyers not as heroes, but leeches. The problem was, a wrongdoing company was a shadowy collectivity, not a leering villain. Although a car with a defective gas tank could kill you just as dead as a madman with a gun, the link between murderer and victim was highly mediated. Many hands labored to put that particular gun into position, most quite innocent of the consequences. There were no Dillingers, no Lindbergh babies, little romance in this arena. When a man electrocutes himself with a defective vacuum cleaner in his garage, the dominant reaction among disinterested third parties is likely to be that he was a putz and the rest of us would be, somehow, more careful. Getting the public to accept a more ennobling vision of the victim was a hard sell.

If some products seemed more guilty than others, the mother of all bad actors was asbestos, a cheap, adaptable mineral that could be fabricated into bricks or corrugated paper or a sprayable insulation. Between the 1920s and the seventies, some 11 million working men and women were exposed to asbestos dust, either in the factories where they made hundreds of insulating and fireproofing products, or when they sprayed, poured, and dabbed it into everything from destroyers to waffle irons, as well as more than 700,000 buildings and 31,000 schools.

Those who breathed the chalklike mineral over a working lifetime were quite simply doomed. Although symptoms often did not appear for twenty-five or thirty years, asbestos caused not only lung cancer but mesothelioma, which could kill in a matter of months, and asbestosis, a scarring of the lungs that smothered gradually, like emphysema.

Scotty Baldwin wasn't sure at first how much the manufacturers knew, but the injuries were real enough. He brought the second successful lawsuit by a worker in an asbestos factory for fatal lung damage. He became the point man for asbestos suits, just as he had in products liability generally.

In the late seventies, Baldwin went to San Francisco to question a doctor named Horton Hinshaw, who was a witness for the asbestos companies in so many cases that the industry decided to depose him once and for all in front of attorneys from across the country. Dr. Hinshaw was installed in a ballroom in the Fairmont Hotel and bathed in movie lights so a video could be shot. In the ballroom were a hundred defense lawyers and fifty plaintiff's lawyers, one of whom was a young South Carolinian named Ronald Motley, who was gaining renown as a trial attorney.

The video director asked each lawyer to stand on an X on the floor and introduce himself. Scotty Baldwin, a little hunchbacked man one lawyer called him "the elf"—went first.

"My name is Scott Baldwin. I am six foot eight and weigh two hundred eighty pounds. I play defensive end, and I'm a senior from Marshall, Texas," he drawled, like a college football player on television.

Bedlam broke out—hoots and hollers from the plaintiff's lawyers, outraged muttering from the defense.

Motley came over and clapped Baldwin on the back.

"You know, I can use a big bruiser like you on my team," he laughed.

When Motley questioned Hinshaw, Baldwin saw what all the fuss was about. Motley's cross-examination was merciless, and he provoked Hinshaw into a number of blunders. Motley was so good, he turned what was supposed to have been a defense deposition into Exhibit A for the plaintiffs. And this after the industry paid all that money for the ballroom and video.

Baldwin and Motley began seeing each other frequently at depositions, and some of Baldwin's style rubbed off on the younger man. Motley was slightly chubby in those days, his dark hair thick on top. He was always the brightest candle in the room, with a kind of star quality about him, even then. Like Baldwin, Motley had an irreverent sense of humor, but didn't seem to use it much in court. Instead, as a self-described "document freak," Motley relied on his virtually photographic memory to overwhelm the other side with facts.

"You're telling them too much," Baldwin warned. "That jury wants a simple story."

Motley listened. Both were from southern backwaters, Baldwin from dusty little Marshall, Texas, and Motley from an industrial suburb of Charleston, South Carolina. Baldwin could see Motley wasn't merely absorbed in asbestos work, he was a fanatic. Nothing else mattered to him. But he was different from other young lions. There was something vulnerable about Motley. And he was, everyone agreed, more than a little crazy.

RON MOTLEY GREW UP IN A TINY, WHITE ONE-STORY HOUSE on Walnut Street in North Charleston, a white working-class neighborhood of one-family homes with small backyards of sandy red-brown soil. He was born in 1944 while his father, Woodrow, called Woody, was in the Pacific with the Coast Guard.

Woody's people were from Blaney, now called Elgin, a rural hamlet near Columbia. The Motleys were "dirt farmers," which in South Carolina meant cultivating whatever the ground could be persuaded to grow. In the Motleys' case, that was mostly cotton and peaches, and Woody's body was shaped by unremitting outdoor labor. He was brown-skinned, with a square-jawed head on a massive frame that finished in arms like tree boughs, big hands, and thick fingers.

Motley's mother, Carrie Montease Griffin, grew up poor in Charleston with six other children. She was known as Tease, after her middle name, and married Woody in 1937 when she was nineteen and Woody twenty-three, having met him through the Baptist church they both attended. She was dark haired and dark eyed, quite beautiful, and Ronald Lee, the couple's first child, inherited both her looks and temperament, which was high strung, unlike the easygoing Woody.

When Woody Motley returned from the Coast Guard, he bought an American Oil gas station amid the warehouses and pawnshops on King Street, a major thoroughfare about a mile from the house. Woody was nothing if not enterprising, and at different times over the years owned a furniture shop, an auto radiator store, and a fuel oil delivery business. But he always had the gas station and did well with it. Tease handled the books.

North Charleston was still in many ways a sleepy little town, dominated by the mammoth North Charleston Naval Shipyard and the Raybestos-Manhattan asbestos factory, both a few miles from the Motleys' neighborhood. Most of the men on Walnut Street worked at the shipyard, whose workforce swelled to twenty-seven thousand during World War II. Some worked at Raybestos, which made asbestos cloth. Woody's little matrix of businesses made the Motleys just a bit better off than their neighbors. Woody had a big '55 Buick when others had Fords, and the first TV on the block.

As the first and for many years only child, Ronnie was doted on by both parents, but was closest to Woody, who took him along to the gas station where Ronnie was supposed to pump gas, but generally played. He would read anything anyone left lying around: magazines, the encyclopedia, Superman and Green Lantern comics. Woody just enjoyed having him around.

The gas station included a little store, where local men lounged, drinking Woody Motley's beer and telling fishing stories, which Ronnie soaked up by the hour. Woody liked company, and relatives and friends were in and out of the Motleys' tiny house. When Woody started making a little more money, he bought a cottage out at Folly Beach, south of the city, and everyone stayed there during the summer. Woody and Tease were the kind of people to whom others turned for comfort when a husband or grandmother died. It was a secure place to grow up, and Ronnie was its center.

It wasn't until Ronnie was thirteen that Mark was born. Ronnie adored the little boy as much as Tease and Woody, and would bring the Motleys' collie over to the baby so he could pat it. At thirteen months, Ronnie and his friend Pat Alderson were delighted to see Mark take his first steps. They had the little boy on his feet in the Motleys' living room as he padded over to Ronnie, who turned him around and sent him back to Pat. The next night, Mark developed a fever, but no one worried until the doctor visited and examined him. He scooped up the baby, who by now was having trouble breathing, and drove him to the hospital, his parents in tow. An emergency tracheotomy was performed, but the child died late that evening, victim of an acute respiratory infection.

By the time anyone remembered Ronnie, he had fallen asleep in the backyard with the collie. An aunt went to gather him up.

"Oh, Ronnie," she said. "Little Mark is not coming home."

Ronnie felt the loss acutely. Children weren't supposed to die, and he spoke of Mark's death even years later. It seemed to have marked him as surely as if Mark were his own child, instead of his little brother. And then, too, just at that moment, his parents withdrew. Woody went to the gas station, threw his remaining stocks of beer into the street, went home, and didn't go back for months. The house was quiet. Tease sat at the window and stared. She and Woody became estranged and, as the years went by, openly antagonistic. Their next and final child, Susan, born in 1958, was learning disabled. Tease, who had smoked Pall Mall cigarettes since she was a teenager, smoked far more now. Woody took up a pipe.

"I just need something to bite on," he told friends.

Ronnie, however, did not withdraw. He became, if anything, more outgoing, more popular, driven to try new things. He was a debater at Chicora High School, and mused about being a reporter or writer. He held strong, if vague, populist views, admired John F. Kennedy, and played an aggressive though not especially gifted brand of basketball, baseball, and football for the high school varsity.

He was an instigator. One night, when he and his friends took Woody's new Corvair, Ronnie climbed into the trunk so his friends could sneak him into the drive-in. Unfortunately, he had the keys in his pocket, and panic set in because of the Corvair's famous airtight doors and windows. His friends calculated the oxygen supply. They figured Ronnie had about ten minutes to live.

"Call my dad," shouted the muffled voice inside. "Get me out of here."

Woody sped over, opened the trunk, yanked out his son, and smacked him in the face.

"You are one damned disgusting sight," he said.

Ronnie started to see a pretty blond cheerleader two years his junior, Sandra Cone, whose father worked at a bank. You couldn't *not* like Ronnie, Sandra thought. He was confident, funny, opinionated, and brash, exciting to be with. He seemed wiser than his years, empathetic, almost as though he could see inside you. And he was shedding a certain residual nerdiness to blossom into a good-looking young man in whom a number of girls were interested.

No dating was allowed by the Cone parents until she was sixteen, after which Sandra and Ron were together a lot, until Ron went away to the University of South Carolina at Columbia, and Sandra went to Winthrop University, a women's school up on the North Carolina border. They wore engagement pins. Ron joined ATO, a major fraternity at the university. Majoring in history, he coasted through college, as he had through high school. Sandra couldn't believe how disorganized he was, yet how much he remembered without really trying. His biology notes were on the back of a series of envelopes. He also started drinking in college, with few ill effects, other than once when he got drunk at a frat party and crashed his father's Buick into a parked bus.

Ron and Sandra were married in 1967 in the Baptist church the Motleys attended, and moved into Woody's little beach house. The grand plan was for Ron to go to law school, but for the time being, he taught fifth grade, then history at Charleston High School, coaching the basketball team until the Vietnam War intruded. He joined the Air Force Reserves, going to Denver for "supply school." Motley thought it about as asinine as everything else in the military, though compared to combat duty in a jungle on the other side of the world, four and a half months in Colorado was a damned passable way to live.

When he returned to Charleston, he decided he didn't want to go to law school after all and, over Sandra's strenuous objections, applied for a job with IBM. He scored high enough on company evaluations that IBM paid him to sit in the Charleston County Library for six weeks and teach himself about computers from an IBM manual, prior to joining the firm.

As he studied, he realized he was making a huge mistake.

"Lord, I hate computers," he told friends.

Rooting around in the stacks one day, he idly picked up a law book and sat down with it. Motley experienced an illumination. Here was logic, for which he had an enormous aptitude that had drawn him to computers, but a logic warmed in human affairs and drenched with the high purpose of politics and history. The attraction was immediate and profound.

His military status allowed him to make an emergency application to enter law school in the fall, even though it was already August. He applied on a Tuesday, drank Friday night with a fellow applicant, took the admissions test Saturday, got the highest score in his class, and won a scholarship to the University of South Carolina Law School at Columbia, where he and Sandra moved two weeks later.

For the first time in his life, Ron Motley was in love with what he was doing. He was a stellar talent at Columbia. Virtually everything he wrote was published in the law review, on which he easily won a spot. Motley was an initiate in the temple of law. He felt the wonder of exercising a part of his mind he never knew he had, not just learning information, but learning to think like a lawyer. There *is* a moment when the mind first penetrates thickets of jargon to reveal the beauty of a potent argument. That is a moment of revelation in the temple.

Meanwhile, out in the real world, Ron and Sandra could barely scrape together the seventy-eight dollars they paid each month to live in a government-subsidized apartment. Sandra worked at a bank to earn their eating money. Ron delivered mail and assembled bicycles. He took a job selling vacuum cleaners. He sold a grand total of one vacuum cleaner. Then he felt guilty about it and gave the family their money back.

"They didn't really have a carpet," he explained to Sandra. "It just wasn't right."

Jennifer, their first child, was born in December 1970. Motley graduated the following June, seventh in a class of 140, despite missing a month of school to work on a friend's congressional campaign. Motley looked at a couple of jobs, then got a call from Solomon Blatt, Jr., who was about to become a federal judge. Sol Blatt, Jr., was the son of the longtime speaker of the South Carolina House of Representatives and a partner at Blatt & Fales, his father's law firm in Barnwell, west of Charleston. Motley accepted a clerk's job with Judge Blatt, and moved the family back to Charleston.

Motley planned to clerk for just one year, but Sandra got pregnant again and so for security's sake, Motley stayed with Blatt an additional year. Money continued to be scarce, and each of Ron's onerous student loan payments was represented by a coupon in a book so thick, Ron and Sandra called it *War and Peace*.

During his clerkship, Motley saw some impressive advocacy in Judge Blatt's courtroom, especially a Chicago lawyer who came in with a products case and really stuck it to the defense attorneys. He was fighting for ordinary people against big companies, which reverberated deep in Motley's populist core.

Then a barrister named William T. Jones appeared before Blatt. Jones needed an assistant and had just been turned down by a young Yale Law School graduate named Bill Clinton. He complained to Blatt that he needed someone of Ivy League caliber to help him with a string of challenging cases.

"That fellow there," said Blatt, pointing at Motley, "is as smart as and maybe smarter than any Harvard or Yale graduate I have ever known."

That was good enough for Willy Jones, who hired Motley. Jones was an old-fashioned, Bible-quoting, theatrical southern lawyer and prosecutor for four little country counties surrounding the town of Greenwood. But prosecuting was part-time work in rural South Carolina and Jones maintained a healthy private practice, leaving Motley to do wills, trusts, and real estate work as well as criminal cases, which he did not enjoy. Even worse was divorce law, an emotionally unsanitary business that had blubbering clients phoning at midnight.

For Motley it was a fast and dirty education, particularly in personal injury work, a Jones specialty. Motley tried his first lawsuits in Greenwood, chiefly train wrecks and car accidents. These suits had a lot of the emotion of criminal cases, the sense of righting wrongs, without the unpleasantness of having to deal with actual criminals. Motley had found his niche.

The move to Greenwood was a pleasant surprise for Sandra and Jennifer, who had nicknamed herself Jiffy. Jiffy now had a younger brother, Mark, born in 1973 and named after the little brother Ron lost in childhood. They lived in a cookie-cutter condominium, but found Greenwood a cozy little city. They were getting by financially. Motley had promised Judge Blatt he would join Blatt & Fales after two years with Willy Jones; however, when the time came to move, Sandra resisted. Greenwood had been an idyllic time for their marriage. But Ron had higher aspirations than assisting a country prosecutor, and moved his family over Sandra's objections.

Greenwood was a metropolis compared to Barnwell, a stick-in-the-mud southern village of five thousand souls surrounded by farms seventy-five miles west of Charleston. The Motleys had their first real house, an asbestos-shingled two-story affair on Manville Road, but since Ron insisted on pressing ahead—with his own money, if necessary—in highly speculative product liability cases, they had to mortgage it every year to pay bills. Sandra allotted herself a $200-a-month salary for being mother and wife so the family would have a savings account, but always had to rob it to keep afloat.

At Blatt & Fales, Motley found a five-lawyer firm that was one of the few in the state that did products cases. Well-connected politically through former speaker Sol Blatt, Sr., Blatt & Fales was nevertheless not on the cutting edge of much of anything when Motley joined in 1975. Motley was determined to change that.

He first sued over fatal fires that consumed mobile homes. These tinderboxes produced toxic smoke, and were soon pulled off the market. He handled suits for pesticide poisoning, then won a big settlement in the case of a heater that leaked fumes and killed some children. He was scoring victories in a legal specialty just beginning to flex its considerable muscle, and by 1976, when Motley was thirty-one, he was lecturing on product-liability law and was about to be elected president of the South Carolina Trial Lawyers Association, the youngest ever.

At that point, he had only read about asbestos cases, which a very few firms handled, until one was referred to Blatt & Fales by a lawyer in Tennessee. Motley and Terry Richardson, who had been hired along with Motley at Blatt & Fales, drove up to Greenville, South Carolina, where the Tennessee lawyers handed over a few folders of material, which was pretty much all there was to the case against the asbestos companies at the time. As they drove back to Barnwell, Motley started reading.

"Hey, Terry. Pull over and let's get a six-pack," said Motley. "You ain't going to believe this stuff."

Thin or not, the folders were plenty damning, and Motley got tremendously excited. And when this happened, he would become animated and make dozens of mental connections to other pieces of the puzzle that he could even now see being assembled, and thoughts came popping out of his mouth to Richardson, who was driving and nodding while Motley bent over a yellow legal pad that he lacerated with his unwieldy Babylonian scrawl.

Asbestos really became a personal mission when he started signing up plaintiffs. Those not yet dead were usually in a pathetic condition. He would travel to their homes or hospital beds and, in either case, found them on oxygen. Most couldn't work and had little hope of ever collecting enough money to provide for their families. It was like discovering a secret race of the oppressed for whom Motley held the key to salvation. No one could fail to be deeply affected by the plight of these ruined working men and women, and he became determined to help. He embarked on a study of pulmonary disease. He bought medical textbooks and read up on the mechanics and physiology of the lung, the proper diagnosis of asbestos disease. He talked to researchers. He learned that while emphysema destroys the tiny air sacs in the lung, asbestosis stiffens them with scar tissue, which also impedes the flow of air. Either way, the result is suffocation.

The defendants in these first cases were Johns-Manville, the largest manufacturer of asbestos products, and Owens-Corning, the second largest. The companies were then settling cases, and Motley made a little splash when he got over $100,000 for one of his clients. Soon he had seventeen lawsuits, all of which settled. It looked like this asbestos business wasn't going to be so tough after all.

The euphoria died when Motley handled his first trial in November 1977 and was humbled by Lively Wilson, one of the leading defense lawyers of his day, who argued the companies couldn't have known asbestos insulation made men sick. The jury deliberated less than an hour.

"I didn't know what the hell I was doing out there," Motley admitted to Richardson.

Using money from cases that settled, a frustrated Motley spent the winter perfecting his mastery of the medical literature. He pored over old workmen's compensation claims and found dozens filed by insulators during the 1950s against the leading asbestos companies for asbestosis. That meant the companies had known workers were getting sick long before they admitted they knew.

Armed with this new information, Motley went to trial in late March 1978 against Johns-Manville and ten other firms in Greenville. Once again, he faced Lively Wilson. Again, Motley lost.

Motley's asbestos jihad was not playing terribly well at Blatt & Fales, especially with Sol Blatt Sr., the firm's superannuated founder. Blatt, though a formidable lawyer in his day, probably never took a deposition in his life and his idea of case preparation consisted of a few phone calls and a visit to the law library. He could not for the life of him understand how Richardson and Motley could be driving all over creation, spending thousands on medical experts and God only knew what else. What Blatt did understand was that the money Blatt & Fales sent out the door on asbestos was never seen again. In 1977, Richardson and Motley had to take out a personal line of credit to fund their habit. The firm wouldn't sink more capital into what looked like a hopeless proposition.

"It's either quit or call up the reserves," Motley told Sandra one night.

Everything, however, was about to change.

In late June, Motley heard rumors about some hot documents involving top asbestos executives that had never come to light because the case settled. During an asbestos conference in New York City, he got a tip that this collection was at the federal courthouse in Newark, New Jersey, and grabbed a cab over there. He found evidence of an old series of letters, but they were held by a defense law firm.

Dead set on getting what became known as the "Sumner Simpson papers," he secured a court order unsealing them. The letters showed Vandiver Brown, corporate counsel for Johns-Manville, and Sumner Simpson, president of Raybestos-Manhattan, which had a factory in North Charleston, agreeing in the nineteen thirties to keep articles on asbestosis out of an industry trade journal, and pressuring a scientist to purge references to asbestos disease from a United States Public Health Service study. This put the final torpedo in the industry's contention that it had no idea its product was hazardous until three decades later—and therefore no reason to warn anyone.

The first success was the reopening of the Greenville case Motley had recently lost, which soon settled. The Sumner Simpson papers started a chain reaction of discovery by other lawyers, one of whom learned that Johns-Manville performed annual chest X rays on employees, but didn't bother telling them they were sick.

Motley also cultivated scientists who tested asbestos products and had firsthand knowledge of the cover-up. When burning at peak wattage, his charm was hard to resist, and he became a master at recruiting informants. Motley would contact the scientist, meet him in some hotel room, and ultimately have him down to Charleston, where he would be regaled with dinners.

Christopher Placitella, an up-and-coming asbestos lawyer in the eighties, attended one of these dinners with Motley and a former industry medical consultant named Thomas Mancuso, who seemed to have experienced some kind of religious conversion.

"He made the guy believe that he was wearing the white hat and it was sort of his citizen's duty to do this," Placitella remembered.

By 1979, the tide was clearly turning. Johns-Manville began settling rafts of lawsuits. Yet Motley still hadn't won a trial. It was quite depressing. The low point came when he took the deposition of Harvey Hewett, Jr., a retired business professor in North Carolina who was dying of mesothelioma from asbestos he'd breathed during a stint in the navy. Motley, a local plaintiff's lawyer named Thomas Taft, and fourteen defense lawyers squeezed into the bedroom where the sick man lay.

While Hewett wheezed and gasped, the defense lawyers got into an argument among themselves. They went downstairs to argue, and wound up outside under a tree, still arguing.

Motley seemed to have disappeared. Taft found him swinging on a child's swing behind the house. He was crying, furious that the defense lawyers were bickering while Hewett asphyxiated before them.

"Those people are fucking buzzards," he said. The professor died a few weeks after the deposition, at the age of thirty-nine.

Finally, in July 1981, five years after he began suing them, Motley won a record $1,857,000 verdict for a former navy boiler attendant named Edward Janssens, a healthy $750,000 of which was punitive damages. *Janssens* catapulted Motley to fame, helped in no small part by his fondness for press attention, which he was already expert at attracting, as when he called Johns-Manville "the greatest corporate mass murderer in history."

On *60 Minutes*, he explained why defense lawyers for the asbestos companies frequently billed as much as $24,000 for a single day of deposition.

"There'll be twenty of 'em in a room, three of 'em doing needle-point or whatever, three of 'em reading the newspaper, one of 'em asking questions, and the rest of 'em twiddling their thumbs," said Motley, sitting with three other lawyers around a table. However, Motley was perched on the *back* of his chair, so on TV he towered over the others.

Suddenly, Ron Motley was red hot. Beginning with *Janssens*, he notched seven straight wins, and by the time he did *60 Minutes*, had won twenty-two verdicts in a row. His firm was involved in over 15,000 asbestos suits all over the country.

If he was developing a reputation as an extraordinary lawyer, some thought he pushed a little too hard, especially when it came to signing up clients. Motley, who didn't take kindly to criticism, dismissed it as jealousy, but a rift began to grow between Motley and some of his fellow litigators.

As Scotty Baldwin could see, there was much to be jealous of. Motley's courtroom style was uniquely his own. His openings and closings were nothing on the page. His power was in his delivery. He could roar like a preacher at a tent meeting, or sound the sweet-est cadences of forgiveness. On his best days, he was a convincing tragedian, and even on his worst, he could be funny as hell.

Though he was not above burlesque touches—like squirting water at defense exhibits or wearing a full set of surgical scrubs, complete with mask, to rag their medical experts—Motley had de-veloped an undeniable authority. He was a physical presence in the courtroom, loping swiftly toward the witness with a document, knowing that in a minute, he was going to tear this guy to pieces in cross-examination, at which he was the equal of any lawyer in the country. And he wasn't afraid to improvise, which one colleague called "working without a net." Many lawyers will dart off on the occasional tangent while questioning a witness. Only Motley would concoct an entire multi-hour opening argument on the spot, while striding back and forth in front of the jury. Nor would he hesitate to scrap a trial plan that had been painstakingly hatched over a pe-riod of months on the second day of the proceedings.

By the time Motley and Baldwin tried a case together in the summer of 1982, Motley was the kind of lawyer other lawyers dropped in to watch. Baldwin was, too, so the Baldwin-Motley trial in Pascagoula, Mississippi, on behalf of a shipyard worker named James Jackson drew a crowd.

Jackson was the first asbestos trial ever in Mississippi, and a great victory. The jury awarded just over $1 million. Motley was flying back to Barnwell when the verdict came in, so he didn't get to see a chastened Lively Wilson, who had beaten Motley so badly in the early days, walk over and clasp Baldwin's hand. Wilson had to be thinking this didn't augur well for the future.

AND IT DIDN'T.

The *Jackson* verdict set off a stampede to sign up clients and bring asbestos cases, so that within a few short years the number of pending lawsuits had shot into the tens of thousands, and by the early nineties, topped one hundred thousand.

But the spiral of triumphs couldn't save Ron Motley's marriage to Sandra. Family life had really disappeared as soon as the asbestos cycle began. He would fly off Sunday night, return Saturday and often enough spend weekends preparing witnesses and meeting co-counsel. Motley was on a schedule that involved three or more plane trips a week, so the firm bought a little turboprop in 1979.

He had no private life, or rather his private life was an ongoing public event. Someone was always with him—lawyers, paralegals, scientists. He was in ceaseless transit among gatherings, court-rooms, hotel conference rooms, judges' chambers, cabs, restaurants, relaxing for a few hours in the hotel bar, trying to slow down, drinking, getting drunk. He flourished in this pressure-cooker atmosphere, cool as a cucumber during the day, something less than that after a few vodkas and grapefruit juice. His brilliance thrived on a manic diet of deadlines and demands, but it wasn't easy to step off the roller coaster and relax with other members of the human race.

The breakup began with awkward long-distance phone calls. There were rumors, and unsatisfactory explanations. Ron was a charming man on the verge of wealth traveling among attractive, often overawed young women. Sandra only needed to know so much, she could guess the rest. After that it was a matter of pride to call it quits. Ron didn't try to defend himself. This was the woman who had helped put him through law school and was raising his children, virtually alone. He wasn't going to say it would be different, because it wouldn't. In 1980, after two tough years, Ron and Sandra officially separated. At Christmas, they told the family, and right after New Year's, Sandra took Jennifer and Mark to live in a rented condo at Wrightsville Beach, North Carolina, where she had friends.

It was quite civil. The divorce wasn't final for several years, and Ron visited Sandra and the kids almost every weekend, staying in a guest room. The worst part of it was, Sandra had basically forgiven him even before she walked out. She couldn't help but think of him as her biggest child, and a needy one at that. He was so obviously not in control of his emotions. The problem with Ron was you loved him even when you wanted to hate him.

Motley didn't take time off to grieve. After *Jackson*, Blatt & Fales was the driving force in asbestos litigation, with more lawsuits than any other firm. By the end of the eighties, they would have twenty thousand cases. They became occupational disease counsel to the Sheet Metal Workers International, the Atomic Workers International, and four other unions, ensuring a steady gush of clients.

With so many new cases, Motley and Terry Richardson went on a small hiring spree so the firm could handle them as well as an explosion of asbestos-related property damage suits. Motley and Richardson's asbestos practice had grown to the point where they were making most of the money at Blatt & Fales, and by hiring six new lawyers, they essentially took over Blatt & Fales. Charles Patrick, one of the new hires, wanted to work in Charleston and Motley readily agreed. Then Patrick called wanting to know where the office was, and Motley said that as soon as Patrick rented an office, that's where it would be. By the time another new hire, Edward Westbrook, showed up in Charleston, Patrick had already moved twice in search of roomier quarters. Another who arrived around this time was Joe Rice, who could try cases, but whose real talent was negotiating, a kind of genius at haggling.

Motley himself moved to Charleston a few years later, by which time Blatt & Fales was dead and Motley, Loadholt, Richardson & Poole stood in its place, named after four of the original five from Barnwell. Later they added Julius Ness, a former chief justice of the South Carolina Supreme Court, as the lead name. By the end of the eighties, Ness, Motley, Loadholt, Richardson & Poole occupied six buildings in Barnwell and two floors of a large, modern office building at 151 Meeting Street in downtown Charleston. It had grown into one of the largest plaintiff's law firms in the world, with 255 employees, including 40 lawyers, and 100 paralegals, secretaries, and assorted assistants.

Ness, Motley's huge inventory of asbestos cases came from "referrals," meaning a firm in some other state brought Ness, Motley into a lawsuit as a partner. In exchange for a percentage of the referring firm's fee, they got Ron Motley, or someone he had trained, to try or settle the case.

Motley and his small nucleus of young lawyers improvised a system for dealing with masses of clients, each of whom was assigned to Rice, Patrick, Westbrook, or whomever, depending on geographic area. To save money, paralegals did much of the case preparation, like reviewing medical records, or locating a sick worker's former factory-mates. It was assembly-line justice, but a viable alternative to somehow getting a lawyer for each of tens of thousands of injured people.

The situation was unprecedented, as were the sheer number of the afflicted. Once the lawsuit was ready for trial, years could pass before anything happened, because there weren't enough lawyers and judges in the world to try the hundreds of asbestos cases being filed every week. The civil justice system was being overwhelmed. It was like those antediluvian Civil War hospitals struggling to deal with thousands of bodies shattered by chunks of speeding lead at Antietam or Shiloh. The state of the art was simply not up to the demands of the moment.

Ness, Motley's annual gatherings of asbestos practitioners from around the country were an opportunity to discuss this legal logjam. In August 1982, the Ness, Motley lawyers were in the Charleston office waiting to drive out to Kiawah Island for one of these confabs when Motley heard on the radio that Johns-Manville had declared bankruptcy. A wave of nausea swept over him.

"Those bastards," he said.

Lawyers began streaming in, all buzzing about the bankruptcy. Charles Patrick ducked into Motley's office.

"Well, Ron, guess I'll be doing wills," joked Patrick.

"No, we'll make it through," said Motley.

Motley's bravado masked shock at what could only be described as a catastrophe. Manville was by far the biggest payer of claims, with intact assets of over $2 billion. The bankruptcy was obviously a strategic move for a still-solvent company facing more than twenty thousand lawsuits. After years of building an airtight case against them, Manville would slip the noose with a legal trick.

To keep Ness, Motley out of the red and recompense injured workers, other targets would have to be found. It took three years of intensive discovery to assemble cases against fifteen other major manufacturers, but by 1985, the firm was ready to take them on.

Johns-Manville emerged from bankruptcy in 1988 with its profit-generating businesses under a new name, the Manville Corporation. That left sick asbestos workers, many of whom died during years of bankruptcy litigation, to compete for the meager assets of something called the Manville Trust.

The Manville bankruptcy forever changed the tenor of what was becoming known as mass tort litigation, large waves of suits filed against a single product. Lawyers like Motley were becoming political actors, and in the future, companies and plaintiffs would increasingly work together to decide how to pay out billions of dollars not only to sick workers, but to others who hadn't even sued yet, disposing in one bold stroke of the rights of perhaps millions of people. It was a momentous turning point, and a lot of people, including plaintiff's lawyers, were damned uneasy about it.

MOTLEY, HOWEVER, HAD NO SUCH QUALMS. HE WAS TRYing to turn the sheer number of injured against the asbestos makers, harnessing an obscure provision in the Federal Rules of Civil Procedure as a tool to try first hundreds and then thousands of suits all at once.

The result was a hideously complex beast called the "consolidated trial," which took place in phases spread over months. As the eighties became the nineties, Motley asked juries in Maryland and Mississippi to decide the fate of as many as ten thousand clients at one stroke. "Massing 'em up" made the stakes so high—awards could run into hundreds of millions of dollars—that neither side could afford to lose a verdict. Most companies sued for peace before or during trial.

Beginning in 1989 in Charleston, West Virginia, Motley did nothing but travel from one large consolidated trial to a larger one, using the same national network of local lawyers with whom he had tried individual asbestos suits. In the asbestos consolidations, local lawyers prepared the facts on the asbestos exposures and medical histories of several "representative plaintiffs," whose stories were typical of others'. Then they brought in Motley, who didn't arrive in town until just before a trial, to deliver his turbocharged version of the "national liability case," which proved the company's wrongdoing. Motley also did the "punitives case," which demonstrated that the defendants—often twenty or more companies—covered up the lethal hazard to workers.

Motley's status in the plaintiff's world was like that of a brain surgeon. First other doctors tested the patient and stabilized his vital signs. Then one morning, Motley walked in, cut him open, fixed his brain, and went home.

Having a local counsel network was what allowed Ness, Motley to become the only truly national asbestos plaintiff's firm, ready to parachute into court anywhere, anytime. They won that niche because no one else wanted it. It was far easier to make money from a finite number of high-dollar cases in your backyard than to do what Ron Motley did, which was live on the road and get a percentage of each local lawyer's fee.

For five years, Motley won every consolidation he tried. Usually, by the time he rode out of town, the local talent had become millionaires.

Ness, Motley took in many millions too. Motley bought an elegant home on the Wappoo River south of Charleston. Shaded by magnolias like the tiny cottage he grew up in, River House, as he named it, was two stories of sandy-brown stone that was cool in summer and had on its east side a rounded glass nose like the prow of a ship. There was a swimming pool and a little guest house Motley converted into an exercise room. The living room contained antique chairs in red and brown upholstery and a nineteenth-century chest that doubled as a coffee table.

Next he acquired the Kiawah Island house, twice as large but half as charming, a $5 million beach house, built to order on the resort. It had a sunken living room with a couch running completely around it. In the middle was a bar, from inside of which a miniature ship holding liquor and mixers glided electrically upward into serving position at the touch of a button.

Throughout the eighties, Motley bought bigger and bigger boats. The first was the *OD1,* for "Orgasmic Delight," which, he told a TV news show, is what he felt when he found a really incriminating asbestos document.

"What does that mean, Mommy?" asked Jiffy, who was watching the show up in North Carolina where she lived with Sandy and Mark.

"It means Daddy's really happy, honey," said Sandra.

The only residents of either of Motley's houses most of the time were three golden retrievers named after types of asbestos. Then he was so struck by a series of Bichon Frises he encountered on the road that he finally bought one of the fluffy creatures, and named him Willie.

Woody Motley took care of Willie when Motley was traveling. It was hard to know which was stranger—barrel-chested Woody cooking three meals a day for a tiny white dog, or Ron chasing Willie around River House, laughing like a madman.

Ultimately, Ron was away so much, Woody assumed permanent custody. When Woody came for dinner at River House, he brought Willie, who had continued to benefit from Woody's cooking until he resembled a small sheep.

"Dad, one of these days Willie's just going to explode," said Ron.

"When I got him he was right *pitiful,*" growled Woody. "He's scared to death now you'll take him from me."

His visits with the dogs and Woody were confined to occasional weekends. Otherwise, Motley traveled constantly for the consolidated cases, which were such behemoths that he began bringing along what became known as the Motley Crew. Touching down in Pascagoula or Baltimore or Beaumont weeks or even months before the trial, a dozen lawyers and paralegals would take rooms at the local Hilton, wiring up a couple with fax machines and computers and extra phone lines for use as "war rooms." From Des Moines came Theresa Zagnoli, Motley's trial consultant, who selected a couple of dozen hopefully typical people from the surrounding community and used them as jurors in mock trials.

Also part of the Crew was Charles Patrick, an expert in asbestos medicine, and Ann Ritter, a brainy Floridian who specialized in scientific issues. Then there was Jack McConnell, a Rhode Islander who opened a Ness, Motley office in Providence. These young lawyers saw their families but sporadically during the eighties. They were sustained by the sense of doing important work, the reasonable expectation that they might well get richer than Croesus, and the force of Motley's charisma, not necessarily in that order. Indeed, the loyalty of Motley's subordinates bordered on the canine. They shared that, along with stories, road romances, workouts at the hotel gym, and meals. And Motley, for whom no family waited in those big empty houses back in Charleston, sat at the head of the table in every hotel restaurant.

RON MOTLEY DIDN'T FULLY REALIZE HIS MOTHER WAS dying of emphysema until the disease was so far along that her future had been whittled from years to months. Her illness was evident by the time of the Manville bankruptcy, and she was formally diagnosed a year later. That didn't keep her from sneaking cigarettes and sucking at them furtively in the bathroom or by a window, even while using oxygen.

Woody knew his wife was having trouble breathing, as she chain-smoked her way through the day, watching soap operas. But Tease hid the full extent of the disease from him. Finally, the doctor called Woody into his office, and told him his wife had advanced emphysema, and she would die of it, slowly, over the next several years. And then, of course, in the last year, everyone knew, even people on the street who saw her wheeling her oxygen bottle in its little cart into a restaurant. By this time she had weakened dramatically, and Sandra, who could come down only every so often from Wrightsville Beach, saw black-and-blue marks on her arms where she had fallen during dizzy spells.

Ron spent as much time as he could with his mother. Sometimes when she spoke, she would stick a pillow under her chest and double over to push out enough breath so she could get a good inhale and finish a thought. Ron, who could not tolerate suffering even in strangers, couldn't stand to watch.

The changes weren't as dramatic for Woody because he saw her so much. For Ron, coming in from the road, these were frozen moments he would retain all his life, the steady strangulation of the wasting process, his mom's weight sinking from 145 to 110 pounds, her skin growing pouchy around her shrinking body. And most distressing, her lustrous dark brown hair, so dark it was almost black, like his, turned white gray, grew stringy, and began to fall out.

Not only is there no cure, there is precious little anyone can do even to make someone with emphysema comfortable. Tease was put into the psychiatric wing of one hospital because it was felt she had given up prematurely on staying alive. But imagine slowly suffocating, not over a period of seconds, as by cyanide gas, or some few minutes, as by drowning, but over the many moments of four or five years. Faced with this, people have been known to commit suicide.

Ron had become an expert on pulmonary disease from studying asbestos. He understood what it meant when one of her doctors told him she suffered from cor pulmonale, a combined lung and heart deterioration. He could read her test results and understand that as the carbon dioxide level in her blood steadily rose, as her hypoxia worsened, the woman he knew was disappearing. In the final stage of the disease the brain operates as though at the top of Mount Everest, deprived of the oxygen the lungs have become too incompetent to provide. At the end, she was frequently confused about whom she was speaking with. She would return to herself for a period, until one day you said good-bye without knowing that that had been her last lucid moment.

Ron saw his mother a number of times just before she died, when she was at Columbia Trident Medical Center in early 1984. On the last visit, he came in late, having flown from the West Coast. He walked to her bed, through empty corridors, and sat by her head, enshrouded with tubes and plastic. The woman he saw there was a miniature of herself, her dark eyes wan, her slenderness shrunken. He sat a moment, then knelt. He felt whatever a boy feels for his mother, because in that moment, the surge of crying takes you back. And he reached a place where a lie has no meaning, and every word spoken is true.

"I'm going to get 'em, Mom," he said. "I swear to you before God, if it's the last thing I do, I'll get 'em."

He stood up, touched her hair, kissed her on the cheek. He held still a moment, watching her chest rise and fall, hearing the pumps and ventilators and monitors humming. Then he walked back down the empty corridors, leaving a woman he would never find again and could never forget. He planned to make certain that the companies that killed her never forgot her either.

THE BODYGUARD

MOTLEY WAS NOT AT THE HOSPITAL WHEN HIS MOTHER died, though he was in Charleston. The funeral was a relatively large affair at a funeral home in North Charleston. His daughter, Jennifer, had been having dreams about her grandmother and didn't want to see the dwarfish body, but her father took her by the hand and led her to the casket, surrounded by wreaths. Then they sat together and wept.

Not long afterward, Woody Motley got rid of his gas station, arranging to "sell" it to Sam Pryor Jr., a black employee who had worked for Motley for years. Woody decided Pryor deserved the gas station, and backed a line of credit with a local bank that enabled it to continue under new ownership. Pryor made monthly payments on the property backed by Woody's line of credit, so that in effect Woody was lending money to Pryor to pay Woody for the gas station. But after Tease died, Woody didn't want to go there anymore.

Months went by and Motley talked abstractedly about suing the cigarette companies, but the asbestos battles still raged, and no one, other than Ron Motley, took his tobacco talk seriously.

He knew already that lawyers had been trying to "get" the tobacco companies for quite a long time, but all they ever got was broke and depressed. For instance, there was a physician/attorney contemporary of Scott Baldwin's named Dr. Larry Hastings.

His fellow members of the Surf Club became convinced Larry

Hastings was a flake when he first took the "Lucky Strike case." In the late fifties, the fashionable Surf Club set considered all of Miami's handful of plaintiff's lawyers outré characters. But when Hastings sued the American Tobacco Company over Lucky Strike cigarettes in 1957, even plaintiff's lawyers thought he'd gone around the bend.

So did doctors.

"What are you *doing*, Larry?" asked one orthopedic surgeon and friend.

Hastings had a habit of going his own way. During his medical student days, staff doctors at Johns Hopkins came into the mental ward one evening to find the catatonics doing the foxtrot, led by Hastings himself, a graduate of Arthur Murray and dance enthusiast.

"I think it helps," he explained. And the catatonics did seem a step livelier.

Hastings's Lucky Strike case was called *Green* v. *American Tobacco,* and it concerned Edwin Green, a trim World War II Navy veteran who had smoked Lucky Strikes for thirty-two years and contracted lung cancer. Green died two months after his case was filed.

Hastings's Lucky Strike case was part of a small flurry of suits filed right after the bad news about cigarettes and lung cancer in the early fifties. The press called it the "cancer scare," as though it had been a false alarm, which was what the companies badly wanted everyone to believe. By 1960, they had already spent a couple of million dollars running a research organization that was supposed to be conducting an "objective" and "disinterested" search for the cause of lung cancer.

But even as far back as 1939, Dr. Alton Ochsner had discovered that smoking had evidently caused seventy-nine cases of lung malignancy in his patients. A 1950 study by British researchers and another by an American team found almost all hospitalized lung cancer victims were smokers, with the heaviest smokers the most likely to die. The American Cancer Society then followed 187,766 men over a period of years and found lung cancer victims were sixteen times more likely to be heavy smokers. That demonstrated the epidemiology of the problem, a statistical association between smoking and cancer in the population.

All of which made cigarettes the only logical suspect in a huge bulge in lung cancer cases that mirrored smoking's rise in the early twentieth century. By mid-century, the bulge was bursting as those who had begun the habit twenty and thirty years earlier began to sicken by the thousands, then the tens of thousands, and finally the hundreds of thousands.

But the spark that lit the fuse of the "cancer scare" was a study by German emigré Dr. Ernst Wynder. Wynder took pure tobacco tar collected from a smoking machine that sucked down fifty cartons of Lucky Strikes at a time and painted this black molasses-like goo on the shaved backs of mice. Of those that survived one year, more than half developed malignant tumors, big, discolored baggy-looking neoplasms. Wynder published his study in 1953 and it scared the tobacco industry to death. Someone had taken the essence of their product, given it to animals, and produced cancer.

"A serious problem of public relations," conceded an official at Hill & Knowlton, a public relations firm, and for the first time in the twentieth century, cigarette consumption dropped two years in a row.

On December 15, 1953, the chief executives of every major tobacco company except Liggett & Myers met at the Plaza Hotel in New York to decide how to stave off the specter of ruin. They invited Hill & Knowlton's chief, John Hill, who suggested they create their own research organization to look into the health charge.

"They set up this institute," Hill remembered later, "and for many years it was in my office and we hired the people."

"This institute" operating from a PR firm's spare rooms was, of course, the "objective" and "disinterested" Council for Tobacco Research, formed within weeks of the Plaza meeting and known originally as the Tobacco Industry Research Committee. Heading CTR was Dr. Clarence Cook Little, an aging eminence in cancer research whose Maine laboratory was known mostly for the high-quality rats it bred for experiments. As the years rolled by and CTR churned out annual progress reports, there was a singular lack of answers to the question of smoking and lung cancer coming from its scientists. They certainly weren't finding them in cigarette smoke, because that was one place they weren't even seriously looking.

CTR turned out to be spectacular public relations, costing a tiny fraction of what the companies spent to advertise the product, though no CTR-sponsored study ever led the scientific community even one step away from cigarette smoking as the primary cause of lung cancer.

From his cramped offices on Flagler Street in Miami, Dr. Larry Hastings was sure this was because it was smoking that was killing all these lung cancer victims, not some mysterious unknown factor, like diet or viruses or car exhaust, as CTR speculated.

Aside from being a practicing physician, Hastings was a product liability lawyer. The tobacco industry was deeply concerned about the product liability phenomenon. Since there was no disproving the smoking–lung cancer connection, the next best thing was to say there was a "controversy" about it. To make absolutely sure that there was a controversy, the companies handed out millions of dollars to CTR researchers and others to look into viruses and diet and car exhaust, to take contrarian positions, to savage the other side in the letters column of scientific journals. And to take the witness stand if and when the wave of product liability suits hit the courtroom.

What the "controversy" really boiled down to was a metaphysical quarrel over the definition of *cause*. Those in the industry's service wielded a kind of medieval logic: How do we *know* one thing *causes* another? Certainly cause isn't just the *association* of one occurrence with another. If smokers get sick, how do we know it's the smoking?

Philip Morris research director Helmut Wakeham summed up the view of the Medieval Logicians some years later:

"The people who eat applesauce die. The people who eat sugar die. The people who smoke cigarettes die. Does the fact that the people who smoke cigarettes die demonstrate that smoking is the cause?"

Statistics cannot prove one thing causes another, merely an association between the two. That was how the companies dodged epidemiological studies like the epic American Cancer Society effort. This of course didn't deal with those rather chilling blackened eruptions on the shaved backs of Ernst Wynder's mice. A CTR official dismissed them as "the wrong material, the wrong tissue, the wrong animal."

From a public health perspective, the industry's position was dangerous nonsense. A reasonable suspicion about a toxic product is always reason enough to pull it from the shelves, and there was much more than mere suspicion about tobacco.

As it turned out, the "cancer scare" didn't create a huge wave of lawsuits, partly because product liability suits were still so novel and partly because so many people smoked, including doctors and lawyers, that believing the worst was simply too much to accept.

The early lawsuits were more like the arrival of the clown car than total war. One of the first was *Cooper* v. *R. J. Reynolds*, filed in June 1954, which charged that Reynolds had killed Joseph Cooper by making false health claims about Camels in ads. However, Cooper's lawyer was unable to actually produce the ads. He had evidently confused Camel's ad campaign with an older one for Luckies. The disgusted judge dismissed the case.

Then there was the *Pritchard* case, tried just weeks before Larry Hastings was to begin his Lucky Strike case but thrown out on a directed verdict, meaning the jury never deliberated.

That left Hastings, who had already had far more success than most suing the railroads on behalf of injured workers. Like Scott Baldwin with his Chevy ignition-and-auto-horn rig, Hastings was one of the first to use "demonstrative exhibits" to tell his story to a jury.

The problem was, Hastings's Lucky Strike case went far beyond the frontiers of the very young discipline of product liability. Cigarette cases were not like other product liability suits. When a car knocks a woman through a window, cause and effect are bound tightly together. It wasn't like the plaintiff smoked a cigarette, began coughing, and died. The injury showed up after thirty long years of exposure. Cigarettes wouldn't surrender their secrets like Chevys. They would have to be pried out by medical witnesses.

But as one of about a hundred doctors in America who were also lawyers, Hastings routinely outmaneuvered the defense on medical issues, and it seemed indisputable that cigarette tar caused cancerous cellular changes.

The companies took Hastings very seriously, assigning squads of lawyers. But after three years of stalling by tobacco, it became clear *Green* would be the first cigarette case to go to a jury. As the trial began in July 1960, the entire industry held its breath.

Hastings had testimony from the venerable Alton Ochsner and Ernst Wynder. But, like Scott Baldwin, Hastings had no internal

corporate documents. It was then unheard of for a company to provide them.

After two weeks, the jury went out, deliberating for ten hours.
They returned on August 2nd. The verdict was so startling, it made
headlines all over the world. The first jury ever to ponder a smoker's
lung cancer came within one pencil mark on the verdict form of
awarding money damages. The front page of the *New York Times*
read, "Jury Links Cancer to Smoker's Death."

The jury ruled Edwin Green had lung cancer, that it was caused
by smoking Lucky Strikes, and that the cancer killed him. It decided, however, that American Tobacco was not liable because the
smoking-cancer connection was not well established in 1956, when
Green's illness was diagnosed.

Even though it was a verdict for the cigarette makers, Hastings
was jubilant. He believed the final *no* on the verdict form was so il-
logical, a new trial would be ordered.

Privately, the industry's leaders were now deeply anxious.

"I understand that Janet has been in touch with you on her
Miami case," an industry lawyer wrote to a scientist as the companies prepared for a retrial in *Green,* "and I certainly hope that you
can be of some good assistance there, since the problem involved is
unique, to say the least."

Millions had smoked Luckies and Camels and Chesterfields, an
ocean of potential claimants. A simple calculus was operating here.
If cases continued to be filed, it would be like Russian roulette.
Every time a jury deliberated, the gun could go off.

Legally, the industry was, if not a sitting duck, a duck with poor
prospects of escape. Its product had no warning label, even though
the companies now knew, if they hadn't in the fifties, that cigarettes
were lethal. Some cigarette ads made claims that sounded an awful
lot like assurances of safety, which could be seen as fraudulent.

At this most vulnerable moment, the industry came to depend
wholly on a small group of trial lawyers to get them out of a colos-
sal jam. Other trials were imminent. One was a case by Melvin
Belli, scheduled to begin a few months after *Green.* Another was a
Missouri action, *Ross* v. *Philip Morris,* on behalf of a man who lost
his voice box after smoking for over twenty years.

Philip Morris was wary of *Ross.* A repeat of *Green* would be seen as confirmation of a trend. As the case got closer to trial, the company brought in a local lawyer named David R. Hardy to handle it. Lyman Field, who represented John Ross, chuckled when he saw Hardy walk into court that first time. Apparently tobacco didn't want to risk alienating the dusty-booted midwesterners on the jury with a slick New York law firm. Hardy's outfit was small even by Kansas City standards, but Hardy was highly regarded and, just as important, he spoke the local dialect. He liked to brag he had never lost a case and wasn't going to start now. There was an authority about Hardy, and charisma. He was a street fighter. He would soon take the measure of the opposition and find it wanting.

LYMAN FIELD HAD AMPLE TIME TO PONDER THE GREAT questions of smoking and health. *Ross v. Philip Morris,* filed in November 1954, didn't go to trial until the summer of 1962. It took about eight years for Philip Morris to get all the clarifications it seemed to require as to just exactly what it was that Field was suing over and to whittle out of the case a count charging fraud and deceit. By 1959 the two sides were still skirmishing over what information Philip Morris would provide, and the wrangling was producing sticky tangles of legal verbiage, like this 1959 docket entry:

"Nov. 16—Judge Ridge enters order granting deft. until 12/1/59 to file suggestions in opposition to application of pltf. for an order compelling deft. to answer interrog. and requests for admissions and suggestions in opposition to motion of pltf. requesting court for an order on deft. to produce designated documents and papers for pltf. to inspect, copy, or photograph."

If Hardy was a street fighter, Field was no pushover either. Born and raised in Kansas City, he was a Harvard Law School graduate who joined the Marines during World War II and survived five of the bloodiest amphibious assaults in the Pacific—Kwajalein, Tinian, Guam, Saipan, and Iwo Jima.

Field and Hardy knew each other fairly well in the little world of law in Kansas City, sharing lunches and anecdotes. A city-bred patrician, Field was tall, slender, and agile. Hardy, about eight years younger, looked Irish and had a twisted nose that could have been broken by a fist. He grew up in a small town north of Kansas City, stood a couple of inches under six feet, and his brown hair still had hints of red. Field belonged to the Kansas City Country Club, while Hardy was a member of its equally prestigious cross-town rival, the Mission Hills Country Club.

Field knew Hardy was going to play rough. Hardy won a pretrial battle granting him almost unlimited license to bring in certain facts that wouldn't play well before a Kansas City jury, such as the treatment of plaintiff John Ross for gonorrhea at age nineteen. But Field had lined up Dr. Alton Ochsner as well as a renowned throat specialist from the Mayo Clinic who had treated Ross's cancer. Field dismissed the scientists for the other side as "trained seals" who would bark the industry's line for a few fish. He was convinced the jury would see through them and he would beat Hardy on the medical issues as Hastings had in *Green*. And Field firmly believed he had a good plaintiff in John Ross, whose laryngectomy had reduced him to speaking by means of an electrical device he held next to his throat, which produced an eerie, metallic sound.

Ross seemed worthy enough of pity when he took the stand before federal District Judge Floyd Gibson on June 18, 1962, the first day of trial, and told his story. Ross had worked for the Better Business Bureau recruiting new members and investigating crooked-sounding schemes. He was diagnosed with cancer in the general area of the larynx in 1952 and operated upon. With his voice box and part of his neck removed, he couldn't shower or take a tub bath or even walk in a heavy rain for fear water would enter the breathing hole in his throat and drown him. Having no way to cough up mucus or blood, he had to remove them from the hole with a forceps each morning or else they might accidentally be expelled during the day with no warning. He couldn't get as much air into his lungs as before, making sports or manual work impossible. He became depressed and self-conscious about appearing in public with his electrical speaking aid. Being unable to speak normally truncated his career with the Better Business Bureau.

He stood in front of the jury and showed them the hole.

"It changed my whole personality," Ross said. "I almost was tempted to withdraw from the human race."

All his misery, Ross contended, was brought on by the fact that he trusted a cigarette company's advertising. For almost twenty years, he smoked Philip Morris cigarettes, which was the brand name of the unfiltered smokes then manufactured by Philip Morris, whose ads featured Johnny Roventini, a tiny fellow in a bellhop's uniform who shouted "Call for Philip Morr-eeees!" but to whom Field referred, whenever possible, as "that dwarf."

Field's case was built around the idea that Philip Morris made its cigarettes sound safe, or at least safer, and thus gulled Ross into smoking them. Field showed ad after ad to the jury. One said "eminent medical authorities" had tested smokers and certified that because Philip Morris had managed to remove an unspecified substance from its brand, "every case of irritation of the nose and throat due to smoking cleared completely, or definitely improved" when smokers switched to Philip Morris. At the bottom, the ad said, "From facts published in authoritative medical journals. Names on request."

Even more to the point was a magazine ad that claimed "you are safe smoking Philip Morris, a finer cigarette scientifically proved less irritating to nose and throat."

There had been dozens of similar pitches and Ross displayed a prodigious memory for the radio shows on which he heard them and the magazines and newspapers in which he saw them. He could remember that in 1936 "they started quite an extensive advertising campaign in national publications." He claimed to have read—and believed—every Philip Morris ad in *Time* magazine from 1936 until 1952.

"I was smoking the Philip Morris product and I naturally was interested in their advertising," said Ross. "I don't believe I missed a one all during that time."

Ross rasped through his electric voice machine as he explained how faithfully he had attended the Country Club Methodist Church, how he had been married to the same woman since 1945, and how he had prospered at the Better Business Bureau.

The parade of Ross's virtues was interrupted only briefly when he explained that while he had been known to use spirits, he had been "classified as a moderate drinker," though there had been a few minor scrapes with the law while under the influence. And later the pastor of his church appeared and said he had never known Ross to take a drink on the Lord's Day, such a loyal parishioner was he.

No, indeed, agreed Ross, he wouldn't hear of it.

"I just had too much respect for the Sabbath," said Ross.

"Never in your entire life took a drink on Sunday?" Field asked yet again as he concluded his presentation.

"No, sir," said Ross.

FOR THE NEXT TWO DAYS, DAVID HARDY DISEMBOW-eled John Ross with dazzling thoroughness, attacking without mercy despite the hole in Ross's neck and the metallic voice. Events that happened some thirty or forty years earlier are rarely clear, and John Ross's recall was no different. Indeed, his memory was unfailingly unreliable. And every one of the hundreds of times Ross failed to re-member something, Hardy's position became more plausible. Why was it that Ross's only clear memories from long ago days seemed to be of cigarette ads?

Because other than that, as Hardy skillfully showed, Ross seemed to have been living in a fog. His first wife's first name was unknown to him, as were the exact circumstances of his first child's birth, who, it emerged under probing, was born out of wedlock. He took several stabs, sometimes into erroneous decades, at the dates of his two marriages and was blurry about exactly what happened to one of his wives. (Did she die while he was married to her? Ross couldn't remember.) Hardy covered Ross's history of "moderate" drinking—"moderate" meant ten to twelve highballs a night, fol-lowed by a round of vomiting—and his unfortunate tendency to en-gage in fisticuffs or wander into the yards of neighbors in his car, his six-month marriage to a chorus girl and his one-month, six-day union with the mysterious Geraldine, of whom he had written on one legal document that his marriage to her "ended in death." But no, it seemed Geraldine, or somebody, Ross wasn't clear who, had filed for divorce in Los Angeles, where the two were then living. Hardy implied Geraldine divorced him because she got fed up with her cantankerous and possibly violent husband getting smashed on bootleg whiskey. Ross offered his own explanation:

"Why, she fell in love, supposedly, with a Hungarian count in Los Angeles, California."

"Fell in love with a Hungarian count?" said Hardy.

"That was the story," said Ross.

The arrests section of Hardy's cross-examination was likewise colorful. Ross seemed to have a habit of frequenting taverns with men friends and then leaving with them in cars, passed out in the backseat. He had an altercation with someone in a lunchroom who said something unflattering about a pal and was arrested for public drunkenness. At these sorts of moments, with Ross fumbling to remember whatever became of some spouse or child or hat or something, Hardy would say, "Were you drinking quite a bit in those days?"

And the answer, generally speaking, was yes. It seemed he never stopped drinking, and this led naturally to a sort of pratfalls section of the cross-examination in which Hardy asked about an incident in the early thirties in which Ross slipped in the shower on a bar of soap and hit his head ("That is one I do not recall," said Ross), an unfortunate occurrence in 1932 where he fell off a chair and was knocked unconscious and collected two hundred dollars from an insurance company, and the way he and his car kept wandering into the wrong driveway at the end of long, bibulous evenings.

It was a three-week trial, two weeks longer than most civil trials of the day, and Hardy had many extraordinary moments, but none showed his shrewdness and ruthlessness to better effect than the six hours he spent interrogating John Ross. Ross's claim to have relied naively on Philip Morris's advertising collapsed when Hardy brought out that the Kansas City office of the Better Business Bureau, Ross's home office, had been filing protests that cigarette company ads were making unsupportable safety claims, with the first target being Philip Morris and the very ads Ross was suing over.

As for his unique ability to retain ad copy and almost nothing else, Ross said it seemed perfectly logical to him that he would have a better memory for smoking-related facts than "some of these various dates and marriages and drinking episodes that you were bringing out here."

"Do I understand you correctly that you think that the content of the Philip Morris ads and your smoking habits would be more firmly impressed on your memory than the first name of your first wife?"

"I never knew the name of my first wife. I never heard it mentioned," Ross protested.

It was as though Hardy had turned the pious family man with the disfiguring disease into Wolfman, of course, none of this had anything to do with whether Philip Morris's ads were all but saying their cigarettes were as wholesome as mother's milk. With Ross's credibility reduced to flaming rubble, no juror would now believe it when Ross said he had relied on them.

Field was unable to rehabilitate his client during his redirect examination of Ross. Not until the very end did Field get off his most telling question of the day:

"Did you ever receive any warning or did you ever read anything or know of anything, any claim made, that smoking caused cancer, before you learned that you had this cancer of the throat?"

"No, sir," said Ross.

THE REST OF THE TRIAL CONSISTED LARGELY OF MEDical testimony similar to *Green*. It is said great trial lawyers earn their money on cross-examination and Hardy wreaked havoc with every one of Field's witnesses, even trying to light up a cigarette in court, an idea quickly nipped by Judge Gibson. In his summation, Hardy called the testimony of the plaintiff's experts "drivel."

The jury went out on the afternoon of July 10, 1962, and returned forty-five minutes later with a verdict for Philip Morris. Coming after eight years of preparation, that ranked as annihilation. One newspaper reported that the jury agreed immediately *that the causes of cancer are a mystery*. They weren't even convinced Philip Morris was Ross's brand. Field never did another tobacco case.

Hardy's victory in *Ross* was so convincing, it boosted the morale of the entire industry and elevated Hardy to the status of conquering hero. In a period of just a few years, he was entrusted with unprecedented power to do whatever was necessary to repulse the enemy.

Hardy became a sought-after speaker by other industries worried about being sued. He had enormous chutzpah. He wrote of how he got himself invited to a conference of cancer researchers and public health officials in Wisconsin in 1967, and lectured them "about the health aspects of smoking, which some have been publicizing as hard facts."

He was tobacco's chief warrior, overseeing the industry's stable of scientists who testified in Congress and in Canada's Parliament, some of whom neglected to mention the cigarette makers were paying them. And he found informants who provided intelligence on unfriendly scientists.

The scientific enterprise Hardy inherited was already big, and he made it bigger and smarter. He helped create industry-wide committees that worked together to present a seamless front to the world. The cigarette companies practiced a joint defense. No mavericks, no splitters. Hardy wanted one message, one voice, one purpose. Survival.

In court he remained top gun. He appeared for American Tobacco in Missouri in early 1970 and won a verdict. He defended Philip Morris against legal icon Melvin Belli in San Francisco and got the case dismissed before trial, a defeat that, one tobacco lawyer exulted, brought Philip Morris to "the bottom of the barrel in our cancer litigation," disposing of the last meaningful courtroom threat.

The *Green* case, meanwhile, hit a series of strange snags. Hastings was allowed a retrial, at which the jury was supposed to consider only whether American Tobacco should pay damages. However, the judge allowed the entire case to be relitigated anyway, and in November 1964, American Tobacco won unequivocally. Hastings appealed, and the appeals court agreed the trial should have been for damages only. Then, in a highly unusual decision, the court decided to rehear the appeal, this time with all of its judges, and the second vote went against Hastings.

So *Green* remained the high-water mark. For twenty-five years, no jury would come that close to hurting tobacco again. Hardy had extinguished the threat. Of the mere handful of tobacco suits filed in the seventies, not one went to verdict. Hardy shut them down just in time. Liability law was changing so fast that if the first *Green* trial had come a few years later, the jury would have been compelled to award money damages.

Due to some fairly extraordinary circumstances, an obscure trial lawyer from Missouri became better heeded than any other figure in the world of tobacco, yet almost no one from the outside world knew his name. David Hardy was now the companies' bodyguard. He had no other client as important and found no other work as compelling. The trials behind him, he entered a new phase, in which he created his most important legacy. This work would be done in law libraries and document rooms, in university dining halls and cocktail lounges, and most important, in hundreds of pages of memoranda. And all of it would be buried, deep in the underground of the industry he protected until the day he died. It would be for another generation to dig it up.

NOT ONLY DID DAVID HARDY STAMP OUT THE LAST EM-bers of tobacco lawsuits in the sixties, the industry's power grew immensely. An Illinois legislator named Dr. Bruce Douglas found this out when he proposed a bill in the Illinois legislature in 1973 to limit smoking in public places to designated areas. Douglas's speech provoked stunned disbelief from the state's elected representatives, one of whom flicked a lit cigar butt at the back of Douglas's head. Others puffed clouds of smoke at him.

Then an army of lobbyists descended on Springfield—so many, the legislature's lower chamber rebelled and actually passed Douglas's bill. But the state Senate voted it down.

Douglas's young son, Clifford, watched from his father's seat in the Illinois House of Representatives as that cigar butt arced into his father's skull. Bruce Douglas just kept right on talking.

If ever a child was born for social activism, it was young Cliff. As an oral surgeon, Dr. Bruce Douglas could have sent Cliff to a private school to get him away from a band of seven Latino brothers who kept beating him up because he refused to join their gang at his elementary school in inner-city Chicago. In 1965, the neighborhood surrounding the school, nicknamed Uptown, had one of the highest crime rates in the United States, and the seven brothers were doing everything they could to hold up their end.

But it was years before the elder Douglas reluctantly sent Cliff to a private school. As a progressive who had stayed in the city and continued to practice in a heavily black neighborhood despite worsening conditions, it wasn't so easy to do. Bruce Douglas had an idealism that didn't yield to threats, or even to the riots that followed the assassination of Dr. Martin Luther King, Jr., in April 1968, which were centered in the West Side, where Bruce Douglas saw patients. A white-owned business, his dental practice was burned to the ground. Although warned to stay away, he set off for what was left of the building with ten-year-old Cliff, but was greeted with sniper fire. Douglas grabbed his son, pushed him to the floor of the car, and sped away.

But Bruce Douglas continued practicing in the inner city, and, at the urging of his activist wife Frederica, went on to represent Uptown in the state legislature.

There were three Douglas children, but only Cliff, the eldest, seemed to inherit his father's lonely moral code. His grandfather was a Russian Orthodox Jew whose family name of Dlugach didn't survive processing at Ellis Island. Cliff felt different, not only because he was white and Jewish in the inner city, but because his body behaved differently. The corner of his eye would twitch or some other part of his face, especially under stress, and he was the butt of vicious teasing. Through an enormous effort of will, he taught himself to maintain control over the tics, which his family wrote off as a folk ailment, the twitches, something you live with.

But he couldn't control his rebellious anger, especially in school, where he interrupted classroom discussions with outlandish questions, got into fights, and engaged in frequent pranks, once taping all the desks together while the teacher was out of the room. He was finally expelled in the eighth grade for pelting the wall clock in the gym with tennis balls until it fell to the floor and shattered.

He was readmitted the following semester, and went on to high school, where he channeled his rage into sports as he would later pour it into social activism. Not until he was in his twenties did Douglas happen to read about Tourette's syndrome, after which a neurologist told him that his twitches and facial tics were indeed caused by a mild case of the disease, which had probably helped prompt his emotional outbursts in grade school. Since there is no effective treatment, Douglas never lost the habit of monitoring himself every minute he was around people.

Douglas used to joke that fleeing thugs in his neighborhood led him naturally to track and field, and after winning the state long jump championship during high school, he was recruited by the University of Michigan, a perennial track power. By the time he left Chicago, the city-bred Jewish boy was usually taken for a WASP from a California suburb. Dark haired, handsome, articulate, and soft spoken, he departed Uptown with something street wise in him, but a quiet, idealistic, Zen street wise. He went on to the University of Michigan law school, where in the fall of 1982, he met Martha Luckham, a classically trained flutist and recent undergraduate at Michigan.

A housemate of Martha's invited Cliff to a Sunday dinner, while Martha invited her then-boyfriend. In Martha, Cliff saw an attractive brunette with poise and gentility. Martha saw a witty young man, in marked contrast to her boyfriend, whose mouth opened only to admit forkfuls of pasta. Martha and Cliff were both immediately smitten. They were soon both lovers and best friends, and moved in together.

Upon graduating law school in 1983 Douglas perhaps reflexively accepted a job with a Park Avenue firm. But before moving to New York, Douglas, who had never been much of anywhere on his own, was eager to travel. Martha encouraged what was to be a solo journey, though she was jealous. Stuffing his worldly assets of $1,500 into a backpack, Douglas embarked on what would become a six-month trip around the world, beginning with two months in Western Europe and Scandinavia.

His real fascination was with Asia, where he traveled for four months and was transfixed: the beauty of the jungle, the imperial culture and ancient poverty, unknowable people who stare and point. And as he traveled—to Cairo, Tel Aviv, Dubai, Bombay, Delhi, Jaipur, Agra, Bangkok, Pattaya, Chiang Mai, Hong Kong, and to Tokyo and Okayama in Japan, where he had lived briefly as a small child while his father taught on a fellowship—he felt like some part of him that had shrunken during law school was throwing itself toward the light.

He traveled with several books, one of which was the biography of another trained lawyer: Louis Fischer's *The Life of Mahatma Gandhi,* which Douglas pored over and highlighted at night and on trains and ferries. He was to read it many times in the ensuing years. He read of passive resistance, civil disobedience, the teachings Martin Luther King, Jr., revered and practiced. He read about Satyagraha, or Truth Force, a term Gandhi coined to describe truth as a natural resource within. It meant not only truth in words, but by example in life. And this, Gandhi wrote, was the foundation of moral political power.

Douglas bracketed and underlined one section of the book:

Millions had read Ruskin and Thoreau and agreed with them. Many Hindus had read them and agreed with them. But Gandhi took words and ideas seriously and when he accepted an idea in principle he felt that not to practice it was dishonest. How can you believe in a moral or religious precept and not live it?

And he was drawn to this remark of Gandhi's:

Any secrecy hinders the real spirit of democracy.

Part of Fischer's book explains Gandhi's thoughts about how to practice law. It is safe to say that few American lawyers have sought instruction on this topic from Gandhi, but Douglas actually read this section as a primer on lawyering, bracketing it in red Magic Marker and printing "legal ethics" next to it:

If a person, wishing to retain him, made a confession of wrongdoing, Gandhi would say, "Why don't you plead guilty and take the penalty?" He thought there was too much litigation for community health and individual morality. "A true lawyer," he declared, "is one who places truth and service in the first place and the emoluments of the profession in the next place only." But the true lawyer, he found, was a rare bird. Lawyers often lied, money talked, and witnesses consciously perjured themselves.

In other words, Gandhi was a lawyer who didn't much like practicing law, and that was how Douglas began to feel as he went deeper into Asia. Compared to what was happening to him now, a conventional legal career suddenly seemed like such bullshit. He waded in the sacred river Ganges, saw the Taj Mahal, traveled among hill tribesmen in Thailand. He lost fifteen pounds, but somehow never got sick. He was virtually broke, having spent most of his money in

Europe, but his eyes were open wider than they had ever been. It was disorienting, exhausting, thrilling. It was freedom.

By the time he returned to the United States, he knew a commercial law firm wasn't his future. Nevertheless, he and Martha, to whom he would eventually become engaged, gathered their things for the move to New York and his new job.

For eight miserable months he toiled at his Park Avenue law firm, drafting the legal instruments that move money from one pile to another, then became a writer for a legal publisher. He got sponsors to pay him to run in the New York Marathon and donated the money to a soup kitchen. He helped with local political campaigns. But being an activist in his spare time just wasn't enough. So he and Martha moved to Washington, D.C., where Martha was hired by a nonprofit group. Douglas volunteered at People for the American Way, a civil liberties organization founded by producer Norman Lear as a counterforce to a growing number of right-wing pressure groups. Once again, the young couple was broke, and lived at first with Douglas's mother, who had remarried and moved to the area.

It didn't take long for Douglas to distinguish himself from other volunteers who were massing at the time to fight the 1987 nomination of conservative Robert Bork for the Supreme Court. For one thing, Douglas was showing up in a suit, not a T-shirt and jeans. For another, he was an attorney, one who was willing, as he wrote in his journal, "to sweep floors just as long as I was sweeping floors in a place where good was being done." It wasn't the kind of thing you could really say to the legislative aides and lobbyists and analysts, but Gandhi had cleaned toilets.

Recognizing a diamond in the rough when she saw one, Melanne Verveer, the policy brains behind People for the American Way, quickly scooped up Douglas and had him appointed staff attorney at the princely salary of $25,000 a year, a charitable act since Douglas was already doing much of the job for free. Verveer could see Douglas had a potent combination of gifts. He could summon up marathon bursts of work energy, was a superior lawyer, and yet had a gentle way with people. In a city ruled by arrogance, Douglas seemed humble. Verveer put him to work analyzing Bork's legal opinions, and after the successful campaign to kill that nomination, Douglas studied up on Douglas Ginsburg, who was also defeated, and Anthony Kennedy, who was finally ratified by the Senate.

It was a high-water mark for the organization, a euphoric series of victories. "People For" had gone up against Ronald Reagan and the Republican right and humiliated them. And Douglas, there among the country's fastest and smartest players, had made a difference. It was a rush.

But his job at "People For" lasted only a few months, the organization reverting to skeletal staffing with the Supreme Court fight over. Douglas heard that an anti-tobacco organization, the Coalition on Smoking OR Health, had just created an assistant director's job, directly under Matthew Myers, who ran the Washington office.

The issue had of course held a visceral appeal for Douglas ever since he'd watched his father fend off airborne cigar butts to introduce his anti-smoking bill. But Cliff Douglas had never considered anti-tobacco work as a career—small wonder since, for all practical purposes, there was no such thing in the late eighties. No one knew this better than Matt Myers, who ran the Coalition on Smoking OR Health out of his law firm and had been fighting the industry in Washington for years.

The point of the Coalition was to focus the resources of the three big smoking-oriented "voluntaries"—the American Cancer Society, American Heart Association, and American Lung Association—on a finite number of key tobacco issues, rather than have each group tilting at its own particular windmill. But the money the voluntaries were willing to spend was pitiful: about $150,000 a year. Not surprisingly, the Coalition hadn't notched any important victories in Washington during its seven-year history.

Myers told Douglas he was pushing the Coalition to be tougher, but it was slow going. Douglas would have to rein in his activism and accept that there was a certain amount of inertia in these giant charitable groups, which were run by stodgy career health bureaucrats.

"With all of its problems, this is the only game in town," said Myers. "And I want to play this game. I want to move this issue. And this is the only way to do it in Washington, D.C."

Douglas nodded. Mostly he was trying to suppress the impulse to tell Myers how amazed he was that he could get paid for such a job.

Douglas found out why the Coalition's track record was so dismal when he began working there on Leap Day 1988, a month before his thirtieth birthday. For the cigarette industry, facing off against the voluntaries was barely a challenge. It was as though the two sides were antagonists from different centuries. The voluntaries were waging an eighteenth-century war, by gentleman's rules. They lobbied, they petitioned, they brainstormed. Meanwhile, the tough boys at the Tobacco Institute were blitzing Poland. Douglas was dismayed to find that while the tobacco people could unleash money and personnel at a moment's notice, the Coalition couldn't respond to an industry press release without three days of review. They were never even in the game.

So Douglas, frequently with Myers's tacit approval, began to work under cover, running what he called "guerilla operations." If Douglas picked up something on the grapevine, for example, he might get John Banzhaf, a law professor who had almost single-handedly forced the industry's ads off the airwaves in 1970, to head off trouble with a press conference.

Eventually, Douglas's job was phased out and he moved to the American Lung Association, where he soon got into trouble for telling a reporter that the American Medical Association was "hypocritical" for giving a pro-tobacco congressman named J. Roy Rowland its most prestigious public health award. The chief executive officer of the AMA called the honchos at American Lung demanding to know who this guy Douglas was, and Douglas was chewed out for allowing himself to be quoted in a newspaper.

The day after the newspaper story, the American Lung Association issued a memo saying its officials "do not make political comments about legislators. PERIOD!"

"Rather than attack a legislator on one subject, find something good to say on another," the memo chirped.

Douglas quit in disgust. But first he excoriated both American Lung and the rest of the Coalition on Smoking OR Health in a scalding exit memo:

> Literally, almost nothing happens. More time seems to be spent bickering over who will be quoted, how the individual organizations' names will be listed, and how the Coalition can be sure that it receives credit to the exclusion of other groups than on important substantive issues.

It was bad enough, wrote Douglas, that the tobacco industry could deploy "unmatchable resources" in Washington, while "the health side does not have even a single full-time advocate/lobbyist" working on tobacco control. Now the voluntaries were too gutless even to speak up in the press.

"The federal tobacco control effort in Washington," he concluded, "has virtually collapsed."

Yet Douglas strongly believed the industry to be morally, if not yet politically, vulnerable. He saw tobacco as a *peculiar industry* by the same logic that slavery was "the peculiar institution": each a compromise with the devil, legal, but indefensible. With tobacco, when other arguments fail, the industry shouts that *cigarettes are a legal product,* meaning too many people are already hooked to abolish them.

But as fed up as Douglas had become with "the voluntaries," he did not lose hope, because he had experienced a small, critical moment of epiphany early in his Washington career. It came in the summer of 1988 at a hearing in the House of Representatives on a new cigarette R. J. Reynolds had developed called Premier. The hearing was strictly routine, although Premier was a bizarre invention. It wasn't really a cigarette at all, but a cylinder containing an aluminum "flavor capsule" and a little bit of real tobacco with a carbon tip that heated, but didn't burn, the tobacco. The press dubbed it a "smokeless cigarette" and Reynolds was trying to get the government to allow RJR to sell it to the American public.

A lawyer for Reynolds named Richard Cooper sat down at the witness table. Since Premier had no more than a twig's worth of tobacco in it, Cooper was asked how much of Premier's nicotine came from the flavor capsule. About 70 percent, said Cooper. The capsule contained flavorings and a "spray-dried tobacco extract."

In other words, it seemed most of the product's nicotine was squirted in at the factory.

No one made anything of this remark except a thunderstruck Douglas, who began squirming in his chair.

"They can't do that!" he whispered to Myers.

Myers shrugged.

"Well, yeah, they can," he said.

The hearing ended, but Douglas could not get Cooper's words out of his mind. The industry always represented cigarettes as chopped-up tobacco rolled in paper, a simple agricultural product, with nicotine being an inevitable part of the package, like butterfat in milk. But here the industry was spraying it into a metal tube where it would be converted to a hot aerosol and sucked into the lungs. What the hell did *that* mean?

On and off for months, Douglas and Myers tossed Cooper's testimony back and forth. Maybe nicotine was a new issue that could galvanize Congress and revivify the moribund anti-tobacco forces. But neither of them could see how this information about Premier could be applied to regular cigarettes with regular tobacco leaves inside. Meanwhile, Premier proved a costly flop and was withdrawn. Douglas felt like he'd gotten a tiny glimpse of something, he wasn't sure exactly what, that just as quickly vanished.

SECRET LABS

IT HAD SNOWED, AN EVENT RARE ENOUGH IN RICHMOND that it seemed to put a strain on everybody and everything. Diana Dollinger had been holed up in her apartment virtually all weekend, scribbling notes, worried she was getting fat. These were neurotic obsessions. She was in fact an attractive, svelte twenty-eight-year-old, an entry-level researcher well thought of by other chemists at Philip Morris.

She left behind a few relatives in the Richmond area when she died very early one Monday in January 1982, but no one claimed to know why she had drunk liquid nicotine, 100 percent pure, straight out of a brown bottle she'd smuggled home from the Philip Morris Research Center. She died a death experienced by several rats at the research center, but few people anywhere in the world. The victim loses control of its limbs and collapses as the bowels and bladder discharge, and the end comes in a wrenching, gasping convulsion.

Diana Dollinger would have had to go to some trouble to get the brown bottle, because nicotine wasn't used in the Physical Research Division building where she was part of a unit that analyzed how tobacco burns, an essential but unglamorous branch of the company's product research. It got William Farone, then-director of applied research at Philip Morris, who supervised Dollinger's unit and others, wondering whether there was a message in her method.

"If you've got a choice, why pick that particular chemical?" he said to another scientist. Indeed, a chemist at Philip Morris would have been among a select few in the country who could appreciate just how nasty nicotine really is. Many at the research center learned the hard way that merely leaving a bottle of the clear liquid open in a warm room brings on a wave of coughing and gagging, followed in short order by dizziness and nausea. A few drops on a small cut on the skin are fatal within minutes unless the victim gets a shot of mecamylamine, which blocks nicotine's effect and is another thing that would be found at Philip Morris and very few other places.

Despite the bizarre choice of poison, there were no stories in the press, and no details in Dollinger's obituary. All of which led to speculation inside the research compound about a cover-up. This of course was more than a decade before nicotine became a routine subject in the media as the Food and Drug Administration tried to reclassify cigarettes as delivery devices for the drug. In 1982, although the scientific community was studying nicotine in a preliminary way, there was precious little awareness of it outside the cigarette companies. It would have looked terrible if the active ingredient in cigarettes was publicly identified as a poison so strong that a woman could kill herself with it.

However, to Farone, this line of thinking led to nothing definite. He heard from another Philip Morris chemist and boyfriend of Dollinger's that she had developed moral scruples about her employer, that she felt so-called safe cigarette work, which concentrated on removing the poisons from cigarette smoke, wasn't really taken seriously at the company. But the boyfriend later denied these statements, and said simply that Dollinger had a history of suicide attempts.

In the end it didn't really matter whether the Dollinger suicide was intended to send a message or was an act of private desperation. For the few dozen at the Philip Morris Research Center privy to the details, the circumstances of her death were profoundly distressing and ignited a debate that Farone remembers "very quickly turned into a microcosm of this broader discussion about are you being used or are you doing something good—all of those kinds of issues that go through your mind when you're working for a cigarette company."

Farone was one of a handful of scientists within whom those

questions caused a dissonance that swelled until eventually he turned on Philip Morris, as did Victor DeNoble, a psychologist performing cutting-edge experiments on the brain effects of nicotine. But for DeNoble the doubts came later. He didn't agonize over Diana Dollinger's death that morning in 1982. The suicide was part of a class of peculiar occurrences at Philip Morris that DeNoble had learned to overlook. He was too deep into his research, and besides, his work was explicitly dedicated to producing a safer cigarette.

"I don't know what happened in the press, you didn't see anything in there," he remembered later. "I think we were told it would be handled by the company, and if anyone were to ask us, that's what we were to say."

DeNoble enjoyed his work at Philip Morris, though he viewed himself as unlike other researchers there. DeNoble likes to point out that he was the son of a plumber, and had it not been for a few lucky breaks, he would never have gone to graduate school in psychology, nor wound up at Philip Morris. But humble origins or no, DeNoble was a brilliant researcher and his plain quality of speech and strong Long Island accent did him no harm whatsoever at Philip Morris, or at the pharmaceutical firms he joined after he left the company.

DeNoble had been scooped up and pressed into service at a time when Philip Morris was determinedly scouring the nation's universities and corporations for top-flight talent, especially in biology, biochemistry, and psychology, and he joined a cast of stars, a group advised by Nobel laureates.

He was then a post-doctoral fellow in psychology suffering the combined rigors of climate and poverty at the University of Minnesota at Minneapolis. An expert on drug dependence, DeNoble was studying how animals self-administer addictive substances, as part of a program sponsored by the National Institute on Drug Abuse. He was twenty-nine but had already published important papers, one of which described how monkeys dosed themselves orally with pentobarbital, a long-acting sleeping pill, and alcohol. This was important because most self-administration work had been done intravenously, while alcoholics, pill-heads, and many others take their drugs by mouth. In the seventies, the University of Minnesota was the proving ground for the techniques NIDA would standardize for use in classifying addictive substances, and in fact was the premier academic institution doing such work. For a young hotshot studying drug dependence, this was where the action was.

In the winter of 1979, DeNoble got a phone call from William Dunn, Jr., the manager of the behavioral research laboratory at the Philip Morris Research Center. Dunn made it clear he was deeply impressed with DeNoble's work in behavioral pharmacology. Not only was Dunn intimately familiar with DeNoble's published work, he knew about ongoing experiments DeNoble had yet to complete, much less publish, which flattered DeNoble, though he later thought it strange. Dunn wanted to hire DeNoble to examine an addictive drug that had so far received little attention in the academy: nicotine. DeNoble didn't know it, but Dunn's views on cigarettes and addiction had been forged long ago. Dunn wrote unequivocally to colleagues in 1972 that nicotine is the reason people smoke, and urged them to "think of the cigarette pack as a storage container for a day's supply of nicotine" and the cigarette "as a dispenser for a dose unit of nicotine."

DeNoble initially told Dunn he wasn't interested. Like anyone in the life sciences, he was highly skeptical about working for a cigarette company. But after realizing that Dunn was offering not only a significant career opportunity but a ticket out of frigid Minnesota, he agreed to visit Richmond, where he learned of the nicotine analog program, a massive effort begun in the mid-seventies. As Dunn and others explained, the company was synthesizing molecules similar to nicotine, hoping to find one that would provide the drug's addictive pleasure without its stimulant effect on heart rate. Company officials made a humanitarian pitch that was hard for DeNoble to resist. In the United States alone there were over 100,000 deaths a year from cigarette-related heart disease, the majority due to gases in smoke that promote arterial clogging. However, nicotine too was thought to be an important culprit, since it caused blood vessels to contract, further straining aging, blocked coronary arteries. Hundreds of nicotine-like molecules had already been created at the research compound's sophisticated chemistry lab, but Philip Morris needed DeNoble to test their effect on animals, and, just as important, to build a model of how nicotine worked in the brain. The company had the capability to denicotinize tobacco, and replacing nicotine with an analog would remove a significant health risk from cigarettes, Dunn explained.

At the end of the day, Dunn seemed pleased with DeNoble.

"See you in April," he said as they shook hands and said good-bye. DeNoble replied he was still not convinced he would take the job.

"You will," said Dunn, smiling gently.

Dunn was right. Not only was the talent at the Philip Morris Research Center world class, but the company was famous for spending money on science. DeNoble said he wouldn't come unless he got a 40 percent raise and $700,000 for his lab. The company offered to double his salary and let him spend $2 million his first year. They would build him a state-of-the-art lab from scratch according to his specifications. He could hire anyone he wanted. DeNoble and his wife moved to Richmond.

Within eighteen months, DeNoble's experiments, which would eventually employ a hundred rats, were so successful that he brought on another superstar academic scientist as co-researcher. Paul Mele was a close friend from DeNoble's grad school days at Adelphi University on Long Island and a specialist in the effect of drugs on the chemical function of the brain. Mele was a physician's son, a designer of elegant experiments, painstaking where DeNoble was prone to jump ahead.

Philip Morris probably didn't count on an uncanny synergy between DeNoble and Mele that produced over a dozen major experimental initiatives in four years. Jack Henningfield, director of the National Institute on Drug Abuse's Addiction Research Center during the nineties, later said it was as though they had packed twelve years of research into four. Within eight months of Mele's arrival in Richmond the pair had isolated two active nicotine analogs, neither of which increased heart rate.

It was, in many ways, a dream job. They were not long out of graduate school, yet had unlimited money and complete freedom— no students to teach, no need to chase down grants—to work on a problem at the frontier of science. If they succeeded, they would have contributed in a historic way to making a product that threatened the health of hundreds of millions of people less dangerous.

The importance of the analog program meant DeNoble and Mele were allowed to be the bad boys of the research compound.

"We were the most anti-establishment—everybody there was wearing suits and ties. Our lab was top secret. You couldn't get into it unless we let you in. Nobody else had animals. We didn't have to answer to anybody. We were literally out of control. We were there, generating data, walking around in blue jeans, with lawyers in suits around, with rat shit in our pockets.

"It was like *Animal House*. We were so loud. Paul and I used to get into these great arguments. It was so loud that on our floor there was a director, and he actually had to move to a different floor because he couldn't work because we were yelling," DeNoble said. (The director was Bill Farone.)

The yelling was the least of it. The Rolling Stones thundered from among the steel behavioral chambers and surgery tables courtesy of DeNoble's boom box. With his long brown hair and cocky air, Mele was even more anti-establishment than DeNoble. After some criticism of their informal attire, Mele and DeNoble installed an "emergency tie case" over which was written, "In case vice president shows up, break glass." Taped all over the walls were syringes filled with mecamylamine, to guard against nicotine exposure. At the front of the lab, visitors were greeted by a huge stuffed rat dangling by a spring from the ceiling with a giant hypodermic needle jammed into its head.

In April 1980, when DeNoble hired on, there was a good bit of the bizarre sprinkled over the research center's patina of high purpose. Smoking was permitted, indeed, encouraged, everywhere. Every morning the "cigarette girl" dropped a free pack of smokes on each researcher's desk. DeNoble remembered standing with Jim Charles, a toxicologist and company stalwart, who was peering at cancerous lesions on a rat's back while he sucked thoughtfully on a Merit. "I turned to Paul and I said, 'This guy's got to be brain dead,'" DeNoble remembered. But Charles was simply living the company's unofficial motto, engraved on every employee's biweekly paycheck: "This is tobacco money."

An authority on how and why people smoke, Bill Dunn was a social psychologist whose work was based on observing human subjects, a thoroughly trusted career Philip Morris man nearing retirement when DeNoble arrived. As DeNoble and others began to lend real weight to the "hard science" side of the discipline, actually reaching into the brains of test animals to record the chemical and other changes that accompany psychological states, Dunn soon saw the psychology unit he had established split in half, with Jim Charles, a Ph.D. in toxicology and pharmacology, becoming supervisor of a new section that included DeNoble.

Dunn and DeNoble came from opposite ends of the discipline, and aside from the fact both had senses of humor—one of Dunn's memos was called "Smoking and Memory: Have We Overlooked Something?"—they were opposites in every other way. DeNoble, a trim, athletic man with dark bushy eyebrows set over a broad, open face, was prone to volcanic bursts of enthusiasm or temper. He listened to Led Zeppelin, drove a ten-year-old van with no muffler, and didn't know Bordeaux from hairspray. Dunn was a white-haired former smoker with a ruined elegance reminiscent of William Burroughs. He was from an old Richmond family, a sophisticate, a classical music lover, a gourmet. The two got along, the elder statesman and this déclassé Long Islander, despite the fact that Dunn could not understand how DeNoble could be so brilliant at science, yet culturally so lowbrow. "You're as close to an idiot savant as I've ever met," Dunn said to him once.

The seven-story research tower in which they worked sits on 472 acres that also contains the gargantuan James River factory, the company's flagship manufacturing plant, a facility a quarter of a mile long that can turn out 600 million cigarettes a day. Visitors to the research tower walk up a staircase lined with exquisite gummy, golden brown tobacco plants on pedestals, their brilliant leaves exuding a resinous musk. DeNoble's lab and most of the psychology section was on the third floor, one floor above a cafeteria and two-hundred-seat auditorium. Across Bell's Road from the tower is the "campus," home to the Physical Research Division that employed Diana Dollinger, the computer center, and several other buildings, with the rest of its acres empty of anything but trees.

One of the first buildings with which DeNoble became familiar was the compound's awesomely efficient incinerator, which was run at night to vaporize lab animals that expired during experiments. Aside from the operator of the burner, perhaps fifty people at Philip Morris knew animal research was under way for the first two years of the lab's existence. "They would fire this thing up about seven o'clock and throw in the rats, whatever they needed to get rid of, and just turn it to powder," DeNoble said. Also to preserve secrecy, the rats were brought to the lab late at night or early in the morning in covered containers, and the lab's windows obscured with brown paper. DeNoble and Mele were to tell the curious only that they were working in the nicotine analog program.

There were other jealously guarded secrets. The sixth floor was called the smoking floor. At one point in the seventies, 960 cigarettes were being simultaneously inhaled by four stainless-steel smoking machines: squat metal drums, six feet across, with ventilation hoods to expel torrents of sidestream smoke. The machines looked like some leftover marvel from the age of steam railroads, with cams and gears and sprockets and syringe-like fittings that did the work of actually drawing in the smoke. The cigarettes, 240 per machine, were clamped onto a rotating wheel, so that each cigarette paused every fifty-eight seconds for a two-second drag at one of eight smoking ports located like spokes radiating from a central hub, where the smoke was held in a chamber. To walk the sixth floor and see a roomful of whirring equipment methodically toking cigarettes at the rate of 48 packs every ten minutes was to feel one had strayed into the very Satanic Mills themselves. The major purpose was to generate large quantities of tar, which was collected in glass vials. However, only a few knew what happened to the tar.

Of course, high levels of secrecy are not unusual in industries like pharmaceuticals where valuable trade secrets and details on products in development must be shielded from prying eyes. But for a company manufacturing a supposedly staid consumer product, the atmosphere of cloak and dagger at the compound was extraordinary and pervasive. So pervasive, that when Philip Morris bought 7-Up and began building the company its own research building in the compound, no one was allowed on the Uncola's construction site without a special permit.

DeNoble was one of a handful with access to most of the studies generated by the various units in the Philip Morris Research Center. Researchers in areas like leaf technology or parasite control, on the other hand, could see data generated by other sections at their level, but not DeNoble's work. Even DeNoble, however, was kept in the dark about much of what was going on in the clandestine labs in Europe, which he was surprised to learn existed.

"They told me about these secret labs in Europe and I went, 'I thought we were the secret lab.' And they said, 'Naaaaah. You want a secret lab? That's the secret lab!'"

Of course, research director Thomas Osdene knew about the labs. Every few months, Osdene, or another trusted subordinate, like Jim Charles, took a trip on the Concorde, bearing a briefcaseful of studies from the States to company labs in Switzerland and Germany, and bringing data—or for supersensitive topics, verbal progress reports—from Europe to company higher-ups in Richmond and New York.

Eventually, DeNoble reviewed some of the paperwork generated by the research in Europe, and so gradually he learned more about the multinational's two labs there. The smaller of the two was adjacent to the Philip Morris factory in Neuchâtel, Switzerland, while the other, INBIFO, the German acronym for the Institute for Biological Research, was in Cologne, Germany. Both were used for the most delicate research, work that needed to be protected from the risk of subpoena in an American lawsuit. INBIFO was the site of numerous experiments in which mice were painted with cigarette tars to isolate carcinogenic constituents and study tumor formation. It was precisely mouse-skin painting that was used to indict smoking as a cause of cancer in the 1950s, and so the industry had been on record ever since as insisting that this test had zero value as a cancer predictor in humans. It would have been rather embarrassing to have to explain why a tobacco company was using this test to study nitrosamines and benzo-a-pyrene, some of the most carcinogenic agents in cigarette smoke, at this late date.

Chemist Ray Morgan lived in the same neighborhood in Richmond as Jim Charles and used to carpool with him. As the company's chief of toxicology, which is the study of poisons and their effects, part of Charles's mission was to lend Richmond's support to the cancer-related work being done at the European labs. Morgan noticed that sometimes, as the men got into the car at the end of the day, Charles had with him a sealed plywood box that he held on his lap as they drove across the research compound to the guard shack, where he left it to be picked up by a courier.

"What's in there?" Morgan asked one day.

"That's something you don't need to know about," said Charles, who despite carpooling and playing tennis with Morgan, wouldn't discuss Philip Morris business with him.

It struck Morgan as odd. Why would the chief toxicologist personally convey a box from the sixth floor to the guard shack? Why wasn't it sent out via the research tower's shipping and receiving department, like any other parcel?

Years later, when Morgan himself began working on the sixth floor, he learned that the boxes had almost certainly contained tar from smoking machines that was being flown to Europe to be painted on the backs of mice.

AS DENOBLE REVIEWED THE VARIOUS STUDIES FROM THE European labs, he was quite startled to read of inhalation studies in which mice, rats, and hamsters were forced to breathe cigarette smoke, and to learn further that these efforts produced cellular changes characteristic of the early stages of cancer. This work was much riskier than mouse-skin painting. If caught doing skin painting, the company could at least argue that skin and lung tissue are very different, as are painting and breathing. It couldn't make those arguments about inhalation studies. Such concealment might even rise to the level of fraud because the cigarette makers had spent so much money to persuade the public that no one had proven the "causal link" between cigarette smoke and cancer.

DeNoble became privy to other queer things. His spacious working quarters were just down the hall from psychologist Frank Ryan, who was filming smokers puffing low-tar cigarettes that had ventilation holes punched into the filter. The holes diluted tar and nicotine in the smoke with air, lowering the yields of those components as measured by the Federal Trade Commission's smoking machines. Ryan's films consisted of close-ups of how each smoker held or lipped the cigarette, so the company could figure out how to place the holes exactly where smokers would be most likely to block them, and so sustain the flow of nicotine. And since the FTC machines, unlike most people, smoked the cigarettes from the very tip and didn't cover the holes, it was easy to fool the government into thinking that smokers were getting less tar and nicotine than they actually were.

The industry had come a long way from 1962, when, as the embattled companies prepared to launch a grand effort to analyze and if possible remove the toxic compounds from cigarette smoke, a British cigarette company researcher lamented that they were really not up to the task, having among them scant scientific expertise. At that time most tobacco companies had herds of engineers, but scarcely any scientists. Over the next thirty years, Philip Morris spent more heavily than other firms to develop a research capability that outshone even that of then–industry leader R. J. Reynolds and which compared favorably to that at drug companies like Wyeth Pharmaceuticals, from which research director Osdene was recruited, one of a number of company employees who came over from the pharmaceutical industry. As far as its research focus, Philip Morris became so much like a drug company that it bought INBIFO, where a number of pharmaceutical firms conducted tests, because it was already doing so much research there on a contract basis. That a pharmaceutically-oriented lab was a frequent destination for Tom Osdene was understandably kept deeply under wraps. After all, why did a company manufacturing a simple agricultural product need so many laboratories?

The answer, as DeNoble soon learned, was that Philip Morris, along with the rest of the industry, had realized in the early sixties that it was in "the nicotine, not the tobacco, business," as a British-American Tobacco researcher said at the time. Two decades later, Philip Morris had become a science-driven company, and as it passed R. J. Reynolds as the sales leader, it expanded its strategy of seeking out the best minds—many of whom might have pursued academic careers had Philip Morris not lured them to its safe cigarette program with the promise of saving millions of lives. Soon there were some five hundred scientists and technicians at the PMRC, organized into two directorates: research, run by Osdene, which included DeNoble, Ryan, Charles, Dunn and others, and development, which was Bill Farone's shop and focused on research more directly oriented to the product. The company was spending $60 million on research a year, and its scientists were the envy of the industry. Then the roof fell in.

DESPITE A FEW TROUBLING DEVELOPMENTS, VICTOR DeNoble and Paul Mele were seeing mostly blue sky and open water as they charged ahead with their work. "We're rockin' now!" DeNoble liked to say to Mele, the only other person in the building who would have the slightest idea what he was talking about. Jim

Charles and Bill Dunn were well practiced at running interference against the corporate honchos in New York, who were understandably ambivalent about anything tending to show that the company not only knew cigarettes were unsafe and addictive, but had pushed the envelope of that knowledge until the company was far ahead of academic and government scientists. By the eighties, the directives coming from New York were increasingly colored by lawyerly concerns; still, the scientific types in Richmond managed to maintain a different perspective.

To develop nicotine analogs, DeNoble and Mele first needed a better model of how nicotine worked than was currently available. They set out using hooded rats, splotchy black and white animals that are common experimental subjects. Some were taken to the surgery table where DeNoble opened their skulls and inserted a cannula, a permanent port through which drugs could drip directly into their brains. Other rats were fitted for intravenous drug administration by passing a catheter down the animal's neck to its heart and out its back, an hour-and-a-half-long surgical procedure. The way DeNoble used the heart catheter was innovative and a major reason for the lab's success. Unlike earlier experimenters who let nicotine trickle into the animal over more than ten seconds, DeNoble set the apparatus to squirt the drug in four-second bursts, mimicking the rapidity with which nicotine from smoke reaches the brain when absorbed into the bloodstream in the lung. When not being experimented on, the rats lived in three rows of steel cages, with a water tank at the top that automatically flushed away droppings. An animal that had outlived its usefulness expired quickly in a special chamber charged with carbon dioxide.

To see if rats would self-administer nicotine, a benchmark test for what pharmacologists call "abuse liability," ten animals were put in self-administration chambers. These microwave-oven-sized boxes, costing $10,000 each, were sealed environments that provided the animals with food and water, a fan for ventilation, a houselight, and had a window for observation purposes. Above the chamber was an infusion pump, a small blue box that passed nicotine, or saline for the control group, from a clear glass beaker atop the pump into the animal. Inside the self-administration chamber were two switches. One wasn't hooked up to anything—it was there to screen out animals who simply liked to push switches. The other switch would give the rat a jolt of whatever was in the beaker. A record of the animal's behavior was electronically recorded and reproduced in several forms—on graphs, numerical printouts, numerical displays—in an adjoining room lined with solid-state monitoring equipment.

The most critical experiment was simple, although it took three months to complete. Would rats work to get nicotine? In other words, if their immediate needs for food and water were met, would they learn to press the lever to get nicotine, and learn to ignore it if it gave them only saline or water, a rough indicator of whether they responded to nicotine as a drug? And press they did, as many as seven times to get one nicotine injection.

"We didn't know where to start, so we started with the dose level in a Marlboro cigarette," said DeNoble. "But since rats arc much less sensitive to drugs, we multiplied it by six." It turned out that rats like nicotine, but nowhere near as much as cocaine, for which they would press three hundred times per shot. On the other hand, rats will press only four times to get alcohol, a drug with an enormous abuse potential for humans. "Rats just don't like alcohol," said DeNoble. "That's why we knew you couldn't make too many analogies from this test. All you could say was this tells you that this drug, nicotine, has a potential in man." But it was certainly, thought DeNoble and Mele, an unmistakable flag of warning. A strong possibility existed that nicotine was addictive, and much more research should be done.

DeNoble and Mele also did what are called acquisition studies. Drug acquisition is the process of learning to like a drug. Pharmacologically-active chemicals—drugs—require such a process. Sugar or saccharine or food does not. They are liked or disliked immediately. With nicotine it took rats an average of eighteen days to learn to like the buzz enough to press the lever regularly. Once they began to enjoy nicotine, they would take an average of seventy-six injections a day.

Then Mele and DeNoble did an experiment in which they gave the rats a free injection every thirty minutes, or forty-eight injections a day. The rats still injected themselves, but now only twenty-eight times, a proportional decrease, meaning the rats were trying to maintain their usual intake of seventy-six shots per day. When DeNoble and Mele further increased the free injections, the rats decreased the number they gave themselves via the switch. DeNoble and Mele began to get excited because this showed a dose-response relationship, something DeNoble had learned from his NIDA fellowship was common to addictive drugs. It meant the animal needed to keep a certain level of nicotine in his bloodstream. The key word was *needed*.

The trick now was to prove that nicotine acted like a drug in the brain—that there were receptors for it there that had to be activated by the drug before it could take effect. Complicating the experiment was the fact that nicotinic receptors are located not only in the brain but in the nervous system all over the body. So DeNoble and Mele gave the rats hexamethonium, which blocks nicotine everywhere except in the brain. The rats continued to press the switches to get their fix. The demand for nicotine was coming directly from the brain, just as does the demand for morphine, alcohol, and cocaine.

"That was the proof," remembered DeNoble. "The crescendo of that experiment was right there."

The self-administration work wasn't merely product research. When DeNoble and Mele wrote up their results in "Nicotine as a Positive Reinforcer for Rats" in 1982, no one had ever gotten rats to self-administer nicotine before. Largely due to DeNobles' programming of the heart catheter, which got nicotine to the brain much more quickly than earlier techniques, DeNoble and Mele had achieved an important breakthrough. They asked for permission to submit their paper for publication in the scholarly journal *Psychopharmacology*. Philip Morris allowed them to submit the paper, but edited out the drug-acquisition and hexamethonium studies, which they felt waved too many red flags. The journal accepted the paper, and then the company's lawyers intervened and forced DeNoble to withdraw it.

Private sector scientists understand that sometimes they must temporarily hold off on publishing research to avoid compromising a product in development. But this was different, DeNoble realized. Philip Morris was deliberately suppressing an important study because it told an unpleasant truth. It was the first real sign of trouble. DeNoble and Mele found it disturbing.

The analog work continued nevertheless, as did all the various experimental ventures on which DeNoble and Mele were embarked. The lab had tripled in size, from about 350 square feet to 1,100, forcing other scientists on their floor to relocate. Money was still limitless. When they needed a new computer system, they were told to just go out and buy whatever they wanted, and wound up spending $50,000. As a joke, they included in one annual budget a request for $278,000 to put rats on the space shuttle for a nicotine experiment. They were a bit chagrined that the request was denied.

Finding a usable nicotine analog was accomplished far more quickly than anyone had expected. Hundreds of already synthesized analogs were sitting on the shelf waiting to be tested, and dozens of these were ultimately patented. Each was a minutely different permutation of nicotine in which one molecule had been substituted for another in the chemical chain. Each went through two initial tests, one to eliminate analogs that increased heart rate and another to see if the analog reached the brain receptors. The third test was to inject the compound directly into the rat's brain. Nicotine-like chemicals produce something called "prostration syndrome." The animal's legs give way, its hair stands on end, it hyperventilates and loses control of its bowels and bladder. Only nicotine produces these effects.

Unlike Diana Dollinger, the rat was getting a sub-lethal dose and recovered in five minutes. In fact, DeNoble noticed, the rat didn't seem to mind. The experimenter could dangle a food pellet in front of the paralyzed animal, which would just stare at it, glassy eyed. The rat was evidently stoned.

By late 1981, DeNoble and Mele had successfully shepherded several analogs through these trials. One was 2-prime methylnicotine, which reached the brain intact and showed no cardiovascular effects. In fact, much to DeNoble and Mele's delight, it slowed heart rate just slightly.

Two-prime then passed a drug discrimination test in which rats were trained to press a switch if the drug they were getting felt like nicotine, another if it felt like saline. Rats given 2-prime pressed the nicotine switch. And 2-prime was four to eight times as powerful as nicotine, potentially far more addictive. Two-prime proved notably free of unpleasant side effects, unlike other analogs, and in fact was more benign than nicotine.

But their euphoria over the analog ended abruptly when DeNoble and Mele had another telling clash with their bosses, this time over nicotine tolerance experiments.

Nicotine is a cholinergic agonist, a poison. The body must develop a tolerance to it, or it will get sick and stop taking it. Therefore the cells change biochemically so they can function when it is present. Eventually, the cells begin to crave nicotine when it isn't present.

In one tolerance experiment, rats were given injections of nicotine in their buttocks over a ninety-day period. At first, at certain doses of nicotine, the rats became so impaired they were unable to press a lever to get a food pellet. But gradually they could function on that amount and by the end of the experiment they were lustily pressing even after being injected with ten times the dose that had once induced stupor.

After their reports on this work made the rounds at Philip Morris, Dunn called DeNoble and Mele in for a chat. He said the tolerance experiments were brilliant, utterly convincing, elegant. However, they were to suspend them and never do any more. Dunn was sympathetic to their heated protests, but the decision came from the lawyers and it was final.

"We found their bodies adjust," said DeNoble. "And that's very dangerous, because tolerance is one of the primary definitions of drug addiction. And here we were showing them that there's massive tolerance."

This setback was sweetened when DeNoble and Mele were given the go-ahead to unveil 2-prime methylnicotine and another equally promising analog for Philip Morris higher-ups even though the testing wasn't finished. This would be done at one of the "Richmond meetings," legendary events for which top brass flew from New York to the research center for a lecture on the latest hot topic in R and D.

On January 7, 1982, DeNoble summarized the accomplishments of his behavioral pharmacology program for Philip Morris president Shepard Pollack, assistant general counsel Fredric Newman, and Hugh Cullman, who had run Philip Morris's foreign operations for years, plus Dunn, Charles, and others. DeNoble described 2-prime methylnicotine, but even this exciting news caused barely a flicker on the poker faces of the executives.

"Okay," said Pollack. "If you've got this analog, and I believe you do, design me a safer cigarette."

A safer cigarette was something DeNoble had been pondering

for two years. So, homework assignment in hand, he returned to the lab that night and quickly sketched what one might look like and included it in a brief handwritten memo to Jim Charles that he fired off on January 8. His diagram called for a sophisticated filter to remove noxious elements from smoke, while the mouth end of the cigarette would hold a series of pads saturated with flavorants and the newly developed nicotine analogs.

DeNoble was very excited about his concept and over the next several weeks peppered Dunn with questions about how it was being received. Dunn just smiled and said the idea was intriguing, and probably do-able. Higher powers were weighing in with their thoughts, he said.

A few weeks later, he told the two scientists that the final answer, unfortunately, was no. There wasn't going to be a safer cigarette based on DeNoble's design, again for legal reasons. But the real bombshell came in September, when Jim Charles dropped in to the lab and ordered them to immediately halt the analog experiments. The company was very happy to have the analogs, but planned to do nothing with them right away.

"They're taking the position that the analogs are going into an in-case-they're-ever-needed status for now," Charles said.

DeNoble and Mele were bitterly disappointed. They had always assumed the company would move aggressively to incorporate such a potentially life-saving innovation into an actual cigarette. They felt duped. And there was not a thing they could do.

"It was simple," said DeNoble. "We couldn't get the analogs anymore. The chemists wouldn't make it. It's not like we could make it ourselves."

Nevertheless, they continued moving forward on other fronts, including the forbidden tolerance work, until January 1983, when the long arm of the New York power center reached out for DeNoble. He was summoned to give a presentation to Philip Morris president Ross Millhiser and his staff at the corporate headquarters on Park Avenue, a highly unusual request. DeNoble had spent weeks preparing for the talk. Using slides, charts, and overheads, he gave a two-hour comprehensive overview of his and Mele's work, which by now had gone on, full tilt, for almost three years. DeNoble and Mele had not only succeeded in isolating nicotine analogs, but along the way had done research that would not be duplicated for more than a decade. They had shown rats would self-administer the drug, that nicotine induced an enormous tolerance comparable to or greater than that developed to cocaine or heroin, and that it acted in some of the same brain sites as cocaine. Taken together, all of this was clearly recognizable as the thumbnail sketch of an addictive drug.

When the presentation was over, there were two beats of silence. Millhiser leaned forward and asked his one and only question.

"Why should I risk a billion dollar industry on rats pressing levers for nicotine?"

DeNoble was stunned. "I don't know," he said finally. "I guess I can't answer that."

DeNoble pondered this exchange all the way home on the corporate jet, but came to no conclusions. There was, unbeknownst to DeNoble, a background to Millhiser's question. A potent new crop of liability suits was being filed against the cigarette manufacturers in the early eighties, of which the most threatening would prove to be a New Jersey action called *Cipollone*. Despite this, DeNoble's work continued, although a team of lawyers from Shook, Hardy & Bacon, the firm David Hardy had founded, arrived at the PMRC after *Cipollone* was filed in the summer of 1983. On an intermittent basis for several months, they had DeNoble and Mele take them through every detail of every experiment, and photocopied their files and notes. The lawyers were very polite. They said simply that there was "some litigation out there" that could be of concern and they needed to get up to speed on the research.

Jim Charles said not to worry about it. At worst, they might have to be relocated to Europe, out of reach of the American courts, or "fired" and moved to a warehouse somewhere in Richmond, where they would work under contract, another legal gambit.

Then, one morning a few days before Thanksgiving, Shepard Pollack, now the CEO of Philip Morris, turned up at DeNoble's lab with corporate counsel Fred Newman. Pollack wanted a tour of the facility. He asked DeNoble and Mele to explain in layman's terms everything they were doing.

Pollack insisted they spare no technical detail, and they spent an hour dutifully guiding him through their work, a kind of miniature version of what they had done for the lawyers from Kansas City. They had even set up a self-administration chamber so Pollack could see a rat press a lever making nicotine squirt into his heart and zoom to his brain.

Pollack asked if this meant nicotine was addictive.

"Don't answer that question," Newman interrupted. "I think that's the wrong question."

DeNoble reassured them that in fact, while a hallmark of addiction, self-administration proved only a drug's potential for abuse.

"Okay, let me ask this," said Newman. "Are these the same tests a government agency would use to define abuse potential or addiction or whatever?"

"Absolutely," DeNoble said. "Don't forget, I was trained by the National Institute on Drug Abuse."

Newman curtly thanked the two scientists and tugged Pollack out of the building. Five months later, Jim Charles called DeNoble into his office. Remembering that he had gotten a promotion at about the same time the previous year, DeNoble figured he was getting another one. Instead, Charles sat him down and told him that as of three o'clock—it was a few minutes after when DeNoble walked in—the behavioral pharmacology program at Philip Morris was over. DeNoble and Mele were told to immediately turn over all notes and documents, kill one hundred rats, close the lab, and get out of the building. The two researchers were given the "choice" of quitting or remaining with the company as factory workers. They quit. But before he left for the last time, Mele stuffed as many documents as he could under his shirt. A week later, DeNoble was escorted back to the lab to open a safe that contained controlled substances, which needed to be disposed of according to special procedures. He found the entire operation—cages, surgery tables, desks, electrical connections, gas outlets, light fixtures—had vanished.

It was the beginning of a purge in which the company systematically rid itself of the scientists it had hired to make cigarettes safer, since such work proved it knew its ordinary cigarettes were hazardous. But the firings, the asphyxiation of rats, the mysterious trips to Europe—none of it could keep such a big genie in his bottle. To Bill Farone, it would seem as though Diana Dollinger's

suicide had somehow foreshadowed a reckoning with the company's true mission. The day she died he asked himself if he was
being used. By the time he found out, the company already had
what it wanted and it was too late.

PAUL MELE AND VICTOR DENOBLE HAD BEEN DRIVING
around in limousines for what seemed like weeks. Not that they were
complaining. Being squired around Richmond by a long-legged
blonde in evening clothes didn't exactly qualify as Dante-esque pun-
ishment. They probably would be having a terrific time had the circumstances of their departure from Philip Morris not been so utterly
deflating. Of course, had that not been true, they wouldn't be getting
the royal treatment.

What the hell is going on here? DeNoble found himself wondering. The limousine would pick them up at about six P.M. at their
homes and inside would be Rhonda Fawcett, one of the lawyers
from Shook, Hardy & Bacon who had visited DeNoble's lab in the
summer of 1983, along with a senior female Shook, Hardy lawyer
and another Philip Morris scientist. Fawcett happened to be an extremely attractive woman, but exactly what she or her employer expected to accomplish was obscure, other than evidently wanting to
soothe away any grudge DeNoble and Mele might harbor against
Philip Morris.

"What can we do to make you guys happy?" Fawcett said on
more than one occasion. "We just feel you guys aren't happy."

So for most of a week, this odd group dined, danced, and bar-
hopped. What with all the cloak and dagger at Philip Morris, De-
Noble's threshold for shock had risen above most people's. One
night, Fawcett invited DeNoble and Mele up to Fawcett's hotel
room for drinks. They declined. DeNoble felt it could be an attempt
to compromise them.

"They're going to throw us in the James River," Mele joked as
they drove away.

But the carousing was a good way to break the monotony of days
spent in a hastily thrown together office in a largely empty building
across I-95 from the Research Center, where the company continued to pay their salaries as they looked for new jobs. Though Fawcett
would later deny that her purpose was anything other than innocent,

nevertheless, DeNoble and Mele couldn't help but wonder if these social evenings were an attempt to see if they were planning to bolt and go public with the rat lab work. Would they try to pay them off?

Things had gotten weird enough. DeNoble decided it was time to go to a lawyer. So the two scientists visited a no-nonsense Richmond attorney who had once sued Philip Morris in an environmental case. They laid out the whole tale of the lab, their research, the shutdown, everything. Could they publish their data? they asked the lawyer.

The lawyer fired off a letter to Philip Morris, asking for a better severance package for the scientists and implying that Mele and DeNoble might go public with their rat research.

In reply, the company coldly informed him that his clients had done sensitive work for Philip Morris which they could not discuss—even with an attorney—under the terms of their confidentiality agreement.

"You guys really hit a nerve," the lawyer said.

Soon afterward, DeNoble got a new job with Ayerst Pharmaceuticals and left Richmond for central New Jersey. It took Mele another five months, but he landed a position with the Armed Forces Radio-Biological Institute in Bethesda, Maryland. Philip Morris was right about the two scientists. They were indeed embryonic whistle-blowers, awaiting the right conditions to be born. Long after their lab closed, at one of the most vulnerable moments in the industry's history, they would re-emerge. Although it would have been out of character for Philip Morris to have done so, in retrospect, it might have been far cheaper to pay them off.

WHILE MELE AND DENOBLE PURSUED THEIR SEPARATE paths, another, similar embryo was gestating in Louisville, Kentucky, headquarters of the Brown & Williamson Tobacco Company, third-largest cigarette maker in America. In fact, the same wave of 1980s lawsuits that got DeNoble and Mele fired got Merrell Williams hired.

Williams was among a gang of paralegals brought aboard to organize Brown & Williamson corporate records that might be requested in an anticipated blitz of discovery orders. They were taught to view what they read in the most damning light possible, to err always on the side of caution.

"We want you to think like a plaintiff's lawyer," Williams's supervisor told him during his orientation at Brown & Williamson in Louisville in January 1988.

The several dozen paralegals who sorted and coded documents were housed at the Hill Street research and development building, a fortress-like brick structure surrounded by a chain-link fence topped with barbed wire.

But the security was directed outward, toward the Hill Street ghetto. Inside, the coders, who took up most of the second floor, worked in what Williams called "a slapstick environment." They were temporary workers, many of them law students, very bright, who sat at community tables amid stacks of paper shooting rubber bands at each other and using homemade foam golf clubs to putt small objects into coffee cups.

The executives of the R and D operation were on the fourth floor, while the third had a smoking machine. Williams couldn't help but notice from his first days at Hill Street that no one minded the store. The coders horsed around. Lawyers were almost never seen. And Williams's own supervisor showed up around eleven A.M.

Williams, who had a doctoral degree in theater, was the only artist among the coders. He was also a bit older at forty-seven, and had, by his own admission, failed thoroughly at everything he tried in life, beginning with being drummed out of the Army for attacking his sergeant with a helmet and proceeding through bouts of alcoholism and depression. A heavy smoker in shaky health, Williams was en route to one of his three divorces and four bankruptcies when he took the paralegal job with Wyatt, Tarrant & Combs, the giant Kentucky law firm running the document project at Brown & Williamson. Nine dollars an hour sounded good to Williams, who was raking leaves and working as a handyman at a car dealership. And, as a Ph.D., he welcomed the chance to do some brain work.

Brown & Williamson, an extremely conservative company, was the last in the industry to sort and code its documents in preparation for lawsuits, an undertaking involving eight million pages of material that was well along by the time Williams came onboard. It was a two-step operation. First, a group of "objective coders" fixed each document with a date, author, title, and so on. Then the subjective coders sorted them into categories designated by letters. The "D" codes all related to disease—addiction-related materials were marked "DA," while cancer got a "DD" and lung cancer "DDA." Documents on marketing cigarettes to children were designated "ABEG." Then they rated each piece of paper on a scale of one to three according to how dangerous it would be if captured by a plaintiff's lawyer, with three being the least damaging. All youth-targeting documents got an automatic "1."

As he read and sorted and coded, Williams grew angrier and angrier. What he was reading were forty years' worth of suppressed studies on nicotine, secondhand smoke, and lung cancer with code names like Ariel, Hippo, Janus, and Wheat. There was a fascinating account of a scientific conference called by Brown & Williamson's parent company, British-American Tobacco, a colossus with affiliates in Brazil, Germany, and Canada.

In 1962, while the American companies were fighting the *Green* and *Ross* cases, British-American brought top scientists from each affiliate to the British seaport town of Southampton to decide what to do about the increasingly troublesome health issue. It was decided to embark on a secret research campaign to either disprove that smoking causes lung cancer or isolate the problem-causing elements of cigarette smoke and remove them, using filters or additives.

Williams read how BAT built a brand-new laboratory called Harrogate, where it planned to carry out one of the largest biological research programs in history, using six thousand mice. Project Janus included dozens of clandestine cancer experiments and went on for thirteen years. Project Hippo dealt with the effects of nicotine and was carried out at a private lab called Battelle.

Williams was amazed that the conferees at Southampton seemed to fully accept that, as one of them pointed out, "smoking is a habit of addiction."

"Nicotine is not only a very fine drug, but the technique of administration through smoking has considerable psychological advantages," noted Sir Charles Ellis, a senior BAT scientist.

Williams began to write down whatever he could remember about the documents as soon as he got home each night. In his spare time, he went to the library and read volumes of congressional testimony on the industry and researched cigarette-related patents. The undertaking became an obsession. Soon, simply recreating from memory was not enough.

One day, he found the door to a supervisor's office open and, curious, walked in. There was an inch-thick stack of documents on the desk. As he glanced at them, he noticed that none of the pages had a Bates stamp. In civil litigation, every page of every document is stamped with a series of nine or ten numbers as an identifier. The lack of those numbers told Williams that Brown & Williamson might never hand this batch over to any plaintiff's lawyer. And that made him much, much more curious.

Williams riffled through the stack and found copies of transatlantic cables from July 1963 between Brown & Williamson and BAT. One was an outgoing cable directed to one Anthony McCormick in London. As he read, his heart began to race:

FINCH AGREES SUBMISSION BATTELLE OR GRIFFITH DEVELOPMENTS TO SURGEON GENERAL UNDESIRABLE AND WE AGREE CONTINUANCE OF BATTELLE WORK USEFUL BUT DISTURBED AT ITS IMPLICATIONS RE CARDIOVASCULAR DISORDERS.

The cable was signed, "YEAMAN."

Williams knew that Finch was Edward Finch, then president of Brown & Williamson. Yeaman was Addison Yeaman, the company's general counsel. Anthony McCormick was a high-ranking lawyer at BAT. And of course the Battelle work was Project Hippo, which probed nicotine's addictiveness and reported that it elevated heart rates.

When that cable was sent, the Surgeon General's Advisory Committee was working on its landmark report, issued in 1964, the first to say unequivocally that cigarettes cause lung cancer. But the Surgeon General hedged on the nicotine issue, citing a lack of detailed studies. Williams now realized Hippo might have changed that.

Thinking like a plaintiff's lawyer, Merrell Williams could see how Yeaman's cable combined with the Southampton meeting would be extremely hard to explain to a jury. It flew in the face of forty years of publicly denying nicotine was addictive. Here were top executives who took it for granted that it was addictive at the time of the *Ross* trial, twenty-six years before the Surgeon General came to that conclusion.

The stack sat on the supervisor's desk for several weeks, while Williams planned how to get it out of the building and copy it. He was afraid some invisible electronic imprint on the paper would set off an alarm, so he came in one Saturday, grabbed a few pages, slipped them into a slit in his overcoat, and walked out, grinning vapidly at the security guard downstairs and holding his breath.

"My daughter's sick, I'll be back, just going to check on her," he told the guard.

The hair he had carefully placed on the remaining documents in the supervisor's office was still there when he came back from the copy shop to return the originals. No one sprang at him from the lobby. No buzzers went off. He made another trip that day and copied more of the stack.

Soon, he was showing up before seven A.M. on weekends, when no one else was working, specifically to steal documents. His natural gift for memorizing plays became invaluable as he mentally marked interesting boxes and folders that he would later pilfer. He picked up a ruined valise at a rummage sale to carry out paper, and later wore a waist-shrinking exercise girdle under his shirt. He jammed documents underneath it and, to avoid telltale rustling, ripped open a bag of potato chips as he passed the guard. He volunteered to break in new coders so he could collect the most sensitive material, allegedly for training, but really for more convenient transport to the copy shop. And finally, just for insurance, he slept with one of his supervisors.

He stole a lot—about four thousand pages. The documents accumulated in his basement, until he decided he had to get them into safekeeping, beyond the reach of Brown & Williamson.

He also typed up a manuscript-length narrative that laid out the corrupt history they revealed, entitled *Intent to Deceive*. Then he placed one set of the documents with a friend in Orlando, Florida, along with a sealed envelope instructing her on what to do with them in the event of his death.

SCORCHED EARTH, WALL OF FLESH

THE CASE THE TOBACCO COMPANIES WORRIED MOST about during the eighties was an epic New Jersey battle called *Cipollone*. It turned out to be a close call, and the industry never forgot it.

Shook, Hardy & Bacon, the firm Dave Hardy built, knew *Cipollone* wasn't like other suits, nor was the consortium of law firms that brought *Cipollone* like other adversaries. These were not quixotic solo practitioners, but three substantial firms with deep pockets. Lead trial attorney Marc Edell brought eight cases, one of which, *Cipollone* v. *Liggett Group, Philip Morris and Loews* quickly became unusually active.

Edell was the first to ask for a lot of documents on a lot of topics, and by the time of trial he had collected five hundred thousand of them, ten times the number amassed by anyone before him.

He was deposing everyone under the sun, including Thomas Osdene and William Dunn from the Philip Morris Research Center. Edell didn't know, of course, that eight months after he filed *Cipollone* in August 1983, two scientists named Victor DeNoble and Paul Mele were relieved of their duties and their nicotine lab shuttered. It would have been quite a revelation, since Edell was digging vigorously into the addiction issue.

There had been concern, even before Edell sued, that Ron Motley himself would get into tobacco litigation because his name was on some late seventies lawsuits that blamed both cigarette and asbestos companies for the lung disease of injured workers. Steven C. Parrish, a young lawyer at Shook, Hardy, heard that Motley and his crowd seemed on the verge of suing tobacco, and that this would be an unfortunate development.

"These are a different breed of cat," Parrish heard people say. "They've been through this against the asbestos industry. They've already got the experts."

Parrish was just getting his feet wet in the firm's tobacco unit. He had joined Shook, Hardy in 1975, the same year Motley joined Blatt & Fales. Like other young associates, he had a reverence for David Hardy, who died in 1976. *Ross* was studied like a sacred text by the firm's tobacco lawyers, and even though Hardy was seriously ill when Parrish came aboard, his philosophy pervaded the place.

"Fourteen-hour-a-day Dave," as he was known, gave the firm both its workaholicism and its brass balls, beginning with his job interview in 1940, at which he casually propped his feet up on partner Edgar Shook's desk.

Wouldn't you throw out a guy who did that? Hardy was asked later.

"No," said Hardy. "But I'd tell him to get his feet off the damned desk."

By the mid-seventies, Hardy had transformed the firm from a small mid-western practice into a national power representing the entire cigarette industry and other corporations of global reach. Tobacco documents, which filled one cabinet at the time of the *Ross* case, were now housed in "the Philip Morris room."

However, much hadn't changed since the sixties. The custom of stapling a rubber chicken to the door of a winning trial lawyer continued. And Shook, Hardy was still composed largely of men and women, who, like Hardy, were from small towns in Missouri. Steve Parrish was from Moberly, halfway between St. Louis and Kansas City. His father was a detective for the railroads, "a railroad dick" as they were unflatteringly known. Growing up, Parrish dreamed of a career in politics. But while at the University of Missouri law school, David Hardy's alma mater, he clerked at Shook, Hardy, and decided to be a trial lawyer.

The firm was small by defense standards when Parrish joined, about forty attorneys. The atmosphere was informal and egalitarian. Parrish liked to say that the only way to tell the partners from the

associates at meetings was by the gray in their hair. He fit in with
the grind at Shook, Hardy, where it was common to find most of the
firm working Saturdays and a good number still hammering away
on Sunday. Compact and fit, with a full neatly coiffed head of dark
hair, his unceasing energy was offset by a self-deprecating quality
notably missing among litigators. He caught the eye of senior partners as much for these personal qualities as for his success in defending the drug company Eli Lilly in a number of high-profile
cases involving DES or diethylstilbestrol, a synthetic estrogen taken
by pregnant women to avoid miscarriage that proved carcinogenic
years later in their children.

His managerial acumen was one reason Parrish assumed command of the Shook, Hardy & Bacon contingent facing off against
Marc Edell in *Cipollone,* where Parrish worked under Murray Bring
of Arnold & Porter, a politically powerful Washington, D.C., firm.
Bring and Parrish coordinated the efforts of seven law firms and
over a hundred lawyers, including David K. Hardy, David R. Hardy's
son, and Rhonda Fawcett.

The money spigot was turned up full blast for *Cipollone,* named
for lung cancer victim Rose Cipollone, a case in which the industry
spent $50 million over almost a decade, delayed producing docu-
ments for years, and buried Edell in pre-trial motions and appeals.
They took numerous depositions, one of which lasted twenty-two
days, and hired private detectives to track down relatives Rose
Cipollone hadn't seen since childhood. But worst of all was what
happened to Rose Cipollone herself. Although withering in the final
stages of lung cancer, she was deposed for nearly twenty-four hours
over a period of four days by industry lawyers. She had lost her left
lung and was so weakened by chemotherapy that she fainted. A half
hour was spent probing whether she ate barbecued dishes, and the
prevalence of spicy foods and butter on the family dinner table.

This ordeal helped drain what little energy Cipollone had left
and she died before Edell had a chance to question her himself.
And so the only information the jury heard from the plaintiff's own
mouth came in response to carefully framed industry questions.
There was little doubt on the plaintiff's side that even if this wasn't
part of a deliberate strategy, the defense viewed it as desirable.

Reporters who covered the trial, held before federal District
Judge H. Lee Sarokin in Newark, New Jersey, were astonished at

the size of the tobacco contingent, which frequently numbered thirty or more lawyers, even for minor procedural matters. They seemed to travel in caravans. Four lawyers no one had ever seen before would fly in, argue a motion, and fly out, never to appear again.

Alan Darnell, who worked on *Cipollone* with Marc Edell, dubbed these tactics "scorched earth, wall of flesh." Scorched earth meant using every trick of the legal process to stall or derail the case. The wall of flesh was the massing of lawyers to intimidate the other side.

Parrish's major role was as behind-the-scenes strategist. It was his task to deal with the damaging admissions contained in the many documents Edell had retrieved. Edell had gotten the Philip Morris smoker psychology study by William Dunn that called a pack of cigarettes "the storage container for a day's supply of nicotine," as well as a Philip Morris research document from 1961 admitting that carcinogens "are found in practically every class of compounds in smoke." Parrish's response was that these were the musings of individuals, not expressions of company policy.

But as the jury went out, Parrish crossed his fingers, convinced that some of the documents could seriously wound Lorillard and Philip Morris, Shook, Hardy's clients.

On Monday, June 13, 1988, the jury came back, and an amazing thing happened. Marc Edell won.

Sort of. In a tortured verdict, the panel ruled Rose Cipollone largely to blame for her own death, but also found that Liggett should have warned the public earlier about the hazards of smoking and awarded her husband, Antonio, $400,000. Much to Parrish's relief, they exonerated Philip Morris and Lorillard, whose brands Cipollone smoked later in life.

Four of the six jurors thought Edell's vaunted documents proved absolutely nothing. Instead, just as Parrish had hoped, they focused on Rose Cipollone's behavior—how awful it was of Rose to hound Antonio into getting cigarettes in the middle of the night—and not on the cigarette makers.

Still, it was the first plaintiff's verdict ever in a tobacco case, and though a mixed bag, proved the industry was mortal. And that got the attention of a lot of plaintiff's lawyers. Nevertheless, with Lorillard and Philip Morris exonerated, it was still a victory for Steve Parrish. Higher courts ultimately threw out the verdict and ordered a new trial. In the meantime Antonio Cipollone died, and neither the Cipollone family, nor Edell's legal consortium, now $7 million poorer, had any stomach for continuing the fight. The suit was dropped late in 1992.

But the documents returned to haunt the industry. A law school professor in Boston named Richard Daynard released them to reporters, and for the first time, outsiders read the private thoughts of tobacco executives about how lethal the product really was, which happened to be diametrically opposed to their public statements.

When Motley got hold of the *Cipollone* documents, he saw in them a familiar, smirking contempt. Juries didn't generally react well to that attitude, he thought. Perhaps Edell didn't handle them so skillfully.

Given the end result, Philip Morris was highly pleased with how Shook, Hardy & Bacon, and especially Steve Parrish, had protected its interests, which, by the late eighties, were extensive. Now the number one American company, Philip Morris had in Marlboro the best selling consumer product in the world, its advertising the globe's most familiar commercial symbol. In late 1988, the company hired Parrish, attached him to Philip Morris International, and sent him to Lausanne, Switzerland, PMI's headquarters and the site of one of the company's two European labs.

In 1990, Parrish was brought to New York and promoted to vice president and general counsel, responsible for both legal and regulatory matters. At the age of forty, Parrish had an office at the top of the Philip Morris building on Park Avenue. He was near the pinnacle of the company he had served so successfully, and that company was looking at a future of unblemished prosperity.

PASCAGOULA, MISSISSIPPI, IS ON THE GULF OF MEXICO, where the air is softened by the coming together of water and sky, which rise together in wispy clouds that float near the surface. Everything important about Pascagoula comes in from the Gulf, like the offshore oil platforms visible from Beach Avenue, where the town's richest citizens live, or the tankers out beyond the oil rigs, or the refineries that dot the shoreline.

Those things make Pascagoula not quite as beautiful as other places on the Gulf, but it is a place where people can find work.

And the biggest employer and biggest single thing in Pascagoula or for many miles around is Ingalls Shipbuilding, which in the early eighties had thirty thousand people on its payroll. Since World War II, the shipyard has built vessels for the United States Navy, growing massive on federal contracts.

Workers at the shipyard handled asbestos in the forties and fifties, and as the twenty-five-year latency period for asbestos disease ended, Ingalls Shipbuilding yielded a bumper crop of lawsuits. Local lawyers filed the cases, but early in the game brought in Ron Motley to try them, beginning with *Jackson* in 1982.

However, the Pascagoulans were merely dabbling in asbestos until Dickie Scruggs arrived on the scene.

Like Motley, Scruggs had learned to "mass up" his cases, raising the ante to the point where the manufacturers couldn't chance a verdict. By sticking to this strategy, Scruggs didn't have to put an asbestos case before a jury for seven years.

Finally, the companies refused to settle a group of cases called *Sciordino,* and in 1991, Scruggs brought in Motley, the acknowledged master, to try them. Though Scruggs and Motley had been on opposite sides of some asbestos issues, Scruggs, who was raised in Pascagoula, rolled out the red carpet for the contingent from Charleston. He had them to dinner at his home on Beach Avenue. Motley and Scruggs went out on Scruggs's boat, the *Bonhomme Richard,* drank beer, pounded each other on the back, and traded war stories. They were a peculiar pair: the impulsive Motley, a brilliant misfit, clambering onto the company jet (the turboprop having been sold) back to Charleston with some beauty on his arm, and Scruggs, who was disciplined, spoke crisply, and had been married to his wife, Diane, for twenty years. Scruggs's character was formed in important part during his time as a Navy fighter pilot, when he and his A-6 Intruder were assigned to the *Franklin Delano Roosevelt,* part of the Sixth Fleet. In October 1973, the fleet's uneventful Mediterranean cruise was decisively interrupted by the Yom Kippur War. The Israelis lost much of their air force early in the conflict, and the Western powers wouldn't allow the United States to resupply Israel from air bases on their territory. So replacement planes flew from the United States across the Atlantic on the wings of tankers, which parked overnight on carriers like the *Roosevelt.*

The next day Scruggs and his squadron mates each escorted a group of five tankers into Israel and the combat zone. This went on for five days, a jerry-rigged but successful operation, and a defining moment for Scruggs, who would henceforth measure all risks against it.

Scruggs left the Navy and attended law school. Finding the life of a corporate defense attorney too constraining after his adventures in the Mediterranean, he set up his own practice in Pascagoula in 1980.

Not long before he did, he lost a trial way out in central Mississippi to a local lawyer named John Barrett, who called himself Don. Despite beginning as adversaries, Barrett and Scruggs soon became good friends, and so when Barrett filed *Horton,* a cigarette lung cancer case against the American Tobacco Company, Scruggs observed closely. *Horton* ended in a hung jury just before the *Cipollone* trial began, which made *Horton* the first case tobacco didn't win unambiguously, and therefore a kind of defeat.

After the hung jury, Barrett and Scruggs got together in Destin, Florida, where both had vacation condos, and talked about tobacco suits, the first real thinking Scruggs had done on the subject. Barrett was determined to have another shot at the cigarette makers.

At the retrial, in the fall of 1990, the jury found the tobacco companies liable for Horton's death, but incongruously, awarded no damages.

It was an extraordinarily frustrating outcome for Barrett. Worse, after two fruitless trials, his legal allies were quitting on him. He had to have help, and the only friendly face he could think of with an abundance of both money and moxie was Dickie Scruggs. So he called him.

Barrett was in mid-pitch when Scruggs interrupted.

"I enthusiastically accept," said Scruggs. "I want to be involved. I will help not only with my time, I'll help financially. And, man, we'll whip 'em together."

"Well, hallelujah," Barrett said. "Welcome to the charmed circle."

JACK McCONNELL OFTEN FELT LIKE MOTLEY'S YOUNGER brother in his early days with the firm. Motley drove him hard, but gave him plum assignments, kept him with him on the road. The Rhode Islander was part of Motley's inner circle, a trusted group of younger lawyers to which Ann Ritter, Joe Rice, and Charles Patrick also belonged.

The Motley with whom McConnell traveled was a leaner, tougher version of the Motley of the early asbestos days, with a physique hardened by daily five-mile runs. He still drank heavily, though his face hadn't reddened as it later would. He wore his black hair combed straight back and sauntered into court sucking throat lozenges, slumping in his chair at slow points during trial, one leg bouncing as he scribbled notes.

His success created an aura that attracted followers, even groupies. Young men like McConnell were fascinated by Motley's strange combination of mental incandescence, reckless courage, and a tormented, almost childlike sensitivity. He could spit in the face of the enemy one minute and cry helplessly over a sick pet the next.

Motley began to confide in McConnell more and more. One night, at dinner in Pascagoula, Motley started telling McConnell about his mother, how she died from emphysema, how she sneaked cigarettes even in her last months in the hospital.

Then he said very quietly, "Jack, someday you and I are going to take on the tobacco industry."

McConnell saw tears, despite the orange cocktail glow.

"You watch," he said.

Motley had begun talking seriously about suing tobacco as early as 1992, when asbestos began chucking in the towel. As he and his little band traveled, Motley tried to build a consensus for his cause. No one thought it was a good idea.

The idea was shelved temporarily when Scruggs brought Motley back to Pascagoula in early 1993 to run one of the biggest civil trials in American history, the *Abrams* consolidated asbestos lawsuit, seven thousand cases amalgamated into a daunting two-stage proceeding. *Abrams* was too big to try in Pascagoula's antiquated courthouse, so it was moved to Exhibition Hall at the Jackson County Fairgrounds, where a small city of construction trailers was built for the lawyers—one trailer for the jury room, two for the defense, and two for Ness, Motley. Most of the Ness, Motley crowd stayed at the LaFont Inn, the town's only hotel.

Motley had a rented condominium. They lived in Pascagoula for four months.

The female Charlestonians didn't understand Pascagoula. There was nothing to eat that wasn't fried. Every morning, clients brought them cakes. A mutt appeared. Fed surplus cake, he refused to leave. Motley named him Garlock, after one of the defendants, and Garlock roamed about, howling. Ultimately, it being realized that the Motley Crew were the only people in Garlock's short miserable life who hadn't chased him with a stick, a paralegal adopted him and Garlock assumed residence in Charleston.

All through the spring and summer of 1993, they tried *Abrams* during the day, met in the trailer, broke for dinner, met again, wrote outlines and briefs, went back to the LaFont, and collapsed. The adrenaline of a huge trial, week after week, was like putting on a show every day. It was an emotional blast furnace. A psychologist testifying in *Abrams* found Motley and his Crew more interesting than the case.

"You guys are so co-dependent," the psychologist told them at the hotel restaurant, "you'll go through withdrawal when this is over."

Motley was the main horse in the courtroom, while Scruggs, who had a magic touch for negotiating, handled the deal-making as defendants weakened and settled.

The high point of the trial came when Dr. Robert Sawyer took the stand. Sawyer insisted small exposures to micarta, an asbestos product used at Ingalls, were harmless. White-haired and scholarly looking, Dr. Sawyer was an effective witness for the defense.

Unfortunately, Motley had come up with a public service video Sawyer did in the seventies for construction workers, which he now popped into the courtroom VCR.

The song "Stayin' Alive" from the movie *Saturday Night Fever* echoed through Exhibition Hall.

> "Hi, I'm Bob Sawyer!" said a longer-haired, younger-looking Sawyer.
>
> *Well, you can tell by the way I use my walk, I'm a wanted man, no time to talk*
>
> "If you're chipping away at an asbestos ceiling without a respirator, you could be chiseling twenty years off of your life," Sawyer warned a worker on a ladder.

Ah, ah, ah, ah, stayin' alive, stayin' alive

"It can cause asbestosis," said Sawyer, "at very low concentrations."

*Ah, ah, ah, ah stayin' aliiiiiiiiiiiiiiii-i-eee-iiiiiii-i-
eeeeeee . . .*

"I notice that's a cut version of the film," Sawyer protested when
the tape ended. "There's a lot of it that's been edited."

"Would you like to see the whole one?" Motley asked. "I've got
the whole one here, sir,"

Nope, that won't be necessary, Sawyer said. He was quickly removed from the stand and no more was heard from Dr. Sawyer.
For weeks thereafter, the door to the Ness, Motley trailer would
spring open and Motley would burst in, thrust a forefinger into the
air, and yodel:

"Stayin' aliiiiiiiiiiiiiieeeeeeeiiiiiiive!"

FOR THE MOST PART, HOWEVER, ASBESTOS LAWSUITS HELD
little challenge for Motley anymore. The liability case was almost
airtight. He was beating the companies like carpets every time out.

"You know what, Dickie?" said Motley to Scruggs.

They were sitting together at the plaintiff's table in Exhibition
Hall toward the end of *Abrams*. Someone was droning their way
through a deposition.

"I'm bored," Motley said.

Scruggs nodded.

"I'm a little bored, too," he said.

Both wanted to get into tobacco. They talked about doing a synergism lawsuit, a lung cancer case involving an asbestos worker who
smoked, as most did. Tobacco and asbestos, each carcinogenic separately, produced an exponentially higher risk of a fatal tumor when
combined. And since the asbestos companies always blamed cigarettes for cancers in asbestos workers, why not haul both industries
into court?

In the middle of the *Abrams* trial, Scruggs dashed up to
Greenville, Mississippi, to help Barrett try a tobacco case called
Wilks, a suit for a retarded schizophrenic. Motley sent jury consul-
tant Theresa Zagnoli to work with Barrett, free of charge.

While Barrett and Scruggs were in Greenville, they were visited by a University of Mississippi law school classmate of Scruggs named Mike Lewis. Lewis had employed a part-time bookkeeper who was a lifelong smoker. She had a series of heart attacks, and because of her long illness, fell into poverty. In the final year of her life she was penniless and had to go on Medicaid to pay her medical bills.

The bookkeeper's family asked Lewis to sue the tobacco company, but Lewis knew his two-man law firm couldn't manage it. In the spring of 1993, Lewis visited the dying woman for the last time. Depressed, he walked out of the hospital that day realizing the bookkeeper's medical bill had now topped $1 million. Suddenly it struck Lewis that instead of suing for the bookkeeper, he could sue for that $1 million on behalf of the state, which wasn't responsible for the bookkeeper's smoking.

In fact, by suing on behalf of the state Medicaid program, a lawyer could attack the tobacco companies on behalf of all the penniless heart attack and cancer victims. And that could cause the industry some real pain.

The following month, he got up the nerve to meet with Attorney General Mike Moore, another law school classmate, to explain his idea. Moore was intrigued, but knew the legislature would never spend money to sue tobacco in ultra-conservative Mississippi. He told Lewis that if he could put together a team of private lawyers with both product liability experience and the money to fund the enterprise, he might be interested.

A number of lawyers had already told Lewis no thanks by the time he called Scruggs, who invited him to visit the *Wilks* trial in Greenville. Barrett and Scruggs sat on their beds in the Hampton Inn and listened with barely restrained glee to Lewis's idea.

"The state of Mississippi did not smoke, did not choose to smoke, and did not choose to have to pay millions and millions of dollars every year on behalf of tobacco-related illness," explained Lewis.

It would be the end of the cigarette makers' most potent weapon, the assumption-of-the-risk defense, the idea that smokers freely choose to use the product, despite its warning labels and

well-publicized deadliness. Though Lewis didn't know it, a law professor named Donald Garner had come to exactly the same conclusion thirteen years earlier, but no one listened. However,
Scruggs and Barrett did, because *Wilks*—like every other individual lung cancer case—was heavy going. In fact, they were about to
lose the verdict.

"I'll tell you how I feel about it, Mike. Like we've been prospectin'
for years and finally just hit a big vein of gold," said Barrett.

Scruggs, Barrett, and Lewis, lightbulbs still glowing over their
heads, then met with Attorney General Moore. In fact, Scruggs had
worked in partnership with Moore before, suing to recover money
the state was owed in cases of asbestos contamination of buildings,
with Scruggs getting a percentage of the recovery. It looked like this
was going to be a whole lot bigger.

ABRAMS WAS APPROACHING A VERDICT WHEN MOTLEY
came into the bar of the LaFont Inn and asked Jack McConnell to
accompany him to a dinner meeting with Mike Moore.

"It's about tobacco, but you can't say anything about that," Mot
ley said.

McConnell begged off. He had been up for days preparing witnesses and was dead on his feet.

Scruggs had already briefed Motley on Mike Lewis's Medicaid
lawsuit idea. Motley got so excited, "I almost had to strap him
down," Scruggs remembered.

Motley had known Moore from the time Moore was district attorney of Jackson County, which included Pascagoula, where
Moore grew up. Moore often dropped in on Motley's trials, and was
close friends with Scruggs.

Moore reiterated what Mike Lewis, Scruggs, and Barrett had
come up with.

"Ron, you are going to be in charge of proving that these guys
are dirtbags, like you're doing with asbestos," Moore said.

"Do you think you've got a shot at that?"

Motley could see that Moore was plenty nervous about their
chances.

Motley said that from what little he had seen from *Cipollone,* he believed he could demonstrate fraud, a massive disinformation campaign about the health risks of smoking.

"I think that's just the tip of the iceberg," he told Moore.

When McConnell saw Motley the next day in the trailer he was still frothing with enthusiasm.

"Looks like we've hit on something here," he said. "Moore's thinking about a lawsuit for the state, a brand-new theory. Goddamn, I want to try it."

Motley, Scruggs, and their staffs began to elaborate the theory for a Medicaid reimbursement lawsuit, designed to be filed by the attorney general of Mississippi, but workable, in principle, anywhere. It would incorporate an idea Motley had pioneered in consolidated cases in which the money damages were based on statistics on the frequency and severity of a particular type of injury—in this case, lung cancer, emphysema, and heart disease—in a population, a so-called "damages model."

The Medicaid idea had at least two attractive features for Motley. It avoided the assumption-of-the-risk argument. And by consolidating the tobacco victims, he would drive up the damages, as he had with asbestos. The third feature, that the industry might therefore be driven to settle, still seemed absurdly far-fetched.

Getting Ness, Motley into the case was crucial because the Mississippi lawyers needed both the big firm's expertise in complex litigation and its financial resources to help front the millions the case would cost.

Ness, Motley was one of the few plaintiff's firms wealthy enough to take on tobacco. Within a year, Joe Rice, the firm's deal maker, would negotiate asbestos settlements worth $10 billion in consolidated cases. Motley and Rice had become the one-two punch that put the firm into the financial stratosphere in the nineties. Ness, Motley, which a dozen years earlier had five lawyers, now had fifty. And Rice, a cocky, gap-toothed North Carolinian fresh out of law school when Motley hired him, was the firm's most powerful partner after Motley himself.

Scruggs—who knew a couple of things about negotiating—had watched him work.

"He leaves nothing on the table," said Scruggs. "Joe's real talent—his pattern—is to argue over everything. Things that are just not worth arguing about, he will create a straight-faced argument not to give it to you. You'll have a 'whereas' clause in there that's totally meaningless, but he'll figure some objection to it, and he'll pile up these nickel-and-dime issues and then trade them back later for something of value."

Rice was now co-managing partner with Terry Richardson, and though junior to Motley, his role was to challenge Motley's tendency to ignore budgets and organizational constraints. So Joe Rice was the key person Motley felt he had to convince to get the firm to spend money on tobacco.

In the fall of 1993, Motley's jet touched down at the Philadelphia airport, where he was met at the terminal by Susan Haines, a paralegal whose cigarette lawsuit, filed on behalf of her dead father, was one of the group that had been handled by Marc Edell. Edell's firm had largely succeeded in dumping its tobacco suits. But Haines refused to let hers die, though she couldn't find a lawyer to take it over.

Motley was impressed by her determination, and intrigued by a cluster of fifteen hundred documents relating to possible misconduct by tobacco lawyers that were a central issue in the case. The documents had outraged the judge, who wrote an opinion so scathing, he was forced from the case for appearing biased.

Around the time of Motley's meeting with Susan Haines, the firm met to talk about tobacco. Besides Joe Rice, there were eighteen other partners to convince, and there was no expert Motley could fly in to argue it was a sound business investment. Almost anyone would have had to agree with Terry Richardson, who told Motley it would be "the world's biggest pro bono case."

Motley didn't even try to make an economic argument for getting into tobacco.

"We've been making a very good living off people with lung disease," he said, sitting at the head of a long conference table in Ness, Motley's Meeting Street headquarters.

"And here's this huge group who have it, the biggest group by far, and nobody's doing anything about it," he said.

He talked about Medicaid cases, secondhand-smoke cases, and other novel modes of attack. Everyone knew what Motley had done with asbestos consolidations, so there was little doubt he could fashion space age legal weapons. Even the youngest lawyers were aware that back in the Blatt & Fales days, Motley had insisted, against strong opposition, on taking asbestos cases, and without that leap of faith, none of them would have jobs. And Motley didn't have to mention his mother, because everyone knew that story.

His immediate objective was to convince the partners that Ness, Motley should take over Edell's *Haines* case, and think about the Mississippi Medicaid suit. Motley proposed a safety net, a $1-million limit on tobacco spending. Only a couple of lawyers would be assigned, and Motley's commitment would be part time.

Finally Joe Rice spoke up.

"Ron, I understand your wanting to do this. But don't tell me you're only going to spend a million dollars and you're only going to be part time on it. Because you never have before, and you sure as hell aren't going to do it on this."

Motley was unfazed.

"You know, Joe, you may be right," he said. "I probably won't. But I'll bet once we start, a lot of good things will come along, even money, because sooner or later, if you kill enough people, the sky may well open and some jury somewhere could get pissed off about it. The point is, we've got the money and people to make it happen. And I think, in the end, we'll be glad we went down this road.

"And I'll tell you one other thing," said Motley grimly. "I personally am going to get into this no matter what. With my own money if necessary. And I'll take any of you who want to join me."

There were some blank stares at that. Everyone suddenly seemed to realize it would not be a good thing if Ron Motley left the firm.

Even so, a third of the partners voted against the tobacco venture. And for the next several years, even those who voted yes would worry that they wouldn't get their usual split of the firm's profits because this crazed Ahab nailed a gold piece to the main-mast, causing a temporary loss of sanity that sent them into uncharted waters after the meanest whale in the ocean.

Nevertheless, for now at least, Ron Motley was in the tobacco wars.

IN AUGUST, THE *ABRAMS* JURY CAME BACK WITH A $12 million verdict for several "representative plaintiffs." Around the same time, one of the local Mississippi lawyers handed a thick bundle of paper to a member of Motley's staff. It was a two-hundred-page narrative in sometimes overheated prose that purported to be a history of tobacco industry misdeeds, especially those of Brown & Williamson. It summarized numerous B&W documents, some of which were extraordinarily incriminating. The local lawyer refused to say how he got it or who wrote it. Its title was *Intent to Deceive*.

Jack McConnell was walking up the steps of the Ness, Motley trailer when he ran into a paralegal talking to the local lawyer about this opus.

"You want to be real careful with it," said the local lawyer. "People could be killed over this thing."

That certainly piqued McConnell's interest, and while Motley was too busy to do more than glance at *Intent to Deceive*, McConnell read it all, lying on his bed at the LaFont. He decided he did not want a copy. This was indeed dangerous material, well beyond even the wildest allegations about the asbestos industry. It was so wild, it sounded fictional.

The next day, he had lunch with Motley in the trailer. Afraid the walls might have ears, they talked in a kind of code.

"You've got to inspect that package," said McConnell. "I knew this stuff was going on, but this is truly amazing."

Motley was enthralled as McConnell described what the manuscript revealed: very early knowledge of how addictive and deadly cigarettes were, proof of a cover-up, plans to remove and possibly destroy incriminating information, a monumental fraud lasting up to the present day.

Abrams went to verdict, and somehow Motley never got to read *Intent to Deceive* and actually forgot all about it. That fall, Motley went to Vancouver for a meeting of the Inner Circle of Advocates, an exclusive group of trial lawyers whose ranks are open only to those with at least fifty civil verdicts to their credit.

While there, a Ness, Motley paralegal decided to jog Motley's memory and faxed him a couple of pages of *Intent to Deceive*.

Motley called back immediately.

"Fax up some more of this thing," he demanded.

This time he read it from cover to cover. Meanwhile, Charles Patrick set out to learn more about the manuscript's author. He concluded that it appeared to have been written by a paralegal named Merrell Williams who had worked for Wyatt, Tarrant & Combs, a law firm in Louisville, Kentucky that helped organize millions of B&W's internal records for smoking and health lawsuits.

Williams also called his manuscript *Affidavit in Expectation of Death,* and the lugubrious title reflected its author's extreme paranoia, for Williams was convinced Brown & Williamson would murder him for leaking its secrets. The manuscript had nine chapters, with titles like "Beneficent Alkaloid Drug," "Lawyers and Science," and "Crusades in Illusion." Each dealt with a different subject, such as suppression of research, nicotine, placements of cigarettes in movies.

The documents themselves were still in Florida, stashed at the home of a friend. After putting them there, Williams did nothing for quite a while. But over time, his conviction grew that this story had to be told. He couldn't send the documents to the media because the coders initialed what they coded and many bore his initials.

Posing, for reasons known only to himself, as a woman, he wrote to Richard Daynard, the law school professor at Northeastern University who had released the *Cipollone* documents. After months of similarly bizarre preliminaries, Daynard flew to Orlando and met Williams in September 1990.

Williams seemed highly agitated. He never showed Daynard documents. He hinted at what he had. He wanted to know if there was some kind of immunity he could get if he brought them to light.

"I don't have any magic wand that can protect you," Daynard warned. "There is no safe way to do what you want to do. You're probably going to get into a lot of trouble. These are powerful, dangerous people."

"Yeah. As if I don't know that," said Williams wryly.

Daynard gave him the phone number of a reporter who might be able to help.

"You're a very brave man," Daynard told him as they shook hands.

Williams met with the reporter about publishing *Intent to Deceive,* but the reporter consulted a lawyer who told him no publisher would ever touch it. And Williams, who was still employed by Wyatt, Tarrant & Combs, wouldn't remain anonymous for long if he publicized the documents, since anyone he sent them to would have to check with B&W to make sure they were genuine.

The law firm laid him off in March 1992. Williams's unemployment benefits soon ran out. He had a quintuple bypass in 1993. Even if the industry didn't kill him, Williams realized, he could drop dead at any moment. In July 1993, as Motley finished up the *Abrams* case, Williams enlisted the help of a hard-nosed Louisville lawyer named J. Fox DeMoisey and they sent a box of Williams's pirated documents to Wyatt, Tarrant & Combs demanding that Brown & Williamson compensate Williams for "distress" caused by working with the documents. If not, Williams would sue and the material would enter the public domain as evidence, which was the whole point of the exercise.

Brown & Williamson sued, which Williams expected. Working with a judge in its backyard, B&W secured a ridiculous court order forbidding Williams from talking about the documents, even with his own lawyer. But not even DeMoisey knew about the sealed boxes in Orlando.

Though the documents weren't public, Williams was named in local newspaper articles that summer, alongside unflattering quotes from B&W's spokesmen. The spokesmen said Williams's "lawsuit" was no more than common blackmail, and the former paralegal merely a petty thief. But somehow, the folks at B&W and even the local reporters missed the point. For Merrell Williams had, in fact, committed an act of civil disobedience.

CIVIL DISOBEDIENCE

WHATEVER IT WAS THAT CLIFF DOUGLAS HAD GOTTEN A
quick glimpse of when his synapses started firing on the concept of
the metal-tube-soaked-with-nicotine that was Premier, he didn't get
another glimpse for a long time. Then one afternoon in April 1991,
he took a phone call at his office from a young woman. He wouldn't
recall much about the conversation afterward except how terrified
she had been.

She was a manager in research and development at R. J.
Reynolds in Winston-Salem. She had seen Douglas's name in a
North Carolina newspaper when he spoke at a tobacco-related
event there and felt he might be sympathetic.

"Let's just say there are things going on around here that I'm
really uncomfortable with," she said.

She was convinced that Reynolds would fire or blackball her for
going outside the company, and made Douglas swear to keep their
talk confidential. She wouldn't give her name. The call lasted
maybe fifteen minutes.

Douglas was a bit puzzled, but definitely intrigued. Within a
week, the woman called back. She believed Reynolds was deforest-
ing large tracts of South America for its tobacco farms, and that a
chemical Reynolds put in cigarette paper to increase the number of
puffs per cigarette could be harmful.

She had spoken out on these things at work and feared

reprisals. She described the Reynolds research center as a malignant place. She wanted out.

"RJR has the largest shredders you've ever seen," she said. Douglas laughed. She said lawyers were in the labs constantly.

The conversation veered from her personal fears to abstruse technical subjects. No matter how far afield she drifted, Douglas didn't push. His only fear was she would hang up. This time, he got her name and phone number.

It was the first step in an excruciating three-year-long courtship, and the whole time Douglas could never be sure the woman wouldn't freak out and never talk to him again. He didn't even know what he was looking for, just that he might learn some important secret about cigarettes. Eventually, the informant began calling him at home, or Douglas would call her at a pre-arranged time in the early evening. The conversations got longer and they began to enjoy each other. Douglas told her bad jokes, and she laughed. Sometimes she called in tears, and he would soothe her. He began as her attorney, because she had a confidentiality agreement with Reynolds and wanted advice on it. He soon became a sort of therapist, a father confessor. He was her friend, but in the end would really be her handler, bringing her story to the world.

He proved faithful to this isolated, terrified woman, never allowing details to surface that might identify her, refusing even to reveal whether she was a man or a woman, so that to this day, only six people know her name. It is no exaggeration to say that Cliff Douglas and the woman he would call "Deep Cough" were about to change the world.

DESPITE HER DOCTORATE IN ENGINEERING, DEEP COUGH was not very articulate. However, she knew how cigarettes were made, and more to the point, had worked on Premier, the pseudo-cigarette that used tobacco extract for most of its nicotine. She told Douglas about her connection to Premier early on, but he didn't know how to follow up, and Deep Cough wasn't even particularly interested in the subject of nicotine. Then one day in November of 1991, Douglas asked if Reynolds used tobacco extract in anything besides Premier.

"Oh, yeah," she said. "The biggest thing they use it in is 'recon.' Reconstituted tobacco."

She explained that Reynolds and the other cigarette companies use reconstituted tobacco sheet, a cheap alternative to leaf tobacco, as filler in the finished cigarette. To make the sheet, tobacco stems, sticks, dust and other junk that in the old days would simply have been discarded are formed into a dry brown sheet of tobacco "paper" from which all the liquids, known as solubles, have been leached out. The solubles are then concentrated into tobacco extract. The dried sheet is later "reconstituted" by spraying back the solubles, including the nicotine-rich tobacco extract, plus a mixture of flavors and humectants, which keep the tobacco from drying out.

"They can concentrate the extract to get any level of nicotine they want," said the woman. "You could have it at five percent, ten percent, fifty percent. It's up to the company."

The finished sheet is chopped up and mixed with other types of tobacco in the cigarette. The recon process helped ensure uniform nicotine delivery from puff to puff and cigarette to cigarette and stabilized nicotine levels in the recon filler material, which naturally has less nicotine than leaf tobacco.

Douglas was scribbling notes. It was like a master circuit breaker had been thrown and all the lights went on at once. The cigarette companies were sucking nicotine out of tobacco, fooling with it, and adding it back in a carefully engineered way. This was not butterfat in milk, as in the industry's favorite analogy. The companies were fine-tuning an addictive chemical to make sure people got enough into their bloodstreams.

"Where do they keep this tobacco extract? How is stored? How do they handle it?" Douglas asked.

"There are vats of it," she said. "There are rooms full of these metal vats that have this stuff in it."

Jesus Christ, Douglas thought. Rooms full of nicotine. *This is it.*

IN THE FALL OF 1991, DOUGLAS TOLD MATTHEW MYERS, his former boss at the Coalition on Smoking and Health, about Deep Cough. Douglas wasn't about to tell the powers-that-be at the big voluntaries about her. Any illusions he might have had on that score were brusquely dispelled by Scott Ballin, the most powerful member of the Coalition's steering committee, when he tried to present an idea for a coordinated publicity and legislative offensive based on the industry's manipulation of nicotine.

"It's a terrible idea," said Ballin, who listed about five reasons.

So it seemed his work on nicotine, and especially with Deep Cough, had to be a straight guerilla operation. Myers helped Douglas fill in the blanks on exactly what Deep Cough's revelations, if true, could mean. It seemed possible that the Food and Drug Administration could regulate the cigarette as a chemical and mechanical system that dispensed nicotine in measured doses. *Drug delivery device* was the shorthand for this. Dragging the industry under the regulatory umbrella would be a historic coup. Beginning early in the century, the companies fought off every government agency that claimed the right to supervise a product that 50 million Americans were putting in their bodies. Other than workplace safety inspectors and environmental officials, no federal employee had any right to enter a cigarette factory, in marked contrast, for instance, to a meat packing plant or dairy. No one outside the companies knew what ingredients went into each brand of cigarettes, or, in any detail, how they were made.

The industry had managed to exempt itself from federal oversight by having almost identical clauses inserted into the Hazardous Substances Act, the Controlled Substances Act, the Toxic Substances Act, and the Consumer Product Safety Act. And the FDA had itself ruled twice, in 1977 and 1980, that even though nicotine was a drug, cigarettes containing nicotine naturally were not a drug. Well, here was evidence, Douglas believed, that Mother Nature had very little to do with it.

In February 1992, Myers, Douglas, and Deep Cough met in Myers's cluttered office at Asbill, Junkin, Myers & Buffone. Douglas hoped to get Myers psyched up about Deep Cough, and thought that having Cough see Myers would embolden her to tell her story, eventually, to both the national press and the FDA.

Prompted by questions, Cough laid out much of what she had told Douglas over many months. Myers was less than impressed. There were several odd moments, moments that would come back to haunt both Deep Cough and Douglas. As he would later notice with other industry informants, Cough couldn't seem to say certain words. She had a special vocabulary to describe anything health-related, especially nicotine-related, and the word she had the most trouble with was *addictive*. Douglas noticed this when she explained that while taste seemed to be partly a function of tar, "you need the nicotine at a certain level, in order to achieve smoker satisfaction."

Myers pounced.

"In other words, they know that smokers need a certain amount to satisfy their addiction?"

Deep Cough smiled. Then she started talking about how a company attorney had instructed her on how to make her reports legally bullet-proof after she wrote one that mentioned the "pharmacological effect" of nicotine. We prefer to call that "smoker satisfaction," said the lawyer.

By the time she came to Washington, she had been laid off by Reynolds, yet it took another eight months before Deep Cough would use the term *addictive*. It was a big deal to her, a forbidden word. It had been a big deal to get her to meet with Myers and Douglas, and Douglas knew it would be a much bigger deal for her to talk to a reporter. But first Douglas needed to find one who wanted the story. He talked it through with one of his running partners, Dr. Sidney Wolfe, who headed the Public Citizen Health Research Group, a watchdog organization founded by Ralph Nader. Wolfe thought the story powerful, but could think of no suitable outlet for it.

The problem solved itself when, late in 1992, Wolfe got a call from an ABC television producer and reporter named Walt Bogdanich who had just been hired by a brand-new news magazine show that would soon debut as *Day One*. The program was Bogdanich's first television job after a distinguished print career, most recently at the *Wall Street Journal* where he specialized in health-related topics. He needed concrete story ideas for *Day One*. Wolfe immediately recommended Douglas, who wasted little time homing in on nicotine. He told Bogdanich there was evidence the industry added something called tobacco extract to tobacco to make sure the cigarette delivered a sufficient buzz. They took nicotine out and re-added it. They manipulated it.

"Wow," said Bogdanich.

He wanted to know about Douglas's sources of information. Douglas mentioned some technical publications, scientific articles, the work of a medical school professor named Dr. John Slade, and his R. J. Reynolds informant, whom he had recently started calling Deep Cough. He talked in some detail about what Cough had told him about the reconstitution process. Bogdanich quickly grasped the explosive premise of the story. And if Deep Cough could be persuaded to talk, here was an insider who could confirm it on camera. If everything was as advertised, it wasn't a question of whether to do the story, but how could you not do it?

Bogdanich told Douglas he was interested. He would get back to him.

This guy got it was Douglas's thought as he hung up. Bogdanich had really seemed excited about it.

DAYS LATER, BOGDANICH CALLED BACK. HE WANTED THE story. He warned that it would take time to get the piece on the air. Since he was brand new to television, let alone to ABC, he would almost certainly have to do several smaller stories first to earn the right to do such an ambitious project.

"Look, we'll make it happen," said Bogdanich. "Somehow, we'll get this story done."

Douglas was elated and he and Martha treated themselves to a pricey dinner. He would have been happier still had he known more about Bogdanich. A steelworker's son from Gary, Indiana, Bogdanich was an imposing figure, a fit six-foot-three-inch investigative reporter with the voice of a natural storyteller. He had already won a raft of journalism awards topped off by a Pulitzer prize for his reporting in the *Wall Street Journal* on how medical labs produce erroneous test results with sometimes fatal consequences. He had previously been the star investigative reporter at the Cleveland *Plain Dealer*. His crowning achievement there came in 1981 when he co-authored a series of articles charging that Jackie Presser, the regional head of the Teamsters union, was not only corrupt but also an FBI informant. Presser was furious that the series had poisoned his chances of becoming Teamsters president and enlisted the help of mob boss Anthony "Fat Tony" Salerno, who put pressure on the paper's owners through powerful lawyer Roy Cohn. The result was that the *Plain Dealer* repudiated the true stories written by Bogdanich and his partner on Presser. Humiliated and angry, Bogdanich left for the *Wall Street Journal* before events vindicated his

Teamsters articles. Presser was indicted, but the saga hurt Bogdanich deeply, and the wound never quite healed.

For a reporter shopping for a big attention-getting story, Douglas's nicotine idea had all the earmarks, but like detectives, investigative reporters worry about credibility. Bogdanich carefully checked Douglas out with congressional staff as well as Sidney Wolfe. As Bogdanich became involved with other assignments, Douglas promised not to give the nicotine story to anyone else.

After six months in which he couldn't get anything on television, Bogdanich aired three pieces that made it clear he understood the medium. By the summer of 1993, he had gained enough stature to discuss his cigarette idea with *Day One* executive producer Tom Yellin. What he proposed was "the story of nicotine," a series of *Day One* segments covering everything from how nicotine poisons workers in the field to its manipulation in cigarettes. What was important, Bogdanich stressed, was that manipulation meant willful behavior, intent. And that, as Douglas had explained, had regulatory significance.

"It's not just that they're fooling around with something that maybe they shouldn't. There are major policy implications," Bogdanich said.

Yellin listened rather reluctantly to Bogdanich's proposal. He had trouble with the manipulation story, which frankly he didn't understand, although ultimately he would become its biggest booster. At that moment, *Day One*'s ratings were unspectacular. Yellin needed a story to put *Day One* on the map and this wasn't it.

Yellin's initial approval was for a segment by Bogdanich that aired in the fall of 1993 on "green tobacco sickness," a form of nicotine poisoning reported by some tobacco pickers. He shot much of it in Kentucky and North Carolina and it taught him what a virulent poison nicotine is. While he reported it, an associate producer named Keith Summa was assigned to begin preliminary work on what became known as "the nicotine spiking story." Douglas provided a lot of leads, and passed along information he had been given by Deep Cough about other places to poke around, such as flavor houses, which sell "flavor packages" that frequently contain tobacco extract to cigarette companies.

Summa was a promising young producer who, like Bogdanich, had a robust social conscience, having worked for the Coalition for the Homeless in New York City. One of his responsibilities there was to monitor conditions in homeless shelters—everything from robberies and murders to blanket shortages caused by attendants who refused to unlock the storerooms on subzero winter nights. Summa would show up at two in the morning in Bedford-Stuyvesant with a couple of volunteers to see what was going down, and blankets got onto the beds very quickly indeed when one of the volunteers was *ABC News* anchorman Peter Jennings, who rode shotgun on these missions for years. Jennings became very fond of this courtly young man from rural New York and got him a job at *ABC News*.

Summa did the bulk of the grunt work on the nicotine story. He sweated through hundreds of tobacco industry patents, isolating scores that showed that the industry was spending a great deal of money finding ways to deliver precise doses of nicotine. Summa didn't have Bogdanich's fire, but made up for it in charm. He contacted Don Barrett, still toiling at smoking and health lawsuits in Mississippi, who was so taken with the young producer that he would keep him tipped off for years to come.

Summa told Barrett his story concerned tobacco companies manipulating nicotine.

"Well, I got the lying bastards to admit it," boasted Barrett, who had gathered sworn interrogatories from the companies explaining how nicotine could be set at varying levels.

In the fall of 1993, Bogdanich turned to the manipulation project full-time, and the main topic of conversation between Douglas and Bogdanich now became: When is Deep Cough going to talk? Finally, she allowed Douglas to give Bogdanich her name and, months later, her phone number. Bogdanich began trying to arrange a face-to-face meeting.

As the reporting reached this critical stage, other interested parties began to take notice. Bogdanich, who was secretive anyway, was being hyper-careful not to tip anyone off to what *Day One* was looking into. Nevertheless, he had to submit a Freedom of Information Act request to the Food and Drug Administration for any relevant information the FDA had collected on "flavor houses" and their sales of nicotine-rich tobacco extracts. That set off alarm bells at the agency. Commissioner David Kessler's tobacco task force was already trying to figure out how the nation's leading public health agency could assert some control over the nation's leading cause of preventable death. Kessler, a brilliant, egocentric pediatrician who also had degrees in law and public health, wanted badly to get a foot in tobacco's door, but his task force was little more than a chat group, devoid of useful ideas. The fact that an ABC-TV news show was looking into nicotine was duly noted and kicked upstairs.

On December 15, Cliff Douglas and Matt Myers had dinner at the exclusive Iron Gate Inn with a high-powered group of Washingtonians that included Dr. Philip Lee, the assistant secretary for health and Kessler's immediate superior, and Bill Corr, Lee's chief of staff.

Douglas gave them a précis of the upcoming *Day One* program, and it was clear to Douglas when he used the words *nicotine manipulation* that this group was hearing them for the first time.

They listened attentively.

"It's going to be a blockbuster," said Douglas of the program.

"Well, I don't know about 'blockbuster,'" said the cautious Myers. "But it's going to be really critical for the FDA and the public debate."

Left unspoken was the possibility that the FDA could use this information to regulate tobacco, but that scarcely needed to be said to this particular group.

Lee turned to Bill Corr.

"We have to look into this," he said.

Myers and Douglas knew already that Kessler's staff had started meeting regularly on tobacco, and Myers had a long-standing relationship with Gerry Mande, an aide to Vice President Al Gore who had recently joined Kessler's staff at the FDA. Not long after the Iron Gate dinner, Douglas gave Myers permission to tell Mande that Douglas had an industry source who knew about nicotine. Almost immediately, Mande called Douglas back and said the FDA would be interested in talking to his informant.

Before he called Douglas, Mande talked to Kessler, who agreed that they had to grill Deep Cough and find out what Bogdanich was working on. It might add up to something the FDA could use to finally throw a lasso over cigarettes. Above all, Kessler didn't want to be blindsided by some startling revelation on a TV show no one had ever heard of.

So began a race between the FDA and *Day One* to get at whatever secrets Deep Cough had in her head. Bogdanich wanted her to tell her story on camera. The FDA feared publicity would unleash a political storm that might kill any chance of ever regulating cigarettes, or embarrass the agency into acting prematurely. Both the FDA and ABC set out to win Cough to their cause, and to convince her that the other side's efforts were misguided.

Cliff Douglas kept a foot in both camps, acting as a kind of static-free communications channel to Deep Cough for the FDA and *Day One*. His role was to steady her, not push one way or the other. Nevertheless, there was little question that Douglas controlled Deep Cough. He was her connection to the big, frightening worlds of official Washington and New York. He could easily have frozen either side out, but deliberately chose not to. It annoyed Bogdanich that Douglas wouldn't favor ABC, even though they were there first. Another part of him understood.

"Cliff is just doing his job, fomenting the revolution," he told Summa.

Bogdanich got the first crack at Deep Cough. On January 6, 1994, after several cancellations, Bogdanich and Keith Summa flew to Cincinnati, where Cough was traveling on business, and had dinner with her on a riverboat on the Kentucky side of the Ohio River. The next day they debriefed her for six hours and she told them about the "G-7" reconstitution process and how tobacco extract was sometimes trucked into Reynolds from flavor houses to be sprayed on the "recon."

Deep Cough was so flighty, Bogdanich was afraid he would never see her again and had a camera crew ready to tape an interview in case she agreed to do it.

"We'd disguise you. Blur your face, change your voice," he told her. "No one will know it's you."

She said no. But promised to think about it.

That night, Douglas got a report from Deep Cough, who was happy with how it had gone. And, she said, she was ready to talk to the FDA.

Douglas went ahead and scheduled Deep Cough's telephone interview with the agency for January 11, dealing, as he usually did, with Gerry Mande in Kessler's office. Not long before the interview, Mande called Douglas and told him he was handing Cough off to a professional at the Office of Criminal Investigations, a branch of the

FDA that looks into criminal acts like product tampering. Commissioner Kessler and his brain trust realized that evaluating the credibility of an informant when the stakes were this high was a job for cops, not lawyers or policy wonks. So Kessler borrowed two detectives from OCI with backgrounds in drug investigations who would work directly under him to lay the foundation for what would eventually become a full-blown FDA probe into the cigarette industry. And their first job was to interview Deep Cough and size her up.

Criminal investigators had never before been brought into an FDA rule-making inquiry, which is almost always a paper chase, a review of documentation or lab results. On the other hand, the idea of the FDA asserting authority over a largely secret enterprise that had never been regulated by anyone was also unprecedented and dictated extraordinary measures.

Gary Light and his partner Tom Doyle were excellent choices to spearhead this mission. At forty-two, Light had spent his career with the army's Criminal Investigative Division at duty stations from Panama to Colorado until he was brought to the FDA to set up their polygraph operation. He was funny, quick-witted and warm, and, like all good polygraphists, had superb interview skills. On the surface, Tom Doyle was a tougher character. A red-bearded native New Yorker and lawyer about nine years younger than Light, he had served with the Secret Service and Central Intelligence Agency.

OCI agents are first and foremost police officers, with badges and guns. The first thing Kessler told Light and Doyle was to put them away. This assignment would require a rather more delicate touch.

Just how delicate became apparent on January 11 when Douglas put Gary Light on the phone with Deep Cough, who was again on the road, this time at a hotel in Dayton, Ohio. She didn't even want Light to know where she was, so Douglas, using a conference call hook-up, dialed her first, brought Light into the call, then hung up.

She told Light she felt like she was being pulled in two directions, by ABC and the FDA. She still hadn't made up her mind about going on television.

"Look, we know you've got something really important to say. You're our number one priority. What you know could be important to the whole country. Now, if you go on TV, Reynolds could sue you and tie you up in court forever. It may totally screw up what we're doing," said Light.

Deep Cough gave Light a thumbnail of how recon is made. She admitted she couldn't describe the process chemically, but she knew where and roughly how it was done.

"CI knows the details of the cigarette production process and is aware of the vats of nicotine that make up the reconstituted tobacco," Light wrote in his report. *CI* meant "Confidential Informant."

The next day, Deep Cough called Douglas. He asked her how it had gone.

"These guys don't know *anything*," she said. "I'm going to have to go through all the stuff I already went over with Bogdanich."

She sounded almost maternal about it, like she wanted to help these poor lost boys, thought Douglas. She was feeling very stressed out, however, about the prospect of the on-camera TV interview that Bogdanich had convinced her to do, now scheduled for January 15 and 16. She told Douglas she wanted to slow things down. It was just too much to deal with at once.

Shortly thereafter, she canceled the interview with Bogdanich, who took it in stride. He knew Douglas would encourage her to complete the ABC project and there was plenty of other reporting to be done. On the sixteenth, Deep Cough spoke again to Gary Light, who hoped that now the FDA would have her to themselves. She gave Light names of key R. J. Reynolds scientists who knew more about nicotine, like Robert DiMarco, a major player in creating Premier.

"It should be noted that the informant has not been interviewed in a face-to-face discussion as of this time," Light reported. Actually sitting down with her was the key to evaluating her credibility, and after more phone calls, a meeting took place in Virginia Beach on January 20. The entire forward thrust of the FDA's nascent tobacco investigation was riding on this encounter.

At dinner that night, Light and Doyle found a very pleasant, single, twenty-seven-year-old woman who had moved from the tobacco industry to a responsible position with the federal government. They adjourned to a hotel, where Cough was subjected to yet another six-hour grilling. Light and Doyle really perked up when she told them how Reynolds had tested the blood, saliva, and urine of employee volunteers who smoked a new ultra-low-tar cigarette, and how one employee was so gung ho, he walked around with a cooler containing his urine samples. This was revealing, because if Reynolds checked nicotine levels in body fluids to develop new products, then the company clearly knew cigarettes deliver a drug.

Light and Doyle returned to FDA headquarters in Rockville, Maryland convinced that Deep Cough was reliable on the basics of the reconstitution process, but knew little beyond that. However, the Cough interviews demonstrated that here was a solid lead worth pursuing, and that the nicotine manipulation allegation, while far from proven, was plausible.

Later, much more knowledgeable sources would back up Deep Cough and teach the FDA the science of nicotine in depth. Deep Cough was important not because she was the most expert industry insider to come forward, but because she was the first. The chain of which she was the primary link would result, more than a year later, in a decision by the Clinton administration to try to end Big Tobacco's exemption from the health laws of the United States.

Walt Bogdanich and Keith Summa got their on-camera interview with Deep Cough three days after Light and Doyle had their first face-to-face talk with her. It was a tortuous session in which Cough's usual difficulty in talking about the forbidden topic of addiction was markedly worsened by her being disguised in a bulky shirt and coat and a floppy cap under TV lights in a roomful of strangers at an airport hotel. It was a kind of Keystone Kops afternoon, what with the cap falling off, requiring new takes, and the planes that screamed by at critical moments, drowning out everything.

In February, the show was assigned an airdate, February 28. Executive producer Tom Yellin was planning to make the nicotine program, entitled "Smokescreen," the third segment of the three running that Monday evening on *Day One*. It would play after a piece about the Kennedy family and another on troubled teens, and Bogdanich wasn't happy about going last.

The Friday afternoon before "Smokescreen" was to air, Douglas got a fax from the Office of the Commissioner of the Food and Drug Administration. It was a letter from Dr. David Kessler.

Technically, it was a reply to a petition from the Coalition on Smoking OR Health, which for years had been asking the FDA to regulate low-tar cigarettes for making misleading health claims. However, Kessler merely used the petition as an opening for a new idea. Although nicotine is undeniably an addictive drug, Kessler wrote, to regulate cigarettes under the Food, Drug, and Cosmetic Act, it must be shown that the cigarette companies *intend* that their products be used as drugs. In the past, the industry has been "given the benefit of the doubt" about this, Kessler noted.

Then Kessler dropped a bomb.

"Evidence brought to our attention is accumulating that suggests that cigarette manufacturers may intend that their products contain nicotine to satisfy an addiction on the part of some of their customers," he wrote.

This can be deduced from "mounting evidence we have received" showing that "cigarette vendors control the levels of nicotine that satisfy this addiction," the letter said.

"In fact, it is our understanding that manufacturers commonly add nicotine to cigarettes to deliver specific amounts of nicotine," Kessler went on.

If the FDA could prove this, the agency could regulate cigarettes. Since addictive cigarettes could never be sanctioned by a government health agency, this "could mean, ultimately, removal from the market of tobacco products." But to avoid what could be profound social dislocation, the FDA would rather work with Congress "to resolve, once and for all, the regulatory status of cigarettes," Kessler concluded.

Kessler's going to regulate tobacco, Douglas thought.

Holy shit.

His second thought was: *He's doing it because of our show.*

Douglas stuffed the letter back into the fax machine and sent it to Bogdanich at ABC. He tried to call, too, and left a voice mail message.

Minutes later, Bogdanich had the fax.

His first thought was identical to Douglas's: *It's a* Day One *letter.*

He grabbed it and ran upstairs to Tom Yellin's office. Yellin had a senior producer with him, and Bogdanich burst in with the letter, out of breath.

"Look at this," he said.

Yellin took the letter. Read it quickly.

"Won't even make the evening news," said Yellin.

"Are you fucking kidding?" Bogdanich said.

"I'm telling you. There's a lot out there today. There won't be any story," said Yellin.

"Tom, this is history. This is history, and this show that we're running Monday made this happen," said Bogdanich.

It was no use. Yellin couldn't be convinced. *He just doesn't get it*, Bogdanich thought.

He ran back to his office, long legs pounding down the fire stairs. He was thinking of his father, who had died just a year and a half earlier of lung cancer. He had tried not to think about it, fearing it would cloud his judgment. But now he didn't hold back. He dialed Stephanie, his wife, at work. Almost as soon as she answered, he blurted out what had just happened. And started crying.

After Stephanie, he called Douglas.

"What do you make of this?" he asked Douglas.

"He's going to regulate," said Douglas. "Kessler is going to regulate fucking tobacco."

"Congratulations. You should feel great," Bogdanich said.

"No, *you* should feel great." Douglas laughed.

Bogdanich ran back up to Yellin's office, and started hammering away again at how this development would just change everything. The government was finally going to do something. Nope, said Yellin. Just not that big a deal.

The phone rang.

"Walt, it's Phil Hilts, *New York Times*," said the senior producer.

Bogdanich took it in Yellin's office. Hilts, too, had the Kessler letter and had heard through the grapevine that *Day One* was doing something on nicotine. He put two and two together and figured they were related. He and Bogdanich talked for a minute or two, and Bogdanich hung up.

"It's going to be on page one of *The New York Times* tomorrow," Bogdanich said. "Kessler's announcement—and he'll probably put in something about *Day One*."

Yellin's enthusiasm for the nicotine story seemed to rise by several large increments. A tie-in with a page-one story in the *Times* was priceless advertising. The nicotine segment, which had been considered completed and "in the can" as of that afternoon, was taken out and refurbished with references to the Kessler letter.

Some narration was read on camera about how the FDA was saying it might now have the legal basis to regulate cigarettes. And all because of *Day One*.

The segment was stitched back together, timed, and trimmed to fit in the allotted eighteen minutes, longer than most *Day One* pieces. The evening of Monday, February 28, 1994, came and Bogdanich was in the same clothes he had been wearing since Saturday. When the broadcast ended at ten-thirty P.M., Yellin waved Bogdanich and Summa and assorted assistants into his office for a meeting. Yellin wanted the cigarette story squeezed for all it was worth. What could they do for a "follow"? Bogdanich offered "the list." This was the official industry-furnished list of the additives and ingredients that went into cigarettes. But by law, one the industry helped write, the public wasn't allowed to know what was on it. The list sat in a safe near the director at the U.S. Office of Smoking and Health, and only the director and certain designees could even look at it.

"Good," said Yellin. "I want that for next week."

All Bogdanich wanted to do was lie down, and now he was being handed a story he thought he would have weeks to report and told to pull it off immediately. But it didn't matter. The show was suddenly very much alive. *Day One*—and nicotine manipulation—were on the map.

THEY GATHERED NEAR THE TOP OF THE BUILDING, THE twenty-second-floor conference room, about as state of the art as any in the world, with a TV that connected to a network called PMTV that showed in-house programming or whatever TV signal the corporation decided to pump through it to Philip Morris facilities around the country. The twenty-second floor was where the most senior people in the company had their offices and did their business, the Chief Executive Officer, the President, the Chairman of the Board, the Management Committee, the Chief Operating Officer, lots of capital letters on the office stationery. One Hundred Twenty Park Avenue was the world headquarters of the Philip Morris Companies, and at the bottom of the building was an art gallery and public space that Philip Morris provided for anyone strolling down Forty-second Street or Park Avenue. Frank Sinatra's generation would say it was classy. Smart. Philip Morris didn't just provide a free public space, they provided a free *hip* public space. That was Philip Morris. The Evil Empire, but with immaculate taste.

Philip Morris Companies is the holding company for Philip Morris Tobacco, Kraft Foods, and Miller Beer, each of which controls a little cluster of companies, each of which has families of brands, and so on down to the individuals who fill each job at PMC, 144,000 people scattered all over the world. And yet not so many compared to Unilever, Bill Farone's old company, with 267,000. Philip Morris wasn't known for size, it was known for strength. It was the strongest member of a strong industry. By 1994, Philip Morris was rolling in money, money Philip Morris literally didn't know what to do with, so every few years it shopped for companies to buy. The company had lobbyists in every state legislature, Congress, and the governing bodies of each of the fifty countries in which it had a presence. Philip Morris, like the rest of the industry, had grown used to the cares of war, not surprising considering the industry had forty years of practice in standing with its back to the wall.

Philip Morris is big on task forces, and had assembled two groups to deal with *Day One,* one from legal and another group from the scientific side of the company, each of which sat down to watch the *Day One* program that ABC had been promoting heavily for days, promising to reveal "something cigarette makers don't want you to know."

Steve Parrish, now senior vice president for external affairs, watched from the twenty-second-floor conference room in New York with the legal group, which included Murray Bring, who had migrated from Arnold & Porter after *Cipollone* to become general counsel, and Chuck Wall, the associate general counsel. The scientists watched the broadcast from their homes in the Richmond area, and were to fly to New York in the early morning the day after the show, prepared to pick it apart. It was Parrish and Bring, but mostly Parrish, who was masterminding this part of the response to *Day One.*

The reason for these rather extraordinary measures was that this little news program had, even before it actually aired, already triggered a monumental problem. Parrish didn't believe the issuance of the Kessler letter about nicotine three days before a *Day*

One segment on nicotine was a coincidence. He figured Kessler had learned key details of the reporting being done for the broadcast, got nervous, and ordered his own investigation. Steve Parrish was one smart chess player.

It was the fifth sentence in the program that rolled through everyone in the room like a shock wave.

"Why are you artificially spiking your cigarettes with nicotine?" asked correspondent John Martin.

"We are not in any way doing that," said an R. J. Reynolds scientist.

That drew groans at Philip Morris, for whom it was downhill from there.

A television interview is like a pyramid. The base is everything said during the ninety minutes or so when the videocamera is actually rolling. The apex of the pyramid is the few words—probably one or two hundred at most—that the source will actually utter during the program. Partly in an attempt to protect Deep Cough's identity by minimizing her on-screen exposure, Bogdanich used only a handful of sentences from a videotaped interview that took close to a hundred pages to transcribe. Another reason was, as both Douglas and the FDA had already learned, Deep Cough was not a good talker. She had trouble putting these arcane technical matters into everyday terms. At one point she took eighty-two words to define what she meant by "waste product." In television news, life histories are summed up in sixty words, and civilizations in two hundred.

Deep Cough appeared and said the forbidden words the industry would never say. On the screen, her baggy clothing gave her a sloppy hip-hop look, and she sat in a kind of twilight, her face blacked out, the pitch of her voice digitally bent to an unnaturally low octave. America heard Deep Cough say ninety words, which took about forty seconds, three sound bites separated by other material. These three "bites" were the payoff to the entire three-year-long dance with Deep Cough.

"They put nicotine in the form of tobacco extract into a product to keep the consumer happy," she said.

"They're fortifying the product with nicotine, is that correct?" said Bogdanich.

"The waste filler, yes they are," she said.

"That's outrageous!" said Chuck Wall at Philip Morris.

The program showed ships unloading in Newark, New Jersey, while the narrator talked about "near pure" nicotine being brought ashore to be mixed with alcohol and applied to tobacco. This drew groans and curses at Philip Morris.

The show built to a confrontation between correspondent John Martin and RJR scientists John Robinson and Joseph deBethezi.

"Why are you adding nicotine to your cigarettes?" Martin asked, springing the ambush.

To his credit, deBethezi didn't even blink.

"We are not in any way doing that," he said.

"You're not adding nicotine?"

"No. We—we don't do that," deBethezi said.

There were interviews with nicotine experts and public health officials—such as the National Institute on Drug Abuse's Jack Henningfield, who called cigarettes "the crack cocaine form of nicotine delivery"—and a short bite from Cliff Douglas.

"The public doesn't know the industry manipulates nicotine, takes it out, puts it back in, uses it as if it were sugar being put in candy. They don't have a clue."

"Neither, apparently, do members of Congress," said the narrator. Cut to a congressional office.

"Well, it disgusts me," said Congressman Mike Synar.

The narrator mentioned industry patents for altering nicotine delivery, and an ad in a tobacco trade publication by a reconstituted tobacco manufacturer promising that the company's process "permits adjustments of nicotine to your exact requirements."

But it wasn't over for Dr. deBethezi. A second piece of the interview had deBethezi admitting that R. J. Reynolds has the technological capability to take all the nicotine out of tobacco.

So you could do it? he was asked.

"Well, as scientists and engineers here in R and D, I think that that could be done. But I think the real issue is that we, as a company, are providing a legal product to people who are looking for a pleasing sensory experience with mild pharmacology."

This was not the way oatmeal companies would describe breakfast mush. DeBethezi was essentially admitting that the company was making cigarettes for people who wanted the drug effect that cigarettes provide. Which was tantamount to saying they were selling drugs to people who wanted a drug experience. That may have gone over the heads of most viewers, but it was crystal clear to those watching that night from the FDA and from Philip Morris.

The show was a startling piece of reporting *and* good television—so good, it was later criticized for oversimplifying for dramatic effect. The criticism was probably a compliment for a show about something called "reconstituted tobacco," a long way from a celebrity special. To the group at Philip Morris, "Smokescreen" was sensational in the old yellow journalism sense. Muck had been raked, and raked in a way that was getting unprecedented attention.

Day One was a statement of the facts of cigarette making that powerful people were already accepting as a premise to dig for more ammunition against this peculiar industry, and the old warriors atop the Philip Morris building knew they were going to fight it the moment the program ended. Everyone in the twenty-second-floor conference room was used to repulsing cancer lawsuits and government agencies. But how to defeat a perception?

Television news had created the hydra and so it would be attacked head-on. *Day One* and ABC would have to be discredited, forced to retract, apologize.

Talk of bringing a libel lawsuit started that night. Just hours before the broadcast, congressional hearings had been announced that would investigate the Kessler and *Day One* charges. As fallout came raining down over the ensuing weeks, the group at the top of the Philip Morris building began planning a massive counterstrike.

THE GUNS OF MARCH

THE DAY AFTER *DAY ONE*, SENIOR SCIENTISTS FLEW UP from the research tower in Richmond and gave Steve Parrish and a group of senior managers a critique of *Day One*'s science, which they said was soft. The company does not add nicotine to reconstituted tobacco, they explained. In fact, comparing the nicotine content of the stems and other material that goes into the recon with the finished product, some nicotine is actually lost. The program was inaccurate, which was precisely what Parrish wanted to hear. That meant there were probably grounds for a lawsuit. And given the intense revulsion the show had inspired in Murray Bring, Chuck Wall, and others who saw it at Philip Morris the night before, that meant a lawsuit was now virtually inevitable.

Parrish, too, was angry about the broadcast, especially the shot of tankers coming into port while the narrator talked about thousands of gallons of nicotine-laced alcohol.

"You know, like tankerloads of nicotine are being smuggled into the country," Parrish said. "The problem with the show was it conjured up the image of the mad scientist standing by the assembly line with the beaker of nicotine."

Parrish hated the nefarious cast of mind the program imputed to Philip Morris. He knew the Philip Morris people and they were no criminals. They were honorable people. They worked like dogs. Their lives were guided by wholesome values, like his own: Parrish, who walked his wife through sleepless nights when his first child became critically ill, would later tell the story of how Philip Morris CEO Geoffrey Bible dropped everything amid the tension of Marlboro Friday—when Philip Morris slashed its cigarette prices and touched off a little war among the manufacturers—and insisted on putting the company helicopter at Parrish's disposal when his little boy drank a bottle of medicine and had to be rushed to the hospital. To Parrish, Philip Morris was a compassionate company, staffed by extraordinarily bright, capable men and women. Parrish was the outside face of that company, not only smart and strong minded, but easy to talk to, easy to be with. It was a measure of the man that Marc Edell, his opponent in *Cipollone,* became quite friendly with Parrish, and met him for drinks or dinner periodically after the trial. Reporters liked him, and unlike most tobacco people, he didn't seem to feel they were Satan's spawn.

But it was too late for meaningful dialogue. Hatches were being battened down. The damage from the broadcast was in the newspapers and, even worse, on the television news every day. First, FDA Commissioner David Kessler testified before Congressman Henry Waxman's subcommittee, which got enormous exposure on every national news outlet. It just so happened that Waxman was probably the most anti-tobacco congressman in living memory, and he exploited this opening for all it was worth. Waxman would hold eleven hearings on tobacco during 1994, seven on FDA regulation of cigarettes. For a period of months, Waxman's staff boasted of "a tobacco event a week."

In fact, there was a kind of snowball effect Parrish had never seen before. It frequently happened that a *60 Minutes* or similar documentary program embarrassed the industry, even ignited a round of hearings. But what was happening now went much farther. Medicine has the concept of a "cascade," a succession of catastrophic events, each triggering a more grave consequence, until—if the process isn't stopped—the patient succumbs. Parrish was witnessing a cascade of adverse corporate events: *Day One,* Waxman's hearings, and a spate of new lawsuits, including ruinous mutations, mounted by adversaries of unprecedented power and wealth. For the first time, the industry saw the entry of the class-action lawyers, the crowd that had tackled asbestos, breast implants, the Dalkon shield, and many other products. And at the head of this new group of antagonists was someone Parrish and

Shook, Hardy & Bacon had been tracking for ten years, a South Carolina trial lawyer named Ron Motley.

Starting right after *Day One,* Parrish met with top operational people every morning at eight-thirty to make sure the patient survived. The company's Washington office, responsible for federal lobbying and political affairs, was patched in on a conference call, and the legal, public relations, and regulatory affairs shops took part from Parrish's office in New York.

After two weeks of these meetings, Murray Bring, the powerful general counsel, took Parrish aside and told him the company needed someone with command authority to cut through traditional fiefdoms and protect the company during this escalation of hostilities.

"Steve, we want you to be the general," said Bring.

Later, Michael Miles, Philip Morris's CEO, approached him directly with the idea. Parrish was the logical person to do it. He had trained at Shook, Hardy during *Cipollone,* the bloodiest legal battle of the eighties. He was well respected, politically canny, and had a background in regulatory affairs.

Parrish would continue his morning meetings, Miles said, but with formal authority over the political, international, legal, and PR operations as a sort of external threat czar, presiding over a task force composed of top people from each of these bailiwicks.

"Everyone will be told, 'Parrish is in charge of this task force. You may be needed on a specific issue and if you are, work with Steve and his group,'" said Miles.

Bring would be a regular in what became known as "the Eight-thirty Group," as was associate general counsel Chuck Wall. Other lawyers, scientists, and lobbyists were called in as needed.

Given that the immediate source of the company's woes was this eighteen-minute TV show, the first thing the Eight-thirty Group did, on March 24, less than a month after *Day One* and the day before Kessler appeared before the Waxman subcommittee, was to sue ABC.

An abrasive New York litigator named Herbert Wachtell was put in charge of a $10 billion libel suit, $5 billion of which were punitive damages. It was the largest libel suit in history, and was filed in Philip Morris's backyard of Richmond. R. J. Reynolds joined in the suit.

Murray Bring announced the action at the National Press Club in Washington. With him were Parrish and Wachtell. Keith Summa and Cliff Douglas sat in the audience.

"The essential allegation by ABC on these broadcasts is that cigarettes are artificially spiked with nicotine during the manufacturing process, in order to keep people smoking," said Bring. "These allegations are not true, and ABC knows that they are not true."

At issue were both "Smokescreen," the February 28 broadcast, and "The List," the March 7 broadcast that reiterated and slightly expanded on the charges in "Smokescreen."

As evidence of damage, Bring cited a dramatic drop in the value of Philip Morris's 800 million shares of stock the day after "Smokescreen," and the congressional and FDA investigations. Bring referred over and over again to the word *spiking*, the use of which, he said, "has poisoned the well."

Walt Bogdanich read about the libel suit in the *Wall Street Journal* on the train to work, then caught the press conference live on one of ABC's internal channels later that morning. He ran over to the office of Forrest Sawyer, the *Day One* anchor, to watch the rest. Sawyer seemed stunned.

Tom Yellin joined them.

"They make cancer sticks. It's a joke. Don't worry about it," said Yellin, trying to calm the agitated Bogdanich.

"I know they make cancer sticks, Tom," said Bogdanich. "I know I don't have anything to worry about as far as the truth, but you have these big guys throwing around some scary numbers."

"Hey, it'll be good publicity for our story," said Yellin.

"I don't trust the money people who are going to have to face this down," said Bogdanich.

Later that day, the complaint was sent over. Bogdanich felt like a thousand pounds had been lifted from his shoulders. The lawsuit was so weak. They had nothing. They were picking nits about the definition of "extraneous nicotine."

He shared his relief with Summa and Yellin. Yet one nerve ending kept quivering. Against his will, his mind pedaled back to Cleveland and that goddamned Jackie Presser story. No, he reassured himself. Not twice in one lifetime.

IMMEDIATELY, AFTER THE *DAY ONE* BROADCAST, COMmissioner David Kessler's tobacco working group, composed of top aides like Gerry Mande as well as investigators Gary Light and Tom

Doyle, began holding strategy meetings almost every day. They divided staff into three teams—one for investigation, one on the science of nicotine, and one on the legal theory of how the industry could be brought under FDA jurisdiction.

With congressional hearings on nicotine manipulation planned for the end of March, meat had to be put on the bones of Deep Cough's allegations rather rapidly, and Doyle and Light's cigarette mission was bumped up from three-quarters to full time. They soon found an anti-tobacco organization in Virginia with a list of twelve former Philip Morris employees, one of whom handed over the company's internal telephone directory. Light and Doyle then called the Research Tower, asking blindly for various people. Every time they hit someone who was no longer there, they tracked him down. That was how they found Ian Uydess.

A biologist who helped develop a process to take carcinogenic nitrates out of tobacco, one Philip Morris never used, Uydess met several times with Light and Doyle in a Richmond hotel. He had been at Philip Morris a long time, eleven years spread over two tours, and had become friendly with many who worked on nicotine projects. He talked about Tom Osdene and Bill Dunn and Bill Farone. And about Victor DeNoble, whose name Light and Doyle had already heard.

By March 12, Light and Doyle had spoken at some length to Bill Farone, former co-director of R and D with Tom Osdene. By the end of the second week in March, they had interviewed both Victor DeNoble and co-researcher Paul Mele at length and were briefing an enraptured FDA staff—including Kessler—about the behavioral pharmacology lab and its odd demise.

For security reasons, Light and Doyle didn't refer to DeNoble by name in briefings or reports. His code name was "Cigarette." Farone was "Philip." Paul Mele was "Patrick," since he was first viewed around St. Patrick's Day. Uydess was "Bio." Cliff Douglas was "Michael Jordan," due to his penchant for fast moves and his hometown, Chicago.

But a code name was all the protection Light and Doyle could offer DeNoble, since the FDA can neither subpoena nor grant immunity, and he stopped returning their calls. It would be only a matter of weeks before he found a more powerful protector.

Farone gave numerous multi-hour interviews to Light, Doyle,

Kessler, and others and became their first real teacher on cigarette design. As a director of R and D and the most senior and scientifically knowledgeable government witness so far, Farone was a big fish. If he wasn't a genius, he was pretty close. He had his own company in California, Applied Power Concepts, which helped invent cutting-edge products, like a "bioreactor" that sped the growth of plant cells so medicines could be quickly harvested.

Kessler and the FDA's scientific staff made full use of his multi-disciplinary talents, and the depth of his chemistry expertise cushioned an anxious Kessler, who knew he was in for a political scorching if he pressed ahead with regulation.

Farone assured them they were on the right track.

"They know the precise nicotine content of every hogshead of tobacco out to several decimal places," he told them. "You think they can't control how much is in a cigarette? *Of course* they can. But there's four or five major ways to do it. Reconstituted tobacco is just one, and it's not really that important."

Soon, Light and Doyle were going around the FDA saying, "It's the blend, stupid," because Farone kept hammering away at how the most basic manipulation tool is altering the blend of the cigarette by varying the amount of the three major types of tobacco, each of which has a different nicotine level. The stalk position of the leaves was also a major determinant, with the higher leaves having a bigger kick because their more developed vascular systems enrich them with nutrients. Deep Cough wasn't wrong, but she and *Day One* had only part of the story. But that wasn't terribly surprising given that it would take a federal agency over two years to fill in the blanks.

MOTLEY, DENOBLE, FARONE, MELE, STEVE PARRISH, MARC EDELL, Dr. Larry Hastings—everyone in the known world of tobacco affairs watched FDA Commissioner David Kessler's testimony at the first-ever hearing on the regulation of cigarettes, which took place March 25, 1994, before Congressman Henry Waxman's Health and Environment subcommittee in Room 2123 at the Rayburn House Office Building, one of several block-long congressional office buildings, each of which has hundreds of rooms arranged along a spider's web of corridors.

At big hearings, the TV and still photographers clad in raggy jeans and sport shirts slump against the rostrum in the committee room, which was what Keith Summa saw when he walked in to find a seat.

Cliff Douglas wasn't allowed to go. His latest employer, the American Cancer Society, had put him on "probation" for daring to operate outside his assigned legislative pigeonhole, even though the Cancer Society hadn't achieved in twenty years what Douglas had in two. Douglas had to watch the hearings on C-SPAN from a cubicle on Pennsylvania Avenue, under house arrest by health apparatchiks. He saw people who had scoffed at him take credit for this breakthrough, while he was forbidden to lobby on an issue he had created.

Nevertheless, he was intensely proud. If this moment belonged to anyone, it was to Douglas and Deep Cough, who saw the hearings at home with her mother.

"No matter what anyone tells you, you did something great," Douglas told her. "And I hope you know that down deep."

Douglas saw Kessler give a bravura performance before Waxman. With the benefit of his month's cram course in cigarette technology, the commissioner assaulted the free-choice argument.

"Mr. Chairman, the issue I will address today is simple: Whose choice is actually driving the demand for cigarettes in this country? Is it a choice by consumers to continue smoking? Or is it a choice by cigarette companies to maintain addictive levels of nicotine in their cigarettes?"

Kessler illustrated the grip of tobacco addiction by pointing out that "even when a smoker has his or her larynx *removed*, forty percent try smoking again."

He showed a chart of patents for boosting the nicotine content of tobacco, and others for nicotine analogs, like those tested by DeNoble and Mele. And he said that while the smoke of modern cigarettes had, on average, less tar and nicotine than those of forty years before, the *ratio* of nicotine to tar had increased over the previous ten years. All in all, nicotine was not allowed to drop below the level needed to sustain addiction. In fact, Kessler told the committee, the FDA's own lab tests showed that the cigarettes officially rated as the lowest in tar and nicotine actually contained the tobacco with the highest nicotine, apparently to make sure enough got through to the smoker. That, Kessler argued, was no accident.

And if intentional, the jig was up. Tobacco couldn't remain a covert branch of the pharmaceutical industry.

Waxman asked about industry studies on addiction, and Kessler said yes, the companies experimented with nicotine on animals. He read the titles of two of DeNoble's scientific articles into the record, but refused to identify the author or give specifics.

"Again, we will give you the facts that we have, and you can assess them and do any investigation," Kessler told Waxman. A little later, Waxman released DeNoble's study on self-administration in rats.

Waxman publicly pounded the industry for not sending its CEOs to his hearing, and finally they agreed to appear. Three weeks later, they dutifully raised their right hands in Rayburn 2123, a tableau that became etched in the collective unconscious of the tobacco control movement. Everyone in that world could remember where they were when the seven CEOs testified.

By then, acting on the FDA's tip, Waxman's staff had contacted DeNoble and Mele, who agreed to testify if Waxman could get them released from their confidentiality agreements with Philip Morris, no mean trick. But the appearance of the CEOs under the white heat of television lights gave Waxman a unique opportunity. Democratic committee members induced Philip Morris's William Campbell to admit that DeNoble's lab was working on nicotine analogs, and to agree to turn over internal files on DeNoble's work. Then Congressman Mike Synar, a young Oklahoman and close ally of Cliff Douglas, who hated the cigarette makers with a passion, moved in for the kill.

"Mr. Campbell, will you release Dr. DeNoble from his confidentiality agreement so that he can voluntarily testify before this subcommittee to tell us what really happened?" asked Synar.

"I don't know of the confidentiality agreement. So I'd have to have an investigation, but then I will answer," said Campbell.

"Will you release Dr. DeNoble from any contractual arrangements that would not allow him to voluntarily testify before this subcommittee?" Synar repeated.

"Dr. DeNoble is quite on record in a—"

"Yes or no?" snapped Synar. "Will you allow DeNoble to come forward?"

"I see no problem and our people will discuss it with you," said Campbell, looking pained.

"No, that's not the question," Synar retorted. "Mr. Campbell, Dr. DeNoble will voluntarily appear if he can get through the agreement that he has with your company. Will you release him from that agreement?"

"Can I check with my counsel at this time?" Campbell asked.

"I just want to know. You're the chairman of the board," said Synar.

"No, I'm not, sir. I'm just the president," said Campbell.

Waxman stepped in, the good cop.

"Mr. Synar, let's just give him a minute," said Waxman coolly.

"All right," said Synar.

Campbell covered the microphone, leaning over to whisper with Fredric Newman, who had visited DeNoble's lab with former CEO Shep Pollack.

"We'll do it, sure," said Campbell.

Within minutes, an ABC-TV news reporter rang DeNoble's wife at work, asking for comment. Other press calls started pouring in. So frightened was DeNoble of exposure, and perhaps retribution, he and his wife jumped into their car and drove from their home in Delaware to Richmond, where they stayed for two days, figuring no one would think to look for them in Philip Morris's backyard.

"I was afraid it wasn't going to be Philip Morris," DeNoble said later. "I was afraid some tobacco farmer was going to come up here and blow my brains out. Some crazed trucker or something."

But upon their return, nothing happened, although they were advised by the FBI to check their cars for bombs every morning and to vary their route to work. Two weeks after the CEOs testified, DeNoble and Mele riveted the committee and millions of Americans with their story of the rat experiments. They speculated on what a free exchange of their research data with the scientific community might have meant for the study of nicotine addiction. Afterward, Steve Parrish held his own press conference at which he pointedly reiterated that DeNoble's reports, standing alone, did *not* prove nicotine addictive. There was, however, no going back. The day after he testified, DeNoble was talking with plaintiff's attorneys eager to recruit him for a potent new generation of cigarette lawsuits.

DON BARRETT WAS STILL SMARTING FROM THREE STRAIGHT whippings by the tobacco industry in Mississippi when he got a strange, anonymous fax one morning in early March of 1994. It said simply, "I admire your work. We should talk sometime." With the fax were articles from the Louisville newspapers about Merrell Williams. Barrett knew instantly that the sender was Merrell Williams.

By then, Barrett had read Williams's *Intent to Deceive,* alternatively entitled *Affidavit in Expectation of Death,* which the Mississippi lawyers were passing around. He had never seen the underlying documents—no one had. But it was obvious from their descriptions in the narrative that this was weapons-grade evidence for tobacco suits.

He knew no one was allowed to talk to this man, but here he was, reaching out to Barrett. Working with a friendly telephone operator, Barrett learned that the fax number at the top of the page belonged to a flower shop in Louisville. By sounding like he already knew Williams, he managed to talk the woman there into giving him the paralegal's home phone number. He called that number.

Williams answered.

"Merrell, this is Don Barrett. Don't hang up!" were the first words he said to him, and before the conversation ended he repeated them several times. Williams was spooked, not sure it really was Barrett. After a few minutes, he warmed up sufficiently to bring up the fact that his mother knew Barrett's father, which was kind of a southern way of being personable. Williams said he might be coming to Mississippi, since his mother lived in Jackson, and promised to call Barrett.

A few days later, Williams rang and they arranged to meet at the Old Tyme Delicatessen in Jackson. Barrett brought Dickie Scruggs and Cindy Lott, another Mississippi lawyer working on the tobacco case.

Williams was gray with fear. Since he didn't know Scruggs, who he imagined, perhaps because of his military bearing, was an FBI agent, he was even less forthcoming than he had been on the phone. Scruggs and Barrett tried desperately to get him to focus on the documents. He spoke in riddles. He might have some documents, then again, he might not. Instead, he wanted to provide more narratives. Forget it, Barrett told him. We need the documents.

Williams was in a quandary.

"I know I can be of help," he said. "And I'd like to help you."

That was as far as he would go, but Barrett and Scruggs now were fairly certain Williams must have, or have access to, another set of the Brown & Williamson files.

Could they promise to prevent harm from coming to him or his wife and children? Williams kept asking. Barrett felt terrible, but the best he could say was that since Williams apparently had proof of bad acts and Barrett and Scruggs represented the chief legal officer of Mississippi, his greatest safety would lie in giving them the material. Williams's position would be much stronger with them as allies than alone.

No resolution had been reached when Scruggs walked Williams out to his car ninety minutes later, but Williams did hand him a chapter from *Intent to Deceive*.

Williams rolled down his window.

"You sure you're not with the FBI?" asked Williams.

"Well, I'm pretty damn sure," said Scruggs.

Williams drove away.

Barrett had a terrible headache.

"I feel like I've got a forty-penny nail in my eye," said Barrett.

"What did he say? Did he say anything?" said Scruggs.

Not long afterward, Williams made a trip to Pascagoula, tugging his boat down on a trailer hitch. He had since learned that Scruggs was legit, so he called him and Scruggs called back, though he was in the Bahamas on vacation. Williams was sleeping on his boat, determined to get away from an apparently malevolent state court in Louisville and the possibility of being indicted there for theft. He soon moved permanently to Mississippi with the help of a $3,000 loan from Scruggs, who also helped him get a paralegal job. Scruggs could see that Williams was not only desperate, but physically ill. Given his history of smoking, drinking, and heart trouble, and the enormous strain he was under, Scruggs was afraid Williams wouldn't survive to see his situation resolved.

The tobacco companies would later heap derision on the fact that Scruggs gave Williams a lot of help—he would soon buy him a boat, car, and house in nearby Ocean Springs—and in so doing, helped himself. This was true. But Scruggs also wanted to protect a man who had taken a tremendous risk and was in extremis, friendless and ruined. With the millions he'd made in asbestos, Scruggs had the means to help and the heart to do it. He became Williams's guardian angel.

Scruggs and Williams met for lunch periodically in early April until one day, Williams said in his cryptic way that he had something he wanted to put in a safe place. Scruggs said he had a former bank building that he used to process legal claims and it had a vault. That would do nicely, said Williams.

But Williams refused to reveal the location of this valuable object until just before the Friday in mid-April of 1994 when Scruggs fueled up his Learjet and flew with his wife, Diane, and Williams to Orlando, Florida. The woman friend with whom Williams had deposited the documents years earlier met them at the airport with two banker's boxes. The plane then flew to Destin, on the Gulf, where Scruggs and his wife got off to spend some vacation time at his condo. One of Scruggs's paralegals, Tammy Cauley, boarded for the flight back to Pascagoula.

Williams and his woman friend were both drunk, cuddled up in the back of the plane with a bottle.

"They're going to try to kill me. If they could get their hands on me, they would," Williams was telling the woman. Cauley figured he was trying to get her into bed.

They landed late at night. Williams and his girlfriend left. Williams wouldn't permit anyone to open the boxes or make copies, but Cauley's instructions were to secretly copy them anyway and lock them up. But the boxes were so heavily bound with packing tape that there was no way to open them without Williams's knowing, so she decided to leave them alone. At around midnight, Cauley dragged the two boxes into the vault of the old bank building, just down the street from Scruggs's office.

The following Saturday, Scruggs returned and, joined by his law partner, Steve Bozeman, and Don Barrett, stood around a table in the bank, feverish with excitement, as Williams brought out the two boxes, still so heavily bound with packing tape that "goddamned Houdini couldn't have gotten out of there," Scruggs remembered.

Williams unwrapped them and, like a crow with shiny things, displayed the documents, one by one. He pulled out a memo by B&W counsel Kendrick Wells proposing that scientific documents be routed through lawyers to make it look as though they were prepared for litigation.

Scruggs had suspected that tobacco probably created a false privilege for its records. But not until that moment did he know how it was done.

The second document was one of those Williams had spotted in his supervisor's office at Brown & Williamson. It was by Addison Yeaman, counsel to the company in the sixties and seventies, a rambling think-piece about nicotine research that contained the sentence: "We are, then, in the business of selling nicotine, an addictive drug effective in the release of stress mechanisms."

"These guys are toast," Scruggs said.

It was like Christmas. Every few minutes, Barrett or Scruggs or Bozeman would exclaim, "My God, look at this!" "No, look at *this*!" "Hold on a minute. LOOK AT THIS!!" There was explosive material on the targeting of women, minorities, and, of course, children, as well as on nicotine manipulation and addiction, and several coding and classification manuals, the blueprints for the whole collection. And everywhere they looked, lawyers were guiding and strategizing.

They browsed until lunchtime. As soon as they went out to eat, Tammy Cauley went in and copied the forty documents sitting out on the table. That night, she returned and copied every last one of Williams's treasures.

Attorney General Mike Moore flew in the next day and viewed a collation of the ten or so hottest documents. Moore was impressed. Williams was scared.

"Have I committed a crime?" he asked.

"I haven't seen any crime committed," said Moore. "You've pointed out a crime."

Over and over, Moore reassured Williams that, at a minimum, he would be physically safe.

"I'm the attorney general of the state of Mississippi. Once I take custody of these documents, you're under the protection of my office," said Moore.

That got through to Williams. For the first time in several years, he believed he might have a future.

"Attorney General Moore, they're yours," said Williams.

Scruggs came back to the office and announced it.

"We've got 'em—legally, I mean," he told Cauley.

That's nice, thought Cauley, who was just then running off an additional two copies.

THE NEXT QUESTION WAS WHAT TO DO WITH THIS WON-derful gift. Moore and Scruggs decided that since Congress had the broadest jurisdiction and Congressman Henry Waxman was clearly an ally, they would turn them over to him. A day or so later, Moore and Scruggs flew a set of the documents to Washington. When they brought them into Waxman's personal office, Waxman literally took a few steps backward, as though they were radioactive.

While in Washington, Scruggs began to fret that keeping copies of stolen documents could make the Mississippi lawyers vulnerable, so he called Steve Bozeman in Pascagoula and told him to destroy all remaining sets. Bozeman informed Barrett of the order from Scruggs, but Barrett convinced Bozeman to give them to him instead of shredding them.

Barrett then turned around and offered his extra set to ABC's Keith Summa, with whom he had become good friends when Summa interviewed Barrett for *Day One*. Days later, Bogdanich met Barrett in Wichita, Kansas, where Barrett gave him what became known as "the small set," three inches or so of the most powerful documents from the Williams collection.

Their colleagues at *Day One* were thrilled at this new coup by Summa and Bogdanich. However, John Zucker, one of ABC's house lawyers, was uncharacteristically negative.

"I see no story here," said Zucker.

Bogdanich said something about begging to differ, and went his way.

He and Summa began reviewing the material, making notes, typing up questions. A few days later, while Bogdanich was on assignment in Washington, Zucker appeared at Summa's cubicle. He told Summa to immediately surrender the documents, plus his notes. He was to dump whatever was on his computer onto a floppy disk, erase the hard drive, and turn over the disk. Summa was aghast. He called Bogdanich and Yellin. They told him to obey Zucker.

When Bogdanich returned, there was a meeting that included Tom Yellin, Zucker, Bogdanich, Summa, Alan Braverman, counsel for ABC, and Roone Arledge, president of the news division. Braverman said if they ran a story based on stolen documents in violation of a restraining order, such as had been entered in Kentucky, Thomas Murphy, the CEO of Capital Cities, which owned ABC, could be jailed.

"No news organization will run this story," said Braverman.

That's insane, said Bogdanich. As long as the reporter himself didn't steal them or encourage their theft, there is no legal problem. Purloined documents are, in fact, a fairly routine source of important investigative stories.

Depressed and frustrated, Summa called Don Barrett and told him they had hit a brick wall. It appeared ABC was going to let one of the greatest public health stories in history pass it by. You'd better send them to somebody else, said Summa.

It was clear to Bogdanich and Summa that the Philip Morris libel suit was having a pronounced negative impact on the network's tobacco coverage. The battle over the B&W documents seemed so irrational, it made Bogdanich queasy. As a precaution he began keeping a journal.

Days later, on Saturday, May 7, *The New York Times* ran a lengthy page-one article based on the Brown & Williamson "small set" written by Philip Hilts, the same reporter who interviewed Bogdanich just before the *Day One* broadcast. Hilts said later that the *Times* lawyers approved the story almost immediately. It was clearly protected by the First Amendment.

This time, Roone Arledge convened a meeting. He was seething.

"So no one's ever going to do what these guys just did?" said Arledge to Braverman sarcastically.

Arledge could see this was an important story and was embarrassed at having been shut out. The logical next step, Summa and Bogdanich realized, would be to beat the competition to the "big set" of documents, the full four thousand pages.

Now Barrett called Bogdanich at home and said Professor Stanton Glantz, a militantly anti-tobacco medical researcher at the University of California at San Francisco, was about to receive the full collection, a golden opportunity for ABC to acquire it from someone with impeccable credentials.

Early Thursday afternoon, Glantz phoned Bogdanich to say that a big box had just arrived by Federal Express. There was no return address, with the sender identified only as "Mr. Butts," after the feisty talking cigarette from *Doonesbury*. Bogdanich flew to San Francisco and copied the documents, and all weekend Bogdanich and Summa camped out on the seventh floor of ABC News at 157 Columbus Avenue reading them, along with a medical school professor and nicotine expert named Dr. John Slade, who thought them "extraordinary."

On Sunday, they interviewed Slade along with Matt Myers, Douglas's old crony. At five A.M. Monday morning, Bogdanich, who had gotten four hours of sleep since Thursday, staggered off to the Empire Hotel for a nap. The show would feature a taped segment on the Brown & Williamson documents, entitled "Cigarette Papers," as well as live interviews with Congressman Henry Waxman and Brennan Dawson of the Tobacco Institute. When Bogdanich returned from his nap, it was still unclear if Waxman would agree to appear alongside Dawson.

Not long before the show was to air that evening, with Tom Yellin and Bogdanich and Summa in the control room in New York, it was agreed that Waxman would answer questions but wouldn't debate Dawson directly.

After the "Cigarette Papers" finished rolling, Dawson and Waxman went at it, and though technically not a debate, it soon became emotionally charged, a drama of diametrical opposites. Dawson, a tall, articulate woman, her eyes blazing, and the balding Waxman, unflappable and effective.

Standing at the back of the control room, with a watch in his hand, was ABC lawyer John Zucker, who was evidently timing the interviewees.

He rushed up to Yellin, who, as series producer, ran the control room during his show.

"You've got to give her more time!" he said of Dawson. "Go back to her! Go back to her!"

Yellin ignored him. As they were about to end the Dawson-Waxman segment, the "Roone phone" rang, which was Roone Arledge's personal line to the control room.

Arledge was excited by what he was seeing.

"This is great," he told Yellin. "But can't you get them to debate?"

Out of the question, said Yellin. Waxman had insisted.

"Okay, well, keep it going," said Arledge.

Afterward, Bogdanich felt *Day One* had regained some of the luster lost when the lawyers killed the original documents story. But then he would think back to Zucker with his watch in the control room and that queasy feeling would return.

MOTLEY WENT INTO A STATE OF PERPETUAL MOTION AFTER the *Day One* "spiking" story aired. The timing was providential. The ABC broadcast and the Waxman hearings came as he and Dickie Scruggs were getting the Mississippi state lawsuit ready to file. Motley turned on his TV set one day to find the whole world going completely crazy over something called nicotine manipulation.

"You get me that transcript. I want it today," he told Jodi Flowers, his latest dark-haired associate, who had been hired specifically to work on tobacco, after *Day One*.

"Aye, aye, sir," said Flowers, who had little fear of anything or anybody, even Ron Motley.

Day One and the attendant burst of publicity around tobacco made Motley restless. It seemed to be taking forever to actually get the Mississippi case off the launching pad and Motley was chafing, afraid someone else would fire the first shot across tobacco's bow. At the end of March, he picked up the *Wall Street Journal* and saw his nightmare confirmed. Several dozen of the best plaintiff's law firms in the country were filing a federal class action on behalf of all 50 million American smokers, charging the cigarette makers with manipulating nicotine to addict them and citing *Day One* and Kessler as authorities.

It would be hard to come up with a bigger class of victims than that, though so far *Castano* v. *American Tobacco* was little more than an imaginative legal concept. It was the brainchild of a New

Orleans lawyer named Wendell Gauthier, who was still signing up recruits willing to make a $100,000 initial payment to fund *Castano*. Motley badly wanted in, and Ness, Motley joined almost immediately. He sent Jodi Flowers and Charles Patrick to an organizational meeting, where Lou Rawls, the singer, and, for some reason, keynote speaker, enthusiastically endorsed suing big tobacco in what Flowers thought sounded suspiciously like a husky cigarette voice.

Flowers sat down, and in a minute an elderly man came barreling into his seat with a great clump of papers clutched against his chest. Flowers felt for the old soul as he pawed through a sort of wasp's nest of legal documents and notes.

Rawls was finished, and Wendell Gauthier took the podium.

"Ladies and gentleman, let's have a very, very warm welcome for Mr. Melvin Belli," said Gauthier to prolonged applause and a standing ovation, and the man sitting next to Flowers smoothed his suit and walked to the podium.

Flowers was glad when she sighted Charles Patrick.

"I almost made a complete jerk out of myself with the King of Torts," she said. It was a new world to Flowers, who had been talked out of going into domestic law by Motley, with whom she had interned during law school vacations.

"You'll spend the rest of your life fighting over knives and forks," Motley had warned her.

So she veered off into product liability and was glad she did, as her friends in domestic law were indeed battling over flatware. Though young, she was Motley's latest protégée, and got the prize assignment of working on *Castano*. It was heady stuff. While she took notes on the speakers, San Francisco lawyer Elizabeth Cabraser was huddled over her cell phone at the back of the conference room, working out the last details of a $3.8 billion breast implant settlement. Everywhere she looked there were high rollers.

Motley himself turned up at a *Castano* meeting not long afterward in Miami. Barrett had brought a small clump of the Merrell Williams documents and read selections to a spellbound audience. Motley was so hungry for the documents, he reminded Barrett of the old movie villain Charles Boyer: "*I must possess eet*. You must *geef* them to me."

Very shortly thereafter Motley got the "big set" from his partners in Mississippi. He spent weeks reading and rereading, becoming better versed than other lawyers, memorizing, working out chronologies, seizing on themes, identifying critical players, scribbling his inspirations in flailing Babylonian arcs on legal pads that Jodi Flowers and Ann Ritter patiently reduced to typed memos.

A "Tobacco Team" began to take shape, which included Jack McConnell up in Rhode Island as well as Motley's inner circle in Charleston. The firm's senior paralegal, Cheryl Glenn, who had waded after asbestos documents in flooded, rat-infested warehouses in Brooklyn and dragged filthy boxes from cobwebbed attics, helped Ritter set up a Tobacco Team headquarters within Ness, Motley. Other lawyers were recruited from the existing ranks, such as Andy Berly, once with the Justice Department, and Susan Nial, a former corporate lawyer from New York.

Orientations were held. Buttons were printed that said FREE MERRELL WILLIAMS. Fancy new shredders were purchased, and the Tobacco Team went through a phase where everyone compulsively shredded everything until finally Ritter told them to stop it. Morale surged. After all, their Maximum Leader had just finished winning or settling nine consecutive multi-million-dollar consolidated asbestos cases.

A small warehouse was rented across the Grace Memorial Bridge in Mount Pleasant, and it began to fill up: the Merrell Williams papers, 327 boxes from *Haines,* forty years' worth of congressional hearings; trial transcripts—thousands of pages just from *Cipollone*—depositions, complaints, exhibits, exhibit lists, interrogatories, briefs, judges' opinions, and records of appellate proceedings from *Green, Pritchard, Ross, Horton, Wilks,* and many others; reprints of newspaper, magazine, scientific, and law review articles; videotapes of documentaries on the cigarette companies, of newscasts, of tobacco company propaganda films and TV commercials from the fifties and early sixties, of focus groups and mock trials; investigative materials gathered by detective agencies on key witnesses and potential whistle-blowers; correspondence between attorneys; internal Ness, Motley reports; tobacco promotional items, current cigarette ads, packs of cigarettes.

Teams of Ness, Motley lawyers and paralegals traveled to

Maine, Wisconsin, Washington, D.C., Virginia, California, Britain, and Germany to interview witnesses or informants. A group of objective and subjective coders worked with the industry documents, while another group of temporary workers scanned material into a computer database. Tobacco Team lawyers lugged boxes home with them, trading memos on which were the important ones and why. Ritter also helped the *Castano* staff set up a document depository in New Orleans in the Energy Building downtown.

And, most significant, Ritter began creating a "liability summary," a comprehensive statement of the case against the industry, topic by topic, in sufficient detail that it would one day grow into a five-foot-tall stack of ring binders. The liability summary was the Tobacco Team's war plan, or its most recent codification, constantly updated and footnoted with documents and testimony.

One pillar of the firm took little part in these elaborate preparations, however. Joe Rice, now co-managing partner with Terry Richardson, stayed out of tobacco, focusing instead on maintaining the revenue flow from asbestos and elsewhere and riding herd on Motley's willingness to gamble more money on the tobacco venture with every passing month.

Of course, anyone who took a look at the Brown & Williamson papers had to admit they made a strong case for taking that gamble. Judges wouldn't like the way tobacco lawyers apparently played fast and loose with certain rules of civil procedure.

"We're going to be kicking their dicks in the dirt" was Motley's more pungent way of putting it.

What Motley saw in the Merrell Williams collection was a detailed catalog of all the ways the industry wronged the country, pointing to many potential areas for discovery. The Williams documents weren't just a road map for discovery, they were the *Rand McNally Atlas.*

All of this was buzzing through Motley's head as he arrived in Jackson, Mississippi, for a critical meeting on the attorney general's case early that spring. Attorney General Mike Moore still hadn't given the final go-ahead on the lawsuit, which was all but ready. Many versions of the complaint had been drafted, but the suit was no less novel for having been fine-tuned. No matter what, a "state Medicaid reimbursement action" was a hothouse flower that might not survive in the great outdoors. The only way to find out was to bring it down to the clerk of the Jackson County Chancery Court in Pascagoula and file it.

Scruggs, Motley, Steve Bozeman, and other lawyers were there in Moore's spacious personal office, along with David White, who ran a public relations firm used frequently by Ness, Motley. The idea was to give Moore one final push.

Moore talked about his young son, Kyle. Tobacco marketing that targeted children angered Americans of every persuasion and was what mattered most to him personally. But, he reminded the lawyers, he held office in a traditional southern state with a conservative Republican governor.

"No matter how worthy, I can't just go off on my own private crusade," he said. "I need to know from you lawyers that this'll stand up in a court of law."

What he heard next wouldn't ease his mind.

"You're going to be in a lot of trouble if you do this," said David White, the PR man.

Not only would tobacco try to defeat Moore at the polls and enlist their front-group hobgoblins to sabotage him, other business leaders would shun him. His money would dry up. It was a prescription for political suicide.

No one had to tell Moore about the poll results on the Mississippi suit. Dick Morris, who occasionally polled for Dickie Scruggs, had surveyed the Pascagoula jury pool in the fall of 1993, just before Morris joined the Clinton White House. Despite Scruggs and Motley's celebrated new legal theory, 60 percent sided with the tobacco companies. Most people couldn't even figure the damn thing out.

For that reason, the action would be filed in chancery court, an anachronistic venue originating in medieval Britain that existed in the U.S. only in Mississippi and three other states. Unlike ordinary law courts, there are no juries in chancery court, and all decisions are made by a judge, called a chancellor, who hopefully would understand this weirdo lawsuit. A chancery court could also order changes in business practices law courts couldn't. Of course, all of this assumed the judge wouldn't agree with the 60 percent of his neighbors who thought the idea didn't make any sense.

Moore looked on impassively as his friend Dickie Scruggs weighed in.

"Time to move," said Scruggs. "We're never going to have a better atmosphere than we do now with what's going on in Washington and nationally."

There are no guarantees, he said, but this is the best legal weapon to come down the pike in a long time. And, he reassured Moore, I'll stand stand behind you, no matter what, to the bitter end.

"I can tell you this," said Motley, charging in. "I don't give a *shit* about polls. Not in this case."

He rose up in his chair.

"I've got two reasons. One is, I've seen the evidence. I've read Merrell Williams's stuff. Nobody's ever seen documents like that. That poll can tell you whatever you want—those folks haven't seen what I've seen. These guys are fuckin' thieves. You put me in front of a judge who's *half*way fair and we've got every chance of winning this case.

"And number two," said Motley. "None of that political-fallout crap is going to mean anything in the long run, because this is the right way to go, and everybody in this fucking room knows that and everybody in the country knows it, and, yes, even down here in the great state of Mississippi they know it, or they're gonna know once we get done educating 'em. And you know it, Mike, or we wouldn't be here. These gangsters have gotten a free ride for forty years.

"We got the theory and the facts and now we got the leader. And you're him. So like Dickie said, it's time to move."

"Well, thank you, Brother Motley," said Moore, to laughter.

"But seriously, I think you've said what's in everyone's heart," Moore said. "I've taken a lot of risks. I'm going to take another one. I do think this is the right thing to do. I know I'm going to take some heat, but I'm going to do it."

The room broke into applause. Moore walked in front of his desk. With the toe of his shoe, he scraped a line in the carpet.

"Now, this is it," said Moore. "Anybody who steps over this line agrees to stick with me till the end, just like Dickie said. Anybody who's not willing to do that, you better leave now."

And one by one, the lawyers stepped over the line.

The MISSISSIPPI CASE WAS FILED ON MAY 23, 1994. With *Haines* and *Castano* that meant Motley now had three tobacco suits. He had been hounding Jodi Flowers to find him a good environmental tobacco smoke suit. Motley was high on ETS suits because a jury was a lot more likely to be sympathetic to a plaintiff who contracted lung cancer merely from breathing the air than a smoker who puffed himself to death. It was, theoretically, another route around the industry's bulletproof assumption-of-the-risk defense.

Not long before the *Day One* broadcast, one fell into his lap when he met a lawyer named Cindy Lott at a conference in Boston. Lott was working on the case of a non-smoking barber named Burl Butler who was dying of lung cancer. In the spring, Motley, Charles Patrick, and Jodi Flowers visited Butler and his wife, Ava, in their home in Laurel, Mississippi.

Butler was gracious, despite the fact that he was in the last days of life, bald, thin, and breathing oxygen. Ava cooked a country-style meal. Jodi Flowers had never met a real live plaintiff before and she was intimidated. The man was dying in front of them. What do you say?

Motley had been in the homes of dozens of dying asbestos workers. They sat around the dining room table and Motley asked Butler how his appetite was, what sort of drugs he'd been taking for pain, for tumor suppression. He knew all the medical terms the Butlers had learned as Burl slowly died. He was concerned and compassionate and Flowers could see the Butlers were taken with him.

Burl Butler still had his sense of humor, but mostly he was pissed off that he was going to die at fifty-three. He told of having a routine physical and chest X ray and the doctor asking him how many packs a day he smoked, and his saying he didn't smoke and why did he want to know? And then the doctor said he had lung cancer. Butler could not believe it.

Then he talked about his little barbershop there in Laurel, where almost all the customers smoked and where he had worked for decades in a gray fog. And how his outrage grew with the black mass in his chest.

"I always knew they were killing those other people, but I never dreamed they were killing me," said Butler.

Butler seemed to need to talk about it. He truly felt hoodwinked. Do you think the cigarette companies knew? Why didn't they tell people?

Motley said he was pretty sure they knew. And pretty sure he could prove it.

"Mr. Motley, if you do take this case," said Butler, "maybe it won't happen to somebody else."

Motley shook hands with Butler at the door. They drove to the airport in silence. Motley sat with a feeling he'd had before, but it was new to Flowers. It was the realization that this first meeting with Burl Butler would almost certainly be the last. And that when all was said and done, that was why it mattered.

PIRATES ON BOURBON STREET

OUT OF THE CORNER OF HIS EYE, CLIFF DOUGLAS SAW people heading toward his table at the cafeteria of the Department of Labor Building on Constitution Avenue in Washington, D.C., where he was attending hearings on environmental tobacco smoke.

He could see several young women surrounding a red-faced man in a blue pinstriped suit. The man was bobbing along like he was heading for a ringside seat, pumping hands along the way. His black hair was slicked back with some brilliantine-like substance.

He got closer and Douglas could see he was wearing shiny black cowboy boots.

Things are getting interesting here at the little ol' Department of Labor cafeteria, Douglas thought.

The man bobbed over, stuck out his hand, and said, "Cliff, Ron Motley. Heard an awful lot about you. It's really a pleasure."

Motley sat down. The two tried to chat but any coherence was sucked out of the conversation by the swirl of activity around Motley, who seemed to be at the center of a vortex of incoming phone calls and faxes.

"I'm sure we'll be seeing each other. If you can come down to Charleston, we'll spend some time. Things are a little crazy now," said Motley, gripping Douglas's hand again. And then he was gone.

Motley wasn't the first plaintiff's lawyer Douglas had met, but Douglas was still new to the breed in the fall of 1994. Douglas had only recently left the world of the private health organizations, most recently the American Cancer Society, for which he had lobbied Congress. Now he was drifting into the orbit of the personal-injury lawyers. It began that fall with a series of missions for Wendell Gauthier, founder of the huge *Castano* class-action suit that centered around nicotine manipulation, Douglas's issue.

Mission was the kind of word Douglas was fond of, which was why Philip Morris saw Douglas as typical of what they called the "anti-tobacco zealot" or "hard-core anti." Douglas had been targeted for a deposition as part of Philip Morris's multi-billion-dollar libel suit against ABC, which Douglas saw as an attempt to intimidate him, pure and simple. Even before the suit, he took some rudimentary precautions. He checked to see if he was being tailed. He bought a shredder and shredded his notes and anything he didn't file. He was careful on the telephone, in case it was tapped. "James Bond stuff," Douglas called it.

A damned unpleasant way to live, was what his wife, Martha, thought of it. Martha resented Douglas's increasingly single-minded pursuit of the tobacco dragon, although she knew he couldn't stand *not* to do it, that his crusade was powered by a deep anger against people he saw as taking advantage of others. She wondered if that anger came from his childhood in Chicago, his own sense of victimization, of being different. She had witnessed his struggle to control those feelings, just as he had fought to control his Tourette's.

Still, she wished for the way things used to be, when she and Cliff would visit bed and breakfasts or discuss books, before tobacco consumed her husband's every waking moment.

Now Cliff was working at home, which for a while was a rented house in Chevy Chase, Maryland, and later, Evanston, just outside Chicago, and finally Ann Arbor, Michigan. Wherever he was he had at his disposal a computer, a telephone, and a fax machine. Period. With those tools, he continued his "guerilla operations" as he had at the health voluntaries, only now as a more or less full-time job.

"That's why when people ask what I do, I can't really tell them," he said once. "Information is power. I sort of broker it to the media. And other folks, of course."

His fax machine zapped industry documents off to the press. He unofficially helped the FDA. He consulted with plaintiff's lawyers, first *Castano* and later Motley's people. He was in the synergism business, as he had been with ABC and the FDA, pollinating back and forth from plaintiff's lawyers to the FDA to Congress to whistleblowers to newspapers and TV.

Although a lawyer, he didn't blend any better with Gauthier and the personal injury crowd than he had with the health apparatchiks in Washington. The PI lawyers loved glitz, slapping backs, and dishing up hale-and-hearty bullshit. Douglas was soft spoken, almost boyish. He always felt like a busboy who'd sneaked into a gala at the Waldorf when he traveled with the plaintiff's people and shared their reliably sterile two-hundred-and-fifty-dollar-a-day hotel suites, dined on their overpriced seafood pastas dripping in cream sauce, and downed beers at the inevitable airport Hyatt cocktail lounges.

The PI lawyers just couldn't figure Douglas out. He kind of bothered them. Lawyers are quintessentially not do-gooders and Douglas was a do-gooder. Most of the high-rolling class-action lawyers grabbed on to tobacco as a potential generator of money and fame, which Douglas didn't seem interested in.

"I like kicking ass," he would say, sounding not at all like Gandhi but a lot like Motley. "And I want these guys to go to jail."

That *Motley* wouldn't say.

Though many journalists on the tobacco beat knew Douglas was *the guy*, Mr. Nicotine Manipulation, at the time he wandered into the Department of Labor cafeteria, he still had no public profile, no permanent employment, and no money at all.

"I don't understand what he does. Most people I know have jobs," said Susan Nial of Ness, Motley one night at a hotel bar in New York City.

She seemed highly suspicious of Douglas. Keith Summa tried to explain about *Day One*.

"He's the guy who started this," said Summa. "Without him, none of you would be doing what you're doing."

Nial's distrust seemed based on the scuttlebutt that Douglas had made a pest of himself trying to get reimbursed for his expenses by the *Castano* group. Indeed, money had become an overwhelming concern for Douglas and his wife. Martha was about to go back to school to earn a degree in business, which she hoped would win her a better job in the non-profit world. That left Cliff as the provider, which meant living from check to check. And it wasn't always easy getting checks from the plaintiff's lawyers.

Douglas took the plunge into self-employment and economic turmoil in August 1994, just a few months before he met Motley in Washington. Fed up with the American Cancer Society, he was hired on a short-term basis by Congressman Martin Meehan, a Massachusetts Democrat, to write up a catalog of the industry's alleged crimes, based on revelations from the Waxman hearings and elsewhere.

The finished document would be a "prosecution memo" outlining how the Department of Justice could seek criminal indictments against industry executives, scientists, and perhaps even lawyers. Such a memo would normally be produced internally at Justice, but the department showed little enthusiasm and Meehan wanted to jump-start the process.

With so much happening that spring and summer, Douglas was eager to get back into the thick of things, and working on the Justice project might heal some of the lingering hurt of being relegated to the sidelines while the world exploded after *Day One*.

He was already working for Meehan when he wandered into the Department of Labor cafeteria in the fall. He had come to Labor to watch his old friend Matthew Myers cross-examine industry witnesses on a new rule proposed by the Occupational Safety and Health Administration that would ban smoking in virtually all workplaces.

The importance tobacco attached to these hearings showed clearly in their order of battle. R. J. Reynolds and Philip Morris dispatched not only an infinity of lawyers, but an ex–acting director of OSHA and a swarm of flacks. They buried the agency in paper. Reynolds alone submitted more than fifteen thousand pages of comments. All of this was supported by full-page newspaper ads on the theme that secondhand smoke is not hazardous. "In any debate, facts must matter," proclaimed Philip Morris in ads whose apparent purpose was to cast doubt on the existence of any facts.

The industry had tried a similar ad campaign in Australia in 1986, but a magistrate found the Tobacco Institute of Australia wilfully distorted studies by independent scientists to make it look like the science on ETS was either inconclusive or pointed away from secondhand smoke as a cancer culprit.

Motley had come to Washington as part of a relief party the *Castano* coalition had mustered at his urging. The cigarette makers were so dominant at OSHA, health and labor witnesses were being pummeled and Myers was overmatched. A call went out for help, and Motley and other *Castano* lawyers responded.

Jodi Flowers assisted Motley. She had heard about the companies' wealth and power, but this was her first taste of it, and she was amazed at their influence, the way they seemed to know in advance what the government's lawyers would ask, and how frightened the OSHA bureaucrats seemed of them.

The *Castano* plan was to sting vulnerable witnesses, but which ones the plaintiff's lawyers planned to cross-examine was never revealed beforehand so the companies couldn't withdraw them. Flowers spent many hours in the OSHA docket office, pulling previous testimony to help Motley get ready.

One tobacco industry paralegal was there every day. One day, Flowers left her stack of printouts to get a drink of water and upon her return discovered the paralegal riffling through them.

"Uh, hello?" said Flowers, staring.

Startled, the little creature trotted away.

"She's probably lookin' for clues 'bout who we're going to do," Motley said when he heard.

If she got any, it didn't show, as Motley and the *Castano* attorneys scored many more points that fall. Duke University economist W. Kip Viscusi expounded on his theory that cigarette smokers who die prematurely save society money. R. J. Reynolds toxicologist Chris Coggins had to explain why RJR spent millions developing the "low sidestream" product Premier if the industry is confident secondhand smoke is innocous. One witness conceded his testimony had been edited by cigarette company attorneys. Others pulled out abruptly rather than face cross-examination. An unhappy Philip Morris withdrew from the hearings in November.

The hearings ended in a draw in early 1995. Though the rule was never issued, a casualty of the Republican takeover of Congress in 1994, the *Castano* team had gone up against the cigarette makers and more than held their own.

"We're a lean, mean fighting machine," said Motley proudly at a *Castano* meeting in December at a New Orleans hotel.

He explained with delight how he had dispatched someone to England to get the smoking policy at the university where an industry witness taught, a no-smoking policy, as it turned out, which embarrassed the witness.

"That's like something they do and they didn't like it being done to them," he said. He called R. J. Reynolds "Joe Coward" and Philip Morris "the Marlboro Mouse" for bolting the hearings.

Motley had expected the show of force he saw at OSHA. What surprised him was that tobacco had already willed into existence a full-fledged alternative to the mainstream science on environmental tobacco smoke—friendly researchers who took industry money, attended tobacco-sponsored symposia, and cited one another in scholarly journals. And, as the Australian experience demonstrated, they were doing it all over the world.

"Man, the asbestos guys were kindergarten teachers next to this bunch," Motley told Flowers.

THE NIGHT FOLLOWING MOTLEY'S "LEAN AND MEAN" oration, Antoine's was filled to bursting. Around one table at the French Quarter landmark restaurant was a group of tobacco company attorneys, while in another room, a much larger group of *Castano* lawyers ate Cajun chowder and drank wine, toasting what seemed like a better than even chance they would succeed the following morning in convincing a federal judge to certify their lawsuit, a first step toward going to court on behalf of millions of addicted smokers.

At a corner table, a reporter for a legal newspaper was cozying up to John Coale, a flamboyant, chunky sparkplug of a man who once called the head of a pro-business lobby "a whore for the insurance companies" during a TV debate. In another corner was Wendell Gauthier, the founder of the feast, the innovator who brought together polar opposites like Motley, the consummate trial lawyer, and Coale, a politically-connected class action lawyer. Gauthier's skill at coalition building was formidable. Instead of three firms coming together as in *Cipollone,* Gauthier stayed on the telephone for a couple of months and hauled in five dozen.

Gauthier was from a town where the spare-time entertainment is hunting alligators. Iota, population one thousand, is bayou country, not far from the Gulf but well west of New Orleans, a place where there is fishing within a hundred yards of every house.

Gauthier had a full head of sandy hair and a soft Cajun voice like butter melting on pancakes in summer sunshine. When he hosted a *Castano* conference, he was the ultimate southern gentleman, a great conciliator with his voice and smile and charm. Gauthier was also an accomplished courtroom artist with many substantial verdicts in air disasters and chemical-plant explosions to his credit. He had organized groups of lawyers before, in the fires at the Dupont Plaza Hotel in Puerto Rico and the MGM Grand in Las Vegas, as well as other mass mishaps. Most of the potentates in *Castano*—Coale, Stanley Chesley from Cleveland, Russ Herman of New Orleans, Elizabeth Cabraser of San Francisco—had sat with Gauthier on these plaintiff's coordinating committees, which managed class actions and mass disasters and usually settled them.

Though Motley had a low opinion of some class-action specialists—he called them "settling lawyers"—he and Gauthier shared an enthusiasm for mock juries, and tried out a version of *Castano* on one. J.D. Lee, a Tennessee lawyer with lots of tobacco experience, and Don Barrett played tobacco lawyers. Motley put on the plaintiff's case and won before two different panels.

"We let poor ol' Barrett be the tobacco industry and he still couldn't win," Motley kidded afterward.

The sham trial was held in Gauthier's own miniature courtroom at his law firm, a little concrete building in Metairie, just outside the city limits of New Orleans. Gauthier's mock court had a wooden balustrade around the jury box and a cabinet full of video equipment with wires that ran to a camera hidden behind an oil painting. Gauthier also used the room to stage elaborate practical jokes.

A *Wall Street Journal* reporter arrived to see Gauthier in the spring of 1994 only to find him missing. Instead there was a lot of excited talk about a new tobacco whistle-blower, who was about to meet with the lawyers. Would the reporter care to sit in?

Naturally he did, and was brought into the mock courtroom, where he was confronted by a surly individual in a white wig who kept demanding to know if he was a cop. The lawyers tried to calm him, but suddenly he stood, pulled a gun from his pants, and leapt across the table.

"I'll kill you, you son of a bitch!"

"No, no!" screamed the reporter. "I have kids!"

Then this wacko pulled the trigger, and like a Daffy Duck cartoon, out came a flag that said BANG!

The psycho informant giggled and stuck out his hand.

I'm Wendell Gauthier. Aah hope you don't mind our little prank.

The practical jokes worked because the "victims" wanted to believe, and Gauthier was surprised at how quickly the law firms said yes when invited to join *Castano,* but, of course, they too wanted to believe. The soil seemed fertile in the post-Kessler, post–*Day One* environment. The companies were running national newspaper ads strenuously denying they manipulated nicotine. *Thou dost protest too much,* Gauthier thought. His confreres in the class-action bar were a cocky and largely undefeated band of pirates. They had done breast implants, heart valves, so many products in fifteen years. They had boarded and plundered many a corporate galleon and prospered. Only rarely did they have to go to trial. Why not tobacco?

The legal action Gauthier filed in the name of his best friend, Peter Castano, dead of lung cancer at forty-seven, was very simple. It sought damages only for addiction, not for any smoking-related disease. That limited the potential recovery to a few thousand dollars per victim—to help them quit and to monitor their health as they aged—but avoided having to fight the Medieval Logicians on whether smoking "caused" each individual's disease. And multiplied by millions of claimants, a few thousand dollars adds up to billions. The mechanics of the suit—how to notify a large class of people that they could join, setting up a medical monitoring program—had been mastered in previous class actions.

With the firepower of sixty-odd law firms, *Castano* had the troops to muster its own wall of flesh, could spend millions a year without breaking a sweat and go toe-to-toe with the industry indefinitely. If they got the suit certified as a class action, anything could happen. The industry might even sue for peace.

That summer, they brought Victor DeNoble to New Orleans, who gave a talk behind closed doors entitled "The Tobacco Industry's Nicotine Research: What They Knew and When." Later,

DeNoble strolled through the French Quarter with a friendly *Castano* lawyer and they stopped at a tavern.

"You know, Victor, you're getting involved in something that's new to you, but I've done this for years," said the lawyer. "So I'm going to give you a little free advice. They'll tell you this is a cause and they're fighting the good fight. Bullshit. It's all about money. Never forget that."

Nevertheless, DeNoble became a guide to the *Castano* lawyers, helping educate them about nicotine and focusing their document discovery. Then he waited, hoping for other ways to be useful.

Gauthier was savvy enough to bring in DeNoble and was savvy about the media, as was John Coale, the rotund Washington lawyer who was also dining at Antoine's that night in December. Between the two of them, *Castano* became an unstoppable publicity machine. Media mobbed their hearings, produced a deluge of hyperbolic articles and television. And now, of course, they had Motley, who was addicted to television interviews.

Perhaps Coale and Gauthier's greatest achievement was to spread the Merrell Williams documents all over the world, which earned them friends in countless newsrooms. After getting a set from Mississippi, Gauthier holed up in his office and selected the hottest fifty. He and Coale kept the pot boiling by leaking handfuls all spring and summer. Documents were faxed by reporters to lawyer friends who faxed them to other reporters until sometimes they were largely illegible except for three or four different fax numbers at the top of the page.

The dinner at Antoine's was a celebration of *Castano*'s success so far, especially the OSHA operation. Gauthier passed out gifts to the young lawyers like Jodi Flowers who did the grunt work in Washington. Motley returned early to his hotel to avoid having to confront a former girlfriend.

Meanwhile, elsewhere in the restaurant, other luminaries were eating and drinking. In the large public dining area next to the *Castano* banquet room were representatives of the two largest institutional investors in tobacco stocks, sharing a table with a tobacco industry analyst, all nervous as cats about the giant lawsuit. In another private room were perhaps a dozen from among the battalion of cigarette company lawyers in town for the hearing. In contrast to the roaring *Castano* affair, the tobacco group ate politely and quietly in a dimly lit rectangular room at the other end of the restaurant, surrounded by framed portraits. For dessert, a large meringue cake was brought in to the *Castano*ites. A chant began: "Send it to them! Send it to them!" With the whole room shouting, a little column led by a bemused waiter wheeled the cake over to where the tobacco lawyers were chowing down. It was like going from the merry Christmas party at old Fezziwig's to the evening meal of the board of directors at the orphanage. The door swung open and the lawyers looked up stonily. "Tell them no thanks," someone muttered from the back.

The cake was marched back to Gauthier's group.

"They won't take our cake?" snorted one of the *Castano* lawyers. "Tell them we'll see them in fucking court!"

RON MOTLEY WOKE UP IN HIS NEW ORLEANS HOTEL room the morning after the fete at Antoine's in rare spirits. After the eight-thirty A.M. hearing in the *Castano* case, he was to rendezvous with Catherine Baen, his fiancée, a former model who was now a civil trial lawyer. Baen was twenty years younger than he, a Texan to whom he had proposed marriage two weeks earlier in one of his frequent impulsive moments, despite the fact they had been acquainted for all of two months. They'd gotten to know each other in Houston, where Baen was a junior local counsel in a major asbestos case Motley was trying. The wedding was set for New Year's Eve in Fort Lauderdale. As with virtually every aspect of his private life, the marriage arrangements were being managed by the staff of Ness, Motley, and the various people who followed him around and made sure his laundry was done, his bills paid, and his messages received and sent.

The hearing was an hour and a half old by the time Motley arrived, which didn't really matter because two other lawyers would do the presenting for the plaintiff's team. Motley was there as an all-purpose troubleshooter, and to rebut certain arguments if necessary.

Griffin Bell, attorney general under President Jimmy Carter, did the lion's share of the advocacy for the cigarette makers. A partner in the Atlanta firm of King & Spaulding, a major force in tobacco defense that represented Brown & Williamson, Bell was pushing eighty and looked it. He stumbled and seemed unfamiliar with class action law and precedent. It was not Bell's finest hour, but he was a southerner, a lawyer of national reputation, and someone who would immediately command the attention of federal District Judge Okla Jones II, a black Clinton appointee of liberal reputation. There were more than thirty lawyers from the tobacco side in the courtroom, so reinforcements were available.

The *Castano*ites were claiming that suits about nicotine addiction would in the not-too-distant future engulf the nation's courts like the current tidal wave of asbestos litigation, causing mammoth delays and wasting judicial resources. The alternative was to look down the road and immediately consolidate all potential suits into one national class action.

Bell argued, quite logically, that there was no proof the threatened deluge would ever happen and that so far not a single nicotine claim had been tested in court.

"Let's have one trial somewhere," remonstrated Bell, "before we bootstrap millions of cases into this court."

While Bell was talking, the "Prosecution Memorandum" Cliff Douglas had written for Congressman Meehan arrived. Upon its release, the memo—actually, Douglas had managed to produce a small book, 111 pages of reasons why tobacco company executives should be indicted by a federal grand jury—was flown by courier from Washington to New Orleans. Copies of Douglas's memorandum made the rounds in the courtroom, accompanied by a buzz of excitement. It had been hand-delivered to the Justice Department that morning, along with a letter signed by seven congressmen.

The *Castano* lawyers were led that day by Dianne Nast, a Philadelphian brilliant at oral argument. Nast reminded Jones that the tobacco companies quite naturally wanted to hold the plaintiffs to single cases. They used their vast resources to delay the trial, impoverishing the much smaller plaintiff's firms, which must win to get paid, while defense firms bill by the hour. For the first time since 1954, she said, *Castano* offered a chance for an even matchup.

Nast talked about the *Cipollone* case, where the companies' delaying tactics had the desired effect of frightening away potential litigants: ten years of trench warfare, blizzards of defense motions and appeals, the deposition that lasted twenty-two days.

Nast was in mid-diatribe when Jones interrupted and asked for a trial plan, a formal road map for how such a complicated case would actually be conducted. It was an unmistakable sign that he was sympathetic.

Motley was pleased.

"Bell looked horrible," he said as he raced back to the Windsor Court Hotel to get members of his firm scrambling on the trial plan.

Motley snatched up a handful of folders and stuffed himself into a taxi that took him to a hangar at Lakefront Airport called Million Air, which handles private jets. Catherine Baen was in the lounge with a friend. Baen was tall, at least a head taller than Motley, and wore a green dress that set off her shoulder-length black hair and dark eyes, a slender, athletic beauty.

Baen and Motley were going back to Houston, where their asbestos trial would soon start again. In the jet, they cuddled like high school kids. Baen massaged Motley's shoulders and Motley propped his boots on an adjoining seat and closed his eyes. The jet cleared the runway and climbed steeply, like a fighter plane. Once at cruising altitude, Motley talked excitedly about a Merrell Williams document that divided legally dangerous documents into categories. "'Youth Targeting' is one," he said. "Another is 'Lawyers and Science.' They got 'Suppression of Research.' I mean, these guys are unbelievable. They're the biggest liars since Goebbels."

He and Baen talked about their wedding and microscopic engagement.

"He asked me every day for three weeks," Baen told her friend. "Then on Sunday, he took unfair advantage of me. He got me drunk. And he asked me on Kiawah, which is such a beautiful spot."

Motley's huge house on Kiawah Island would soon host an extravagant wedding reception with music by the Fabulous Thunderbirds, a nationally known rhythm and blues band.

Motley looked around the plane. "Where's my puppy? Where's Willie?"

"I had to fly commercial down here, so I couldn't bring him," said Baen.

"Why can't Willie come?" said Motley, feigning hurt.

"That's okay," he said, perking up a moment later. "Just means you're going to have to show me that twirling video."

He turned to Baen's friend. "She used to be a twirler in high school. Did you know that? Now I have *got* to see that video." He laughed.

From the airport in Houston, they took a cab to the Four Seasons, where Motley had rented a condo for the duration of the asbestos trial. Baen continued on to her apartment. Every member of the hotel staff knew Motley and he greeted them like long-lost cousins. Several congratulated him on his upcoming marriage. His fiancée was a very lovely young lady, said the man at the front desk.

"I'm a lucky man," said Motley solemnly. "A very lucky man."

JENNIFER MOTLEY WAS IMMEDIATELY DUBIOUS ABOUT HER father's engagement. She couldn't believe it could be a good thing to marry somebody after knowing them two months. She also got the feeling neither her dad nor Catherine especially wanted her to meet her stepmother-to-be. The two finally met at a restaurant in Washington, D.C.

What did you think? someone asked Jennifer.

"I thought she was very tall," said Jiffy.

Motley's son, Mark, went to the wedding. But Jiffy made a stand. After all, she never got an invitation. She had plans to go skiing and she went.

Then came the reception at Kiawah, a spectacle of pharaonic proportions, with hundreds of guests. Jiffy, who had blossomed into a witty, sparkling young woman, came with her best friend from college. In the backyard, a big top-style tent the size of a large auditorium had been hung with chandeliers. On one side was Texan food, drink, and decor for the bride's family. On the other, a South Carolinian ambience for the groom. Jiffy could see there wasn't much mingling. She found Baen a cold fish. The whole thing seemed doomed.

Looking in from the edge of the tent was Cliff Douglas. Douglas had flown in with Martha to attend a Ness, Motley conference on tobacco evidence that brought together *Castano* people with Dickie Scruggs and other Mississippi lawyers. It was a chance for Douglas and his wife to have a brief, low-rent vacation in sunny Charleston before Cliff pushed on to Washington, and Motley had invited them to the reception.

Cliff and Martha stood on the lawn, gaping.

J. D. Lee, the Tennessee lawyer, strolled by.

"Just a gathering of five thousand of Ron's very closest friends," he chuckled.

"I guess," said Douglas. He figured the party must have set Motley back a quarter of a million dollars. And he thought the house grotesquely large, a monument to its cost.

Martha found the size of the gathering oddly sad. *Maybe he doesn't have a personal life,* she thought. Motley seemed surrounded by groupies.

Motley was hugging everyone, male and female. He came by to welcome Martha. He was half drunk, but his eyes were alive, a piercing, analytical gaze, as though trying to figure her out.

TO A NORTHERNER, THE COURTHOUSE IN LAUREL, MIS-sissippi, seemed like a museum exhibit on rural southern justice, with its chipped plaster walls, dirty, scuffed floor littered with wrappers and cigarette butts, and a partially disassembled Jones County seal nailed over the judge's bench. Six blurry oil portraits of judges hung on the courtroom wall. Ancient tungsten lighting dappled the room and a vending machine in the hallway sold orange Nehi in bottles.

State justice is worn and pockmarked in Mississippi, especially in Laurel, a lumber milling town where this hearing on a secondhand smoke case was about to take place. Unlike northern states where the system is underfunded, in Mississippi the system has never really been funded at all. The judiciary is just one more thing, like police, public health, and schools, for which each year the state is barely able to squeeze the money from its pauperized citizenry.

This mid-January morning in 1995 in Laurel, Motley was representing Burl Butler's family in the secondhand smoke case. In the last weeks of his life, Butler lived in an oxygen mask, barely able to rise from his bed. About a week before he died in the spring of 1994, a helicopter appeared over his clapboard house on Decatur Street, circling at low altitude. Butler's grandchildren were playing on a rope swing in the big oak in the backyard and scampered toward the house in fright. Ava, Butler's wife, ran outside. The chopper was so low, she could see the men inside through its open door. And she saw what looked like a videocamera.

On Wednesday, May 6, the helicopter returned. The sound of its beating rotors reverberated in the dying man's room on and off that afternoon. This time, Ava was too busy tending Burl to go outside. The tobacco lawyers were apparently waiting for Butler to die so they could immediately make a motion to attend the autopsy. Challenging the idea that a plaintiff's death was due to lung cancer—or that the cancer was caused by cigarettes—had been a key ingredient in the successful defense of numerous cigarette liability cases, including *Cipollone*. But whether they would ever have gotten their order will never be known. The helicopter did not return Thursday. After a series of violent seizures, Butler died early that morning, Ava at his side.

Ava complained about the helicopter to one of the local lawyers, who called Jodi Flowers at Ness, Motley. Flowers tried to chase down its tail numbers, but the craft was never located.

A few months prior to the helicopter incident, a white van began showing up in front of Butler's barbershop, which was in a small shopping center about a mile and a half from his home. The men inside the van videotaped everyone who went in or came out of the barbershop for several days. Occasionally, they videotaped right through the window of the shop.

The barbershop was the kind of place in which politicians love to be photographed kibitzing with the common people, a men's club where discussions of politics or fishing rambled through hot summer afternoons. As many folks came in for the conversation and air conditioning as for the seven dollar haircuts.

There were four barber's chairs and three surviving barbers. On the wall were moose antlers, pictures of men standing with deer carcasses, a photo of John Wayne. After Butler got sick, the shop went no-smoking. Before that it had been so smoky, the ceiling turned yellow and sticky. It was still discolored where a coat of white paint had missed the edges.

"That stuff dripped off the ceiling," said one customer. "Dripped on my head."

"That's how he lost all that hair on the side," said Jimmy Sherriel Clark, now the head barber, shaving white hairs off the back of the man's neck.

"It won't only kill you, it'll make your hair fall out," said another barber from the next chair.

"Maybe that's why business been so poor," said Clark. They laughed.

As a result of the helicopter incidents, the barbershop surveillance, and some other less than tactful behavior by tobacco company law firms and their creatures, Ava Butler was an angry, resolute woman, determined to fight her husband's lawsuit to the bitter end. And Ava was quite spry, a good bet to see the case all the way through.

On the day of the hearing, she came into court with a daughter and sat in the second row of the mostly empty courtroom. Motley arrived and ducked into a room down the hall to prepare.

Circuit Court Judge Billy Joe Landrum, a thick, balding man in his sixties, strode in at ten after ten and told everyone he wanted to get the show on the road.

This hearing was to determine if the judge would compel Brown & Williamson to turn over the Merrell Williams documents as evidence, including the "subject coding index" Motley had gotten so excited about on the flight to Houston.

Judge Landrum waved his hand as though he didn't understand what all the fuss was about.

"Well, why should we sit around here arguing about it?" he said. "You guys get together on the procedures and I'll review 'em in camera."

"Okay," said Motley, a little startled. Having the judge read the collection and decide what could be introduced had been his fall-back position all along.

"Uh, we don't have them here," said Gordon Smith of King & Spaulding, representing Brown & Williamson. The judge beckoned them both into his chambers. When Motley came out he looked content.

He walked over to Ava Butler and patted her. "You've got a man up there in heaven smiling down at you right now," he said.

"JUDGE, MY NAME IS MIKE MOORE, AND I'M THE ATTORNEY general of Mississippi," said a short, bullet-headed man standing at the podium wearing a wide tie covered in black, yellow, and blue splotches.

Shortly before the Butler hearing, Moore was in his hometown of Pascagoula to block an attempt by an imposing array of blue and gray suits to kill his tobacco lawsuit at the pre-trial stage.

Moore sought to inspire Judge William Myers not to be cowed, as had many local judges, by such a display of force. So you began with the fact that Mike Moore was not just some lawyer, but the top law enforcer in the state.

"This case reminds me of cases I used to try here against co-caine dealers," said Moore.

As traffickers in addiction and disease, tobacco *ought* to be compared to the Cali cartel, scag dealers, illegitimate businessmen, he said passionately.

Moore called his novel Medicaid lawsuit "the most important public health case ever brought in America." Two states, West Virginia and Minnesota, had already filed similar suits and eight others were considering doing so, a fission reaction that could change how the industry operated.

But Moore really started preaching the sermon when he spoke of all the children in Mississippi whom the industry must woo as "replacement smokers" for the one million a year who quit or succumb.

The symbol of this infamy was the cartoon figure Joe Camel, which had been spectacularly successful in penetrating the illicit children's market. One study found that Joe was recognized by thirty percent of three-year-old kids and ninety-one percent of six-year-olds.

"About the same percentage as recognize Mickey Mouse," said Moore.

About the same as Mickey Mouse! Those words conveyed the radiant heat of the youth issue. The implication that tobacco was preparing three-year-olds for lives of slavery was the backstage pass that was already putting this obscure southern attorney general on the national stage. The study that empowered Moore with those electrifying statistics was a unique piece of work by Dr. Paul Fischer, formerly a professor of pediatrics at the Medical College of Georgia in Augusta, where Fischer and other doctors spearheaded research into cigarette marketing and children. By the late eighties, Fischer's group was heading away from the cigarette companies' position that children experiment with cigarettes mostly because of peer pressure, followed by family influences. It turned out that the more familiar the teen was with cigarette advertising, the more he smoked.

Then one day, after his two-and-a-half-year-old son picked up a straw and pretended it was a cigarette, it dawned on Fischer that smoking might take root in early childhood, long before teenagers fool around with cigarettes.

But no one had ever examined very young children on the subject of cigarette ads. And Fischer could find only one marketing study on essentially preverbal children, which used a game. So Fischer and his colleagues invented a board game in which the children were given cards with logos for different products—Joe Camel, the Marlboro Man, the Disney Channel symbol, the golden arches of McDonald's, the Nike swoosh—and told to match the cards with colorful pictures of twelve products on the game board. On the board were Mickey Mouse, sneakers, a telephone, a TV, a cigarette, a hamburger, a pizza, a glass of cola, a car, and others.

Two hundred and twenty-nine boys and girls aged three to six played the board game at ten preschools in Atlanta and Augusta. The results were published in the *Journal of the American Medical Association* in December 1991 and amazed even ardent anti-tobacco-ites. Not many children knew the Marlboro Man, but by age three, almost a third had no trouble matching Joe to the cigarette, and by age six, practically all could, an almost identical success rate for matching the Disney Channel's Mickey Mouse silhouette logo with Mickey himself.

Since young children don't read magazines and there are no cigarette ads on TV, Fischer concluded that kids became familiar with Joe Camel via "environmental" sources, such as billboards, T-shirts, movies, and placards in stores.

The companies' intent was irrelevant, Fischer believed. Merely making children that young aware of cigarette brands was pernicious.

But the implication of Fischer's study grew more ominous in light of two other facts. Though the industry contends it spends $5 billion on marketing each year solely to get adults to switch brands, only ten percent do so annually. Secondly, and even more important, the first cigarette a child smokes regularly usually becomes his brand of choice *for the rest of his life*.

The conclusion—that the companies weren't recklessly throwing away billions on the few adults who might switch, but carefully investing in what they themselves called the smoker's lifelong "brand franchise"—was inescapable.

Motley had seized on Fischer's study and would soon adopt him as a witness. During 1995, Motley and Jodi Flowers, who was put in charge of the "youth project" at Ness, Motley, found that R. J. Reynolds, makers of Camels, had collected information on the smoking habits of fourteen-year-olds. Meanwhile, Gary Light and Tom Doyle at the FDA were learning about an RJR unit called Strategic Research, whose brightest light was a marketing genius named Richard Nordine.

Reynolds had known since the early seventies that Marlboro was edging out its brands by capturing a disproportionate share of child smokers, to whom cigarette companies were not allowed to advertise—"I believe unfairly," complained one executive, who wrote in 1973: "Realistically, if our company is to survive and prosper, we must get our share of the youth market."

At Strategic Research, Dick Nordine came up with two concepts that guided Reynolds during the eighties. One was the "young adult smoker," who was identified as being over eighteen in company reports. But in fact, Nordine was attacking a Marlboro strategy he almost certainly knew applied to youngsters twelve years old and probably younger. The other concept was "First Usual Brand Young Adult Smokers," or FUBYAS, which was the key group to capture—young people who were about to seize on a "first usual brand," which they would likely smoke till the end of their lives.

It became RJR's mission to make sure that more FUBYAS chose Camel, a declining brand smoked largely by old men who were, for obvious reasons, dying off. A cartoon Camel registered strongly with focus groups of "young adult smokers," and thus the Joe Camel ad campaign was launched in 1988, though one focus group warned that Joe "may be appealing to an even younger age group." The results were spectacular. The brand took off.

When Paul Fischer's study appeared, it created quite a stir, and focused a great deal of unwanted attention on Reynolds's marketing practices. But it was Fischer's usefulness to lawyers like Motley that got him into trouble, as Reynolds sued to get his notes and backup materials, allegedly to check for fraud or bias. They also went after the names of the children, who had been guaranteed confidentiality.

After two years, Reynolds won the legal struggle, but the victory was hollow. Paul Fischer had already become the Deep Cough of the youth issue, and his study radically altered the terms of the debate.

Others took his work even farther. It seemed that for very small children, it wasn't so much a matter of pushing a particular brand, as getting them used to the idea of smoking. Then, as they became a little older, they might be more disposed to handle cigarettes, and so enter a relationship of "friendly familiarity" with the product.

By the time Mike Moore spoke at the hearing in Pascagoula, Fischer's Joe Camel study had been cited hundreds of times in the media and legal briefs, and had significantly lowered America's tolerance for tobacco companies.

Three-year-olds know about Joe Camel—*the same as for Mickey Mouse!*

Four lawyers stood up for the tobacco companies and argued to Judge Myers that the Mississippi case belonged in circuit court, not chancery court. This was an end-run around product-liability law, one said, hitting the table with his fist. But none had any rejoinder to Moore's Joe Camel salvo.

The final speaker was Jim Upshaw, local counsel for the American Tobacco Company since the days of the *Horton* trial. Upshaw didn't care at all for Moore comparing his client to a dope baron.

"We are a legal product," said Upshaw. "We are not marijuana. We are not cocaine. We are not heroin. We do not sell our product in back alleys. We do not sell our product under bridges. We pay excise taxes."

Upshaw was a broad, bearded man with gray and white hair. He wore a black suit with wide lapels and white pinstripes.

They want to strip us of our legitimate defenses, he boomed, and for you to *assume* we're liable for Medicaid costs for all these people without proving it in individual cases. Outrageous, Upshaw snorted.

Between Upshaw's bellowing, trains passing a few hundred yards away, and intermittent drilling from the floor above, it was getting a bit noisy in Myers's courtroom. The racket seemed only to catalyze Upshaw's indignation.

"They're not asking for a new remedy, they're asking for a new *right*," Upshaw fairly shouted.

"It's not the job of this court to solve all the ills of society," hollered Upshaw amid the clatter, train horns, and drilling.

Afterward, as the attorneys filed out, Don Barrett, also a member of Moore's legal team, wished Dickie Scruggs a merry Christmas.

"Upshaw looked like Johnny Rocco today," said Barrett. "In fact he sounded like Johnny Rocco. That was his whole argument. 'Things are going to be my way, see? See? See? See?'"

Barrett stuck out his chest and made a tough Edward G. Robinson face, thumbs hooked in his lapels. Scruggs and others gathered around chortling, because Upshaw, in his black pinstriped suit, did look a little like a twenties gangster.

"Rocco don't like that, see? And what Rocco wants, Rocco gets!" said Barrett, strutting about.

But Rocco didn't. A month later, the judge in the *Butler* case de-privileged the Merrell Williams documents. A month after that, on February 21, 1995, Chancellor William Myers ruled against the tobacco companies' pretrial motions, setting the Mississippi AG's case on the road to trial. Motley, Scruggs, and Moore were over the first hurdle.

A TROPICAL SHITSTORM

CLIFF CALLED THEM "PANEL DISCUSSIONS." EITHER HE or Martha would bring up some burning topic and toss it back and forth while they lay together in bed, just before turning in.

"Panel discussion. Okay?" said Cliff as Christmas 1994 approached, and with it, his deposition in the ABC libel case.

"Okay," said Martha.

She called it "the wide-eyed Cliff look." His hazel-green eyes actually dilated when he was excited about something. That was what was looking at her right now.

Douglas explained that he knew Philip Morris would try to get him to tell who Deep Cough was.

"If the court rules I have to reveal her identity, then I either tell them or I go to jail," he said.

"You're going to tell me you'd go to jail," Martha guessed.

"Right," said Cliff.

She sighed, put her head back on the pillow.

"Yes," she said. "I can see that you would."

Cliff turned out the light.

"I'll come visit you," she said.

"Very funny," said Cliff.

The deposition took place at a Marriott in Bethesda, Maryland. Douglas, who couldn't afford a lawyer, was defended by two provided free of charge by Ralph Nader's Public Citizen Litigation Group.

Philip Morris's Herbert Wachtell seemed to lose no opportunity to demean Douglas. He ridiculed Douglas's claim that what he could reveal about Deep Cough was limited by his lawyer-client and journalist-source relationships with her, the latter a result of his role as facilitator of the *Day One* broadcast.

Wachtell bullied Douglas for giving what he considered disingenuous answers and got into long arguments with Allison Zieve, one of Douglas's counsels, whom he accused of signaling Douglas not to answer certain questions.

"Look, I know that ABC made false statements here, participated in by your client, and did so with malice!" Wachtell shouted. "I know all of that, but I'm going to prove it, including proving it by this deposition."

"I'm going off the record," declared Zieve. Over Wachtell's protests, Zieve immediately declared a lunch break.

She had to give Douglas a respite from the ordeal, which was exacerbating his Tourette's. His eyes were blinking and there was even a hint of twitching, not particularly noticeable to a casual observer, but troubling to Douglas, since he feared it made him look nervous.

The heart of Philip Morris's libel claim was that "adding back" nicotine-rich tobacco extract to the reconstituted tobacco sheet was not "spiking" or manipulation. According to Philip Morris, the latter would be true if "extraneous nicotine" were added, but this nicotine wasn't extraneous to the tobacco since it was merely "solubles" separated out during the recon process that were now being reunited with the dry tobacco sheet.

Wachtell tried to get Douglas to admit he had no expertise in cigarette manufacturing and that neither he nor ABC ever had information proving Philip Morris lathered nicotine from an "outside source" onto reconstituted tobacco. But perhaps most important, Wachtell tried to show that Douglas hated the industry so fanatically that he recklessly fed ABC misinformation that made a quotidian manufacturing process seem sinister.

Douglas realized later he should have just conceded his dislike of the industry. What could be more obvious? But Wachtell's attempts to humiliate him got his blood up, so he fought tooth and nail about everything.

Lunch did not improve the atmosphere. When the lawyers reassembled, Wachtell questioned Douglas about a report he had written for the American Council on Science and Health in which he referred to Deep Cough as a "he." Did that mean Deep Cough was a man?

No, said Douglas, he used the pronoun *he* colloquially, as a convenience. He flatly refused to answer further.

"So you are declining to tell us whether that is a true or a false statement, is that correct?" asked Wachtell.

It wasn't a matter of true or false, Zieve objected. This was a detail that could help identify this person.

This went on, in fact had already gone on, for hours, as Wachtell went sentence by sentence through the American Council on Science and Health report and other writings and statements Douglas had made about Cough and *Day One*.

"I'm sorry, sir, but I can't breach my attorney-client responsibility," said Douglas.

"Spare me the platitudes," said Wachtell.

"Let's bear with the insults," said Zieve indignantly.

"This is not an insult," Wachtell shot back.

Wachtell's frustration seemed to grow. He asked the same questions over and over, sometimes four or five times in a row, learning nothing as Douglas parried every thrust.

In fact, despite the video camera staring him in the face, Douglas actually felt himself relaxing.

Wachtell, who sat out of the camera's view, turned away to refer to his notes for a moment.

Suddenly, he whirled, thundering into Douglas's ear, "Who is the former RJR manager, Mr. Douglas?"

Startled, Douglas thought perhaps Wachtell had lost his mind. Did he really think screaming at him like an interrogator in a banana republic jail would spook him into giving up Deep Cough?

Douglas said nothing. He looked straight ahead.

The deposition descended further into bedlam that afternoon, but Douglas felt strangely immune, as though watching from a distance. Wachtell began shouting at Roger Witten, one of ABC's attorneys.

"Herb, don't shout at me," said Witten. "Don't shout at me now, don't shout at me tomorrow, and don't shout at me ever."

Zieve asked Douglas if he needed a break.

"No," said Douglas, a half smile on his face. "This is great."

And he meant it, too. Douglas realized Wachtell hadn't gotten shit from him all day.

"Why were you doing all this?" Wachtell finally asked at about half past six at night.

"I thought this was an important issue, sir," said Douglas.

"Did you think you would be happy with the program that would ultimately be shown?"

"That would be speculation, of course," said Douglas. "Walt Bogdanich is a brilliant journalist, as I came to learn. I had great faith in his ability and in that of his staff. And with my participation—"

"To steer them the right way?" Wachtell interjected.

"That they would do a good job of doing the investigation, yes sir," said Douglas.

"You were confident that if you were participating and collaborating, you would not be unhappy with the result, is that correct?"

"There was no way of knowing that, sir," Douglas said evenly.

"You didn't have any doubt about it, did you?" Wachtell said.

"I did not know, sir."

"You didn't have any doubt about it, did you?" Wachtell repeated.

"About what?"

"Whether you would be happy with the final product."

"There was no way of my knowing," said Douglas. "I was very hopeful that this would be a good piece of investigative journalism."

"Did anything happen in connection with the preparation of the final product which caused you to lose hope?" Wachtell asked.

"There was a time when I wasn't sure it would air, yes sir," said Douglas.

"Did you ever lose hope that if it aired, you would be happy with it?" asked Wachtell.

"Sir, I never lose hope," Douglas replied.
"No further questions for today," said Wachtell.

DISCO LIGHTS SWIRLED AND A ROCK BAND BLASTED THE
walls of a network soundstage on the western edge of Manhattan as
two men pushed their way through the crowd at the annual ABC
Christmas party. Keith Summa and Walt Bogdanich did not look
jolly. They had just seen a public statement ABC was considering is-
suing to settle the lawsuit with Philip Morris, the latest in a series
of drafts ABC's law department had floated over several months.
But this one had the word *apology* in it, and Bogdanich and Summa
were dumbstruck.

They had come to meet Paul Friedman, the network's vice president for news. They located him near the bandstand, where they
shouted into each other's ears.

"We're talking about *apologizing?* What the hell are we apologizing *for?*" hollered Bogdanich.

"It's just the lawyers," Friedman hollered back. "I'm going to see
what I can do about it. Please don't worry. I'm sure it won't be
issued."

Neither Summa nor Bogdanich had much taste for the festivi-
ties. Summa went to a bar and had numerous bourbons. Bogdanich
waited at Pennsylvania Station for the train to his home on Long Island. Standing in the station's seedy waiting area, among half-
drunken teenagers returning from a rock concert, Bogdanich felt
utterly dejected.

It wasn't just this eagerness to settle, even before ABC had done
any significant discovery. Everything about the case had felt wrong
from the beginning, starting with the choice of the Washington-
based Wilmer, Cutler & Pickering as ABC's lead counsel. Though a
Beltway powerhouse, Wilmer, Cutler had no profile in First Amendment law. They did happen to be the law firm of Alan Braverman,
ABC's counsel, who Bogdanich suspected had killed his story on
the Brown & Williamson documents.

However, Friedman begged Bogdanich not to get his own
lawyer.

"We hang together or we hang separately," Friedman would tell him. "If you go out on your own, it'll be taken as a sign of weakness and they'll exploit that."

That made a certain amount of sense. Because ABC's legal case still seemed strong, especially given a surprising opinion by Circuit Court Judge Theodore J. Markow in Richmond, Philip Morris's home turf.

"Philip Morris's description of reconstituting tobacco undercuts its argument that 'we simply don't add nicotine.' It does add nicotine that could be left out," Markow ruled on December 30.

"Why? If the purpose is benign, Philip Morris wins. If to addict, it loses," Markow wrote.

ABC was pushing hard to get Philip Morris to turn over highly sensitive "motive/addiction" documents that could prove the company's purpose was not "benign." If it could show *Day One* was factually accurate, the network could avoid revealing Deep Cough's identity, which Bogdanich was just as determined as Douglas not to divulge.

"All they can do is put me in jail," said Bogdanich. "It would be different, you know, if there were a firing squad involved."

On March 8, 1995, Bogdanich endured the first of an eventual ten days of depositions, over fifty hours of questioning that finally limped to a halt on May 25. Even Philip Morris's Steve Parrish, who received intermittent progress reports, was surprised at how acrimonious the lawsuit was becoming. Wachtell mocked and taunted Bogdanich, but this time he was up against Steven Sachs of Wilmer, Cutler & Pickering, a seasoned trial attorney who simply would not put up with him.

"You really need some kind of help, Herb," Sachs said after a Wachtell tirade accusing him of improper interruptions.

Wachtell never shook Bogdanich as he interrogated him on every step of the reporting on *Day One*. However, there were other ordeals during the spring of 1995. Bogdanich's American Express records were subpoenaed in an attempt to locate Deep Cough, an unprecedented intrusion into a reporter's news-gathering methods. But instead of one month's bills, seven years' worth were accidentally turned over.

The journalism community evidently stood with Bogdanich, because just before he was deposed, "Smokescreen" won the George Polk Award, one of the most prestigious honors for an investigative

report, and helped ABC win the Du Pont Columbia Gold Baton, a
high honor for television journalism.

Also, two focus groups in Raleigh, North Carolina, the heart of
tobacco country, each voted eleven to three for ABC, a positive result largely confirmed by a telephone poll conducted in Richmond,
where the trial would take place.

Other aspects of the case were not going so well. Philip Morris
stonewalled on producing documents. Others were sent on a dark,
oily, smelly paper that made them unusable. And there were persistent rumors that ABC was trying to settle the lawsuit. ABC brass
told reporters who asked about it, off the record, that there were
certain "problems" with the *Day One* show.

Bogdanich heard this through the grapevine. It wasn't Philip
Morris that put the knot in Bogdanich's stomach. No one at the
network seemed to be defending the show.

Then one day Bogdanich picked up the phone, and without so
much as a hello, a voice on the other end said, "You're a fucking asshole if you don't hire your own lawyer."

It was Seymour Hersh, the renowned investigative journalist
who uncovered the My Lai massacre during the Vietnam war.
Hersh, who was one of Bogdanich's heroes, had been in a similar
situation once.

"When the stakes are high, their interests ain't your interests,"
he said.

Bogdanich got a lawyer. He had the undeniable feeling he was
being set up.

ALL THE TO-DO ABOUT UNCOVERING DEEP COUGH'S IDEN-
tity would be nullified, of course, if Cough could be convinced to
appear voluntarily in the lawsuit to tell what she knew. After un-
successful attempts to telephone her, it was decided Keith Summa
would try for a face-to-face contact. But it had to be done in a way
that wouldn't lead Philip Morris to her doorstep. That was where
the Fairfax Group came in.

When the libel suit began, Wilmer, Cutler retained the Fairfax
Group, a well-respected investigative agency that was experienced
in high-profile corporate battles, to handle detective chores.
Summa and Bogdanich were already careful on the telephone and,

when they tried to reach Deep Cough, used phones in offices other than their own. Fairfax's operatives, who had checked the backgrounds of Democratic vice-presidential hopefuls in 1988 and 1992, told Summa that Philip Morris probably already had his personal phone and credit card records, had gone through his trash, and were following him.

"It's a high stakes situation and they do surveillance in high stakes situations," a Fairfax agent told Summa.

So Fairfax took charge of getting Summa to Deep Cough in a secure manner.

Nothing was left to chance. Summa was picked up late one afternoon at his Manhattan apartment by a youngish man in a sports car, behind which was a tail car to ward off pursuit. From LaGuardia Airport, Summa flew under an assumed name to a southern city, where, as promised, an older man in a brown trench coat and hat was waiting at the bottom of an escalator.

"You Mister Summa?" he asked gruffly. "Follow me."

Summa thought the trench coat part was a bit over-the-top, but did as instructed. Another tail car followed into early evening traffic. Summa's driver executed a series of high-speed U-turns across six lanes of traffic, abrupt lane changes and other frightening maneuvers.

Meanwhile he gave Summa surveillance pointers, like always face away from a pay phone while talking so you can see who's following you.

"Right now I'm trying to lose the tail because the one way to know you're not being followed is when you lose the car trying to follow you. If you lose them, you lose the guy who's really trying to follow you."

His eyes kept flicking up to the mirror.

"Look!" He jerked his thumb. "We shook those dumb bastards!"

Summa was driven an hour southwest to another city, where he rented a car under a second phony name and rode several more hours to a dumpy motel where a reservation had been made for him under yet a third alias. He paid cash for everything.

The motel was on the outskirts of the town where Cough lived, and the next morning he drove to see her. After waiting in the car to make sure he hadn't been followed, he walked across the street and nervously rang the bell. Cough's mother answered.

"I saw your car across the street. I assumed you were from Philip Morris," she said.

Summa was a little shocked that Cough and her mother were so paranoid until he remembered that *they* really *were* being hunted.

Cough wasn't home, the mother said, but she would try to reach her and find out if she would talk with Summa.

Summa went back to the fleabag motel and waited. All day, the mother kept saying her daughter hadn't made up her mind. Summa stayed another night, and the next morning checked with the mother from a pay phone at a Dunkin' Donuts. Summa could hear what sounded like sobbing in the background.

"She won't talk to you," the mother said.

Given the history of their dealings with this informant, Summa wasn't exactly surprised. He called Bogdanich and the lawyers and told them they would get no further help from Deep Cough.

BY THE SPRING OF 1995, IT APPEARED ABC WOULDN'T need her. Philip Morris finally began to provide information on the cigarette-making process, which was furnished under a confidentiality order that expressly excluded Walt Bogdanich, even though as a named defendant he had a right to see anything in the case.

To help review documents, Wilmer, Cutler hired a former vice-president for research and development at Brown & Williamson who had left the company under less-than-friendly terms. His name was Jeffrey Wigand, and Wigand traveled frequently in the spring and summer of 1995 from his home in Louisville to Wilmer, Cutler's offices on M Street in Washington, where he sat in the wood-paneled Sequoia Room going through boxes of paper. Wigand also put ABC's lawyers through short courses in cigarette manufacture, lecturing as many as seventy attorneys at a time.

Wigand was no stranger to teaching lawyers, or journalists for that matter, about tobacco. In late 1993, he reviewed Philip Morris documents for a *60 Minutes* program. In May 1994, he was smuggled after hours into a back entrance at the FDA building in Rockville, Maryland, and conducted to the top floor office of Commissioner David Kessler to educate Kessler and his staff on cigarette design.

Wigand liked to say he had "the keys to the kingdom," and
Kessler badly wanted in. Wigand, an extraordinarily bright man
with a doctorate in endocrinology and biochemistry, found the commissioner an apt pupil.

"I could sit there, and as fast as I wanted to move, he could ab-
sorb it," Wigand remembered. "His eyes opened up like saucers
when I talked to him."

Unlike other FDA sources, Wigand insisted Kessler himself be
present when he was interviewed, not just Kessler's subordinates.
Wigand became the FDA's navigator, helping interpret reams of
technical information. Code-named "Research," he spent five
days in May and June 1994, more than seventeen hours of discussions that took eight hundred pages to transcribe, explaining
how tobacco plants were bred for nicotine content, the uses of additives, and, most important, how to heighten the "impact" of
nicotine with ammonia compounds, the state of the art in tweak-
ing nicotine.

The beauty of ammonia was it didn't increase the amount of
nicotine in the tobacco. Adding ammonia compounds changed the
nicotine from a "bound" to a "free" state, making the drug more
readily available to the brain. The increased potency of the cigarette would be felt by the smoker, but wouldn't register on the machines that measured tar and nicotine levels. It was exactly like the
difference between powdered cocaine and crack, a way to get a
stronger high from a smaller amount of dope. One very important
ammonia compound, Wigand said, was diammonium phosphate,
or "DAP."

As soon as Wigand mentioned DAP, Mitch Zeller, the FDA's
chief of policy, had a flashback. Right after *Day One*, Zeller and
other FDA staff had toured Park 500, a Philip Morris reconstituted
tobacco factory south of Richmond that was the biggest manufacturing facility Zeller had ever seen in his life, with hundreds of
pipes running into enormous tanks and presses. Philip Morris
wanted to show the FDA it wasn't spiking cigarettes, although
Zeller and his colleagues were such novices that nicotine could
have been slurping through those pipes and they would never have
known.

Out on the factory floor was one old banged-up-looking pipe.
Zeller said to himself that if they were adding nicotine, it wasn't

through that one because it was wrapped in bright yellow tape and stuck out like a sore thumb. On the tape was printed DAP.

Zeller asked what "DAP" was.

"Just one of the flavors we add," said the Philip Morris tour guide.

Actually, Wigand told Zeller and Kessler, DAP was one of the secrets of Philip Morris's success. He walked Kessler through a Brown & Williamson manual he had put together, a kind of nicotine cookbook that explained the chemistry of using ammonia in cigarettes, and another document that said ammonia was probably the major reason Marlboro was such a dominant product. Simply put, you just got a better hit from a Marlboro.

ABC's lawyers also grasped the importance of Park 500, and were interested in anyone who could tell them more about it. One source called in late March 1995 and two lawyers met with this informant, code-named W.

W had maintained testing and measurement equipment at Philip Morris during the late eighties. W told the lawyers he was surprised *Day One* hadn't mentioned Park 500, since he "knew that Philip Morris created the facility to assure that its cigarettes would provide smokers a consistent high." W himself wasn't particularly thrilled about being around nicotine. After a few hours of breathing fumes from nicotine-rich vats at one company lab, "he sometimes would have to find a bathroom and throw up."

"The employees are highly segregated, with few employees knowing more than just their immediate area of concern," W said. Most significantly, W reported that Philip Morris used a Hewlett-Packard machine he called a "5880" to test tobacco extract at fifteen-minute intervals for nicotine and other substances, which implied that nicotine levels were, in fact, carefully set.

"W told us that he thought the Philip Morris employees were 'good churchgoing people,' but that the company was responsible for killing people," the lawyers reported.

BY LATE JUNE 1995, HERB WACHTELL AND HIS COL-leagues had guessed, by counting the blank spaces in ABC documents where pronouns had been blanked out, that Cough was a woman, but apparently still didn't know who she was. Just then,

with an October trial date looming, the political climate deterio-
rated significantly for Philip Morris. And Wachtell's old friend Cliff
Douglas was part of the reason.

Douglas had gotten a call from Gary Light at the FDA saying
that an anti-smoking group in Houston had a cache of very powerful Philip Morris documents.

"We have copies," said Light, "but we can't use them because
they're under seal. So I thought maybe you could be helpful on this."

Douglas went to Houston and got the material, which came
from eighties-era smoking and health suits, and two days later
launched one of his patented synergistic juggernauts. He leaked the
papers to Philip Hilts at *The New York Times,* who had broken the
story on the Merrell Williams collection, and Hilts wrote a strong
front-page article that appeared June 8.

What Hilts got was two thousand pages of material, thirteen
years of reports from William Dunn's behavioral research laboratory
on how the company studied the drug effects of nicotine on people,
not just rats. There were experiments in a metallic silver chamber
measuring nicotine-related brain-wave activity. Blood sampling
work was done on smokers, as well as saliva testing, for which nicotine levels were checked before, during, and after smoking.

"They concluded," Hilts wrote, "that for most smokers, a low
level of nicotine in the blood 'triggers the smoking response,' that
is, a desire to light up."

Bill Dunn thought hyperactive children might be predisposed to
seek nicotine in their teen years, and reported that his unit had "already collaborated with a local school system in identifying some
such children in the third grade."

All in all, it was a devastating story for Philip Morris, whose
stock dropped again. The documents could obviously be a critical
support for ABC's defense.

That was fine, but despite the *Times* article, the leaked documents were still under seal and, as Douglas liked to say, needed to
be laundered before the FDA could use them. So Douglas delivered
a set to Congressman Henry Waxman, who stood on the floor of the
House of Representatives and read hundreds of pages of highly
technical material into the *Congressional Record,* making them
public information.

The Philip Morris collection debuted at a perilous moment.

That summer, President Clinton was poised to make a major policy decision on tobacco: Would he authorize an FDA rule regulating cigarettes as nicotine-delivery devices, or heed the advice of "moderates" who wanted him to let the industry regulate itself under mutually agreed upon but toothless guidelines? Clinton was thought to be leaning toward the latter.

As Clinton teetered, he got two strong shoves toward regulation. One was Douglas's splashy release of the Philip Morris collection. The second came from Ron Motley and Dickie Scruggs, and theirs was almost certainly the decisive shove. In April, Scruggs got a call from Dick Morris, who had surveyed attitudes toward the Mississippi AG's case and was now Clinton's pollster.

"How's your case?" asked Morris.

"We're out here by ourselves on this thing," Scruggs told him. While Motley was enthusiastic, Scruggs thought the Mississippi suit was stalled. He had hoped the Justice Department might make a move, but they hadn't. A way had to be found to keep the pressure on at the national level.

Scruggs considered Morris a genius, someone who could "always tell you where political north is." Morris thought attacking the big, bad tobacco companies on the issue of youth smoking could dispel the notion that Clinton always waffled on tough issues, but Clinton had to be persuaded it wouldn't cost him the South in the '96 elections. Morris needed money for a poll to prove it.

"I think getting the President involved could be our way in," Scruggs said enthusiastically.

With $10,000 from Motley and Scruggs, Morris polled the five largest tobacco-growing states early that summer and learned that as long as the focus was on preventing children from smoking, there was strong support for regulation, even in the heart of tobacco country. If there was a showdown, Clinton could win.

And then, at the end of July, Douglas picked up the newspaper and read that the Justice Department was presenting evidence to grand juries in Washington and New York. His prosecution memo had borne fruit.

He let out a whoop, jumped on top of his desk, and started dancing.

The Washington investigation dealt with potentially false statements by cigarette company officials—including their CEOs—to regulators and Congress, while the New York probe concerned tobacco's failure to disclose its own knowledge about nicotine addiction to stockholders, an investigation sparked by the Philip Morris nicotine documents Hilts had written about. By the end of the year there would be five grand juries investigating the industry.

In early August, Clinton made his decision. He announced the FDA would proceed with a new rule bringing cigarettes under its jurisdiction. On August 11, the FDA published an official notice of its proposed rule in the *Federal Register,* and cited Douglas's Philip Morris collection four dozen times via the *Congressional Record.* Kessler's team footnoted the Merrell Williams documents, now safely in the hands of the University of California at San Francisco's medical library, even more heavily, as well as the Joe Camel study. There was no turning back now. The feds were in the game.

EVEN AS PHILIP MORRIS'S POSITION WEAKENED, ABC was running full tilt away from confrontation. At the end of June, the *Washington Post* reported the network had offered to settle the libel case "with a statement in which the network would apologize" for *Day One*. Bogdanich, who had gotten caught up in the enthusiasm of the Wilmer, Cutler trial lawyers, was plunged into gloom.

As July progressed, the libel case began to move quickly. Wilmer, Cutler now had a substantial body of material on Park 500 and it was damning on the issue of nicotine control. On July 10, ABC moved for summary judgment, asking the judge to throw out the libel suit on the grounds that *Day One* was demonstrably true.

Exactly three weeks later, Thomas Murphy, ABC's president, told a group of financial analysts that a settlement might be near. On the same day, after weeks of speculation, the Walt Disney Company announced it had acquired ABC.

On August 10, ABC general counsel Alan Braverman faxed Michael Nussbaum, Bogdanich's lawyer, a "proposed statement" ABC would read on the air. The target date for the deal was August 18, when ABC's motion for summary judgment would be argued.

"Things could happen very fast now," Braverman told Nussbaum.

Bogdanich read the statement. Though not as abject as earlier versions, it was still an apology and therefore unacceptable, which is what Nussbaum relayed to Braverman.

The next day, Philip Morris asked Judge Markow to close the August 18 hearing to the press and public. That would be grossly unfair, objected Steve Sachs, who had defended Bogdanich at his deposition. Because the network's case was based almost entirely on sealed Philip Morris documents, ABC had been forced to stand silent for eighteen months while Philip Morris publicly smeared Bogdanich's reporting. Markow agreed not to close the hearing.

At ABC, Bogdanich waited anxiously for news. He was poised to take a week's vacation, which he had long put off because of the volatile situation. Around five P.M., Braverman reached Nussbaum and told him the deal was "dead." Nothing would happen right away, and Bogdanich needn't worry. Bogdanich promptly left for Seabrook, South Carolina, with his family.

Bogdanich tried to decompress. He sat in the sun and played with his children. A dedicated runner, he ran daily despite the muggy heat, which by midweek had reached a hundred degrees. He was panting and drenched in sweat when he swung his big frame into a phone booth one afternoon to check his messages. He had one from Nussbaum saying call immediately. The settlement was going down as he spoke.

Game, set, and match, Bogdanich thought as he took off like a rocket for his vacation town house, more than two miles away, cutting through a golf course. *They got me out of the loop, then they brought the hammer down.*

When he arrived, his wife and children were still at the swimming pool. He had to sit down and inhale slowly to calm himself. Then he rang Nussbaum, who said he hadn't seen the latest draft of the agreement, but it was definitely an apology. Bogdanich called Cliff Douglas.

"You better mobilize the people who believe in the truth to get the message out that this is wrong," Bogdanich told him. Douglas immediately began making press calls.

His wife, Stephanie, returned with the children, and they embraced and cried. Bogdanich's options were stark. He could quit, sue ABC for compromising his interests, or stay. He decided to stay, but he and correspondent John Martin refused to sign the apology. Nussbaum had compiled a long list of ways ABC had allegedly sold out Bogdanich's interests, which he now traded for a concession: a public statement that Bogdanich had not signed the apology and had been awarded a new long-term contract as a sign of ABC's continued faith.

Details of the deal began to leak on August 18. Three days later, Diane Sawyer read the rather lengthy apology on *World News Tonight*.

"We now agree that we should not have reported that Philip Morris and Reynolds add significant amounts of nicotine from outside sources," she said. But ABC contended that the central premise of *Day One*—that nicotine is carefully controlled—remained true.

Philip Morris's Steve Parrish and the "Eight-thirty Group" had planned a response to Sawyer's announcement well in advance, including press briefings and weeks of full-page ads in major magazines.

APOLOGY ACCEPTED, they exclaimed in bold letters.

All fall, Bogdanich and stunned journalists all over the world puzzled over why ABC humiliated itself. Was the company simply shedding legal risk in preparation for its takeover by Disney? Was someone pulling strings at some level that even they, who were insiders, were unaware of? As Bogdanich looked into it, there seemed no end to the layers of onion peel surrounding the truth.

BY THE TIME ABC APOLOGIZED, RON MOTLEY'S MARRIAGE was breaking up. In fact, Catherine had walked out in June, after less than six months of married life, an unsurprising outcome considering she barely knew her husband.

Motley was inconsolable. He called a reporter from Mississippi, where he was driving along the Gulf Coast in a van with other lawyers, en route from some hearing.

"She's gone, man," he said. "I don't know why. I found somebody and the next thing I know she's gone."

Instead of a honeymoon, Ron and Catherine had tried an asbestos case together in Houston right after their marriage. They lived at the Kiawah house upon their return to Charleston, but were rarely together there. Catherine almost always seemed to have family members around. She returned frequently to her native Texas. Once she flew home for a doctor's appointment.

When a friend met Motley in Boston, where he was giving a

speech, he was sleeping little and taking numerous prescription medications. After the speech, he made calls from his hotel room, trying to scare up someone he knew to have dinner with. Failing, he strode from the room, dashing into an elevator filled with women in evening clothes.

"Where the hell are we going?" the friend asked.

"Just following those short skirts," he said. Outside, they wandered a few blocks around the Four Seasons hotel.

"You should slow down," the friend suggested. "You're going to wind up like Belushi."

"I'm staying really busy," he said. "I'll be all right."

A psychiatrist suggested Motley go through "experiential therapy" at a retreat called the Pocket Ranch in northern California, and he was hurting so badly, he took off for seventeen days right in the middle of a big asbestos trial. He thought it might get Catherine to come back.

He found himself talking to the group about little Mark, his brother. And so they staged a symbolic reburial. At a small Buddhist shrine in a field, Ron squatted down and talked to Mark about what he had hoped to do with him as they grew up, and how he regretted not demanding to go to the hospital to see him before he died, although he knew it would have been impossible to watch him clawing for breath. And in some strange way, the Pocket Ranch seemed to help for a while, although Catherine never came back.

WORK WAS ALWAYS AN EFFECTIVE BALM FOR MOTLEY'S wounds, and events suddenly began moving quite quickly in the Mississippi attorney general's case.

It started on a Sunday late that summer, when Ann Ritter got a phone call at home from Dickie Scruggs, who was almost hyperventilating with enthusiasm. He had just learned that Jeffrey Wigand, the former Brown & Williamson executive who helped ABC review documents, might agree to be a witness in the Mississippi case. A week or so earlier, Wigand had secretly taped an interview with 60 Minutes. Once it was broadcast, Wigand might testify.

A criminal lawyer representing Wigand had contacted Scruggs and told him generally what Wigand might say. Scruggs thought it was dynamite.

Ritter coordinated document analysis for Ness, Motley and spoke regularly with Scruggs, to whom she funneled any media-worthy material, which Scruggs would then leak to the press.

Scruggs told Ritter that his chief concern was that Wigand was covered by a very stringent confidentiality agreement.

"What do you think, Ann?" he asked her. "Can we pursue this guy?"

Ritter called a legal ethicist who worked frequently with Ness, Motley, then called Scruggs back. Scruggs could proceed, she said. According to Mississippi law, under which the attorney general's suit operated, they were entitled to contact such a witness.

"Ron's going to shit. He is going to be so excited," said Scruggs. But he cautioned Ritter to keep a very low profile on Wigand. Ritter agreed.

The next day, Monday, immediately after the Ness, Motley switchboard opened, the receptionist received a bizarre phone call.

"There are four bombs in the Meeting Street and in the Church Street office," said a mechanical voice that seemed to be speaking underwater.

"Mr. Ron Motley and Ann Ritter, they shouldn't mess with the tobacco industry. These bombs will go off today," the voice said. Then the line went dead.

Three minutes later, Motley's secretary heard the same message when she checked Motley's voice mail.

With both Ritter and Motley out of town that morning, Jack Draper, who handled telephone security for Ness, Motley, took charge of evacuating the firm's 151 Meeting Street headquarters and another office across the street. A swarm of law enforcement officers de-scended on the scene, including the FBI and two Air Force bomb squads.

The calls were quickly traced to a pay phone in front of a Fam-ily Dollar store a few blocks away.

"This is quality stuff," said an FBI agent after listening to the electronically disguised voice on Motley's answering machine. "That's no prankster. That's professional work."

However, sweeps for bombs found nothing either at the firm or at the homes of Ritter and Motley.

When Ritter learned of the bomb scare later that day, it struck her as an extraordinary coincidence that it came within twelve hours of her conversation with Scruggs. Even more worrisome was the possibility that her own telephone was tapped, since she had spoken to Scruggs from home.

She did not feel any better the following day, when investigators told her that with modern high-tech surveillance equipment, her home phone conversations could be monitored from a remote location without any physical sign of bugging on her phone line.

When Motley learned of the bomb threat, he ordered that security be strengthened. "Proximity card" readers that would admit only those who had a special plastic card implanted with a digital chip were installed in Tobacco Team areas. All tobacco-related paper was to be shredded. No exceptions.

Though Motley personally didn't believe the tobacco companies themselves were responsible for the bomb hoax, it made little practical difference.

"Everyone needs to understand that this case is not like anything else we've done," Motley told Ritter. "Whoever did this, doesn't matter who—they're dangerous."

A bomb scare turned out to be the perfect introduction to the Wigand saga, which did nothing but get more peculiar with every passing day, even as it became clear that Wigand was becoming not only the Mississippi state case's star witness but perhaps the corporate world's most famous whistle-blower—albeit a reluctant one.

However, for quite a while it appeared Wigand would never go public at all. For much of the fall, the interview Wigand taped with Mike Wallace of 60 Minutes sat in the can, until CBS executives finally chose to deep-six it, a decision that leaked into the New York Daily News, along with the inflammatory details of the interview itself.

Both Wallace and executive producer Don Hewitt, however reluctantly, publicly supported the interview's suppression. Later, they would decide killing the show was the wrong thing to do. But that was later.

The official reason for this self-censorship was the fear that Brown & Williamson might sue CBS News for encouraging Wigand to break his confidentiality agreement with Brown & Williamson. Yet no suit had been threatened, much less filed, by Brown & Williamson.

But there was another level. Negotiations ongoing at the time the program was killed enabled the Tisch family, which owned both Lorillard Tobacco and CBS, to sell the network to Westinghouse. As with ABC's libel suit, it seemed that legal risk was being shed for the sake of a corporate acquisition.

But what made it all so *devilishly* interesting was that while Lorillard/CBS was dancing with Westinghouse, and Lorillard/CBS was fencing (supposedly) with Brown & Williamson, Lorillard/CBS was also buying six cigarette brands from Brown & Williamson, a deal worth an estimated $100 million. Not even to mention the fact that key executives and corporate lawyers involved in killing the original CBS segment stood to gain handsomely if the Westinghouse deal was consummated.

CBS did air a substitute tobacco segment on November 12, 1995, the date the original was to appear, but minus the lengthy Wigand interview that had been its heart. Wigand's extremely high rank while at Brown & Williamson made the story of the interview's suppression instantly huge. It got huger in January 1996, when the *Wall Street Journal* ran a story by Pulitzer prize–winner Alix Freedman based on a deposition of Wigand taken by Ron Motley elaborating on his allegations.

That story really got the legal department on the eighteenth floor of the Brown & Williamson Tower in Louisville buzzing like wet bees, especially since the deposition had been leaked to the *Journal* despite being under court seal. To add insult to injury, the *Journal* immediately put the depo on the Internet.

Brown & Williamson demonstrated a crude nasty streak in going after Wigand, with little result except to financially and emotionally punish him, which was what the company no doubt intended.

"I won't even call him *Mr.* Wigand. He's just Wigand," said corporate spokesman Joseph Helewicz at the beginning of one interview, as though the depth of his contempt would poison public opinion against him.

Wags at the Food and Drug Administration dubbed B&W *the stupid company* and the Wigand imbroglio showed why. First, they sent attack dog lawyer Gordon Smith to appear opposite Mike Wallace on *60 Minutes,* a severe mismatch if ever there was one. The company had public relations specialist John Scanlon dredge up a dreary parade of largely minor and occasionally imaginary offenses.

Scanlon then gave a five-hundred-page dossier of dirt on Wigand to the *Journal*. But instead of tossing off a negative piece about Wigand, who had been an important source for two *Journal* reporters, the paper incinerated the dossier in a front-page story.

A month later, Scanlon was subpoenaed by a federal grand jury investigating tobacco company intimidation of a government witness, namely Wigand, who by then had given testimony to two federal grand juries and investigators at the Department of Justice's antitrust division. In fact, Justice took Wigand under its wing, sending prosecutors and FBI agents to Louisville, where Wigand would educate them on the cigarette business, as he had done so effectively elsewhere. Then Motley began to dig up a lot of documentary evidence supporting his story. Which was pretty wild.

THE WIGAND DEPOSITION WAS THE FIRST IMPORTANT skirmish of Motley's young career in tobacco litigation and it was a baptism by live fire.

It took place in Pascagoula on November 29, 1995. Dickie Scruggs had met Wigand in New York just as the storm was breaking over the *60 Minutes* program. Scruggs impressed Wigand as someone who could protect him legally, whom he could trust. Wigand impressed Scruggs as a potentially devastating witness.

The Wigand deposition was a big event for Pascagoula, indeed for America, since Wigand had come forward as the tobacco control wave was hitting a crest of public support, and as vice-president for research and development for B&W from 1989 until 1993, a $300,000-a-year position with every imaginable corporate perk, Wigand was in a position to know a lot of secrets.

Given the bomb incident at Ness, Motley and Wigand's notoriety, Scruggs flew him in the night before the deposition and put him up at his home on Beach Avenue, where armed security men conducted sweeps for bugging devices and explosives. The next day, Wigand, Scruggs, and a film crew from *60 Minutes* were out on Scruggs's spacious lawn, where Wigand paced, trying to figure out whether to go through with the deposition.

If the fortified revetment on Beach Avenue wasn't enough to give Wigand pause, there was the fact that as soon as he arrived at the courthouse in Pascagoula, he would be served with a court order from Kentucky forbidding him, as per his confidentiality agreement, from discussing his tenure at Brown & Williamson under penalty of imprisonment. So Wigand could go to jail in Louisville if he testified in Mississippi, or be held in contempt in Mississippi if he didn't give his deposition. Jeff Wigand was scared.

He started out angry. As the company never tired of pointing out, he had an ax to grind, as whistle-blowers always do. In Wigand's case, he had been fired, in March 1993. The company's version was he had been abusive to coworkers. Wigand's was he had pushed B&W president Tommy Sandefur too hard to develop a safer cigarette. The two sides wound up in court, with the result that in order to keep his severance and health benefits, which he desperately needed since he had a young daughter with spina bifida, Wigand had to sign a confidentiality agreement that was draconian even by tobacco industry standards.

Wigand's background was with companies like Merck, Pfizer, and Union Carbide developing and marketing medical devices. He had set up Carbide's medical products marketing operation in Japan, drawing on his fluent Japanese. His command of the language was one of several skills he brought back from his first stint in Japan, during his military service in the sixties. Another was judo, which he studied with Kobayashi, a great master. He competed at the level of a fifth *dan* black belt, at that time quite a distinction for a foreigner, and sparred with the U.S. Olympic Team. He also became proficient in kendo, or sword fighting, and karate. He was one hundred and sixty-four pounds and fast as lightning.

He found martial arts strengthened mind as well as body. (Not that it didn't have practical advantages, like when he put a judo wrist grip on a would-be pickpocket in Atlantic City.) Wigand moved through the American corporate wilderness unafraid. Just as Cliff Douglas was catalyzed by the experience of Asia, Wigand's soul was formed in Japan.

He was different from the rest at B&W. He came with twenty years of experience in health care. He actually worried about health and wouldn't back down. He was not a good fit for the parochial corporate culture of Louisville: a short, defiant Bronx tough guy who carried himself like Jimmy Cagney, spoke three languages, meditated, could kill you with a single blow, and thought what the firm needed was a crash program to make a safer cigarette. Jeff Wigand was just plain wrong for *the stupid company*.

While embittered, Wigand never wanted to be an anti-tobacco hero. He insisted CBS get his permission before broadcasting its interview with him and hadn't given it when his new role was thrust upon him by the revelation in the New York *Daily News* that he was CBS's hitherto anonymous source. Prior to that, Wigand was happily teaching Japanese and chemistry in a public high school in Louisville.

Motley called what happened after Wigand's cover was blown "a tropical shitstorm." He was sued for millions of dollars for fraud, theft, and breach of contract by Brown & Williamson before an openly hostile judge in Louisville. His marriage collapsed, forcing him from a cozy suburban home into a Louisville apartment, which was broken into, as was his car. The Israeli armor-piercing bullet was left in his mailbox. In 1994, a computer-generated voice twice left death threats on his answering machine.

So now Wigand had two guards who protected him around the clock and checked his car for bombs each morning. No matter what the outcome of events, he was certain to be in court for years. There was no evidence that the threats and other acts of terror were Brown & Williamson's doing, but the company was probably happy if people concluded that *whistle-blower* and *martyr* were synonyms.

A lot of that flashed through Wigand's mind as he paced back and forth on Dickie Scruggs's lawn.

"It's up to you, Jeff," Scruggs said. "Nobody's going to blame you if you say no."

Wigand was thinking: *My marriage is ruined, they fired me, I'm being threatened and harassed. Plus they're already after my ass.*

"Ah, fuck it," said Wigand. "Let's do it."

It was an electric moment for Scruggs. He clapped Wigand heartily on the back.

"All right, man. I'll tell Mike," he said, meaning Attorney General Mike Moore.

The national press had turned out in force, and Moore, Wigand, Motley, Scruggs, and the rest of the state's legal team had to run a gauntlet of camera crews to get into a former warehouse on the outskirts of town that served as a temporary courthouse while the regular courthouse accommodated a trial. As Wigand entered the building, a lawyer shoved the Kentucky court order into his hand.

Motley met Wigand that day. The Jeff Wigand he saw was a tired, haunted man, whose personal space would soon shrink to the size of the furniture-less apartment in Louisville in which he began living not long after the deposition, and where he slept on a futon on the floor. He could be, as one reporter termed it, "prickly." He was certainly blunt, a quality often praised but little prized in the corporate world. Ron Motley was also known for speaking his mind. The South Carolinian and the Bronx native began that day what soon became a strong friendship.

Motley was handling the deposition because he was known to be fairly impervious to bullying. The tobacco lawyers he would face were expert at derailing the depositions of hostile witnesses by having one or two of their number repeatedly raise shrill objections while the rest of the wall of flesh loomed in the background. After spending weeks using breaks from his asbestos trial in Houston to master the Brown & Williamson material, Motley, who frequently would take a full day to prepare a critical witness, had only a few minutes with Wigand before the deposition began. He outlined his game plan, which was to build gradually toward the most damaging charges, and then, without warning, dash like bloody hell for the finish line, dropping every bomb in Wigand's considerable arsenal.

"I'm just going to stomp over 'em, and to hell with their objections. 'Course, they just make 'em up anyway," Motley told Wigand.

Besides, Motley knew that under the law, he would probably be right. A deposition was only a fact-finding tool. Its admissibility was not at all automatic. That gave Motley considerable latitude in questioning, and most objections were supposed to be reserved for trial.

"They're going to bleat like sheep, but just ignore it. You focus on me," said Motley.

"Yup," said Wigand, sipping coffee from a foam cup.

Dick Scruggs poked his head in the door.

"Let's go, guys."

There was no way either Motley or Wigand could have been prepared for the spectacle that awaited them. There were twenty lawyers for the other side plus attendant staff, bringing the total size of the tobacco war party that filled the long, narrow main room of the one-story cinder-block building to about fifty. As the attorney general of Mississippi, Mike Moore was not used to playing the underdog in a roomful of lawyers, but that was how he felt as Motley addressed the camera to begin the videotaped deposition.

After the tobacco side took twenty minutes trying keep the deposition from taking place at all, Motley cut them off. "I'm not a very patient man," he said. "My middle name is not Job."

He began by having Wigand explain that B&W is the American subsidiary of the British American Tobacco Company, the second biggest tobacco concern in the world after Philip Morris, and that he had been recruited in 1989 with instructions to give priority to safe cigarette work.

Shortly after he joined B&W, however, Wigand distributed a fifteen-page report on a meeting in Vancouver of chief scientists from BAT subsidiaries around the world. The report so infuriated Kendrick Wells, B&W's assistant general counsel, Thomas Sandefur, the president, and Raymond Pritchard, chairman of the board, that they demanded an immediate meeting with Wigand. There were just too many references to taboo topics.

Motley asked Wigand what was said at the meeting. Thomas Bezanson, who ran the show for the tobacco side that day, popped up.

This would divulge attorney-client matters, he said.

"You may answer, sir," Motley told Wigand.

"Just a moment," said Bezanson. He threatened to have someone call Judge William Myers.

"This record is sealed," said Motley. "That is all the protection you need."

Bezanson said the judge's case management order allowed the judge to be summoned if the deposition strayed into attorney-client matters. He insisted the deposition be suspended. Motley said he would get off the subject of what was said at the meeting.

In fact, Motley had no intention of backing off. The issue of lawyers doctoring science to protect the company in lawsuits was the heart of his case. And no one had ever gotten an insider to explain how the companies did it. They had struggled to get Wigand as a witness, struggled to get him to testify despite court orders and threats and lawsuits. This was the moment of truth, the point when the wave either broke or continued in to shore.

Motley turned once more to Wigand.

"As a result of this meeting that you described—I don't want to know what happened at the meeting—but as a result of the meeting that you described, was there any change made in the minutes of the meeting in British Columbia?"

"Yes," said Wigand.

"What change was that?" Motley asked.

"I object," said Bezanson. "I believe you are continuing on in the course of disclosing attorney-client privileged matters."

"I think you ought to go off the record and talk to the judge. This is going to be problematic," said Joe Colingo, local counsel for R. J. Reynolds.

"The order doesn't say that," piped up Mike Moore, who had virtually memorized the case management order for just such an eventuality.

"Well, the order doesn't not say it either," retorted Colingo. "The rules say you can."

All along, Motley knew his trump card was that this was a plaintiff's deposition. That meant the plaintiff's lawyers, Motley's firm, were paying the court reporter and video crew. And that meant he could call the tune.

"I don't agree with your interpretation," Motley said firmly. "I'm going forward with this deposition. If I'm wrong it will be stricken later."

"That is not what the case management order proposes," said Bezanson, losing the battle to keep his voice low. "Pursuant to Paragraph Nineteen, I instruct the court reporter to suspend operations until we have had an—"

"There's nothing in this order that says the court reporter listens to anything you say," said Motley wearily. He then turned to Wigand, who was sitting on a wooden chair in the witness box, fascinated by the skirmishing.

"Sir, will you please answer my question and tell me whether or not, as a result of that conference, without telling me who said what, was there any change made in the composition of the minutes which you previously described as prepared by Mr. Thornton?"

"I continue to object and instruct not to answer," said Bezanson angrily. "There is a telephone right here. We can call the judge."

"You got thirty lawyers. Go get him on the phone," said Motley. Motley pivoted back to Wigand.

"Answer my question, please, sir," he said.

"Can I ask you to repeat the question?" Wigand said.

Suddenly several people started talking at once. Bezanson shouted, "Under the case management order—"

Motley turned on Bezanson and spoke to him as though to a misbehaving child.

"Sir, if you continue to disrupt this, I'm just going to walk up there close and let him state his answer for the record. And whether you hear it, I care not.

"Will you please tell me so I can hear what your answer is?" Motley said to Wigand.

"Could you please repeat the question?" Wigand said quietly.

"Yes," said Motley, striding right in front of the video camera.

He leaned directly into the witness box.

"Did they *change* the minutes?"

"Yes, they did," said Wigand.

"Did they eliminate twelve pages of the minutes?"

"Roughly twelve pages of the minutes."

"And what did they eliminate, the stuff that said cigarettes were harmful?"

"They eliminated all references to anything that could be discovered during any kind of a liability action in reference to a safer cigarette. Statements were made that anything that alludes to a safer cigarette clearly indicates that other cigarettes are unsafe, and it furthermore would acknowledge that nicotine is addictive," said Wigand.

For the first time in almost half an hour, there was a silence between question and answer. Bezanson still objected more than a hundred times in the remaining 120 minutes of the deposition—but they were standard two-sentence objections. Round one, anyway, was over.

Wigand's statement was a hydrogen bomb. As B&W's chief scientist, he had in-depth knowledge of all research and product areas. That he would have had a great deal of contact with top lawyers like Kendrick Wells and with president Sandefur was a matter of common sense. Here Wigand undermined a key tenet of the industry's defense, which was that incriminating scientific reports reflected the views of underlings, not company policy. Wigand was saying

that Sandefur, the $12-billion-a-year tobacco company's top deci-
sion-maker, had said on several occasions that "we're in the nicotine delivery business," which certainly would be interesting news
to the FDA.

Wigand had tales that would have made Victor DeNoble feel
right at home. Here, too, executives were boarding planes bent on
various obscure missions. In Richmond, tar was apparently being
sent to Germany to be smeared on mice. In Louisville, Wigand
claimed, an executive smuggled seeds for a high-nicotine tobacco
plant into Brazil in a pack of cigarettes that was grown and later
blended into Viceroy cigarettes.

The lawyers at Brown & Williamson seemed omnipotent. Although Wigand ran a research and development department with
243 scientists and workers and a $40-million budget, he was denied
access to files on earlier B&W research. Kendrick Wells screened
all scientific material from BAT's main laboratory in Southampton
before anyone at R and D in Louisville, including Wigand, was allowed to see it. Some of the British reports were shipped in only to
be shipped right back by a nervous Wells.

By the time the questioning turned to additives, Motley had hit
his stride, playing directly to the jury that might one day see the
videotape.

"Sir, at any time did you learn that Brown & Williamson was
using a form of rat poison in pipe tobacco?" Motley asked.

"Object to the form," said Bezanson.

"Yes," said Wigand.

"What form of rat poison was that?" asked Motley.

"Object to the form," said Bezanson.

"It is a compound called coumarin," Wigand replied. "It was
contained in the pipe tobacco—"

"Object on trade secret grounds and instruct not to answer,"
Bezanson interrupted.

"You are objecting that the man is revealing that you used *rat
poison* as a trade secret? You may answer, sir," said Motley.

"Object to the form," said Bezanson.

"Go ahead. If they used rat poison in pipe tobacco that human
beings were taking in their bodies, I want to know about it. Will you
tell me about it, sir?" said Motley.

"Object to the form," said Bezanson.

"I was concerned [about] the continued use of coumarin in pipe tobacco after the coumarin had been removed from cigarettes because of the FDA's not allowing the use of coumarin in foods with additives," said Wigand. "The reason why it stayed in pipe tobacco is the removal would change the taste of the pipe tobacco and, therefore, affect sales."

When it was over, Scruggs and Moore were jubilant. Wigand was exhausted. He shook hands with them and Motley and got out of the building as fast as he could.

NOT LONG AFTER THE DEPOSITION, MOTLEY AND WIGAND tracked each other down. Each was in a hotel room far from home. Things were going a bit better for Wigand. Public relations man John Scanlon had been subpoenaed, which made him feel more adequately protected. He was on his way to winning visitation rights with his two girls.

Motley's personal life, on the other hand, was a train wreck. Catherine and he were about to divorce. He was drinking far too much. His mood was lower than it had been in years.

Months later, as Mississippi's case was upheld by an appeals court and an even stronger effort in Florida began to go forward under the protection of a special law that was sneaked through the legislature, Motley called Wigand again. There's no question we did a historic thing, Motley said. What you said changed the way people think in this country. And things will straighten out for you. Eventually, Motley told Wigand, even tropical shitstorms blow over. Wigand laughed.

Wigand became a regular guest at River House. Motley was interested in picking his brain, but their strong relationship had deeper roots, a tie between two irascible men who, it happened, were both recovering from doomed marriages.

"It's the symphony of the souls," Motley said of his bond with Wigand. Wigand found River House was somewhere he could relax and banter with Motley and play with his tiny white dogs. He was protected. And Motley didn't want anything from him that he wasn't more than willing to provide: help in hitting back at people who had made his life a very unpleasant place to be.

Motley would later call 1995 "the year of momentum." Scruggs saw it, too. They were breaking through—with the President, the FDA, new states like Florida filing suit. They had signed up important witnesses. They were starting to amass the evidence they would need to win at trial, but Motley knew there was more to the story. What he had seen so far was just a small chunk of an iceberg that extended deep into very cold water.

FLYING EMPEROR OF TORTS

CLIFF DOUGLAS COULD FEEL THE STORM SURGE AS 1996 began, too. He had, after all, played a major part in creating it. But he was haunted by some unfinished business from 1995. The ABC apology had left the impression—one the tobacco companies immediately exploited in the press—that the nicotine manipulation charge was a phony, which Douglas was eager to dispel.

Given the rather grim precedent of the libel action, Douglas had no luck in getting the press to dig further into the arcane science of cigarette manufacture—until someone gave reporters a copy of ABC's sealed motion to dismiss Philip Morris's suit, a stunning document that detailed the case ABC would have made had the matter gone to trial. Filled with engineering jargon, it recounted how tobacco extracts with different concentrations of nicotine are manufactured and used in the reconstitution process. A lengthy article about the motion appeared in the trade publication *Legal Times*, and was the subject of a segment on ABC's *World News Tonight*.

Then someone slipped Douglas notes of an interview by ABC's lawyers with the informant "W," who had maintained testing equipment at Philip Morris's huge Park 500 reconstituted tobacco factory, and Douglas leaked them to this reporter for an article in *The Nation* magazine.

The *Legal Times* and W stories aroused fury at ABC, and an internal probe was launched to learn who the leaker was. Interestingly, Philip Morris and ABC agreed to limit the probe to non-lawyers, which automatically made Walt Bogdanich the prime suspect, though he heatedly denied the charge.

But that didn't stop a stream of memos and calls from ABC's legal department demanding Bogdanich tell what he knew about the leaked documents. There was even talk of more depositions.

Bogdanich knew who the culprit was and wanted no part of what he viewed as a witch hunt. So he stalled any attempt at a formal meeting with ABC legal.

After several delays, a meeting was scheduled for April 10 at five P.M. between Bogdanich and his lawyers and ABC general counsel Alan Braverman and Paul Friedman, vice-president for news.

At four-thirty P.M., Roone Arledge, president of the news division, brought Bogdanich and his attorneys into his office to discuss the situation.

Bogdanich knew Braverman and Friedman wanted to interrogate him and he had no stomach for it. He had gone into a deep depression after the apology, and the vindication of his reporting by the recent disclosures was the first ray of hope in quite a while. He believed ABC executives saw him as a troublemaker, and was using the W leak as an excuse to get rid of him. Well, let them, he thought.

"Enough is enough," Bogdanich told Arledge. "Even if I talk to them about this, tomorrow it'll just be something else."

Arledge thought Bogdanich a brilliant reporter. He wanted to keep him at ABC. He tried to mediate.

Perhaps, he acknowledged, the network should have done more to protect him.

"I don't know," Arledge sighed. "Maybe we shouldn't have settled."

He seemed to think that if the meeting with Braverman and Friedman took place, the result would be bad for Bogdanich or bad for *ABC News*, probably both. By then it was after five-thirty P.M. Arledge suggested Bogdanich put it off for another day.

But Bogdanich didn't want to be the one to call Braverman and Friedman, as it would look like another stall tactic. Arledge thought a moment.

"Consider it canceled," said Arledge. "Go on home, Walt."

The meeting was never rescheduled. On April 12, Walt Bogdanich presented *ABC News* with a letter of resignation but stayed on to finish a Peter Jennings documentary about tobacco lobbying before beginning a new job as a producer at *60 Minutes*.

But there was, perhaps, another layer of onion peel wrapped around the *Day One* story.

The actual sale of ABC to the Walt Disney Company wasn't formally completed until after Congress passed its sweeping relaxation of the laws governing electronic media, the Telecommunications Act, which was enacted in February 1996.

Just the prospect that such a bill would pass and wipe away barriers to the ownership by a single company of different telecommunications media helped fuel the merger not only of ABC and Disney but of Westinghouse and CBS. During 1995, while ABC and Philip Morris were alternately negotiating and litigating, the telecommunications bill was the subject of intense lobbying, in which ABC counsel Alan Braverman was intimately involved. A reporter in ABC's Washington bureau was told that the ABC lobbyists had been instructed never to discuss what they were doing with anyone from the news division.

The key man for ABC to lobby, since he controlled the bill's fate, was Thomas Bliley, chairman of the House Commerce Committee. Bliley represented Richmond, Virginia, and he had long borne the nickname, by virtue of his unblemished record of allegiance to his district's most powerful corporation, of "the congressman from Philip Morris."

WHILE WALT BOGDANICH FOUGHT HIS FINAL BATTLE AT ABC, Cliff Douglas was working as a kind of whistle-blower therapist and handler, using the same gentle touch he had developed with Deep Cough. Three Philip Morris employees were considering releasing sworn affidavits on their experiences at the company. The FDA gave them Douglas's name and phone number and two of them called him.

Douglas soon flew to Richmond and met Ian Uydess, a former Philip Morris scientist. He spent time, too, with Jerome Rivers, a one-time factory supervisor. The third prospective whistle-blower was William Farone, but Douglas wasn't involved in bringing him out.

Douglas spent most of his time on Uydess, a forty-nine-year-old biologist who needed careful handling. Uydess was an unlikely giant killer, short, balding, with a reedy tenor voice. He didn't want to hurt anyone, especially close friends from his days at the Philip Morris Research Center, where he worked during two tours between 1977 and 1989.

His best friend there was Frank Gullotta, who did human experiments on the brain effects of nicotine that were in the documents Douglas leaked to *The New York Times*. Unfortunately, all those people Uydess liked so much were the same people about whom he had valuable information, information he was putting in his affidavit. Predictably, once the affidavit became public, Gullotta never spoke to him again, which hurt Uydess deeply.

Another of his friends at Philip Morris was Victor DeNoble. DeNoble was relieved to hear Uydess's affidavit dealt with, among other things, nicotine research. Uydess could confirm some of what DeNoble told Congress because the two of them had occasionally chatted over coffee in the research tower in Richmond.

When Uydess phoned DeNoble, DeNoble was supportive. Udyess seemed scared shitless, DeNoble thought.

Nevertheless, DeNoble couldn't resist calling back a few days later with a fake southern accent.

"Mr. Uydess?" said the southerner. "This is Congressman Tom Bliley. From Richmond?"

Uydess gulped.

"What the hell you *doin'*, boy? Don't you know I grow tobacco down here?"

Uydess muttered defensively. He didn't find it amusing when DeNoble revealed who he really was. And he continued to worry about tobacco company retribution before and after the three FDA affidavits were released on March 18.

Uydess would certainly have found it comforting to know that at the Philip Morris offices in New York, Steve Parrish was strongly encouraging the company not to go after him, Farone, and Rivers.

"We had seen what happened with the Wigand situation, which did not go well. To put it mildly," he laughed. "And I just didn't think there was any mileage to be gained out of that."

So when someone at a large gathering of Philip Morris R and D staff asked Parrish about the three whistle-blowers not long after they came forward, he said the company would attack their version of the facts, but wouldn't conduct a personal vendetta against them as individuals. Parrish had no idea how that would go over, and was pleasantly surprised when he got a warm round of applause.

However, Uydess's perhaps illusory fear of being hounded by Big Tobacco was soon replaced by his very real anxiety at having to deal with the media machine, which pursued him ferociously even before his identity was publicly revealed.

Cliff Douglas accompanied Uydess for a period of several days, during which both CBS and ABC romanced him for an exclusive interview. Uydess had trouble making up his mind. Douglas hoped to steer him toward his friends at ABC, but Uydess agreed to meet the 60 *Minutes* people first in Washington.

Hard on the heels of the public relations disaster surrounding the suppression of the Wigand segment, Mike Wallace personally courted Ian and his wife Carol at a hotel suite in the capital. Also there were Ann Ritter and Douglas, who called Summa from an adjoining room.

"I'm in here with Mike Wallace. I'm doing what I can," Douglas told Summa.

Douglas knew very well he wasn't going to outcharm Wallace, the symbol of investigative journalism to most of the nation and anchor of one of the most popular television shows in history. If the idea was to get your message to as many Americans as possible, it almost had to be Wallace.

Meanwhile, at the sight of this roomful of powerful people, all genuflecting to her and Ian, Carol Uydess had an anxiety attack and had to be taken, briefly, to the hospital.

She recovered in time to accompany Ian to dinner that night with Peter Jennings at his penthouse apartment in New York, a soirée arranged by Keith Summa.

Douglas had to suppress a chuckle at the sight of Ian and Carol chatting with Jennings as the anchorman worked the crank of his sushi machine and cracked open bottles of wine. The Uydesses laughed at Jennings's impression of Bono, of the band U2, and got a bit teary as they talked about why Ian was going public. Afterward, Uydess helped Jennings wash up the plates.

Quite a day for a corporate scientist from Richmond—Mike

Wallace and Peter Jennings fighting to be your personal media guru. Uydess picked Wallace, who interviewed him in Pascagoula soon afterward, appearing also, along with Victor DeNoble, on the *Larry King Live* show.

Though King never asked about the heart of Uydess's story, what Uydess called "the inner company" at Philip Morris, Motley and Ritter thoroughly questioned him about it during four days in Charleston that spring. Uydess told them how a circle of hand-picked scientists conducted certain investigations "'behind the scenes' on a strict 'need-to-know' basis," as he put it in his FDA affidavit.

"Most of this stuff had to do with smoking and health or the behavioral impact of nicotine," Uydess told Ritter and Motley.

"But tell me this," asked Ritter, whose father had been a research psychologist and who had an aptitude for technical subjects. "Why collect so much information? I mean, measuring brain-wave activity, hiring you and all these biologists, the DeNoble stuff. It couldn't do anything except get them into trouble."

"You have to understand, Philip Morris loves to know," said Uydess. "They want to know the truth. It's part of who they are. They don't like just *kind of* knowing. They want to *know*."

Then, before flying home to Richmond, Uydess barbecued at River House with Motley, Ritter, Bill Farone, and Jeff Wigand, formally joining Ness, Motley's growing roster of potential witnesses.

As for Victor DeNoble, he did not make the cut, despite his riveting story. Motley believed he had been seriously damaged in a deposition the year before at which Philip Morris hit DeNoble with allegations of compromised research results, citing a former assistant's claims that nicotine was dripping out of the rats during the self-administration experiment. Also problematic were DeNoble's reports to higher-ups, which did not classify nicotine as addictive.

So DeNoble came to Charleston and gave Motley ammunition to counter Philip Morris's charges, which he found absurd. He was angry that the Motley crowd seemed to have turned out to be fair weather friends. However, from Motley's point of view, there was too much at stake to risk on a witness who already carried so many negatives.

By now, however, DeNoble, at age fifty-two, was souring on the idea of being a witness in lawsuits. He had been out of the corporate research world for four years, and had taken a job with the state of Delaware, making sure mentally retarded adults got proper care in group homes.

DeNoble's view of plaintiff's lawyers had toughened a great deal in the two years since his friend in New Orleans warned him that "it's all about money."

"We, as experts, we're the suckerfish. Motley's the whale. They throw crumbs out to us. The day you lose that perspective, you're in trouble," DeNoble said.

THE MIDDLE OF MARCH 1996 WAS A SORT OF CRESCENDO point, a moment of critical mass. The week before the affidavits of the three FDA whistle-blowers were released, the Liggett Tobacco Company, smallest of the five major manufacturers, announced a settlement with Wendell Gauthier's *Castano* consortium and, two days later, a separate deal with five attorneys general suing the industry.

Both pacts were largely symbolic, since Liggett was almost bankrupt, but they were a considerable psychological blow to the industry, since it was the first time any cigarette company had settled a smoking and health lawsuit. However, while the attorney general's cause became stronger every month, the giant national *Castano* class action was thrown out of federal court two months after the Liggett settlement, and the influence of the *Castano* lawyers rapidly waned.

Wendell Gauthier and his team immediately went into state courts to file "sons of *Castano*" class actions, which were modeled on the defunct federal suit, but Motley withdrew from the consortium, feeling the "sons" actions were losers. He wanted to focus instead on the attorney general suits, plus *Butler,* and another secondhand-smoke case he had picked up, an Indiana lawsuit called *Wiley* v. *RJR Nabisco Holdings, et al.*

That was plenty of litigation for a law firm that, with sixty lawyers—twelve on the Tobacco Team—was large for a plaintiff's firm, but quite puny by defense standards. After all, Shook, Hardy & Bacon alone had four hundred lawyers, fifty in its tobacco unit, plus a thousand paralegals, science experts, secretaries, and others who backed them up. And Shook, Hardy was small compared to Jones, Day, Reavis & Pogue, Reynolds's national product liability counsel, with its eleven hundred lawyers in the U.S., Britain, France, and Saudi Arabia. All told, the industry had more than 400 law firms on its liability payroll. To call that an army of lawyers is hardly an exaggeration.

Meanwhile, the pace did nothing but increase for Ness, Motley, and especially for Ron Motley. By the summer of 1996, a couple of states were filing suit every month. Four AGs sued on three consecutive days in August. By year's end, Ness, Motley represented eleven of eighteen litigating states, in addition to its commitment to the *Butler, Wiley,* and *Haines* cases.

Although much of the workload was carried by local counsel in each state, most of whom had previously worked with Motley on asbestos cases, key proceedings usually involved Ness, Motley people, so that all of the Tobacco Team's attorneys, paralegals and others were traveling almost constantly.

But Motley himself was the number one frequent flier. As the end of 1996 approached, a typical five-day period found him going into six or more states.

Despite the marathon schedule, spirits were high on Motley's jet.

"I'm a lawyer! I follow court orders! I have a little dick!" shrieked Jodi Flowers, the slender, brown-haired junior attorney who frequently traveled with Motley, imitating a defense lawyer at a deposition they had just finished in Beaumont, Texas, as she waded past boxes to the little refrigerator just behind the Cessna Citation's cockpit.

Motley laughed.

"Hey, remember what we used to say, anytime we did an asbestos guy," Motley said, "and we'd mess that guy up bad, man. And we'd start goin', 'Put 'em up, fuck 'em up! Put 'em up, fuck 'em up!'"

Such enthusiasm was not always shared by others at Ness, Motley. The Tobacco Team seemed to be gradually inhaling the rest of the firm's staff—and its resources, more than $1 million a month, Motley's hard-won first million having been expended years earlier. The Tobacco Team now took up the entire fourth floor of the Meeting Street headquarters in Charleston. Motley frequently traveled with two other lawyers, a paralegal, an attorney or two from allied firms doing tobacco work, and perhaps the odd television producer.

That the rotating group of Ness, Motley Tobacco Team members who routinely flew with Motley was living in a bubble was obvious, and it was equally clear it was Motley's bubble. He was the one indispensable man. If he needed the plane, it was his plane. If he needed a lawyer, the lawyer was detached. And from all of this, not one dime had come back to the firm. It made people very nervous.

And, as corporate CEOs, Vegas-level entertainers and anyone else traveling in bubbles soon learns, a strong instinct for self-deprecation does not flourish on private jets. The air is thin at 41,000 feet. If there was a game plan, it was known only to this flying emperor of torts. Improvisation was the rule, and changes of itinerary numerous.

One trip had been rerouted so many times that the jet was just leveling off after takeoff from Charlotte, North Carolina, when Motley, already scribbling furiously on a legal pad, became vaguely aware of someone signaling from the cockpit.

"Yessir?" he shouted forward.

"Uhhh, you want to clue me in a little bit here?" said the pilot, twisting backward.

"Boston," said Motley. "We're going to Boston."

"Thanks," said the pilot.

Whole months were disappearing in an atmosphere of frenzy more akin to the Rolling Stones on tour than lawyers on business. There were depositions, hearings, speeches to legal or health groups, presentations to Canadian provinces, and foreign countries interested in suing.

These were Motley's gigs. It was off the jet and then by van or limo to the event of the day. Then back to the limo, back to the airport, and on to the next city for another limo to a hotel, where everyone ate at the restaurant and drank at the bar. This could go on for three, four, sometimes seven or even ten days at a stretch, with the twin-fan jet, nine-passenger Cessna Citation III fueled and ready at every stop. While it was going on, no one did laundry and Motley didn't even carry his own coat. Keith Summa called it "the 1996 lawsuit tour."

Motley liked to say it was really all the same case. A deposition of an expert in the *Butler* case would also serve the state suits, and vice versa. As far as Motley was concerned, the plane wasn't flying to physical places, but connecting the dots in his mind that formed the grand mosaic of the One Big Tobacco Case, the one with all the right pieces. Documents, judicial decisions, input from an expanding network of industry employees turned plaintiff's advisors—it was all coming over the transom so quickly that the mosaic was changing daily, necessitating a lot of improvising. And Motley thought of himself as the master improviser.

BUT THE BURDEN OF WORK—AND RESPONSIBILITY—SOME-times threatened to overwhelm him. In addition, he often felt alone and unhappy and, unless he was preparing for some morning proceeding, drank rather too heavily at night.

This produced some memorable moments, as when Motley, just arrived from Beaumont, strode magisterially toward the reception desk at the rear of the huge atrium of Atlanta's airport Hilton, gripping a big red plastic cup of vodka and juice he had procured in the private jet terminal.

Setting it down carefully, he put his elbows on the counter and, leaning in toward the clerk, asked very gently "Do you want me to sing?"

He then delivered a couple of heartfelt verses from "The Star Spangled Banner" until being led away by members of his entourage.

But a few days later, Motley's mood improved significantly when he learned of an important breakthrough in discovery.

He was back in Charleston, driving to the airport to fly to a deposition that evening in Vermont, when Ann Ritter called his cell phone and told him that Liggett Tobacco had cleared him to look at several hundred of their documents the following day at a law office in New York.

Motley was elated, since he had been after this particular batch of material for years. It concerned a shadowy body made up of the general counsel, or chief attorney, from each company, plus the industry's most trusted outside lawyers, a group known as the Committee of Counsel.

Officially an organ of the Tobacco Institute, the Committee of

Counsel was actually a kind of super-executive for the industry, making policy in politics, science, any area that bore directly on survival. Through liaisons, the COC controlled the Council for Tobacco Research, and a whole network of groups with inoffensive names like the Ad Hoc Committee, the Research Liaison Committee, the Industry Technical Committee. Very little was known about any of them, except that all dealt with smoking and health and were run by the same dozen or so attorneys, at the head of which, throughout much of the sixties, was usually David Hardy, who had helped set some of them up. No one was allowed to know more, since their activities were protected by attorney-client privilege.

In Motley's developing theory, the Committee of Counsel was the heart of darkness, the unholy of unholies. He compared it to the Commission, which directs the New York Mafia's Five Families, although unlike the Commission, the COC sometimes dealt with even petty details, dispatching operatives to Asia in search of pliable researchers.

Ritter told Motley that if he could get himself to New York, Liggett would show him capsule summaries of Committee of Counsel meetings, something no outsider had ever seen.

"If I get the minutes of the general counsels, those motherfuckers are dead. They are dead," said Motley as he hung up the phone.

"They've never produced a single page about this," he said excitedly. "Which is in and of itself damning. This is where the skeletons have got to be buried."

Liggett, of course, was not offering these treasures out of the goodness of its heart. Its chief executive, Bennett LeBow, was trying to use them as an escape hatch from the attorney general suits. A newcomer to the cigarette business, LeBow desperately wanted an agreement between Liggett and the attorneys general to shore up his Liggett I pact, because so many more states had sued since then.

LeBow had no particular interest in the cigarette business when he bought Liggett in 1986, just a fondness for making piles of money. He had grown up in a tough neighborhood in West Philadelphia yet founded and sold his first company by the time he was thirty. In the mid-eighties he was "a deal guy," as he readily admitted, a sort of second-tier corporate raider, with an unsavory reputation for hijacking failing companies, sucking out any remaining value, and casting away the dry bones. The pugnacious LeBow outlasted his critics, making millions along the way. Liggett had seemed a good investment.

"It had been for sale and no one wanted to buy it," LeBow recalled. "I looked at it and said, Hey, you know, the cigarette business is a great business. What the hell are you talking about? It's a pure deal. And at the time, there were a few lawsuits around. A few. The owner didn't want to put up with those lawsuits."

As time went on, LeBow learned more about the cigarette business, and a lot more about lawsuits. The same group of lawyers had handled Liggett's cigarette-liability work for decades, but then LeBow got to know and trust a new lawyer named Marc Kasowitz, whose firm specialized in product-liability defense but had never represented the tobacco industry.

In September 1994, LeBow suggested that Liggett's longtime tobacco counsel, James Kearney and Francis Decker, whose old law firm was about to fold, simply transfer to Kasowitz's firm. Then an extraordinary thing happened. A letter arrived from Philip Morris offering to pay all Liggett's legal fees if he used another firm that already did cigarette work.

Kearney and Decker recommended he take the offer.

"In the back of my mind, I said, 'This is bullshit,'" said LeBow. "My lawyers are recommending I take Philip Morris's money? Who's going to look after my interests?"

Since Liggett, which had archaic brands like Chesterfield and L&M, was in rocky shape, LeBow took the money, about $8 million a year. When he decided in late 1995 that it didn't make much sense to risk losing billions in smoking and health lawsuits, he turned to Kasowitz to negotiate what became known as the Liggett I settlement. But after Liggett I, lawsuits continued to proliferate, while LeBow became convinced the other manufacturers had decided to destroy his tiny firm, using their superior muscle to undercut Liggett's brands to punish him for making a deal. With under 2 percent of the market, Liggett's financial position deteriorated steadily.

The final straw came in August 1996, when the *Wall Street Journal* broke a story about how Mike Moore and Dickie Scruggs were quietly circulating a bill in Congress that would grant the industry blanket immunity from civil damages in return for complying with FDA-style regulations and paying restitution, a so-called "global settlement." Although the bill never went anywhere, the idea of a global settlement worried LeBow, because bankrupt Liggett wouldn't be able to come up with the money. If there were to be negotiations, he wanted his company to get a special dispensation, a better deal.

So Kasowitz made a frantic call to Mike Moore and Dickie Scruggs, hoping, in effect, to cop a plea. Liggett would give up dirt on its four much bigger brothers in return for a settlement of all pending attorney general suits, and, Kasowitz hoped, preferential treatment in the future.

The dirt was in the documents, and the attorneys general had deputized Motley to make sure it was filthy enough to let Liggett off the hook. The first thing Motley had requested of Liggett was the minutes of the Committee of Counsel. It had taken months of demands and several previous trips to New York, and now it looked like he would actually get a shot at them the day after his Vermont deposition.

"We going to New Yo-ak!" he said to his staff on the plane, which was about to take off from Charleston.

Someone cheered. Everyone understood the significance of what could be waiting for them there.

"But first, we've got this little deal to do in Vermont," Motley added, as he strapped himself into his seat.

THERE WAS SNOW ON THE GROUND AND ICE ON THE runway when the little jet touched down in Burlington just after dark, and in the wind and bitter cold the plane's rear hatch opened and disgorged luggage, boxes of documents, laptop computers, a printer, and an overhead projector, all of which were lugged out to a van.

Motley had flown into the cold to question one John Craighead, M.D., a heavily credentialed lung pathologist from the University of Vermont College of Medicine. Craighead had served with the industry's Council for Tobacco Research and Motley planned to show him that CTR's Scientific Advisory Board, of which he had briefly been a member, was a panel of eminent dupes. Along the way,

Craighead was expected to offer his opinion that Mississippi barber Burl Butler died from inhaling secondhand smoke.

Motley called what he was about to do with Craighead a "trial" as opposed to a "discovery" deposition. He didn't expect to learn anything new about CTR from Craighead, who had been there only a year. The major purpose of the affair was to read a long succession of damaging documents into the record and capture Craighead's reactions of disgust and amazement on videotape for the jury.

The deposition had a hallucinatory aspect. It began at six-thirty P.M. and didn't end until after midnight. Having landed just forty-five minutes before, the Motley party had to conduct it on empty stomachs in a basement room of the Burlington Sheraton that gave out through sliding glass doors onto a walkway carpeted in faux grass.

Surrounded by cartons of documents, paralegal Sandra Burley flanked Motley at a big rectangular table, and like a skilled scrub nurse, her upper body never stopped twisting as she expertly found each piece of paper and stuck it into Motley's hand as he asked for it. The industry's lawyers took up the rest of the table.

Craighead, whose full gray beard and sideburns made him look like a Civil War general, did indeed look disgusted as Motley read from reports and memos. He seemed especially appalled when Motley told him that the Council for Tobacco Research was in fact classified for tax purposes as a *trade association,* not a research group, since its work benefitted industry attorneys.

Motley went on to show that the Scientific Advisory Board, which since CTR's founding in 1954 had boasted many noted experts on cancer medicine, was the heart of the deception that CTR represented. The industry claimed—and had repeatedly told Congress and the American people—that the SAB made research grants free of industry interference in an effort to understand the causes of cancer.

Craighead had believed this, too.

"Were you ever told that lawyers were pre-reviewing the grant applications before you had a chance at look at them?" Motley asked.

"No," said Craighead.

"Were you ever told that lawyers for the tobacco companies were refusing to fund certain studies that the Scientific Advisory Board agreed were meritorious?"

"No, I was not told that," said Craighead grimly.

Motley read a sample of what he called his "CTR's greatest hits" documents, such as a memo from a vice president at Lorillard Tobacco who wrote that CTR's purpose wasn't research but "public relations, political relations, position for litigation, et cetera."

A visibly angry Craighead said he had not been aware of these things when he joined CTR in 1976, and had he known, wouldn't have participated.

Then the tobacco lawyers spent three hours counter-attacking, quizzing Craighead on numerous obscure studies on environmental tobacco smoke to undermine his expert credentials.

"The next is 'Indoor Burning Coal Air Pollution and Lung Cancer, a Case-Control Study in Fuzhou, China.' The lead author is Luo Ren-xia," one cigarette lawyer recited.

Craighead coldly dismissed these. He hadn't read them and didn't care. Many hadn't appeared in reputable journals and some, he pointed out, "are in foreign tongues."

The next morning, Motley chuckled with delight as the van drove through sooty snow to the Burlington airport, highly pleased with his little tutorial on CTR.

"Did you see how red he got? Oh, my God, he was pissed!" he said.

But now he was eager to get to the Committee of Counsel documents in New York, where he would meet with Marc Kasowitz, LeBow's lawyer and trusted lieutenant.

Of course, all Motley would actually be allowed to see of the Committee of Counsel material was a "privilege log" containing summaries, not the COC documents themselves, which involved lawyers from other companies. Either those companies had to agree to waive their attorney-client privilege, or someone had to get a court order *deprivileging* the material.

So Motley wanted to get Liggett to send selected documents to various courts where Motley or the attorneys general had cases pending. Then Motley would try to puncture the privilege.

To do it, he needed to show that lawyers were injected into scientific areas so the companies could argue later that smoking and health research—especially work pointing to the industry's long-standing knowledge that its products were deadly—didn't have to be turned over to the government or plaintiff's lawyers. Documents created to further illegal acts, such as hiding evidence, would qualify for the "crime/fraud exception" to the privilege.

This was a formidable cloaking device. There can be no practice of law unless attorney and client can communicate freely and confidentially. Courts will not push the privilege aside without compelling reasons. What an attorney does for his client is not a fact in the case, it is how facts get *into* the case, just as a lawyer's closing statement is argument, not evidence. A lawyer is an officer of the court and if he advocates in bad faith, he breaks the law. But because of the privilege, the likelihood is that no one will ever know that except lawyer and client. It is an honor system.

The attorney-client stratagem is brilliant because the evidence sought by the plaintiff is, by definition, *not* evidence. The odds are no one would ever suspect the privilege had been so deeply perverted.

What gave it away was something called "Special Projects," a Council for Tobacco Research program that lawyer Marc Edell first stumbled over during his epic *Cipollone* case.

Oddly, Edell found no references to Special Projects in CTR literature, then discovered that some scientists who passed themselves off before congressional committees as public-interested smoking and health researchers were being paid by the lawyers to work on these Special Projects.

Special Projects, Motley had learned from industry documents, was in fact a secret research fund controlled by David Hardy and other lawyers. Research guidelines for "Special Projects" were contained in a green loose-leaf notebook called "the Green Book." The basic idea was to generate a massive body of work leading away from cigarettes as a cause of illness and toward *diet or viruses or car exhaust. Any* other cause.

A great deal of the research was of questionable legitimacy, what Bill Farone dismissed as "funky science in support of tobacco." For instance, there was an obsession with studying identical twins. One of the industry's scientific allies believed dietary deficiencies caused *all* cancers, an idea that even a CTR official called "idiotic."

The net effect of those "Special Projects" that were actually published was to foster the impression that there was *still,* at century's end, some uncertainty about the deadliness of cigarettes. In coordination with the Tobacco Institute, which periodically launched nationwide ad campaigns, Hardy and industry heavyweights like R. J. Reynolds's general counsel Henry Ramm masterminded a disinformation campaign.

But Hardy was also concerned about research by the companies themselves that by the late sixties indisputably linked cigarettes not only to lung cancer but to emphysema and other illnesses. Don't write these things down, Hardy warned. Any internal document that seems to "tacitly admit that cigarettes cause cancer or other disease would likely be fatal to the defense" of a smoking and health suit, wrote Hardy in August 1970.

"The psychological effect on judge and jury would undoubtedly be devastating," he observed.

Though *Ross, Green* and the other early cases had faded away, Hardy, as the industry's bodyguard, was preparing for the next generation of suits. The *Green* and *Ross* lawyers were not allowed any internal tobacco documents. But, Hardy noted, new laws were making it likely that courts would order company records to be turned over to the plaintiffs.

"I can anticipate rulings which would leave us defeated by our own hand," Hardy wrote ominously.

Thus began a policy of censoring the language used in internal communications—witness Deep Cough's inability to say the word "addictive"—and attempting to cloak scientific reports in privilege by having lawyers watch every phase of research.

The heart of the disinformation campaign was CTR, Motley had realized. And controlling CTR was the Committee of Counsel, with its incessant quest for friendly scientists—"the most elaborate search for favorable research, experts, and witnesses that the world will probably ever know," as one judge called it.

After *Cipollone* was dropped, Edell continued to try to get the industry to turn over a group of fifteen hundred Special Projects documents in the *Haines* case. A judge was about to deprivilege them, but the companies got him kicked off the case for appearing biased.

The judge's opinion quoted tantalizing snippets from Committee of Counsel minutes, which helped convince Motley to take the *Haines* case in 1994 for the chance to get at the "Special Projects" documents.

But Motley didn't fully grasp the crucial significance of the Committee of Counsel until just before the Craighead deposition, when he came across an intriguing document by two British tobacco company scientists who toured the United States right after the 1964 Surgeon General's report, the first to say smoking caused cancer.

The two scientists wrote up a kind of damage assessment on the American situation for their superiors in Britain, which came to be known as the "Trip Report," in which they discussed a "powerful Policy Committee of senior lawyers." The Policy Committee, later the Committee of Counsel, "determines the high policy of the industry on all smoking and health matters—research and public relations matters, for example, as well as legal matters—and it reports directly to the presidents." And one of the several organs the Policy Committee controlled, the Brits reported, was the Council for Tobacco Research.

All of which heightened Motley's anticipation as he, Burley, Susan Nial, and Grant Kaiser, a lawyer with the Texas attorney general's suit, reached the Burlington airport for the flight to New York City.

There Motley telephoned Marc Kasowitz, a fiery, silver-haired Connecticut native, with whom he had formed a close working relationship.

"Tell me some *fucking* good news," Kasowitz said.

Motley laughed. He told him he would be in New York in two hours and that he hoped it would be Kasowitz who had good news for him.

MOTLEY AND HIS PARTY SPENT THE AFTERNOON PORING over thousands of pieces of paper, many handwritten, and some virtually illegible. It was frustrating. One document from 1966 seemed to show that sensitive scientific reports from the British were sent "back-channel" to the home of Brown & Williamson counsel Addison Yeaman, who was then also head of CTR. Other material was apparently related to Committee of Counsel documents quoted in the *Haines* case, but it was hard to tell from the privilege log. After five hours of this, his eyes bleary and head aching, Motley realized he would have to come back another time and see more.

Motley and his retinue were joined at a restaurant that evening by Keith Summa, who had become quite friendly with Motley after ABC made him a kind of roving tobacco producer-reporter.

When Summa came in, he refused to let the check girl take his coat.

"He's afraid his bag of grass'll fall out of there," cracked Motley.

Motley ordered separate tumblers of ice, vodka, and grapefruit juice. "I'll just assemble 'em myself," he told the waiter. He then proceeded to get volcanically drunk, staring blurrily across the table at Summa, with whom he exchanged insults and high-fives during the course of a besotted dinner punctuated by seal barks of laughter.

"Keith, you know, a half-full balloon you buy at the zoo gets more air time than you do," said Motley.

Summa, tall, courteous, dark haired, youthful, smiled back. "Ron, you need a new tune," he said.

"They tell you I'm gonna have a speaking part in a movie?" asked Motley, referring to two independent film producers he was friendly with.

"You don't ever shut up, so it's got to be a speaking part," said Summa.

Everyone else at the table watched, as though at a sporting event, especially the women, who seemed fascinated by the locker-room atmosphere. After the dinner and cutting contest were over, the group rose unsteadily to its feet and began weaving around the large circular table in the general direction of the coatroom, which at that moment seemed far, far away. Motley and one of his party crashed to the ground in a drunken bear hug.

The evening continued at the bar at their hotel, where Summa was soon deep in an emotional tête-à-tête with Motley about his breakup with Catherine Baen.

"I've got no one," he said. "I can do all this, but I've got no one."

He began sobbing.

"She left me," Motley said. "She really hurt me."

He reached for Summa's hand, and Summa clasped it warmly between his.

"You know you're among friends," Summa said gently.

Motley wiped his eyes, got up, embraced Summa.

"You are my brother," he said. "You know that? You are my brother."

He looked at the others at the table. "I'm okay," he said, strength returning to his voice. He bade everyone good night and floated off through the bar, into the lobby toward the elevators. He stood, swaying slightly before the doors. They opened and he disappeared.

THAT FALL, MOTLEY NOT ONLY TRIED TO FIGURE OUT WHICH documents to get from LeBow, he attended some of the negotiations for what was becoming known as the Liggett II settlement.

A number of these sessions were held at the offices of Arizona Attorney General Grant Woods, who had recently filed a tobacco lawsuit. Having a spy who knew the layout of the enemy's camp certainly made sense to Woods, but Moore and Scruggs weren't terribly certain they wanted to do another deal with LeBow. They were fast becoming obsessed with their idea of a "global settlement" with the entire industry and were afraid a side deal with Liggett, the hated traitor, could wreck it.

Ron Motley argued passionately that the attorneys general simply had to have the Liggett documents if they wanted to pose a credible threat to big tobacco. They were the crown jewels of the case. His enthusiasm and the strong support of Woods, who pulled a lot of weight with other attorneys general, ultimately carried the day.

However, Woods wanted not only documents but public admissions that the product was deadly and addictive, and he and the chief private lawyer for Arizona, Seattle attorney Steve Berman, pushed hard for them. Berman became, with Marc Kasowitz, a key drafter of the settlement document. Berman had begun challenging Ness, Motley's dominance in the attorney general suits, and had done very well, signing up Arizona, Washington, Illinois, Indiana, and others. The quiet, youthful Berman worked brutal hours to make up for his firm's small size, arriving at his office at six A.M. and staying until nine or ten P.M. six days a week.

The other chief negotiator was Joe Rice, Ness, Motley's managing partner and deal maker. Rice specialized in the financial aspects of settlements, and having put together several multibillion-dollar asbestos deals, he knew how to make one happen.

Although other attorneys general, such as Christine Gregoire of Washington and Richard Blumenthal of Connecticut, played roles, Woods emerged as the heavy in the negotiations. Woods had a unique profile. He was a Republican from a heavily Republican state and the first Republican attorney general to sue tobacco, but his politics were much closer to those of a liberal Democrat. Woods did things his way. He spent his lunch hours playing basketball with his staff, had his own weekly radio show, and loved Elvis Presley so much, he sneaked off during a Liggett negotiating session to visit Graceland. He didn't give much of a damn what people thought, which gave him credibility with Kasowitz and his people, and he became a kind of enforcer in the negotiating process.

To Woods, it was critical that LeBow publicly acknowledge the industry's wrongs, because even if inadmissible in court, such a confession would have enormous public relations value. Of all the elements of the deal, the "admissions"—that nicotine was addictive, that cigarettes killed, and most critically, that the industry targeted children—were the toughest things for LeBow to swallow, especially since he could very credibly argue he wasn't around when the lies were told. LeBow wanted to hedge, at least on the child marketing issue. For Christ's sake, LeBow would say, children don't buy *Chesterfields*. No one under the age of fifty has bought a Chesterfield since the Korean War.

"Ben, either you're the white knight or you're the black knight. There is no gray knight," Woods said to LeBow in Phoenix. "And what you're trying to do here is be the white knight, so you've got to *be* the white knight."

LeBow resisted and the issue was temporarily shelved, but in the end, he came around. Throughout the fall and winter, the negotiations continued, a portable affair held in Phoenix, Washington, D.C., New York, and elsewhere. Through it all Motley dashed into and out of New York, as Kasowitz's people culled documents and organized them into categories.

The talks were supposed to be secret, but in fact *ABC News* producer Keith Summa had shadowed the very first session in Phoenix, promising to keep the secret in return for getting a tip just before the deal went down.

BY EARLY 1997, THERE WAS A DRAFT AGREEMENT SPELLing out what Liggett would have to do to satisfy the attorneys general. Not only would the company make admissions, it would also print "Smoking is addictive" on its products, turn over its documents, and make its scientists and executives—including LeBow—available to plaintiffs in smoking and health suits.

By March, the haggling had to do with satisfying the specific needs of various states, especially Minnesota, whose attorney general, Hubert Humphrey III, known as "Skip," had been the lone holdout in "Liggett I," the earlier and much smaller settlement.

Motley pressed steadily ahead with the document selection. By the evening of March 19, all the pieces were in place. Woods, Moore, and the other attorneys general were in Washington, D.C., where a regularly scheduled meeting of the National Association of Attorneys General was in progress. Steve Berman, Joe Rice, and Dickie Scruggs were there, too, putting the final touches on the deal by telephone with Kasowitz and his team.

Motley had set up a war room at the Regency Hotel in New York, and had seven staffers working double duty, helping him prepare for a deposition the following day and also working over the logistics of the documents transfer. As evening fell, he was on the phone to his partner Rice every few hours for the latest news.

At Kasowitz's offices on Avenue of the Americas, attorneys were still making final document selections, and duplicating machines all over midtown Manhattan were shooting out multiple copies of twelve banker's boxes of records that were to be flown out the following day. Two dozen documents had been flagged for the judges to look at immediately. Kasowitz called them the "Motherfucker Documents," the most shocking in the collection.

There had been a lot of scheming about how to get this payload to the courts before the industry could block the transfer. The final plan was the brainchild of Motley and Dickie Scruggs. On the morning of March 20, Scruggs would have his Learjet on the flight line at Teterboro airport, a very large private airfield in northern New Jersey, just across the Hudson River from New York City. Also on the tarmac would be Motley's Cessna Citation III and another jet owned by a Texas lawyer. The idea was that vanloads of documents would be blasted across the Lincoln Tunnel to the airfield, the three planes would load up, and just as the settlement press conference began that morning, this little plaintiff's air force would taxi down the runway and hit cruising altitude at about the same time the other tobacco companies realized, too late, that today was D Day. They would gnash their teeth and rush off to court, but by then the squadron would be beyond recall, well on the way to its targets.

The targets were courts Motley had chosen because they had procedures to expedite the review of documents: the Florida attorney general's case in West Palm Beach, the *Butler* secondhand-smoke case in Laurel, Mississippi, and the federal court in Texarkana, Texas, home of that state's attorney general suit. Motley's plane would leave first, bound for Laurel. Then Scruggs's plane would hit Florida and finally the Texas jet would bomb Texarkana.

Motley was in his room at the Regency in New York when he switched on the television at just after six-thirty P.M. the night before the big day to see Tom Brokaw on *NBC News* report that an agreement would be announced the following day between what were now twenty-two attorneys general and the Liggett Tobacco Company.

"Liggett will turn over a treasure trove of what are said to be highly incriminating documents by industry lawyers to the attorneys general," said Brokaw.

"I don't fucking believe this," said Motley. "Shit."

Scruggs, Moore, and Motley had gotten wind of the leak just before the broadcast and tried to talk correspondent Bob Kur out of doing the story. But Motley didn't really believe it would happen until he saw it. He stalked from the room.

Cliff Douglas was also staying at the Regency, having come to New York to help Motley get ready for his deposition. He was downstairs in the bar having a drink and a sandwich when Motley stormed past him.

"What's up, Ron?" asked a puzzled Douglas.

"We're fucked, that's what's wrong," said Motley, who kept walking.

"What do you mean?" asked Douglas.

"The deal is dead," said Motley, and hurried off.

As it turned out, the deal was only damaged. Moore and Scruggs blamed Kasowitz for the leak. Motley was furious at Kur, especially since *ABC News*'s Keith Summa had kept his promise and sat on the story. Kasowitz was convinced Moore leaked the story to force Liggett to actually send the documents. Heads cooled as the evening wore on.

"Ron, we're almost there," said Kasowitz, who was in Alabama putting together a separate settlement with a group of private lawyers. "Let's finish this thing. We've just come too far to quit."

Motley agreed, and went back to his room to continue preparing for his deposition, which was of Philip Morris senior vice-president for research Cathy Ellis, an important figure. Now that the secret was out it was anyone's guess what would happen the next day at Teterboro airport. Douglas spent most of the night in his room, taking press calls about the settlement.

In Washington, there was chaos. By midnight there was still no final draft of the settlement agreement and Minnesota attorney general Skip Humphrey, who was ideologically hostile to settlements of any kind, couldn't seem to make up his mind whether to sign it.

Morning came and the press conference announcing the deal kept being put off. By one P.M., there still were no signatures on the agreement, and Humphrey was refusing to come out of his hotel room. Finally, at three P.M., several attorneys general managed to convince him that the process had to be brought to an end. The press conference was set for four P.M., and as the twenty-two AGs, led by Mike Moore, walked into the ballroom of the Hilton and stepped onto the stage, staffers were faxing each other the signatures of Bennett LeBow and the attorneys general to close the deal.

But by then, lawyers for R. J. Reynolds had gotten a North Carolina state court to bar Liggett from sending out the documents.

Nevertheless, a very determined paralegal from the offices of Kasowitz, Benson, Torres & Friedman named Joseph Hawry, known affectionately at the firm as "the Bagman," was in a white van driving through the Lincoln Tunnel en route to Teterboro airport. There was time to load only one plane with documents, and that was only a first installment of six boxes—it had proven impossible to get all twelve boxes selected and copied by morning.

The boxes were stowed in the tail of Motley's Cessna and Hawry climbed aboard. Three hours later he was at the Jones County regional airport near Laurel, but by then, the North Carolina court had ordered that distribution be stopped.

When Hawry called from Mississippi, Aaron Marks, one of Kasowitz's lawyers, phoned a Mississippi lawyer who worked with Motley and told her that as soon as the judge in Laurel faxed up an order formally requesting the documents and indicating Liggett would not be violating the North Carolina order, Hawry would drive them to the courthouse.

An hour later, the fax machine began kicking out a piece of paper that began "In the Circuit Court of Jones County," and after a few more lines came through, Marks rang Hawry's cell phone.

"You're good to go," said Marks.

The next day, Friday, an exhausted Motley returned to Charleston. For several days, a battle raged as Berman and Motley dispatched lawyers in a dozen states to fight the industry's attempts to squelch the transfer of the documents to other courts that were to receive them. Those battles ended the following week with the industry losing every one. The lone Cessna that flew to Laurel was now followed by a series of shipments by overnight courier, until all twenty-two states had all twelve boxes of material.

In the three months following the Liggett II settlement, the number of states suing the industry almost doubled. The stakes were getting very high indeed, both for Ron Motley, whose firm was still hemorrhaging money, and for an industry facing three attorney general trials in the next six months, an industry whose future had never looked darker.

The week before the Liggett deal was announced, Motley's partner Joe Rice got a phone call from Meyer Koplow, a product liability defense lawyer whom Rice had known for years and who now represented Philip Morris. Rice wasn't surprised to hear from Koplow, with whom he dealt occasionally on asbestos cases. Whenever the two talked, Rice would tell Koplow that he ought to prevail upon his cigarette client to start thinking about making a deal. They're going to have to do it sooner or later, Rice said. The AGs aren't going away.

Koplow wanted to know if Rice could bring Attorney General Mike Moore and the other people who mattered from his side to a face-to-face meeting with industry representatives.

"If you're bringing the right people, I think I can bring the right people," said Rice.

Phone calls with Koplow continued into the weekend, when Koplow told Rice who he was bringing: J. Philip Carlton, a retired North Carolina Supreme Court judge; Arthur Golden, a close friend and former law partner of the CEO of R. J. Reynolds; and

Herbert Wachtell, senior partner at Koplow's law firm and lead lawyer for Philip Morris in the ABC libel suit.

These people, Koplow said, had the authority to speak on behalf of the four major cigarette companies, which was all of them except Liggett.

Rice had also been talking with Moore and Dickie Scruggs all week. Moore wanted to know if Rice thought this Koplow guy was for real. Rice thought so, but the only way to find out for sure was to have the meeting. There was nothing to lose by listening. Well, then, go see these people, said Moore, and Scruggs concurred. A time and a place were set: Tuesday morning, March 18, at the airport Sheraton in Charlotte, North Carolina. Rice would fly there directly from the Liggett negotiations in Washington. He was to tell no one about his conversation with Koplow, or about the meeting, not even Ron Motley, his own law partner.

As he packed his bags that weekend, Rice kept wondering what the trigger was, what had prompted this historic change of course.

Why talk to us *now*?

T E N

JACKSONVILLE

BY THE TIME JOE RICE GOT INVITED TO SIT DOWN WITH the industry, the only tobacco warriors who had logged more air miles than Rice and Motley were Dickie Scruggs, Mike Moore, and Steve Bozeman, Scruggs's indispensable staff man.

Various permutations of Bozeman, Moore, and Scruggs flew in Scruggs's Learjet for more than two years, pursuing a mission closely allied to that of the Motley Crew's Citation. If Motley was Patton, which *he* thought he was, then Scruggs and Moore were the diplomatic corps, appearing in almost every state capital to sign up attorneys general. A forty-thousand-mile recruitment drive.

It was cleaner cut in the Lear than on the Citation. Moore was courteous to a fault—always "shoot," never "shit." There was a lot of cop in Mike Moore. He had been a district attorney in Pascagoula for two terms, attacking a corrupt county commissioner system that had run things there for thirty years. Moore was threatened. Annoying, nosy people like him could be, and were, thrown into the Pascagoula River. That mission required more than courage, it took fervor. There was fervor in the Lear.

Moore is Catholic, and grew up thinking Father Patrick Quinn, one of his teachers, was as close to a saint as he'd ever see. Other progressive priests preached public service, but Quinn left Pascagoula for eighteen years of missionary work in Mexico and died there. To

Moore, Quinn wasn't a symbol of commitment, but its living, breathing embodiment.

To his developing moral compass, Moore added a theatrical flair that he developed as district attorney of Jackson County, which includes Pascagoula. Once he prosecuted a newspaper editor who allegedly hid the gun in the attic that killed his wife. To get up there, the editor would have had to climb a rickety old ladder, which the defense argued was far too flimsy for the purpose. For his summation, Moore dragged in the ladder, gingerly climbed up twenty feet, and orated, swaying above the jurors.

Verdict for the prosecution.

Moore was one of the shorter attorneys general, and in group pictures, he and Dennis Vacco of New York and Daniel Morales of Texas could count on being placed in the front row. Rangy Dick Blumenthal and bulky Grant Woods, the back. But as the first attorney general to sue tobacco and builder of the Medicaid lawsuit juggernaut, Moore was in charge. No doubt about it.

He and Bozeman and Scruggs barnstormed throughout 1995 and 1996, signing up states to sue, caucusing in the hallways of attorney general meetings until twenty-five or so AGs were yammering in the corridor and nobody was listening to the speaker in the hall.

Scruggs spent millions to keep himself and Moore in the air.

"The companies have an army. We need an army," Moore told each attorney general. "We've got to equal out the influence, the money, all the tools of war."

Tobacco's response was to preemptively sue anyone *contemplating* a Medicaid action. That infuriated the AGs. This was a group that contained Rhodes scholars, first in their law school class, people who chose public service from many other life options. The preemptive suits were a serious strategic error. Tobacco sued eight AGs and every one of them sued back. Motley signed up most as clients. Steve Berman grabbed others, as did Richard Heimann, a *Castano* lawyer who joined the attorney general lawsuit game by partnering with Don Barrett.

Scruggs and Moore watched each other's back. Together, they were like high school buddies, flipping each other pieces of gum, sharing significant looks. Suddenly they were the main event. They hit the national stage knowing nothing, so they were unafraid, just as they had been unafraid to sue the industry.

In the summer of 1996, Douglas ran into Scruggs and Moore in

Palm Beach, Florida, where all three were attending a multi-day conference on tobacco suits. The Mississippians pulled Douglas aside, and for two hours over breakfast, they talked long-term strategy. Very long term.

"We want you to think about the endgame," said Scruggs. "What happens if we get a chance to negotiate something with the industry? What would you want us to get from them?"

They absolutely must agree to unfettered FDA jurisdiction, said Douglas reflexively, including the power to lower the nicotine yields of cigarettes.

Even while he struggled to formulate a wish list, he was fighting his own astonishment at the question. *Endgame.* Scruggs was thinking *years* ahead, spinning scenarios like chess problems. While Moore had an extraordinary ability to communicate passion and sincerity, Scruggs and Motley, Douglas realized, were probably the closest thing the plaintiff's side had to strategic geniuses.

"So where to after this?" Douglas asked at the end of their breakfast.

Moore made a swooshing noise and flew his hand through the air like a plane.

"Up, up, and away," he said.

In fact, the only thing worrying Moore was a plane crash. There had been several unpleasant incidents. En route to one meeting, one of the Lear's engines flamed out and they plunged twenty thousand feet before it relit.

Moore brushed that off, too.

"We're on a mission from God," he said, and there was little doubt he meant it.

Now Scruggs and Moore waited in Washington for a report from Joe Rice. And for the next meeting, if there was to be one.

AS 1997 BEGAN, PHILIP MORRIS'S STEVEN PARRISH realized how badly they had underestimated Mike Moore, his doggedness, his charisma, his caliber as a leader. Moore had created not only a legal threat, thanks to Motley and Scruggs, but a political storm center feeding off a sense of moral outrage felt across the country. By seizing on child targeting as his battle cry, he had outpoliticked tobacco. Moore and his message would have to be dealt with.

The process that brought Joe Rice to Charlotte just as the Liggett deal was being cemented really began when R. J. Reynolds appointed a new chief executive officer named Steven Goldstone. Goldstone had no real background in the cigarette business before joining Reynolds, and that may have been why he had the temerity to suggest, in March 1996, that the manufacturers of the peculiar product couldn't continue as "kind of an outlaw industry" and would have to strike a bargain with their many enemies.

But Geoffrey Bible, the pugnacious chairman of Philip Morris, was sending a different message.

"We will fight in court and we will win because we are right," said Bible in a xenophobic speech to Philip Morris workers in which he compared the anti-cigarette activists to Nazis and the tobacco industry to the Allies. He said this in April 1996 to rally the troops, but he also believed it. An Australian who dropped out of high school and went to work at age fourteen, Bible was an outspoken battler in the mold of tobacco autocrats like Joseph Cullman III, who had turned Philip Morris into an imperial power. Having Bible on the front lines reassured the diehards that nothing would be given away on his watch.

He was their Nixon, so he could go to China. Even while sounding the charge, Bible was reaching out to Chuck Wall, Steve Parrish, and Murray Bring, the in-house lawyers, because as a new chairman and Australian, he wanted to find out just how bad the situation really was. Bad, Parrish told him—the FDA, class actions, the Justice Department, the attorney general suits.

As the leader of the "Eight-thirty Group," Parrish could afford to be a dove. He told Bible that the cost of war had gone well beyond what was going out to hundreds of law firms giddily billing away at $250 an hour. Or the fact that damages in any AG case could easily reach the billions, and that some of the weaker sisters in the industry wouldn't even be able to post an appeal bond for that amount to contest an adverse verdict.

"The real question is, what's the immediate impact from a PR and congressional relations standpoint of a four-billion-dollar judgment in Florida?" Parrish would say. "And then, jeez, you've got a dozen more trials after that."

Suddenly the air was full of real hatred toward the cigarette men. The industry had become the political stalking-horse of choice, a dangerous place to be. Parrish watched in dismay as elected leaders and electorate bonded on a common field of shared injury. Senator Frank Lautenberg had struggled for years to quit, and Florida Governor Lawton Chiles smoked as a ten-year-old. Washington Attorney General Christine Gregoire, who had teenage children, was enraged to find Joe Camel ads offering free concert tickets in *Rolling Stone*. Everyone knew the AGs were talking about something real.

Having the governor of Florida walk into court and say your company is a drug pusher, addicting children to a lethal substance—as Lawton Chiles did when Florida filed suit—gave real weight to the label "outlaw industry." If nothing else, it made for some very ugly television on the twenty-second floor of the Philip Morris building.

It was time for Nixon to head for Beijing. It began with a Philip Morris retreat in Bermuda in July 1996 attended by all the warlords—Geoffrey Bible, Chuck Wall, Parrish, Herbert Wachtell, Mark Firestone, who ran regulatory affairs, and others. They were trying to figure out whom they needed to negotiate with. Should it be done through a group of governors? Would the White House get involved? Would it have to come from Congress?

For several days, about ten of them met in a rather small, sweaty conference room amid a lot of blond wood at a resort hotel. Bible's habit was to hold his views until the end to avoid warping the discussion. On the last day, Bible, who had taken notes throughout, put down his pen, put his elbows on the table, and interlaced his fingers.

"Look, obviously I've given this a lot of thought, and I think that if there's any way that something can be done, we ought to explore the opportunity," said Bible in his Aussie accent. "And I think we need to move forward."

No one disagreed. The group started talking about how to begin a peace process.

In August, Jacksonville lawyer Norwood Wilner won a $750,000 verdict against Brown & Williamson in the *Carter* case, the first damage award against the industry since *Cipollone,* and that prompted a phone call to Geoff Bible from Martin Broughton, the chief executive of British American Tobacco, which owned Brown & Williamson.

Bible and Broughton convened a meeting of tobacco company

chiefs that summer at which the question quickly became: What would the companies be willing to give up in exchange for peace? Task forces were set up to study all the important areas—restrictions on advertising, FDA regulation, ingredients disclosure, and, most important, immunity from lawsuits. That was priority number one.

News of the impending Liggett settlement in March 1997 pushed the industry's concern into high gear, and helped prompt Philip Morris lawyer Meyer Koplow's phone call to Joe Rice, the first time the biggest tobacco companies had ever extended a peace feeler to a plaintiff's lawyer.

Joe Rice entered the first of what were to be many conference rooms at an airport hotel in Charlotte on March 18. There was a round of handshakes, and at about one P.M. everyone sat down. Mike Moore's cause had enlisted fifteen additional states in one year for a total of twenty-two and was moving toward trial in almost all of them. The duct-taped, untried, weirdo lawsuit cooked up three years earlier by a bunch of hicks from Mississippi and South Carolina had matured.

But the biggest thing the AGs had going for them was never their theory of law—it was that they were attorneys general. As Rice took his seat, Golden, Wachtell, Carlton, and Koplow were aware that this guy with the shaggy hair and snaggle-toothed grin who played Reba McEntire on his office boom box spoke for almost half of the top state law enforcement officers in the nation, who in turn represented 134 million American citizens.

Rice was backed up by Edward Westbrook, from Ness, Motley. Opposite them were four negotiators for the industry, three of whom would be at every important meeting from that day forward. One was J. Philip Carlton, a former North Carolina Supreme Court judge who resigned in disgrace over an influence-peddling scheme but had close ties both to North Carolina governor Jim Hunt and the Clinton White House. "The Judge" ran a firm that mediated disputes for major corporations and was the only negotiator who spoke for the entire industry.

Representing Philip Morris were Meyer Koplow and Herbert Wachtell, at whose New York offices Rice had spent months negotiating a major asbestos settlement. Koplow was an Orthodox Jew, and negotiating schedules tended to be built around his religious observances. He was a precise and circumspect man, a conciliator who buffered the acerbic Wachtell, leader of the Philip Morris team in the ABC libel suit. Wachtell was given to saber rattling. His negotiating style, Rice liked to say, was "fix my problem and screw your problem."

The other negotiator was Arthur Golden. He and R. J. Reynolds's CEO, Steven Goldstone, had gone to law school together, rose to partnerships together at the Wall Street firm of Davis, Polk & Wardwell, and remained close friends.

Wachtell and Carlton did most of the talking. They underlined that they had full authority from the highest levels of the industry to negotiate.

"We think," said Herb Wachtell, "that there is a window of opportunity here, and it's a historic one. And we know that to make it happen there are going to have to be concessions on our part."

Rice said that if Wachtell and his people were serious, they had better move fast, because Mississippi's trial was set for July. The industry would need to have their top executives involved to get the attention of the AGs.

"You'll need to convince us that the people you're bringing don't want to ban the product, because we can't live with that," Wachtell replied.

Rice could see that the industry was already thinking of a comprehensive package, including Food and Drug Administration jurisdiction and restrictions on the right to sue, all of which implied an act of Congress. *Wow*, he thought. *Where is this going?*

WHILE THE ATTORNEYS GENERAL TRIED TO NEGOTIATE THEIR way out of tobacco litigation, Cliff Douglas was digging his way into it. He was appointed co-counsel in the Mississippi state suit, assisting with the deposition of whistle-blowers like William Farone, former director of applied research at Philip Morris. And he continued to work with the *Castano* lawyers.

Motley thought Douglas's legal experience too slight for him to play a major role in trial preparation, such as taking depositions. Indeed, Douglas had virtually no hands-on courtroom background.

Motley tended to see Douglas as a bit starry eyed, sort of a precocious kid.

"You know more," Motley told Douglas during a night of heavy

drinking in New York after a deposition at which they had both appeared. "But I'm the man."

That became a running joke between Martha and her husband.
Douglas would come in, all sweaty from digging in the garden or
some other manual task.

"You're the man," Martha would say.

"No, but I know more," Douglas would reply.

Nevertheless, Motley wanted to employ Douglas's expertise on
nicotine manipulation, and an opportunity soon arose when Motley
got a court order in the Mississippi state suit for Philip Morris
to produce the so-called "ultra-sensitive/trade secret" Philip Morris documents that had been turned over to ABC during the libel
suit.

The "UTS" documents were considered the case's most incisive
discovery, and were still under seal when Douglas went to
Pascagoula in February 1997 to sift through them.

He browsed the documents in the former Ritz Theater, a pink
building with a gaudy sign that Philip Morris was using as a trial
headquarters. Due to Douglas's activist history, a "baby-sitter" sat
three feet away to make sure he didn't make notes or copies. By the
second day, the baby-sitter wasn't paying much attention, and Douglas began scribbling.

Some of what he read dealt with what Philip Morris did with
hundreds of thousands of pounds of nicotine-laced tobacco stems,
a waste product from a denicotinized cigarette Philip Morris made
in the late eighties called Next. Next was a dismal commercial failure, and after spending $300 million on it, PM was stuck with the
nicotine they had sucked out of Next's tobacco. So they soaked tobacco stems, which are low in nicotine, in the nicotine, making
something called "ART stems," or alkaloid-reduced tobacco stems.

No one at *Day One* ever saw this material, which was returned
to Philip Morris once the libel case was settled.

Given Herb Wachtell's belligerent questioning at his deposition,
Douglas now experienced an overwhelming sense of vindication.
The documents told how stems were soaked in nicotine in special
silos at the Next manufacturing plant, packed into hogsheads,
trucked to other plants, and blended into test versions of Benson &
Hedges and Marlboro cigarettes. Consumer panels rated the cigarettes for taste, and the research department tried to determine if

cigarettes prepared from the stems gave a different drug or sensory impact than other forms of tobacco.

Philip Morris, however, had told federal investigators that all the nicotine from Next had been thrown out.

If a jury had seen what he was reading, Douglas felt certain ABC would have been exonerated. These memos were talking about adding nicotine from an outside source—namely the Next process—to stems and putting them in cigarettes, exactly what Philip Morris had forced ABC to apologize for saying.

Since the memos remained under seal, Douglas couldn't share this information freely. All he could do when he got back to the hotel was prepare a detailed memo for Ness, Motley and the other attorneys in the case that was a road map for what to ask for. Then he called Martha.

"I've seen stuff that's pretty damned incredible," said Douglas.

ALTHOUGH HIS CASE AGAINST THE INDUSTRY WAS LESS than fully formed, by the end of March 1997, a fully rested Motley itched to try it out on a jury.

He discussed the idea with Jeff Wigand during his frequent visits to River House, the smaller of Motley's two Charleston homes, where he and Motley talked tobacco, watched basketball games, and played with Motley's new bichon puppies, Chase and Catch.

There were occasional bursts of insults.

"You're a fucking Ph.D. and you can't run the VCR?" laughed Motley as Wigand fumbled with the remote control.

"It's your house, so it's probably broken anyway," said Wigand. "You bought the most expensive one. *And* it doesn't work."

"If *you're* in my house, it's probably booby-trapped," said Motley.

"If they were going to booby-trap your house, it'd be in the liquor cabinet," Wigand shot back.

Wigand was actually thinking of moving to Charleston from Louisville, where an angry tobacco supporter menaced him at an office supply store, and where several times after the *60 Minutes* debacle someone on the street yelled, "Hey, mother*fucker!*"

Motley encouraged him to move, to start a new life. Wigand encouraged Motley to get into a tobacco trial as soon as possible.

Motley decided to team up with Norwood Wilner, who had won

his first tobacco contest in August 1996, a verdict that made head-lines as far away as Sweden and helped convince the industry to start its peace process. Motley would partner Wilner in his next case, *Connor vs. R. J. Reynolds*, to begin April 7.

Dozens of reporters who had worked the Liggett story began ar-riving in Jacksonville, including Keith Summa of ABC News and NBC's Bob Kur, whose Liggett scoop the night before the settle-ment ruined the maiden voyage of Motley's Air Force.

They found an unglamorous family involved in an unglamorous lawsuit in unglamorous Jacksonville, a humid place of glass sky-scrapers surrounded by sandy sprawl and diced up by brown rivers that wind off into swamp.

Jean Faye Connor's family was working class. Almost everybody they knew smoked, and so did they. As a small child, Jean Faye would stand in front of a mirror with a pencil, puffing languidly in the style of fifties movie stars. There is nothing very remarkable in her story, except that she eloped when she was seventeen, by which time she had graduated from the mirror to real life.

After thirty years of three packs a day, Jean Faye discovered a mysterious lump on her neck, which she showed to her younger sis-ter, Dana Raulerson, at lunch one afternoon. Somehow, Dana knew right away Jean Faye had cancer. Tests were done, a very advanced cancer found, and she was given six months to live. She actually lived longer, over two years, on a regimen of toxic chemicals and ra-diation. Dana helped take care of Jean as death approached.

"Jean was on oxygen at this point. But what would happen is she would get these attacks where she couldn't breathe very well, even with oxygen. She would get really scared and she would think that the oxygen wasn't on and I would have to show her it was. She would get so anxious that she would make her breathing even worse. I would sit on the couch with her and I would rock her and hold her real close to my chest and say, 'Breathe with me.' And I would breathe at a real slow and paced rate to help her calm down, to help her get into not hyperventilating, into normal breathing again.

"Then she got to a place where she couldn't swallow because of the cancer. I knew, I mean, she was dying. She had turned in-ward. The last time she had spoken was the day before. She had an anxiety attack and got scared. At this point she was in a hospital bed that had been brought into the apartment, and we were having a change. We had some diapers and things underneath her.

"The last thing I remember my sister saying was, we were changing her diaper and I said, 'Jean, you're just going to have to cooperate.'

"She was laying there like deadweight. So here's this little, bitty, nothing of a person, because my sister was small to begin with, and now she was almost *no* weight. I said, 'Jean Faye, you're going to have to cooperate. You don't have a big ass anymore, but I still can't pick you up.'

"And she picked up her hand and she said, 'You better watch out what you say.' She still had that fight in her. Like, 'I'm still the big sister. So watch out what you say.' And I said 'I know, I know.'"

A few nights later, Dana, a recovering alcoholic, left her sister's side to attend an Alcoholics Anonymous meeting. Jean Faye seemed to be resting comfortably, her children spread all over the little house. When she returned two hours later, Jean had drifted off to death, breathing lightly, even at the end.

IN THE LIVING ROOM OF THE CELEBRITY SUITE AT THE Jacksonville Hilton was a long wooden table, heaped with what looked like party favors for a chain-smokers' dinner dance. There were candy bars, sodas, potato chips, cans of pudding, cookies, and a clear plastic garbage bag filled with packs of cigarettes.

Ron Motley was in the bedroom, two hours from entering the national spotlight in his first tobacco trial, along with Woody Wilner, who had stung Brown & Williamson for $750,000 in the *Carter* case, his very first tobacco suit. When Motley decided to make *Connor* a practice run for his own cases, Wilner had been only too happy to have him.

Motley strode into the living room, where his staff was working over a black spiral notebook, the script for the opening. In it were the major points he would cover in large type, and next to that a column of film clips, charts, and other visual aids.

"You ever see that movie, *Patton*," he said to no one in particular, "where Patton's on the battlefield and he says, 'God help me, I love it'?"

No one replied. Motley walked back out.

In the plastic bag were Salems and Winstons, which Jean Connor smoked for over thirty years until she died at forty-nine. Some of the other stuff on the table would figure in Motley's opening statement, which was two hours away, but only Motley knew how. He kept having new ideas.

He materialized again.

"Okay, now I want you to figure out our ten best exhibits," he told Laura Norris, a senior paralegal.

"I want the one on doubt. Doubt and controversy. I'm going to let you pick 'em. Okay? How 'bout—Rodgman, of course. But just the page that's the best."

Wilner and Motley were relying heavily on memos by former R. J. Reynolds scientists Alan Rodgman and Claude Teague, Jr., to support their key allegation, which was that Reynolds, like the other companies, hid damaging research about cigarettes, especially in the fifties, when it could have made a critical difference.

By the time *Connor* was ready for trial, Wilner had filed over one hundred individual smoker's suits in Jacksonville, scoffing at the conventional wisdom that they were unwinnable. Wilner's brilliant victory in his first case seemed to prove his theory, which was that the companies had psyched out the plaintiffs' lawyers by crushing them in the early contests, artificially choking off the flow of suits. He believed that if you kept trying cases, the industry would lose enough of them to abandon its scorched earth policy and begin settling.

All of which was fine, except that prior to *Carter*, not only had Wilner never tried a tobacco case, no one could remember the last time he'd sued over a defective product. The fact was that while Wilner was a gifted litigator, he made his mark defending asbestos companies.

Wilner knew it made eminent sense for his eight-lawyer firm to be backed up by the Ness, Motley colossus and its nationwide tobacco discovery. And so in late March, an advance team was dispatched from Charleston to set up a war room at the Hilton, just across the St. John's River from the Duval County Courthouse and the Omni Hotel, where Jones, Day, Reavis & Pogue, the R. J.

Reynolds lawyers, had rented a floor. Motley brought not only Jodi Flowers but Charles Patrick and Kim Vroon, a tall, cheerful Chicagoan. The war room was manned by six secretaries and paralegals. Motley installed himself in the Celebrity Suite. The Marines had landed.

Wilner and Motley got along fine, though they had little in common. Where Motley was hyperactive, Wilner was earthbound, with an easy laugh. He had grown up in an upper-middle-class Jewish home in Miami, a background more northern than southern, and now lived in a modest ranch-style house on the Ortega River.

Six foot one and solidly built, Wilner had gone to Yale, later getting a master's in engineering to go with his law degree. He loved technical subjects and had a bit of the high school science teacher in him. You might be standing around waiting for a flight at an airport and you'd get a pop quiz: So, what's the engine configuration on a Boeing 737? On an Airbus 300? Good. An MD-80?

It was only a few blocks from the Duval County Courthouse to the modern brown two-story building that houses Spohrer, Wilner, Maxwell, Maciejewski & Stanford, close enough so that on warm days Wilner rode to court on a pink bike with a white basket. Nothing fancy about Woody Wilner. He didn't believe in surveying juries after a trial to see what had gotten through. He didn't think much of jury consultants. He wasn't particularly high on polling or focus groups. "We're just not going to worry about that" was a stock answer on such topics.

Wilner's lack of worry sometimes worried Motley. Especially when, days before trial, Circuit Court Judge Bernard Nachman severely limited what they could tell the jury about the industry's conduct.

Nachman's ruling dealt with the critical issue of preemption. The 1969 Federal Cigarette Labeling and Advertising Act placed the words "Warning: The Surgeon General has determined that cigarette smoking is dangerous to your health" on every pack, and the Supreme Court later ruled that Congress considered that to be all the companies needed to say from 1969 onward about smoking's hazards. In its 1992 decision in *Cipollone,* the high court said sick smokers could still sue, but were preempted from claiming the industry failed to warn them after 1969.

Naturally, tobacco lobbyists had helped draft the 1969 bill. David Hardy considered it his crowning achievement. He knew warning labels were the best thing that could happen to tobacco. In return for fourteen little words, the industry could argue it was absolved for whatever it did to its customers after 1969.

The *Cipollone* decision meant that for practical purposes, only those who got hooked before the law took effect could sue. That limited the pool of litigants to a group that, due largely to the product they were suing over, would die off completely in the foreseeable future.

Trial courts often felt compelled to draw puzzling boundaries between pre- and post-1969 corporate activities, which was exactly what Nachman did, chopping out the entire post-1969 fraud case. And there were other reasons to believe Wilner would not repeat his triumph in the *Carter* case. Unlike Grady Carter, who made many failed attempts to give up cigarettes, Jean Connor quit the first time she tried, making it hard to get a jury to believe she was addicted to nicotine.

Then, too, Motley had long viewed Jacksonville as a fundamentally evil place for a tobacco lawsuit. Ness, Motley focus groups showed that a cigarette lawsuit, with its opaque scientific and legal issues, would do better in Ph.D.-rich Palm Beach than blue-collar Jacksonville. Those results helped convince the Florida attorney general's office to file its Medicaid action in Palm Beach. But Jean Connor had lived, died, and would sue in north Florida.

Wilner and Motley split up the trial, with Motley handling the truncated conspiracy and fraud case while Wilner educated the jury on the science of lung cancer. They were also splitting the two hours allotted per side for opening arguments, but Motley didn't believe Wilner would finish on time.

"Please save me forty-five minutes, Woody," he said, slicking back his black hair with his fingers in the bathroom of the Celebrity Suite.

What about exhibits for the opening? Motley demanded.

"Well, we've got both the Tobacco Institute ads. The 'Cigarette Controversy' blowup," said Jodi Flowers, Motley's R. J. Reynolds expert.

"What about the controversy documents—the 'we can create controversy every darn day of the week'?" asked Motley. "I like that."

"Frank Colby," said Flowers, naming the RJR scientist who wrote it.

"Who said we manufacture controversy?" Motley asked. "'Doubt's our product.'"

Flowers shook her head. "That's Philip Morris."

"Shoot!" said Motley.

"Well, you don't like 'We can maintain controversy every darned day of the week'?" Flowers retorted. "That's catchy."

"I want something strong on nicotine. Pick the strongest nicotine one," said Motley.

"How about 'We are a highly ritualized segment of the pharmaceutical industry'?" said Flowers, quoting a 1972 memo by researcher Claude Teague.

Motley said he wanted to take a pack of Salems, tear it open, take out a cigarette, hold it up. Then he would tell the jury that they had to solve a mystery—what's in the smoke? There wasn't anything listed on the pack to help them. Now, why was that? he would ask. He would compare Salems to cookies manufactured by RJR Nabisco, corporate parent of Reynolds Tobacco. Well, gosh, Snackwells list their ingredients, he would say. No secrets there. Everyone started rummaging through the packages on the table.

"I've got baby food locked in my trunk," said Kim Vroon. "You want some baby food?"

Jodi Flowers began reading from a box of cookies: "Niacin, iron, thiamine mononitrate."

"Ingredients!" barked Motley.

"Sugar," said Flowers.

"Sugaaaaar!" said Motley in a spooky voice. "Cocoa! Do not burn, will kill you!"

Motley grilled the room about the *Kueper* case, another lawsuit against Reynolds successfully defended by Paul Crist, the head lawyer in *Connor*.

"Crist does an excellent job of saying, 'This is a diversion,'" said Theresa Zagnoli, Motley's jury consultant, an energetic dark-haired Iowan. "Their thing will be 'What does this have to do with Jean Connor?' And I think what they'll do is, they'll just beat that to death. What you can do to easily take charge is say, 'Everything has to do with Jean Connor.'"

"Yeah," said Motley.

"The other thing is, go slow. You know a lot, you can bury the jury in all this *stuff*. So, slow and easy. Okay?" said Zagnoli. "So I want you to do two things."

"Okay," said Motley.

He turned to face the group around the table. "Y'all want to go eat, girls? Y'all want to go eat? Kimmy?" Most of the room went down to the Hilton's buffet. Motley wolfed down barbecued chicken and iced tea. When they came back up, Zagnoli was on the phone, looking a bit haggard.

Shouted Motley from the bedroom, "Help me find my boots. I'm kicking ass."

Someone went to help him. There was some giggling. Motley emerged, wearing black ostrich-skin boots to go with his dark blue suit, and it was quiet. "Let's go," Motley said.

"Ready?" he said to Zagnoli. The phone rang again.

She made a face.

"What's wrong?" Motley asked.

"Nothing," she said, grabbing the receiver. Motley started walking out. The entourage followed. Then he stepped back in. After years together, Theresa Zagnoli was like a younger sister to Motley. He kept waiting, looking at her as she cradled the phone against her shoulder.

"You sure you're okay?" he said finally.

"I'm fine!" she said, exasperated. "Go! Do your thing. I'm fine. Go do what you do."

They kissed.

"I love you," said Motley.

"I love you, too," said Zagnoli.

Then he was in the hall.

SHARING THE HARD, WOODEN BENCHES OF COURTROOM Number Two with the media, the financial analysts, and the Connor family was a trial complement of thirty tobacco lawyers, most on the right of the shallow spectators' section, including a couple from Shook, Hardy & Bacon, the strategic nerve center. Others sat beside Dan Donahue, Reynolds's deputy general counsel, at a long table arranged perpendicular to the defense table.

Donahue scrutinized a photograph accompanying a newspaper

article on Merrell Williams while another tobacco lawyer looked over his shoulder.

"He looks like a little saint," said Donahue with contempt. "All he needs is a little sunlight coming through."

Wilner began his opening statement. It took him about fifteen minutes to arrive at one of his central arguments, that Jean Connor used cigarettes as intended and died as a consequence, that "there is no instruction on the product that says, 'Don't smoke more than this.'"

"Objection," said Reynolds's Paul Crist. "Preempted."

Wilner was trying to talk about warnings, he said. Judge Nachman sustained the objection. Within minutes there were more objections, and before long, Crist was cutting into Wilner's opening virtually at will.

Worse, Wilner seemed to irritate Nachman beyond any rational measure. When Wilner began explaining negligence, Nachman scolded him for instructing the jury on the law. Four sustained objections later, Nachman told Wilner he "disliked being interrupted," then embarrassed him by explaining how to do an opening statement.

By the time Wilner sat down an hour later, his presentation had been perforated over twenty times by objections, and half of his exhibits had to be yanked off the easel. More important, if it kept up like this, Nachman's evident contempt for Wilner almost had to rub off on the jurors.

Motley couldn't believe it. He had never seen a lawyer ripped into like that during an opening. He mentally revised his own statement to excise anything that might draw Nachman's ire.

So much for the script.

"Now, R. J. Reynolds is a drug company," said Motley, walking back and forth, "and I'm going to prove it to you. They may also be a tobacco company, but they are a drug company. They sell a drug called nicotine and they sell it in cigarettes. They sold it to Jean Connor."

There were objections, but few were sustained. Motley seemed to have charmed Nachman, clowning with the bow-tied judge during jury selection. And if Nachman often deferred to Crist and his team of tobacco heavyweights, he also knew Motley was a legendary figure in tort law. *Connor* was a punitive damages case, and one of the major precedents in punitive damages was *Janssens*, Motley's first asbestos verdict, which he had won in this same Duval County Courthouse in 1981.

It didn't hurt that when Motley had earlier needed a copy of the *Janssens* decision brought to Nachman's chambers, it was delivered by Evan Yegelwel, a lawyer friend of Motley's who happened to go to Nachman's synagogue.

Nor could it hurt that Yegelwel sat in the front row throughout Motley's opening.

Motley told the jury how the conspiracy was hatched at the Plaza Hotel in December 1953, and how the first conspiratorial act was to issue the "Frank Statement," announcing in hundreds of newspapers that the newly created Tobacco Industry Research Committee, later the Council for Tobacco Research, would spare no expense to penetrate the smoking and lung cancer "mystery."

"I will prove that R. J. Reynolds launched a campaign to create doubt and controversy so that cigarette smokers could feed their state of denial," said Motley. Then he read from the "Frank Statement":

"'We accept an interest in people's health as a basic responsibility, paramount to every other consideration of our business. We believe the products we make are not injurious to health.'"

He tore open a pack of Salems, but, absurdly, had to ask the jury to pretend it was a 1969 pack to get around Crist's preemption objections. He mentioned a couple of documents and company scientists, scribbled the names of a few carcinogens on butcher paper, and it was over. Seventy-five percent improvised, it was mostly an exercise in damage control after Wilner's disastrous beginning.

Then Paul Crist stood up, a graying, rumpled midwesterner. Far from being improvised, what he said drew on forty years of collective tobacco trial experience. Jean Connor's cancer is *not* of a type associated with smoking, Crist said. There's no way of knowing if it started in the lung because the plaintiff didn't bother to do an autopsy. And anyway, Jean Connor was fully warned. She even admitted that she knew cigarette ads were taken off of television because it was a hazardous product.

Over and over, Crist's gruff, deliberate voice spoke what seemed like common sense. How addictive can cigarettes be if fifty million people have quit, one of them Jean Connor, who did it on her first try? Where is the withdrawal, the intoxication, the ODs?

"I think when the day is done that you will conclude that smoking behavior is what smoking behavior is, and I think that you will conclude that labels don't change the nature of smoking behavior," said Crist. "It remains what it is. Those of you that smoke, those of you that know smokers know what it is and you know that it can be difficult for people to quit."

On to "this question of whether or not cigarette smoking causes lung cancer." Inhalation studies have never produced cancer in animals, Crist said, a bald untruth. He dwelt on the 1964 Surgeon General's Report as though it were the last word on cigarettes and disease, and asserted that it was merely the Surgeon General's "judgment" that cigarettes cause cancer.

And, no, Crist said, Reynolds didn't market to children. Yes, Winston ads appeared on *The Flintstones,* but he showed the jury newspaper clippings billing the show as "an adult-oriented" cartoon.

Crist sat down.

It was masterful. Every base had been touched. And even though his two-hour statement was packed with distortions, it rested on a feather bed of platitudes about how smoking just plain isn't something people should sue about, because *everyone knows you shouldn't smoke.*

The next day, Wilner's chief medical and scientific witness, Dr. Allen Feingold, did little to right the balance.

Motley had bumped into Feingold in asbestos trials and found him stubborn and convincing. But in tobacco, Feingold's expertise came primarily from wide reading and the fact that as a pulmonary surgeon and chief of medicine at South Miami Hospital, he saw a steady stream of lung cancer victims. A native Canadian, Feingold was a curly-haired, bearded, little Jewish man with what probably sounded to Jacksonvilleans like an upper-crust northern accent. Wilner and Feingold were best friends, having worked together frequently in defense of asbestos cases.

Wilner offered Feingold as an expert on both lung cancer and addiction, though he had no research credentials in either. Feingold testified for almost four days on the history of the lung cancer epidemic in the United States, how carcinogens attack the lung, how nicotine acts on the brain. He recounted all the major studies in smoking and health and was thorough to the point of inducing stupor. He brought along boxes of books and studies, which piled up around him, until his small bearded form began to disappear.

Not so his resonant baritone. Indeed, Feingold could not seem to stop talking, even when the judge told him to please stay out of arguments between Crist and Wilner.

On Friday, Motley flew home to Charleston to meet with his staff and prepare Dr. Victor Roggli, a pathologist with whom Motley had worked on a number of asbestos cases.

"I am singularly unimpressed with Allen Feingold," he told Ann Ritter upon arriving. "He's just too argumentative."

The Monday following opening arguments was Feingold's last full day of direct testimony. Afterward, Motley, Wilner, and Feingold strolled back from court to Wilner's firm, enjoying the hot sunny afternoon. They sat around Wilner's roomy office preparing for the next day.

"Does Wynder '50 and Doll and Hill '50. Does the mouse-paint and then goes into, right after the mouse-paint, we go into the 'Frank Statement,'" said Wilner, narrating how Feingold would handle the lung cancer studies, including Ernst Wynder's 1953 experiment that produced tumors by painting mice with tar.

After a bit more of this, a restless Motley got ready to leave.

Feingold stepped in front of him.

"What about cross, Ron Motley? What do you see there? They'll ask weird details, right?" asked Feingold, even though Motley had already briefed him on what to expect in cross-examination.

"I mean, the big picture would be, you hurt the man, that's what I'd do. I'd talk about, you don't have any time for your patients 'cause you're always testifying. He's probably got everything you ever said in a deposition. And he'll pick nits," said Motley.

"Nitpicking," said Feingold.

"You ain't got nothing to worry about," Motley reassured him. "Just stay calm. There's nothing he can do to you. He'll have every deposition that you've ever given in these cases, but you've been consistent. I mean, goddamn, that's what I hated about you! You're always fucking consistent."

Feingold laughed.

"Consistently wrong. But you were consistent," said Motley.

He apologized that he would have to miss court the next day to take a deposition in Baltimore for the Florida AG's case. He shook hands with Wilner and Feingold and left.

The next day, to no one's surprise, Feingold did not finish his direct testimony in the morning, but was still sawing away until well past three in the afternoon. By then, Paul Crist, a smoker who chewed gum at the defense table, was chewing twice as fast, as though he'd rather be chewing on Feingold's throat.

As soon as his turn came, Crist sprang up, and began shredding Feingold's professional credentials as a smoking and health expert, his lack of formal background in toxicology, pathology, oncology, cardiology, biochemistry.

"The fact of the matter is, Dr. Feingold, that your primary medical specialty is testifying as an expert witness in lawsuits, isn't it?" said Crist.

No, said Feingold, though he acknowledged he had been listed as an expert in thousands of asbestos cases, earning over $2.5 million and spending a thousand hours a year on them.

Crist threw out a series of essentially rhetorical questions. Didn't Feingold really believe that quitting smoking was no more difficult than losing weight? Wasn't it true that most people smoke the same number of cigarettes over a period of many years, unlike addictive drugs that produce tolerance and require escalating doses? Didn't he agree that since the 1964 Surgeon General's Report, which did not find nicotine to be addictive, and the 1988 report, which did, the main element that changed was the definition of addiction, and that the '64 definition is still considered the "classic" definition and still valid?

Feingold gave a firm no to each.

Then Crist pulled out a thick sheaf of paper.

Did Feingold remember appearing in an asbestos case called *Colt* v. *Armstrong* in Dade County, Florida?

No.

"Let me show you, Dr. Feingold, a copy of a transcript of a deposition of May 13, 1992, of I. A. Feingold, M.D. That's you?"

"Yes," said Feingold warily.

"Dr. Feingold, let me ask you if you remember giving these answers to these questions. 'Question: Do you think cigarette smoking is an addictive disease? Answer: That is a very interesting topic,'" Crist read.

"'Cigarette smoking is not exactly addictive. The classical definition of an addictive substance is still valid in that it is a substance which is associated with the development of tolerance,'" Crist continued.

"'Cigarette smoke does not have that feature. A great majority of people smoke a fixed number of cigarettes over a great many years, hence do not have any tolerance component to their behavior.

"'Question: Do you think for the average adult smoker who's smoked many years that the choice to continue smoking is less of a free choice?'" read Crist.

"'Answer: In most patients, in almost all people who continue to smoke today, there is a very important psychological reason why they do so and why they decide to do so every day. It is very much a matter of—*just like losing weight*. It's a matter of *free choice*, but not all people can accomplish it. It is very much a matter of free choice.'"

Crist clapped the document shut and dropped it on the table.

"Did you give those answers to those questions on May 13, 1992, Dr. Feingold?" he snapped.

"I did," Feingold said.

"And, Dr. Feingold, that's after you had already been involved in learning about this for probably a decade?"

"That's correct."

And hadn't Feingold himself smoked until he was twenty-nine? Yes, he had.

"And with respect to your smoking, Dr. Feingold, you made the decision to quit smoking and you did so, didn't you?" asked Crist.

"Absolutely," said the plaintiff's addiction expert. "I made the decision and I did so."

"Your Honor, this would be a good time to break for the evening," said Crist.

By then, most reporters had left. And to the extent that he was still visible from behind his wall of books, the jury seemed to be avoiding eye contact with Dr. Allen Feingold.

THAT NIGHT, GROUPS OF REPORTERS AT THE OMNI HOTEL sat up late, discussing the trial. Was the plaintiff's case running off the rails already? Most didn't think so, although there was broad agreement Feingold had been an unmitigated disaster.

At about two A.M., Carrick Mollenkamp, a correspondent for the financial wire service Bloomberg News, rang the room of ABC's Keith Summa.

Bloomberg's London bureau had picked up an early edition of a *Wall Street Journal* article that said secret "global settlement" negotiations had been under way for two weeks. These were unprecedented face-to-face talks between the cigarette companies and the attorneys general of several states, led by Mississippi's Mike Moore. The *Journal* piece said hundreds of billions of dollars in restitution were under discussion, along with what sounded like an industry-friendly compromise on Food and Drug Administration jurisdiction over cigarettes. Disturbingly, the two sides were said to be moving not only toward settling the state Medicaid actions, but protecting Big Tobacco from all smoking and health lawsuits.

Summa immediately trotted down the hall to Mollenkamp's room and read the story on the Bloomberg reporter's laptop while Mollenkamp, chain-smoking and sipping coffee, made calls, but came up empty at such a late hour. He sent e-mails and a short dispatch to his editors. Summa ducked back to his room but had no luck with ABC's Washington bureau and went back to tell Mollenkamp.

"I'm going to have to go out there," said Mollenkamp. "I've got to put some meat on the bones."

There meant Tyson's Corner, Virginia, a nondescript suburban corner of greater Washington where the negotiators, according to the *Journal*, were holed up in a couple of hotels. Mollenkamp packed and grabbed the first flight out early that morning.

By nine A.M., the media room at the Duval County Courthouse, a small cinder-block cave equipped for the giant *Connor* press corps with a TV feed from Courtroom Two and folding tables for laptop computers, was buzzing about the global story. Attorney General Mike Moore issued a bland communiqué confirming the talks, but said little else.

None of this was news to Motley, who had since learned both of Joe Rice's initial meeting with the industry and some even more significant sit-downs that followed it. Joe Rice, however, told his partner little about day-to-day events so Motley could focus on getting the state suits ready for trial.

The secret, obviously, was out. Reporters and camera crews showed up in Tyson's Corner and became a feature of the negotiating process from then on. But aside from Mollenkamp, the other reporters in Jacksonville stayed with the trial, which remained hot. *Summa*, for instance, had gotten pieces about the opening statements on both *World News Tonight* with Peter Jennings and *Nightline*.

Crist spent the day cross-examining Feingold. The next morning, Motley put on his science expert, Dr. Victor Roggli, a pathologist at Duke University medical school.

Roggli was a southerner with impeccable credentials, and through him Motley began to lay out his cover-up case. The major evidence was a series of reports by Alan Rodgman and Claude Teague Jr., former senior scientists at Reynolds. Teague wrote a lengthy study, entitled "SURVEY OF CANCER RESEARCH with emphasis upon POSSIBLE CARCINOGENS FROM TOBACCO," in which he noted:

> There appears to be a growing suspicion, or even acceptance, among medical men and cancer researchers that the parallel increase in cigarette consumption and incidence of cancer of the respiratory system is more than coincidence.

Teague's report was a strong sermon indeed from a top company scientist in 1953, a time when Reynolds still ran ads in *Life* magazine showing doctors in lab coats smoking Camels.

When Alan Rodgman, RJR's chief scientist, updated the health picture in 1962, things were immeasurably worse:

> Obviously the amount of evidence accumulated to indict cigarette smoke as a health hazard is overwhelming. The evidence challenging such an indictment is scant.

Rodgman pleaded for biological tests, which Teague had recommended in 1953. Rodgman protested that studies done by Reynolds "remain unpublished because they are concerned with carcinogenic or co-carcinogenic compounds. . . ." How could the company say the case against cigarettes is unproven and yet refuse to own up to results obtained in its own labs? He argued that the risks of being candid were worth taking:

> What would be the effect on this company of not publishing these data now, but being required at some future date to disclose such data, possibly in the unfavorable atmosphere of a lawsuit?

What effect indeed? By the time the plaintiff's case ended on April 23, the jury had heard a great deal about R. J. Reynolds's research. It had learned about work at a company facility nicknamed the "Mouse House" that produced emphysema in cigarette-smoking rabbits in 1969, and of inhalation research with mice, hamsters, and dogs that did in fact produce cancer, including one study sponsored by the Council for Tobacco Research that CTR's lawyers tried to water down.

They saw a spectacular $200,000 Ness, Motley computer animation of cellular DNA under attack by smoke-borne carcinogens, a grainy early-sixties clip of Barney Rubble and Fred Flintstone sneaking out to smoke Winstons behind the house, CAT scans of Jean Connor's chest, and a triptych of freeze-dried lung sections, one mottled gray with cancer cells.

The last image on their TV monitors was of a skeletal Jean Connor, supported by a nurse, shuffling unsteadily down a hospital corridor in a white bathrobe two weeks before she died. The courtroom was silent except for the sound of Jean Connor's feet as her chthonic face bobbed toward the lens.

"The plaintiffs rest, Your Honor," said Greg Maxwell, Wilner's assistant.

THE DEFENSE OPENED WITH DR. DAVID TOWNSHEND, Reynolds's head of product design, who had become the Wyatt Earp of Winston-Salem for helping beat back two other lawsuits with testimony virtually identical to what he would say in *Connor*. It was the heroic story of how Reynolds tried to improve the product despite incomplete knowledge about what it was in cigarettes that was killing people, what Townshend called the "moving target" of the scientific frontier.

Townshend gave a day and a half of cheerful testimony. He flatly denied the company's cigarettes were designed to deliver particular nicotine yields. Although numerous memos made it plain that Reynolds learned how to push up nicotine while holding down tar, Townshend blamed that on wrongheaded public-health officials who thought it might make for less deadly cigarettes.

The sandy-haired Townshend had a kind of yuppie charm that impressed the jury, and words like *deadly* never dirtied his lips. He spoke of smoking and health "issues." At one point, he put up a chart of "Controversial Compounds," which were in fact nitrosamines, benzo-a-pyrene, and other major smoke carcinogens, substances he admitted the company had known of for decades.

Townshend had a seemingly endless supply of colorful graphs and illustrations, prompting Motley to walk into the press room and exclaim, "Dr. Townshend, do you have a chart of your past lives?"

Cross-examination didn't start until past five in the afternoon. Motley waded in, sucking a throat lozenge.

Is doing research and development on health "issues" the right thing to do? he asked.

Townshend allowed that it was.

"Well, is it the right thing to do to tell a half-truth?" asked Motley, to an immediate, sustained, objection.

Townshend had said Reynolds published tar and nicotine numbers in the fifties until forced to stop by the Federal Trade Commission, as though the government had blocked RJR from sharing health information. Over heated objections, Motley now forced him to admit that the FTC intervened because RJR was making misleading claims about tar and nicotine.

Motley asked if Townshend remembered appearing in the *Rogers* trial in Indianapolis in August 1996.

"Do you recall testifying under oath, 'I can't'—talking about yourself—'accept the idea that cigarettes cause cancer'?"

Crist objected indignantly. The lawyers huddled with Nachman. The judge said he didn't see why Motley should be allowed to ask that question.

Motley was flabbergasted.

"It goes to credibility, Judge," he said carefully.

After a day and a half of hearing Townshend talk about his

saintly dedication to a healthier cigarette, the jury might be interested to learn he didn't actually believe the product caused death.

Nachman relented and allowed Motley to try again.

"Doctor, the last question hopefully that I'm going to ask you today: Is it your opinion, as you sit here today," Motley said, "do cigarettes cause cancer, yes or no?"

"Objection, Your Honor," said Crist, claiming the witness "has not been qualified in this area."

Sustained.

"Dr. Townshend, we read to the jury sworn answers from interrogatories of R. J. Reynolds where they denied that cigarettes are a scientific cause of lung cancer. Do you agree or disagree?"

Objection. Sustained.

Motley was furious. He flipped through pages of his yellow pad.

"Have you ever provided an opinion under oath as to that?" he asked.

"Objection, Your Honor. I think it's irrelevant," Crist shot back.

"No, it's not irrelevant," said Nachman.

Thank you, Lord, thought Motley.

He turned to the jury.

"Have you ever offered an opinion in a court of law under oath as to whether or not cigarettes cause lung cancer?" he said.

"I've offered my personal opinion under oath," Townshend said quickly.

More objections. Nachman couldn't seem to make up his mind what to do. Finally, Motley was allowed to read from the transcript of the *Rogers* trial in Indianapolis:

"'Would you agree with me, sir'—this is the question—'that if a product causes cancer, just accept that hypothesis for a moment, that it causes cancer, and is designed and intended for human consumption or inhalation, that would be a dangerous product?'

"Your answer was," Motley continued, "'I can't accept the idea that cigarettes cause cancer. I don't know that. And it may be that cigarettes cause cancer, but scientifically, I don't believe it has been shown scientifically that cigarettes cause cancer.' That's the end of your answer.

"The question is: Did you give that answer under oath to the question I asked," Motley demanded. "Yes or no?"

"I believe I probably did, because that answer is consistent with—"

"All I asked you was yes or no," said Motley.

No further questions for today, Motley said wearily, and sat.

Everyone filed out of the courtroom except Motley, Wilner, and their staffs. Still steaming over his arcane struggle with Townshend, Motley didn't move from his seat for the next hour, writing page after page of notes.

There was a palpable sense of frustration.

Woody Wilner walked about the chamber saying, "Anybody know the answer?"

"Anybody have a clue?" piped up Motley.

"Does anybody know the answer to this question 'Do cigarettes cause cancer?' I don't know," said Wilner. "Nobody knows. It's a mystery! Everything's a mystery when it comes to cigarettes."

"We just don't know much about it," said Wilner. "He's the head designer at R. J. Reynolds. He's Numero Uno. He's the Big Cahuna. And he doesn't know whether the product causes cancer. Not only doesn't he know—*he's not even qualified to answer the question.*" Wilner walked in circles, waving his arms. People laughed.

"Who *is*? Is there someone *bigger than you*? We go up to him and say 'Is there someone more *important* than you we need to ask? Let's bring him down. *Smarter* than you? Well, did Dr. Rodgman know the answer? The fabled Dr. Rodgman.'"

"He's their top guy and he doesn't know the answer. That's an incredible admission," said Wilner.

"I know it is," said Motley.

Wilner continued muttering as Motley and his people worked.

"We've taken a survey and most of 'em *want* to get cancer." He ambled back and forth. "They *like* their cancer. Don't take it away from them."

Townshend would be by far Reynolds's most important witness, Motley and Wilner agreed, and a frontal assault on this slick, likable expert might put the case away for the plaintiffs. So the next morning, Motley turned up the heat. In particular, he wanted to end the shadow dancing around words like *risk* and *health issues.* He wanted to unmask Townshend for the jury, to show them not

Crist's dedicated scientist but a charlatan, a company man who denied obvious medical truth.

Jodi Flowers and Kim Vroon had labored into the night, locating Townshend's euphemisms so Motley could strip them away.

Townshend had told Crist he was on a Canadian expert committee on making smoke less toxic, a panel that he said "focused on product modification and how product modification might reduce harm."

Did he mean harm to humans? Motley asked.

"Specifically, talking about harm reduction to smokers, because cigarette smoking certainly is a risk factor for a number of diseases," said Townshend.

"No, sir, I'm not talking about a risk factor. You used the word *harm*," said Motley.

"And that is what I meant by the word *harm*."

"When you use the word *harm*, Dr. Townshend, do you concede that cigarette smoking has harmed at least one human being?"

"Mr. Motley . . ." sighed Townshend, shaking his head.

"Judge, can I have an instruction for him to answer that question, please?" said Motley.

"Answer the questions put to you, sir," Nachman said.

The court reporter read the question back.

"Your answer?" Motley asked.

"I don't know," said Townshend.

"You don't know, Dr. Townshend," said Motley grimly, looking at the jury. They seemed vaguely interested, but were otherwise impossible to read.

Crist and Townshend had harped on how the carcinogen benzo-*a*-pyrene is not only in cigarettes, but in other combustion products such as the char on a broiled steak or diesel exhaust. Motley got Townshend to admit that only tobacco products have tobacco-specific nitrosamines, or TSNAs—highly dangerous, lung-specific carcinogens known to produce cancer cells in lung tissue. TSNAs, Townshend reluctantly acknowledged, were in the Salems and Winstons Jean Connor smoked, and this fact was known to the company in the seventies.

Townshend had also crowed about how over a forty-year period Reynolds's crack scientists sharply decreased tar and nicotine levels, as determined by FTC tests. Under prodding, he now admitted that

the FTC announced in 1994 that its testing method, which was borrowed from the industry, was unreliable and the numbers worthless.

Motley summed up.

"You testified about all the work that Reynolds has done in response to what you said were health claims or hypotheses," he said,
a chart mapping lung cancer deaths nearby.

"But between 1960, when it was reported there were thirty-five
thousand deaths, and 1997, where there's a hundred seventy thousand deaths—it didn't do much good, did it?"

"I'm not sure I understand your question to me," Townshend
began, "you mean as a chemist—"

"That's a big increase," Motley said.

"Are you asking me is the number difference—"

"Yes, sir."

"Whether it's large?"

"Yes, sir."

"The number difference is large."

A break was called for lunch.

"We kicked their dicks in the dirt," said Motley buoyantly as he
clumped down the fire stairs with a couple of reporters and Jodi
Flowers.

He heard Carrick Mollenkamp shouting from the landing
above: "Hey y'all. FDA came down! It just came down!"

Everyone ran back up a few steps.

A federal judge in North Carolina had ruled that the FDA could
regulate cigarettes as nicotine delivery devices, said Mollenkamp.
There were high-fives and yelps of delight.

"Now you can have every fucking expert take the stand and say,
'I agree with the FDA, and here they looked at these same documents the jury's getting and these fucking guys are drug companies,'" Motley said excitedly.

Outside, the air was hot and sticky, but to Motley it seemed like a
beautiful new world was spread out for him there by the St. John's
River.

BY THE END OF APRIL, AS THE DEFENSE WRAPPED UP ITS
case, the press ranks had notably thinned. Some reporters had been

dispatched to cover the global settlement talks, which moved to a different city every few days.

At the very end of the trial, excerpts were read from the deposition of Jean Connor's former husband that perhaps shed a little light on why she didn't try more seriously to quit. After admitting he couldn't remember the dates of his two marriages to Connor, though he noted that "it wasn't a two-week deal or nothing," he confirmed that Jean Faye was a chain-smoker. Then again, he himself smoked up to three and a half packs of cigarettes a day. Not surprisingly, the two didn't criticize each other much on health matters.

When it did come up, it was usually because Jean had done something that winded her and "her lung couldn't hardly breathe all the time, and I heard her say, 'These things are killing me.' And I said, 'Well, light another one.' 'I will as soon as I finish this one.' I said, 'Okay, light another one.'"

Connor's mother remembered Jean Faye watching "those dancers on TV on Saturday or Sunday night with those Lucky Strike cigarettes" during the fifties, when Jean Faye was a little girl. Once, she caught her standing with a pencil in front of the mirror and demanded to know what she was doing. Little sister Dana had spoken up and said, "She's trying to be like those girls on those Lucky Strike commercials and in those ads and billboards."

Dana sat fingering rosary beads during closing arguments. Had it gone well? How could you tell? Two jurors had long since departed, one after being stricken with some kind of attack, the other because of a sick mother-in-law. That left a bare-bones jury of five women, one man and no alternates to decide if Reynolds marketed an unreasonably dangerous product, and if that product killed Dana's sister, Jean. If they believed the company did what it did knowingly, they could assess punitive damages.

Punish Reynolds, Wilner and Motley urged. Send a message. It was a big job they were asking the jury to do. "You can change history," said Motley. But Crist beat the drum of "common sense" one last time. This woman smoked. She didn't have to. He asked them to do a much smaller, easier job: to look at Jean Connor. Implicit in Crist's message was, you know Jean Connor because you *are* Jean Connor, and *you* know you don't have any right to come in here and get money just because you smoked. The jury would have to stretch to get to where Wilner wanted them to go. All they had to do for Crist was look at themselves.

Most of the wayward reporters had returned by the time the verdict came down on May 5, although the atmosphere was less than electric. The thunder of the global talks had nearly drowned out the rather sad case of Jean Connor. There had been a moment when it seemed Jean Faye's death somehow could have changed the world, but the moment passed. In the end, as had happened so many times before, the jury heard enough about Jean Faye to blame her, not enough about Reynolds to hate them. The Connor family lost.

A room had been set aside for post-verdict press conferences, but Dana wouldn't go in until Reynolds's Dan Donahue left. Dana had given no interviews during the trial. Now she spoke for an hour in a cold fury.

"R. J. Reynolds lied under oath," she said under the TV lights. "David Townshend lied under oath."

Motley was ashen, but Wilner refused to admit discouragement and spoke quietly to reporters of his next case. Then he walked outside and could be seen bobbing slowly up Liberty Street in his shirtsleeves, heading back to his office, enjoying the late afternoon sun.

Within an hour of the verdict, several reporters who had been virtually living in the press room in the Duval County Courthouse were on a plane to Dallas, where a new round of global settlement talks was just getting under way. None would return for Wilner's next trial.

PEACE NOW AND FOREVER

MOTLEY AND WILNER MADE THEIR WAY TO DALLAS THE afternoon after the verdict. Though chastened, Motley was determined to continue, feeling he now had even more reason to push ahead with the attorney general lawsuits, the secondhand-smoke suits, and others that hopefully wouldn't suffer the fatal weaknesses of *Connor*.

Motley walked up to the Terrace Room, just above the lobby of the Fairmont Hotel, to find Joe Rice, Mike Moore, Dickie Scruggs, a large group of attorneys general, and a contingent from the moribund *Castano* national class action, now splintered into a dozen "Sons of *Castano*" class actions in state courts. Hovering outside the room were Carrick Mollenkamp, Keith Summa, and other reporters.

The negotiating was not going well that day. For one thing, there was a deep chasm between the *Castano* lawyers and the AGs' camp that went back to the very beginning of the global talks in April. Motley called the *Castano* lawyers "the Girths," and you could see why, as Russ Herman, a New Orleans *Castanoite*, and John Coale, the very savvy Washington lawyer, approached the conference room, walking side by side, arms waggling from their ample middles.

The Girths included Hugh Rodham, a Florida lawyer more famous as Hillary Clinton's brother, Maury Herman, Russ's brother, and Stan Chesley, who was actually quite slight of stature. When the Hermans gathered with Rodham and Coale, others in the room maneuvered carefully, and the scene took on the overstuffed look of those portraits of Gilded Age plutocrats in waistcoats and watch chains.

The AG-*Castano* chasm resulted from the fact that the AGs thought the Girths' lawsuits meritorious in theory but of little real consequence, and mostly an effort to stay in the fee game once their pioneering national class action was shot down. They were included in the negotiating process, as Scruggs later explained, "so they wouldn't come in afterward and try to sabotage it."

None of this stopped the *Castano* party from thumping conference room tables and demanding their right to be heard. While Motley deeply respected *Castano* founder Wendell Gauthier, who was recuperating from cancer surgery and following the talks by telephone, some *Castano*ites represented what he never wanted to be—tanned, pinky-ring-wearing caricatures of the personal injury hustler, beating a path to the plane crash to sign up victims.

The global settlement negotiations had been in progress about a month by the time Motley joined them in Dallas in early May. The first full-scale bilateral negotiating session between tobacco and the plaintiffs had been held April 3 at a hotel in the Crystal City section of Arlington, Virginia. Joe Rice, Dickie Scruggs, and Steve Berman were the legal talent for the attorneys general. They would be present at every negotiating session from then on, as would John Coale, Hugh Rodham, and other *Castano*ites. Moore's negotiating team, in addition to himself, comprised attorneys general Grant Woods of Arizona, Bob Butterworth of Florida, and Christine Gregoire of Washington, along with Matthew Myers, Cliff Douglas's old comrade-in-arms, representing the health community. Within a few weeks, Connecticut attorney general Richard Blumenthal was added. None had any interest in banning the product. That much—and not a lot more—they agreed on.

Washington Attorney General Christine Gregoire was a bit surprised to learn that the anti-tobacco forces were at Crystal City not only to settle their own lawsuits but to formulate national policy on cigarettes. So she and the other AGs quickly decided it wise to use their newfound clout to extract whatever they could in every area.

Moore had told lead negotiator J. Philip Carlton that the acid test would be whether his side could produce Geoff Bible and Steve Goldstone, and there they were, among the approximately thirty-five people gathered around a conference table, way down at the opposite end of the room from the AGs. They soon launched into a lot of vague but conciliatory diplomatic rhetoric.

"We're prepared to make fundamental changes to the manner in which we do business," said Bible, whose large head, with its massive chin and gray hair parted on the left and swept back, sat on a smallish body.

Goldstone was the very image of a Wall Street lawyer, slender and elegant, thin lipped, balding, with a pointy nose, wearing gold-rimmed glasses. He was concerned about the image of their peculiar product. Goldstone wanted to rid the tobacco enterprise of the hateful label "outlaw industry."

"I don't want to go to cocktail parties and have people asking me why I kill people," he said.

Moore responded with a challenge.

"I wanted to have you here so I could look you in the eye and assess whether you're serious," he said. "As far as I'm concerned, the tobacco companies are addicting our kids. I've got a trial date coming up. I don't have time to go through a waltz with you. If we detect for one minute that you're not serious, we'll walk out."

Bible and Goldstone left and the tobacco lawyers made their pitch. Everything was on the table, they said: FDA jurisdiction, disclosure of ingredients, and a substantial payment. As a sign of good faith, they immediately offered to do away with their billboards.

Jesus, thought Rice.

Grant Woods, who had played the heavy in the Liggett talks, went last. You'll do away with billboards, but what about cartoon characters, like Joe Camel, and human models, as in the Marlboro Man? And, said Woods, he wasn't going to give up anyone's right to sue.

Arthur Golden, the RJR negotiator, hemmed and hawed. There was obviously a disagreement between Philip Morris and Reynolds on advertising. The industry said it needed time to think.

The next morning, they met again, and Golden immediately conceded both controversial advertising symbols, plus the broader principle of human and cartoon figures. The companies would also agree to "virtually" all the terms of FDA regulation.

Moore and Scruggs were caught totally off guard. Scruggs felt like a kid in a candy store. What else should they ask for?

In fact, Steve Parrish had urged that the industry immediately make a present of the cowboy and the camel, a spectacular gesture to provide momentum. So what seemed incredible to Scruggs and company had, in fact, been carefully hatched months before.

Golden also said, as diplomatically as he could, that refusing to limit the right to sue tobacco was "a nonstarter" for the industry.

Then Wachtell began stem-winding.

"What we really want, what all of us want, is peace now—total peace—now and forever," he said.

The industry was giving up a lot, including its constitutional right to advertise as it saw fit. A severe limitation on civil liability was a fair price. Wachtell was getting worked up, turning red as he laid out a long list of types of lawsuits he wanted to bar in the future.

Then each attorney general spoke. Gregoire was seething as she awaited her turn. "There was an aura in the room that we were dealing with Herb Wachtell and that not a cross word could be said to him," she remembered. Now she attacked.

"Look, I'm not going back to my citizens and tell them they don't have a right to sue one of the worst violators of consumer protection laws in our state's history," she said, looking directly at Wachtell.

The following Monday, they reconvened in Chicago for five days of talks, still in secret, a near miracle considering the number of participants. There, the breach between the *Castano* crowd and the attorney generals' camp grew wider.

The attorneys general wanted the issue of how much the industry should pay left until the end, because otherwise the industry would think it could buy its way out of making health concessions. That position infuriated Russ Herman, Stan Chesley, and other *Castano* lawyers.

"You know, Dick, at some point you're going to have to have the guts to say to these guys, 'Show me the money,'" Herman shouted at Scruggs. "That's how you know people are serious. Now, when are you going to get it done?"

"Nobody's going to talk to my lawyer that way," said Moore, and left the room, followed by everyone else, just as Gregoire walked in.

"What in heck happened here?" she asked.

To satisfy the class-action lawyers, there was a short preliminary discussion of a global payout. Five billion dollars over five years, said the industry, a laughably small amount and one that would ultimately expand more than seventy-fold.

Meanwhile, Grant Woods was getting a little fed up with the constant declarations of unswerving good faith by the industry, when back home in Arizona, the companies were pushing a bill in the legislature to prevent towns from enacting strong local anti-smoking measures.

"We're willing to go forward here, but let's be honest. It's just business as usual with you people," said Woods.

When they broke for lunch, Robert Fiske, former Whitewater prosecutor and one of the Philip Morris negotiators, approached Woods and asked for more detail about the Arizona bill. Gregoire came over and said that her state was also busy fighting off a pro-tobacco bill, one totally at odds with this alleged new philosophy.

"I'll see what I can do about this," Fiske promised.

The two camps went off to separate catered lunches, both paid for by the industry. As the AGs were finishing theirs, Fiske walked in and took Gregoire and Woods aside.

"Those bills are dead," he announced.

Woods called one of his legislative contacts. The bill had been withdrawn. Woods found it somewhat unsettling.

"I knew they could pull strings, but, man," he said to Gregoire. "Some guy in a hotel room makes a phone call and this thing just disappears from the map."

Cliff Douglas, already deeply concerned about a global pact, heard the story a few weeks later.

He had a different interpretation.

"That should tell you how badly they want this," he said.

ON APRIL 16 CAME THE CATASTROPHE AT TYSON'S COR-ner, Virginia, where the attorneys general and the tobacco wizards arrived for a morning session at the DoubleTree Hotel to discover their secret negotiations were no longer secret, thanks to the *Wall Street Journal* article that prompted Carrick Mollenkamp to fly in from Jacksonville.

Unfortunately, most of the other AGs also found out about the talks from the *Journal,* and Scruggs, Rice, and the others had to do a lot of explaining on the phone.

Due to the unwanted publicity, there were all kinds of state officials, private lawyers, camera crews, and other fauna at the Fairmont Hotel when Motley rolled into Dallas from the *Connor* trial on May 6. By afternoon, things were tense in the Terrace Room, which was above the lobby and gave out onto an outdoor swimming pool where one reporter, sick of staking out the hallway, was turning laps.

Joe Rice could see that there were just too many people in the room, many of whom had no clear idea of what had already been hammered out and were eager to renegotiate some pet point. Speeches were being made in a spiraling competition to see who could talk toughest about tobacco, especially with the press around.

Scruggs led the group through the latest offering from the industry lawyers, eleven draconian limitations on who could sue tobacco and under what circumstances. Meanwhile, the tobacco side was at its headquarters at Jones, Day, Reavis & Pogue's Dallas office, on the nineteenth floor of a metallic tower a few blocks from the Fairmont.

Hoping to make progress away from the increasingly chaotic larger group, Scruggs, Rice, and Moore had been holding periodic small-group meetings with Arthur Golden, Meyer Koplow, and Philip Carlton. Moore and Scruggs were in one of these little huddles at Jones, Day when Rice rang Scruggs's cell phone.

"You'd better get your ass back here, Woody and Ron are getting everybody all whipped up. They're talking 'em out of it," said Rice.

Motley and Wilner, the only people in the room who had done a cigarette trial, were attacking the industry's demand for the abolition of punitive damages in tobacco suits, and they had the AGs spellbound. It wasn't the money damages, Motley was saying. Having punitives in the case allowed evidence of conspiracy and fraud to come in.

"I'm the sumbitch that's going to have to try these cases," said Motley, "and that's how you can go in and poison the well. That's where you get to the jury—on the punitives evidence."

Connor proved how badly you need conspiracy and fraud documents, he said, because the industry was so adept at playing on the common-knowledge theme, the argument that everyone knows the dangers of smoking.

"The irony is that the industry is using the fact that they are killing hundreds of thousands of people as a defense for killing hundreds of thousands of people," he said.

That resonated with the attorneys general, and they began ripping into the eleven points. Another problem was an industry requirement that the amount that could be paid out in lawsuits be capped. As usual, Grant Woods helped tip the balance.

"I've got a major problem with this. The deck's already stacked in favor of the industry," he said.

John Coale, the *Castano* lawyer from Washington, D.C., charged out of the room cursing.

"They keep moving the goalposts," Coale said to Keith Summa. "Every time a new player comes in he brings his own list of nonnegotiable demands."

Coale seemed upset that Wilner and Motley actually wanted to try these cases.

By the time Moore phoned into the Terrace Room from Jones, Day, Reavis & Pogue, the galley slaves had sawed their leg shackles off and were about ready to knock the centurions overboard and seize the ship.

Said Moore to Woods, "These guys want you to come over and tell them face-to-face that you're willing to kill the deal over this stuff."

"Fine," said Woods, "but I'm not the only one."

Woods went up to his room, packed his bags, and checked out, thinking it was probably over. Meanwhile, other attorneys general were in front of the Terrace Room dispensing the official party line to members of the press. No, the talks have not broken down. Yes, *of course* we'll meet again tomorrow. Just then the elevator door opened and out came Grant Woods, dragging his suitcases.

That didn't go over very well. Motley, Wilner, Woods, Gregoire, Russ Herman, and others went over to Jones, Day at about three P.M. and told the tobacco people that their eleven points wouldn't wash.

"We can talk through other issues, but we believe in the jury system," Woods said. "Whatever the jury believes these people are owed, they are owed."

Woods made no effort to sugarcoat it.

"I want you to know that I have respect for you all as lawyers. But I think we're at the end of the line."

Rice was upset, as were Scruggs and Moore. This was unrealistic, Rice thought. The industry wasn't going to make concessions without protection.

"We're going backwards," he told Motley at the hotel.

The next morning, the industry gave up on capping the payout in smokers' suits. But after Motley's speech of the day before, that was no longer enough. The idea of revamping the civil justice system for the benefit of the tobacco industry was profoundly distasteful to most of the attorneys general, though not, Woods noticed, to the *Castano* lawyers.

"These guys are pretty much counting the money at this point, aren't they?" Woods said to a colleague.

There was a conference call later that day that brought the Dallas group together with the other suing attorneys general, who by now numbered thirty, their numbers swelling almost weekly as more states sought to get in on a possible settlement windfall. The conference line crackled with ideas and volcanic rhetoric.

Scruggs boiled as he listened to the call in his room with Moore and other AGs. Who the hell *were* all these people? He walked over to Rice's room, where he heard the rest of the conference. It was decided a delegation would go over to Jones, Day and say that the AGs couldn't agree on a counter-proposal on civil liability.

Scruggs closed the door to Rice's room.

"Joe, that's it," said Scruggs. "I'm not going out there again."

Then Moore came in, and Scruggs exploded.

"Mike, you're letting them run all over you. The Prohibitionists are having the last word and nobody's shutting 'em down. You're not taking control of this fucking thing," he said.

Moore tried to calm him. These were necessary growing pains, he said.

"Believe me, Dickie, I'm as frustrated as you are," Moore said. "But we've got a couple dozen AGs with us now and we've got to address these issues."

"We *already* addressed them," said Scruggs.

"Well, we got to do it again," said Moore.

"Then you do it," said Scruggs. "I'm out."

And Scruggs left the hotel and went to the airport, so angry he forgot his luggage.

MIKE MOORE DIDN'T SMELL AN AMBUSH WHEN HE WALKED into the ballroom at the Sofitel Hotel near the airport in Chicago a few weeks after the meltdown in Dallas.

This was supposed to be a gathering of men and women of goodwill, an exchange of views with public-health professionals, health apparatchiks from the American Cancer Society and the other big voluntaries, plus what Dickie Scruggs called the "hard-core anti-tobacco people," organizations with names like Californians Against Death by Tobacco, most of which had limited memberships. Scruggs saw these folks as the Trotskyites of the movement, more interested in being right than getting anything done. Trying to deal with them was like debating a group of emigré revolutionaries. Most of their energy was dissipated in attacking rival sectarians for lacking true proletarian zeal.

So Scruggs had passed on going to this particular meeting. No, thanks, he told Moore. I'd rather have a root canal.

Moore wanted to build bridges to the grassroots health groups, whose support would be critical if and when the global package got to Congress. And since those opposed to a global deal would be there, notably Michael Ciresi, chief lawyer for Minnesota attorney general Hubert Humphrey III, Moore didn't want to leave the job of defending the settlement to Matt Myers, who had to attend as the health representative on the global negotiating team.

A large ballroom was filled with long rows of tables placed end to end, behind which sat a throng of Ph.D.s, M.D.s, M.B.A.s, M.P.H.A.s, and the odd L.L.B. waiting for Moore and Myers to feed them the details of the global talks, which the health people felt they owned, or should own, even though they had never sat at the negotiating table and never would have been asked. Those in the ballroom on May 28 were earnest and well credentialed, but the tobacco industry had easily neutralized them and people like them for five decades.

Many wore yellow buttons reading NO GLOBAL BAILOUT with a

picture of a bomb with a lit fuse. Others had on NO MOORE SELL-OUT buttons.

Cliff Douglas was there, too, sitting on the far left, near the back. He nursed a strong presentiment that this "exchange of views" would probably be an exercise in futility. Like virtually everyone else in tobacco control, what angered him most about the "global settlement" was its secrecy. Tobacco was too important a subject to be negotiated by invitation only behind closed doors.

Moore himself wore a NO GLOBAL BAILOUT button.

"I'm a Johnny-come-lately. I'm somebody who doesn't know as much as you do about these issues," Moore told the crowd.

He explained that he got involved because of his son, Kyle, a ten-year-old, and his seventy-six-year-old father, who had smoked for sixty years and still hadn't quit.

"If I ask you a couple of questions in this room today, I want you to be honest with me. I don't want you to hold back. Everybody in this room, if you had your druthers, would you ban the product in America? Raise your hand," he asked.

Only a few hands were raised.

"How many think we ought to put them out of business by bankrupting them?" he asked. Many more hands shot up.

"That means we hurt 'em, right? So part of this process is—let's tell the truth, we're gonna be frank today—part of the process is, these are sorry, *no-good*-for-nothing rotten *scoundrels* who have killed *millions* of people, am I right?" he asked. The room lit up with applause.

"And there's a feeling in every one of us in this room, that, *by God*, they ought to *pay* for it, am I right?" Moore shouted.

"Amen" came back the response.

"We ought to *punish* 'em, am I right? We ought to make 'em *pay*! Huge sums of money! Even if they can't afford it? Right?

"People ought to serve time in *jail*, right?" he hammered.

"Yeah!" people shouted.

"You know our United States Justice Department's been working on that for how many years? Anyone been indicted yet?"

Silence.

"If I win my lawsuit one hundred percent, you know what I get? Judge gives us a big chunk of money and they change the way they do business in Mississippi," he said.

He explained the benefits of a national solution, one that offered federal regulation and restricted advertising, and how the attorneys general were trying to build in financial penalties for the cigarette makers if youth smoking didn't drop.

Then Tom Pursell, one of the Minnesota lawyers, stood up.

"What's the rush?" he said. "Mike Moore wants to make the argument that you settle now or more kids will start smoking. What about the kids who wouldn't smoke if we held out a little bit longer *and got this right?*"

Tumultuous applause. Pursell got a prolonged standing ovation.

The health people wanted Moore to sign on to various "core principles" and declarations. Why didn't he put his faith in the legal system? Because the courts have never given sick smokers justice, said Moore, and the AG lawsuits could still flop in court. The questions from the floor were valid, but the tone got nastier.

Who gave you the right to make health policy for the country? How could anyone give this bunch of killers amnesty in the courts?

"Well, I don't know any deal in history where you didn't give anything up," said Moore evenly.

"Yup, you've been suckered," muttered a man way in back wearing a NO MOORE SELL-OUT button.

Moore conciliated.

"In talking to people here, I've heard good ideas about youth access and I'd like more," he said.

"Hey, I'll *show* you how it's done. There are people here who've been doing this a long time," barked someone from the American Association of Public Health Physicians.

Moore started to color.

"Why are we cutting a deal with a terrorist killer organization?" said a woman whose brown cloth coat was covered with patches for political causes.

Moore shot Myers a look and left the ballroom. When he came back, he said little else. It seemed that the position of the "hardcore anti-tobacco people" was that if it was any good, tobacco wouldn't do it. If tobacco would do it, it couldn't be any good.

Afterward, en route to the airport, Moore called Scruggs on the cell phone.

"How was it?" Scruggs asked.

"I got no ass left at all, man," Moore said.

Douglas drove home to Evanston, where he and Martha had moved from Washington. He thought about the ruckus he had just witnessed, which he had largely stayed out of. What was the point? Moore didn't want to hear it anyway. He was going to get his deal come hell or high water. The Mississippian was already parroting the industry's line, pretending that the radical paradigm shift that began with *Day One,* the cascade of damning evidence, had never happened, and that juries would continue to exonerate the cigarette makers, all so he could argue that making a deal with the devil on the devil's own terms—i.e., defanging the plaintiff's lawyers—was the best that could be done.

Sitting in the car, Douglas realized he had to get more directly involved in tobacco litigation, so juries would see what he saw. He also knew he had to break his alliance with Motley and Scruggs. He now swore to do everything he could to kill the global deal.

Meanwhile, Moore and Steve Bozeman, Scruggs's law partner, boarded Scruggs's Learjet for the flight to New York, where the global talks had moved after Dallas.

Moore had brought Scruggs back into the fold right after the disaster in Dallas. From then on, they had agreed, a small, hand-picked group would do the negotiating. They worked out a punch-list of issues and went back to the table in New York the following week, this time without Grant Woods. Woods found out and showed up, furious at being excluded, but soon calmed down and joined the process.

Often, Moore and Bozeman, who had been a sailor on a destroyer escort for the *Franklin Delano Roosevelt* while Scruggs and his fighter were aboard the carrier, would work through these two- and three-hour hops on the Lear. Tonight they had a bourbon and Coke and relaxed. After dueling with the industry all week, the last thing they had expected was to be bayoneted in the ass by the health community, their supposed trenchmates.

Nevertheless, Moore thought his "mission from God" might finally be approaching completion. Steve Parrish, especially, seemed to have realized that it was political common sense to get on with a deal. Parrish would often approach the AGs after some harsh posturing by the industry and say, Uh, guys, don't pay too much attention to that. Let me see what I can do.

Moore and Bozeman landed at Teterboro in New Jersey and took a limousine to New York, where they would sit down again the following morning with the cigarette makers.

In the limo, Bozeman was reading from a big book of quotations he kept in his briefcase.

"Here's one," he said. "Somebody negotiating with Napoleon said this: 'We will negotiate to the gates of hell. But no farther.'"

Moore smiled.

"Boze, you be sure to let me know when we get there," he said.

BY JUNE 1997, THE GLOBAL SETTLEMENT NEGOTIATORS were in Washington, and by the second week, a deal was imminent. The media ranks swelled. Last-minute filings brought the number of suing states to forty, plus Puerto Rico. In the several days before June 20, the sessions stretched into marathons.

Motley, who had been preparing for trial in Mississippi, arrived and stayed at the ANA Hotel with the attorneys general, advising the AGs on what the cigarette makers should be required to publicly disclose of their internal documents.

The actual deal-making was taking place at the industry's headquarters, a suite of conference rooms at the Park Hyatt Hotel, a salmon-colored structure across the street from the ANA. Periodically, Moore, Scruggs, and others jumped into taxis and rode off to lobby members of Congress and the White House. One crucial White House meeting almost didn't happen. Asked for his identification at the guardhouse, Grant Woods produced the Elvis Presley driver's license he'd gotten at Graceland during the Liggett talks. The guard did not think it was funny. They were detained. Grimmouthed phone calls were made. Security clearances were reviewed. Mike Moore just shook his head.

In the Roosevelt Room, Woods, Moore, Scruggs, and industry negotiators met with White House deputy counsel Bruce Lindsey. The cigarette makers were adamant about extricating themselves from punitive damages and class-action suits, which were the thin end of the wedge depressing their stock price. Several attorneys general were equally adamant in opposition. Scruggs and Moore had wracked their brains to come up with what Scruggs called a "bright shiny thing," something the industry could give up that would allow the AGs to accept losing punitives and class actions.

Lindsey suggested the companies fork over another $50 billion as a sort of giant fine for past illicit behavior on the condition that no one could ever sue them again for punitive damages for anything they had done in the past. The industry people swallowed hard, but accepted it.

That was fine, Scruggs said, but even so, the most liberal AGs still would have trouble with the deal unless the White House endorsed these changes to the civil justice system. Some argued that if you're going to cut the tobacco demons the fattest legal break in American history, what do you do for the good guys? Lindsey reluctantly agreed that the White House would issue a statement providing political cover to the AGs.

The AGs approved the Lindsey compromise during a conference call, and later, Lindsey read Scruggs the promised White House statement, which said that given the global settlement's public health gains and the $50-billion punitives payment, its civil liability provisions were acceptable. Unfortunately, said Lindsey, he could not let them have a copy of the statement.

On the morning of June 20, final changes were being made to a sixty-eight-page "Proposed Resolution," which both sides stayed up all night to draft and redraft.

On first reading, it was a seminal victory for the anti-tobacco camp. The industry had accepted FDA jurisdiction. It would pay $368.5 billion over twenty-five years to the AGs, would no longer use human images or cartoon characters in its ads, would run only black and white ads except in adult publications, tear down its billboards, ban vending machines, put $5 billion a year into a fund to pay off sick smokers who sued them, dissolve the Council for Tobacco Research and the Tobacco Institute, place more prominent warning labels on cigarettes saying, "WARNING: Cigarettes are addictive," "WARNING: Cigarettes cause cancer," and "WARNING: Tobacco smoke causes fatal lung disease in nonsmokers," among other things, and pay fines if underage tobacco use didn't drop by thirty percent in five years and sixty percent in ten years. The industry would accept no smoking policies in public buildings and most workplaces, except restaurants, bars, and elsewhere in the "hospitality industry."

The Proposed Resolution would be activated when the President signed legislation incorporating its provisions.

Unfortunately, there was fine print. For the FDA to actually do any regulating—for instance, to ban a toxic ingredient—it would have to hold hearings, have a comment period, submit to judicial review, give Congress an opportunity to intervene, and at the end of all that, the companies could ask to reopen the process. Most of the fines for youth smoking would be waived if the industry showed it was acting in good faith. The trade associations could be re-formed. The holding companies of the cigarette makers, which had most of the money, were made immune from lawsuits.

However, by Friday morning, as verbal snarls were untangled, the Proposed Resolution was as far as the exhausted negotiators could take the peace process after eleven weeks of talking. The drafters hoped to unveil the pact that weekend in Jackson Hole, Wyoming, at the summer gathering of the nation's attorneys general. More urgently, Mike Moore's trial date was less than three weeks away and he refused to change it.

On Friday morning, the announced times for press conferences came and went. An enormous clot of reporters formed just outside the industry's little conference-room complex on the mezzanine level of the Park Hyatt. Present were newspapers that hadn't been seen at a tobacco event all year as well as longtime hands. Security men manned a red velvet rope dividing the narrow corridor in half. On the other side, reporters could see Stan Chesley walking around with a cup of coffee and Motley scowling into his cell phone.

He was scowling at a last-minute hitch that threatened to wreck everything. He and Scruggs had been working on two remaining areas of contention, document disclosure and whistle-blowers, both largely resolved.

Except for Jeffrey Wigand. The industry insisted Wigand would have to be discussed some other time. No, Scruggs and Motley said, it has to be now. Motley called in Wigand's personal attorney, Laura Wertheimer, from her office on Massachusetts Avenue.

At about noon, with the press mob growing, Wertheimer came out of the conference room at the Park Hyatt and told Motley that

Brown & Williamson wouldn't budge. It was willing to let other whistle-blowers go. But not Wigand. Motley walked across the street to the ANA Hotel and told Scruggs and Moore what had happened.

"I think we better call off the press conference," said Motley.

Scruggs and Moore agreed. It seemed Brown & Williamson would risk their shot at "peace now and forever" to continue a purely private vendetta. Then again, it made a kind of sense.

"Wigand was a particular raw nerve for them," Scruggs said later. "He was so crucial to Brown & Williamson's credibility, their public image, and they had invested millions to take him out. *Millions*. And literally put their corporate image on the line to wreck this guy."

It seemed to Scruggs that B&W's major concern was that, with his legal muzzle removed, Wigand would hit the lecture circuit and bite at them at every opportunity.

Motley went back across the street to the Park Hyatt and told the other attorneys general that Moore wouldn't sign unless all claims against Wigand were dropped. The AGs—Gregoire, Woods, Florida's Butterworth, Connecticut's Richard Blumenthal, and New York's Dennis Vacco, a late addition to the negotiating team— immediately backed him. Then, caught up in the spirit of what they had just done, they broke into applause.

Just beyond the velvet rope, reporters heard the applause and assumed there had been some fantastic final breakthrough. An "arb," Wall Street lingo for an arbitrageur, a trader who profits from small discrepancies in market prices, whipped out his cell phone.

"It's going down," said the arb.

But it was not going down. When the AGs' Wigand ultimatum was presented to the industry, their jaws dropped. The media horde was informed that the press conference had been postponed yet again.

Scruggs, Motley, and Moore believed fiercely that no one had suffered as much as Wigand, that no individual had had more to do with getting them where they were now. Scruggs and Motley were personally close to Wigand. To desert him now would be flagrant hypocrisy.

Tobacco negotiator Phil Carlton decided to go over the heads of Brown & Williamson to the parent company, British American Tobacco, and personally entreat BAT's chief executive, Martin Broughton, to give up Wigand. Broughton was said to be on a train in England somewhere, incommunicado for the next ninety minutes.

Located at last, Broughton evidently didn't think the sight of Wigand roasting slowly on a spit was sufficient reward for risking BAT's worldwide empire. All tobacco's lawsuits against Wigand would be dropped in return for Wigand's promise not to comment publicly on tobacco issues during a "cooling-off period."

When it was understood the Wigand issue had been resolved, there was another hearty round of applause from the sleep-deprived attorneys general.

Keith Summa had been communicating steadily with Motley inside the conference room via cell phone. The moment the thing was signed, Motley would send Jack McConnell to alert Summa so he'd get a scoop.

McConnell, who was in Washington for a Democratic party fund-raiser, had with him his eight-year-old daughter, Catherine. As an excuse to leave the room, which was closely guarded, he was planning to say Catherine needed the bathroom. But Catherine was terrified of the mob outside.

Motley had known Catherine since she was a baby. He knelt down in front of her, and slowly raised Mr. Buzz, his tickly right index finger. Mr. Buzz approached her stomach.

"Mr. *Buuuuuzzzzzzzz*," he tweaked, "wants to know *whatzzzz* you're *doingggggggzzzzzzzz herezzzzzzzzzzzzzzzzz*."

Catherine giggled. McConnell took her by the hand, and she grinned back shyly at Uncle Ron as McConnell led her past the velvet rope, through the press herd, and found Summa.

"They've just signed," he said. "They're going across to announce it any minute."

Summa called it in to New York, ahead of even the financial wires.

Minutes later, the attorneys general conducted a triumphal march from the Park Hyatt across 24th Street to a large ballroom in the basement of the ANA, enveloped by a walking forest of television boom-mikes. Scruggs and Motley were in the thick of the procession. Moore ignored a public relations consultant's advice to keep his lawyers separate from the AGs. However, the *Castano*ites were kept to the rear.

Each attorney general made a speech in the ballroom. Moore called it the "most historic public health achievement in history." Most of the rhetoric was similarly torrid. Florida's Butterworth whipped himself into a lather on the theme of the Marlboro Man riding off into the sunset on Joe Camel.

There were no plaintiff's lawyers on the dais. They stood behind a rope to the left of the stage.

Butterworth was still talking when a commotion broke out in the clump of lawyers behind the rope. It was a bearded Jeff Wigand literally burrowing his way into the attorneys as he made a beeline for Dickie Scruggs, whom he embraced, smiling ecstatically. Then he hugged Motley.

"Thank you very much," Wigand said. "God bless you."

"I'm proud of you," said Motley, eyes full of tears.

Wigand and Motley and Scruggs stood quietly and listened to the speeches.

Then one of the Ness, Motley ladies smiled warmly at Motley and said, "Your mom's smiling down at you right now."

In the ballroom were two hundred members of the press—cameramen, still photographers, magazine writers, book authors. Wigand had gotten everyone's attention by barreling in like a crazed assassin, and now, as the press conference ended, the media herd followed him out and backed him against a wall opposite the ballroom.

He explained he had been at his lawyer's office not far away when Motley called to tell him he was a free man and to come on down.

"I feel incredibly relieved and happy," he told a reporter as more and more microphones twisted toward him like angry snakes.

Then he excused himself, wiggled free, and dashed for the nearest doorway, which opened onto a small auditorium that sloped down to a stage. He peered out from behind a snack cart. But the press horde had roared upstairs to hear Ralph Nader.

In the ANA lobby bar, Motley grabbed Scruggs's arm.

"Let's have a drink," said Motley.

"Let's have a lot of drinks," said Scruggs.

But Moore and Scruggs had a final errand. They had to run a copy of the Proposed Resolution over to the White House. They had trouble getting a cab so late on a Friday afternoon. When they arrived, Bruce Lindsey had already departed to join President Clinton in Denver, where he was attending an international economic conference. Domestic policy advisor Bruce Reed had been left behind to receive what Scruggs called "our Holy Grail."

Reed congratulated Scruggs and Moore. Then he handed them the statement Lindsey had promised.

It said President Clinton appreciated the work of the attorneys general and would review it, but that as of now, the President had "not concluded whether it is in the best interests of the public health."

There was no mention of civil liability or punitive damages. Nothing Lindsey had promised was there. No cover for anybody.

Moore and Scruggs were amazed.

Reed told them to have faith and within a couple of weeks, the White House would endorse the plan.

Scruggs and Moore got a cab back to the ANA for the victory celebration.

"They screwed us," said Scruggs. "'Wonderful work. Thank you very much. Good night.'"

Moore thought Clinton would come around. It didn't dampen their spirits much. There was still a lot to celebrate.

THE GLOBAL DEAL GOT A BANNER HEADLINE STRETCHING all the way across the front page of the *New York Times,* like the Kennedy assassination or men walking on the moon. In retrospect, June 20 was the pinnacle, as good as it was ever likely to get for the big-business style of plaintiff's law practiced by Motley, Scruggs and the others. Two weeks came and went, as did two months, and there was no White House endorsement. Clinton decided he wanted to toughen the pact.

Keith Summa got in to see domestic policy advisor Bruce Reed at the White House and asked him about the global deal.

"We don't feel this has to go this year," Reed said.

Influential health figures, like David Kessler, who had left the FDA to become dean of Yale Medical School, attacked the Proposed Resolution, while an unholy alliance of cigarette lobbyists and attorneys general stumped for it. Senate hearings were held at which Matt Myers admitted it wasn't perfect, but called it fixable, a big step forward.

Pass our bill, protect the children, let's start saving thousands of lives now—that was the tune sung all summer long by Scruggs and Moore. It quickly began to sound tinny in the halls of Congress, which had no intention of passing a piece of legislation shipped in from a hotel across town. The drafters of June 20 counted on the pact's huge pot of guaranteed money to be the honey that would summon the bees, but since much of the money was tax deductible—meaning taxpayers would subsidize it—the bees didn't much like it. For liberals, it was a sweetheart deal for tobacco. The tobacco states loathed it because it didn't protect tobacco growers. The rest of the Hill waited to see which way the leadership would go and the money would flow. And everyone waited for Clinton to bless a global settlement bill. But he never did.

While Congress wrestled with various bills based on "the global," the individual AG cases ground onward. With Joe Rice's help, Mike Moore settled Mississippi's lawsuit on July 3 for $3.36 billion, freeing Moore to lobby for the global deal. To ensure that Merrell Williams would be freed, as Wigand had been, Scruggs and Moore once more had to threaten to walk out.

By that time, opposition to the global settlement had grown into a raucous chorus. Minnesota attorney general Hubert Humphrey III, the only suing AG who didn't settle, asked angrily during Senate testimony in July what right anyone had to settle his lawsuit for him.

He said the deal was full of loopholes. Not only class actions, but any grouping of more than one tobacco case would be banned, extinguishing consolidated trials—like Motley's *Abrams* case.

It was an odd moment for Motley, who was in the audience in the Senate that day. He was a pioneer of advanced legal methods, yet traditional allies, like Dick Daynard, Ralph Nader, even Trial Lawyers for Public Justice, a liberal group that Motley had helped form in the seventies, now pilloried him for limiting the right to sue.

Senator Edward Kennedy read a letter from his brother, Senator Robert F. Kennedy, to a tobacco official in 1967:

"Thanks for meeting with me," Bobby Kennedy had written, "and I appreciate your commitment to reducing youth smoking."

Afterward, Moore and Jeff Wigand, both of whom sat with Motley at the hearing, met for lunch. Despite the apparent frostiness of the Senate, it was a cheerful meal. The southerners were eternal optimists.

Moore said he was due at the White House at four P.M.

"You want me to go along so you don't say anything wrong?" asked Motley.

"Yeah, you're perfect for that job," snorted Moore.

Moore imitated Humphrey's nasal voice.

"'We've got this problem with punitives.' Hell, he's only saying that because he's running for governor."

Just then Scruggs walked in.

"How about her?" he said, indicating a brunette in culottes out at the bar. "They're all wearing these skimpy little things."

Someone expressed surprise that so few questions had been asked about the fees the lawyers would collect for the global deal.

"Yeah," said Wigand sarcastically, "why don't they do this for free?"

"Until I met you I *would* have done it for free," said Scruggs. "If I was going to get involved with you, I said I've got to get paid. Mr. Irascible. Isn't that the word?"

Wigand grinned.

"That's the word," he said. In fact, he was less irascible than usual. He was about to move out of Louisville and take a condominium in Charleston, across town from his friend Motley. The global settlement had furnished Jeff Wigand with a new life, though at the considerable cost of his old one.

It was a new life for Moore and Scruggs, too, as they tried to master the game of national politics in week after dreary week in Washington. They ascended to a slightly higher level of comprehension when they realized that many of their supposed Democratic allies did not even *want* to solve the cigarette problem.

Of course, the anti-tobacco Trotskyites were savaging "the global." That did not surprise Moore, given his experience in Chicago.

But Scruggs was stunned to learn from Beltway insiders that

Vice President Al Gore wouldn't support *any* anti-tobacco plan. He wanted to be able to run for President against the demon cigarette companies in 2000.

"You have to understand," Senator Tom Harkin told Moore that summer. "This is a good issue for us."

"DR. DUNN, AROUND PHILIP MORRIS YOU WERE KNOWN as the Nicotine Kid, right?" the plaintiff's lawyer asked William Dunn, Victor DeNoble's one-time boss at the research center.

Thunk!

Flap whap a *whap*-whap . . .

Thunk!

What is that goddamned noise?

That's what Cliff Douglas was thinking, up on the twenty-sixth floor of a Richmond office building as he tried to concentrate on Dunn, a Ph.D. who couldn't seem to remember anything useful about much of anything from his days at Philip Morris. DeNoble's work was evidently a complete blur to him.

Thunk!

Flap whap a *whap*-whap . . .

Thunk!

A dark object of some kind kept banging into the conference room window at Hunton & Williams, a law firm representing Philip Morris that was hosting Dunn's deposition. The research tower where Dunn ran the behavioral research lab was just a few exits down I-95 from the tinted windows where *something*—

Thunk!

What the holy hell is *that*?

The Dunn proceeding was part of Douglas's decision after the fracas in Chicago between Mike Moore and the health community to get more involved in lawsuits. With Dunn, he was backing up one of the "sons of *Castano*" lawyers. But he had also started taking depositions himself.

"Do you believe that cigarette smoking causes cancer?" a plaintiff's lawyer asked the white-haired Dunn.

Thunk!

. . . Jesus! thought Douglas, glancing at the window. Some kind of *dark blur* over there . . .

"I don't believe that anything that I did at Philip Morris at the research center had any bearing upon the question that you asked," Dunn replied.

That opinion seemed so extraordinary that it got Douglas's attention, despite persistent interruptions by a bunch of rampaging—

Thunk!

Vultures.

Thunk!

Flap whap a *whap*-whap . . .

Earlier, he had noticed these enormous birds hovering out in the distance and thought maybe they were hawks.

But now that they were actually crashing into the window one by one—

Thunk! Thunk!

alighting there and padding around, flapping their huge black—

. . . flap whap a *whap*-whap . . .

wings, he could see they were vultures. Turkey vultures, to be more precise, with reddish heads, making that peculiar hissing sound they make, folding and unfolding their wings, capering about the windowsill like it was their rumpus room. Right smack-dab in the middle of Dunn's testimony.

There were four vultures out there now, two feet from the lawyers and Dunn. Everyone was watching them, instead of paying attention to Dunn, who was himself studying them.

"Don't you think it's wonderful that Hunton & Williams has pet vultures?" Douglas stage-whispered to the *Castano* lawyer.

Douglas began mentally drifting, wondering how Philip Morris would respond to the charge that its scientists attract vultures. They'd argue they're *not really* vultures. Your Honor, those good-sized animals caroming off the top of our law firm could be *any* species of ugly carnivorous bird.

A marvelous spectacle, as he told Martha that night on the phone: that a flock of vultures would ignore all the carcasses in the city of Richmond to attend the deposition of William Dunn, aka the Nicotine Kid.

Thunk!

IN THE EARLY FALL, DOUGLAS BEGAN SPEAKING AT GATHerings of cancer victims and their loved ones, at which he discovered something that fascinated him: Not only had the cigarette companies succeeded in getting juries to believe smokers had freely chosen a smoky suicide, but many lung cancer victims believed it, too. They were actually ashamed to be wasting away from this awful disease, because *nobody has to smoke cigarettes*.

A few months after Douglas's brush with vulture culture in Richmond, he gave a talk to an audience of forty-five or so cancer victims in Bethesda, Maryland, many of whom had thoroughly bought into the "free choice" argument. They were about to die, and believed it was their own damned fault.

Douglas, who by now had spoken all over the world, from Dublin to Beijing, had concocted a special half-hour-long speech to help relieve the psychological component of their suffering, entitled "Addiction: The Tobacco Industry's Lethal Weapon."

Of the people taking their seats that night at the Marriott in Bethesda, Maryland, there were a number of women wearing wigs to hide the fact that chemotherapy and radiation had eaten their hair. Others had to be helped up the aisle.

"It has been said that among cancers, lung cancer in particular has a stigma attached to it," Douglas told the audience, who belonged to a group called the Alliance for Lung Cancer Advocacy, Support, and Education, or ALCASE.

"If I have one goal today, it is to debunk the gross misconception that lung cancer survivors who smoked are somehow 'guilty,' and lay the blame where it belongs," he said.

"You need to understand that the chief preventable cause of lung cancer is the tobacco industry," he said.

No, Douglas repeated, it isn't your fault. A cigarette, he explained, is so much more effective a nicotine delivery device than, for instance, nicotine chewing gum, that if you put the gum up against a cigarette in a fair fight for the smoker's nicotine receptors, the cigarette wins hands down every time.

And that, he explained, was what had happened to them. Cigarettes always won—over the gum, the nicotine patch, their shame for being too "weak willed" to quit, over exercise programs, occasional bursts of optimism and other vectors that seemed to be leading them, however briefly, to a healthier life.

The humble cigarette truly was, said Douglas, quoting Bill

Dunn's most famous memo on nicotine, "among the most awe-inspiring examples of the ingenuity of man."

At the heart of its ingenuity is its efficiency, he told them. The three-tenths of a milligram of nicotine in each puff of a Marlboro cigarette reaches the brain in about four seconds. The speed—faster than intravenous injection—is due to the large surface area of the lung, which quickly transfers the drug to the pulmonary artery.

To maintain enough nicotine in the bloodstream, the average smoker has one cigarette roughly every half hour, each of which provides ten .3-milligram hits. Given an average intake of thirty cigarettes over sixteen hours of wakefulness, the smoker is shooting up three hundred times a day, pharmacologically speaking.

Philip Morris, Douglas told the cancer victims, spent forty years making sure every hit is perfectly metered—manipulating the blend and the recon, using chemicals like ammonia, adding dilution holes in the filter—so that quitting is impossible for all but 5 percent of those who try annually, a success rate that is no better than for junkies trying to kick heroin.

So that's why you never got to the top of the mountain, up where you could draw breath without this monkey on your back, Douglas told them. You were no match for such an ingenious drug delivery system.

Ingenious but for one fatal flaw: Every hit comes from a filthy needle, ten shots of nicotine *and poison* every half hour.

How long ago did the companies know there was something . . . well, *peculiar* about their product? Douglas asked.

Douglas held up a reproduction of one of the old Philip Morris ads that John Ross sued over back in 1962. These dated from the thirties.

" 'You're bound to inhale sometimes,' " Douglas read, " 'but you can have this proven protection.' "

"You're *bound to inhale*? These guys are *warning* you about inhaling a product that is meant to be inhaled," he said. "The beef industry doesn't warn you that you're bound to swallow pieces of steak."

"They knew *something* was wrong a long time ago," said Douglas.

He told the cancer victims about the industry's cover-up of its knowledge about nicotine addiction, and about Deep Cough. They listened raptly as he narrated how Herbert Wachtell tried to pry out Deep Cough's identity, how Wachtell screamed at him.

"That deposition was taken right over there," said Douglas, pointing down the hall. "Right here in this very Marriott."

But the message Douglas drove home over and over again was, *It is not your fault*. After all, he told the victims, the industry first enticed most of you with this "drug cocktail" at the age of twelve and a half.

"So try to take whatever feelings of guilt or anger you may be harboring and aim them not at yourself, not at each other, but at the guilty party—the makers and sellers of cigarettes," he implored.

And then, Douglas gave his trademark closing:

"Remember: 'If you think you're too small to be effective, you've never been in bed with a mosquito,'" he quoted.

Afterward, there was a stream of sometimes tearful cancer patients and their escorts.

A woman named Susan Levine approached and introduced her daughter, Deena, to Douglas. Pale and thin as a wraith, Deena wore a scarf to cover the absence of what had once been flowing chestnut hair, and the scarf seemed huge on her head.

Susan explained that Deena, who was twenty-seven, started smoking at fifteen, and was diagnosed with cancer at twenty-six.

"You have no idea how important it is for us to hear what you said," said Susan. "It was simply wonderful."

Douglas got a little choked up. He said that made him very happy.

Then Deena thanked him and took his hand in hers. She kissed him on the cheek.

Douglas gave Susan his card. Five months later she called. Deena had died. But Susan had become an anti-tobacco political organizer, and soon she would begin giving speeches of her own.

IN JULY, MOTLEY'S PEOPLE TOOK THE REAR HALF OF the Brazilian Court Hotel, a Spanish-style resort in West Palm Beach, to get ready for trial in August in the Florida attorney general's case.

A last-minute decision was made to have Motley depose Geoffrey Bible of Philip Morris, and Motley sat in his room for two days reviewing thousands of pages of material. The day after Bible, he deposed Steven Goldstone of Reynolds, and got Goldstone to come closer than any cigarette company official ever had to saying flat out that cigarettes cause cancer. And yet even in this new era of peace, Goldstone was still careful to phrase it as a matter of his personal belief, leaving the company an out. Both depositions generated a lot of media coverage.

But those stories had to compete with another one that capped perhaps the worst episode in Motley's legal career. The family of Mississippi barber Burl Butler was suing their lawyer and champion, Ron Motley.

The charge was quite serious: that Ness, Motley negotiated away the Butlers' rights to punitive damages in the global deal. Roe Frazer II and Shane Langston, two of the Butler family's Mississippi lawyers, were alleging that Motley's firm weakened the Butlers' legal position to suit their higher purpose in the attorney general suits. That would be a breach of ethics.

"Ava Butler isn't going to get any of that $50 billion for past punitive damages," Frazer indignantly told a reporter from his office in Jackson.

Frazer claimed Ness, Motley used the *Butler* case as a vehicle to conduct discovery for the state cases. Therefore, the Butlers, and by extension Frazer's firm, were entitled to some of Ness, Motley's as-yet-unawarded global legal fees.

Ness, Motley countersued, charging Frazer with trying to extort those fees. In fact, the Charleston firm had considered pulling out of the case in December of 1996. They saw unaccountably large sums of money being spent by various Mississippi lawyers who appeared to do little work. One signed pleadings and sent bills though no one in Charleston knew who he was.

When Ness, Motley tried to withdraw, Roe Frazer flew to Charleston and demanded that the South Carolinians not only cut him in on the AGs' fees, but open their tobacco files to him. He hinted that if they didn't, their liability material might fall into the hands of competing lawyers. (Frazer later denied pressuring the Charleston firm.) It was decided it would be simpler for Ness, Motley to stay in the case, which was set for trial for the following summer.

However, in the spring of 1997, Judge Billy Joe Landrum, who had been favorable to the plaintiffs, was forced off of *Butler*, and a new judge took over who not only smoked cigarettes but had been known to do so on the bench. The trial date was pushed back a year.

Of course for Ron Motley, *Butler* was simply part of the One Big Tobacco case he was putting together. *Butler* benefited from discovery in other cases, and those cases benefited from *Butler*. But the scandal of Ness, Motley allegedly negotiating away the rights of Burl Butler's widow was played up in a *Wall Street Journal* article by legal correspondent Milo Geyelin that came at a time when the global deal was being roundly condemned. And there seemed little doubt that if the pact became the law of the land and abolished punitive damages in tobacco suits, the Butler family's case would indeed be compromised.

Down in West Palm Beach, Motley was deeply humiliated, especially when Ava Butler herself publicly excoriated his firm. He had always felt a strong personal commitment to the Butlers. At hearings in Laurel, Mississippi, Motley and Ava Butler would sit with their arms around each other. Motley got so depressed over the *Journal* article, he became ill.

"I don't mind being called a rich plaintiff's lawyer," said Motley one night, "but for them to take that poor lady and her family and turn them against me and say the things they have about me is just more than I can bear. It's really hurt me profoundly, more than I can ever describe. For Milo to write that article, and make it look like I'm some rich motherfucker, you know, depriving a widow of some money, is—I'm not ever talking to him or the *Wall Street Journal* again as long as I live."

In the end, Joe Rice stepped in and stared Frazer down. Ness, Motley left the *Butler* case, the Mississippi contingent got no money from the Charleston firm, and the claims and counterclaims were all dropped.

At the same time, Rice was also helping to work out an $11.3-billion settlement of the Florida case, which was announced on August 25. Motley didn't learn of it until the night before, when he and the rest of the trial team were summoned to dinner with Governor Lawton Chiles. But the *Butler* squabble presaged even uglier things to come. The ink wasn't dry on the Florida settlement before the trial team began fighting over how the fees would be divided, first in the newspapers, and then in court.

Motley would always feel Florida was the one that got away. Jury selection was under way at the time of the settlement, and just as he had predicted, Palm Beach County's well-educated citizenry was hostile to tobacco, with the potential jurors' responses on questionaires running about 70 percent in favor of the plaintiffs.

They had a sympathetic judge and a superb trial team suing under a special law rammed through the Florida legislature in late 1994 that prohibited the companies from arguing that smokers "assumed the risk" and chose to use cigarettes, thus denying the companies their most potent weapon. Ness, Motley's Andy Berly, and trial team members Wayne Hogan and W. C. Gentry, old allies from the asbestos wars, had spent months de-privileging industry documents with a "special master," a court-appointed senior lawyer who supervised discovery. Three weeks before the settlement, Motley's team finally got eight of the Liggett documents released to the public, including some Committee of Counsel material.

Also released was a 1964 memo that suggested that if the results of a proposed public opinion survey showed most people knew smoking was dangerous, they could be given to Congress or the Federal Trade Commission, but if unfavorable, "they could be destroyed and there would be no record in any office of the nature of the returns."

Shook, Hardy lawyers were in court just before the settlement arguing strenuously that the judge must not allow jurors to connect them personally with the fact that Shook, Hardy had been charged in the Florida suit with abetting a civil conspiracy.

And then, just as Motley seemed about to succeed in pulling the tobacco lawyers into the case, it was over. But there was no time to dwell on it. He was being summoned to Texarkana, where the Texas attorney general's lawsuit was in crisis, with trial just weeks away. And after two days of rest back in Charleston, that is where he went.

DON'T GET IN THE CAR

RON MOTLEY HAD A DATE WITH DR. THUO, AND WAS FLYING down the highway in a blue Suburban through a bleak corner of Arkansas that got poorer and hotter and flatter north of Texarkana.

He was on his way to give a urine sample to an Oriental man in a corrugated hut, and if that seems strange, everything about the Texas attorney general's lawsuit was strange. The plaintiff's team was housed in a former mental facility called Pinewood on the Texas side of the small city of Texarkana, half of which is in Arkansas. Pinewood's gym had been converted into a giant vault in which boxes of evidence were stacked twelve feet high on steel shelves.

Ness, Motley's staff slept in small bedrooms formerly occupied by the "clients" in the squat brown stone and metal building. The firm's offices were in the wing marked "Adult Unit." Conferences were held in the "Group Room." The isolation chamber where violent patients had been restrained still had its steel door and tiny window, only now the door stood open and inside the room were envelopes and computer paper and toner for the copying machine.

Motley hated Pinewood, and drove off on this unexpectedly long road trip to see Dr. Thuo.

"I've escaped from the Loony Bin and I'm wandering around Arkansas," he told his secretary back in South Carolina on his cell phone. He explained that he was suffering from a recurring infection and needed a urine test.

Thuo awaited him in a metal-roofed shed in Ashdown, a town just over the Arkansas line that consisted of a couple of stores, a gas station, and a Chinese restaurant. Motley strode behind the Chinese restaurant and found a small Vietnamese man in black jeans, black cowboy boots, and a work shirt. Motley went into the bathroom and came out with his beaker of urine.

"How you pay for this?" Thuo demanded.

Motley handed over fifty dollars in cash, which seemed to please Thuo. Thuo said he treated "minor emergencies."

"I do thirty-five urine tests a day," he exclaimed.

Motley left Thuo stuffing the bills into the cash drawer of the minor emergencies clinic behind the Chinese restaurant on the plains of Arkansas.

"You'll never believe what just happened," he told Jason, his tall blond ex-Marine assistant and driver, as he climbed back into the Suburban.

"'I worldwide known for urinalysis test,'" Motley quoted. "This guy is maybe four foot eight, with boots."

"Think that story might get better after a few pops?" he said. He stared out the window as the flatness rolled by.

Now it was back to the Loony Bin, as everyone called Pinewood. Local police guarded the parking lot, and internal security was overseen by a former bodyguard for the Saudi royal family, but amounted to little more than requiring visitors to wear badges. The real threat wasn't from tobacco company spies, but the unstable metabolism of the trial team. Houston lawyer John O'Quinn, whose name almost always appeared next to the adjective *flamboyant* even in friendly press accounts, was the supposed leader. Ness, Motley had been retained only as consultants to Texas Tobacco Litigation, the limited partnership that was actually prosecuting the Texas attorney general's lawsuit and which was being funded by a consortium of five Texas law firms, one of which was O'Quinn's.

A month before the trial date, Motley had been called in to fill an apparent leadership vacuum since O'Quinn's time was still largely taken up with breast implant and other litigation.

"I hope he realizes that he's not going to be able to just walk in and learn this in two weeks," Motley said.

Now, in mid-September, O'Quinn was on the scene, but so was Motley and there was no love lost between them. O'Quinn clearly prized his lead counsel status. Then, one night, the police stopped O'Quinn's car at Pinewood for allegedly driving erratically and O'Quinn, who has had well-publicized difficulties with alcohol, was packed off to a drying-out facility in Houston. The next day there was an emergency meeting and Motley was appointed interim lead counsel. Not long after that, O'Quinn returned and was reinstated. He could be seen through the open door of his office at Pinewood, a big man with slicked-back hair in a gray football T-shirt. The name JOHN O'QUINN had been pasted over a sign that said ART THERAPY.

The Five Firms all had rather sketchy organizations in the field. John O'Quinn, Walter Umphrey, Harold Nix, Wayne Reaud, and John Eddie Williams were good lawyers, and O'Quinn was among the top rank of trial lawyers in the United States. But to fight tobacco at the level of an attorney general's lawsuit took staff—lawyers, but also skilled paralegals and secretaries who'd spent years learning the case. And so the call went out not only for Motley but for the tobacco trial machine he had created.

A number of the Ness, Motley lawyers who had been living amid the glitz of West Palm Beach now were faced with trying a lawsuit in dingy Texarkana and dutifully moved into the Loony Bin or the Holiday Inn or an apartment, about thirty lawyers and support personnel altogether. The tobacco industry law firms set up their main operations center in an empty bank building in the city's boarded-up downtown and filled it with some eighty lawyers and staff, while individual firms rented space in several other buildings. The companies were spending millions in Texas, which had the distinction of hosting the largest civil trial in history.

As the trial date approached, both sides scrambled feverishly to put together mammoth kitchen-sink exhibit lists, containing every possible memo, X ray, and newspaper article they had the remotest chance of using. The gold standard for stockpiling evidence in an attorney general's tobacco suit was Minnesota, where Mike Ciresi's law firm had amassed and analyzed a warehouseful of industry documents, but Texas was a close second. When it was finally delivered to federal District Judge David Folsom, there were thirteen thousand items of evidence on the plaintiff's exhibit list, while the defense listed thirty-eight thousand.

Having done this before in Mississippi and Florida, the industry was well organized, but the plaintiffs were by any measure poorly prepared, owing largely to the relative inaction of the Five Firms in key areas over much of the previous year. The appearance of Motley, who brought with him discovery from Mississippi and Florida, helped, but didn't change the fact that there was no grand strategy for presenting the case to a jury and no clear chain of command.

"This case is such a mess," said Motley privately. "It should never go to trial."

Motley himself had moved into the Bridal Suite at the Holiday Inn. "I refuse to stay in that Loony Bin," he said.

Just a few days before his encounter with Dr. Thuo, Motley began his Texas odyssey by flying to Beaumont, near the Gulf Coast in east Texas, to take a deposition. But the deposition was postponed, so he visited with Walter Umphrey and Wayne Reaud, Texas trial team members and old comrades from the asbestos days who maintained dueling palatial offices across the street from each other.

Umphrey's quarters included a vast foyer paneled in wood like an outsized Edwardian study, on top of which he landed every day in the helicopter he flew from his cattle ranch, making the entire building vibrate.

He was jowly, brown skinned, and his hair had gone white, but when he emerged from his inner office to greet you, stepping over a crate of onions next to his secretary's desk, his handshake was iron. Inside the Umphrey edifice, Motley, Umphrey, and Reaud prepared for a key hearing in Texarkana. Motley was worried because the Five Firms had failed to get the judge to review any of the "crime/fraud" documents, the ones the industry claimed were privileged and which Motley felt were the essence of the conspiracy. In Florida, the trial team had spent months working with a special master to get these documents "tee'd up" for trial, but with jury selection set to begin on September 29, less than two weeks away, none of this work had been done in Texas.

Motley was also worried about whether to go to Dallas to talk to a business ethicist and potential witness, or to Texarkana, and didn't know what to do about his girlfriend, who called from the hotel four times during his meeting with Umphrey, crying more hysterically every time.

"Jesus, I can't take her to Texarkana," said Motley. "She'll go nuts."

Umphrey, Motley, and Reaud walked over to the Beaumont Club for a buffet lunch of barbecued beans, chicken, mashed potatoes, and cherry cobbler. They sat around a big circular table.

Walter Umphrey began to narrate the adventures of his boyhood friend Oscar, who it seemed had a habit of venturing south of the border for long weekends of whoring, a practice that had already killed off two of his friends.

"Bad hearts," said Umphrey.

Oscar entertained Mexican hookers at the rate of four a night, and to prolong his capacity for ecstasy, Oscar, a mechanic by trade, used a special aphrodisiac.

"You just put this stuff on the head of your dick," rumbled Umphrey. "He could keep it hard for twelve hours."

Motley laughed and said nothing, perhaps awestruck by a feat of storytelling more tasteless than anything he could come up with even while drunk.

When they returned to Umphrey's office, all was confusion. Judge Folsom had changed the subject of the upcoming hearing, necessitating a scramble to prepare to argue on a new topic. Charles Patrick was already in the air on a Ness, Motley plane bound for Dallas when he got a message from a flight controller to proceed instead to Texarkana.

Given the chaotic situation, Motley felt he had no choice but to do the same, so the crying girlfriend was put on a jet to her hometown on the Gulf, never to be heard from again.

But the event everyone was talking about was the postponed deposition, which had been rescheduled for Saturday morning. There were wild rumors about what the deponent, a lung specialist named Dr. Gary Huber, was going to say. The Texas team, especially Wayne Reaud, who first made contact with Huber, was in a state of high excitement.

"If what this guy knows gets out, it'll blow the lid right off this thing," Reaud told a reporter after lunch.

Reaud was a portly man with a wavy head of gray hair. He had gotten to know Huber through Huber's nutrition clinic at the University of Texas at Tyler, where Huber had been on the medical school faculty. For months, Reaud drove 225 miles north from Beaumont to Tyler to consult Huber about his weight.

Huber's pretty young wife, Mary, didn't believe Reaud was so terribly interested in her husband's nutrition program. She believed Reaud wanted Gary Huber for a very different reason.

For years, Huber had been a tobacco industry consultant on secondhand smoke and earlier was director of the Harvard Project, an exhaustive study of cigarettes and lung disease heavily funded by the cigarette companies. A brilliant scientist who would eventually publish over 150 scientific articles, Huber had proved the academic catch of a lifetime for the industry, a dream front man. By the summer of 1997, when Wayne Reaud told Ron Motley about his developing relationship with the lung specialist, Huber had been associated with tobacco and the industry's leading lights for twenty-five years. There was a strong presumption that Huber knew where bodies were buried.

Motley was very interested in pursuing Huber, but it wouldn't be easy. He had been paid as a consultant to tobacco law firms through much of the eighties and nineties, which meant the industry would undoubtedly claim it owned the contents of his brain. Huber would have to be strongly inclined to change sides and tell what he knew, because his life would certainly be turned upside down.

Motley's people began calling Huber and then Motley called Huber and then Motley flew to Tyler in the summer of 1997 for a visit. He came with a group, but Huber knew immediately which one was Motley when he walked through the door of his house, surrounded by attractive blond women. He was charmed, indeed starstruck by Motley, drawn in by his magnetism. He reminded Huber of another extraordinary personality he had known: David R. Hardy.

Motley went up to Huber's loft-like office at Tyler Junior College, sat in one of his black Harvard University chairs, and Huber started talking and didn't stop for almost eight hours.

Motley was fascinated, but also, Huber felt, testing him, trying to see if he was telling it straight. Because if the story was true, no one had ever heard anything like it.

GARY HUBER AND RON MOTLEY HIT IT OFF PARTLY BE-cause, as Huber liked to say, both were from the wrong side of the tracks, but Huber's background was so low down and impoverished it made Motley look like Rockefeller. Huber grew up near Spokane, Washington, in a shed-like house that had dirt floors, until he was in high school. His father was a well digger with a second-grade education, and his mother took jobs wallpapering so she could eat the paste, which was made of flour and water. Huber, long limbed and six foot six inches, escaped by getting a basketball scholarship to Washington State University. He went on to medical school at the University of Washington, where he was so proficient at research that he was the only student with his own technician and electron microscope. Harvard took him as an intern, and he specialized in pulmonary medicine. He remained at Harvard for fifteen years.

In 1971, Huber was approached by Dr. Gilbert Huebner, who bore the unlikely title of "medical director" of the Tobacco Institute. Huebner proposed that Huber research lung disease at Harvard with industry support. Huber and his colleagues resisted at first, but the industry was persistent, and flexible. The scientists could study what they pleased about smoking and health and publish the results without interference. The industry would donate research cigarettes, smoking machines, and technical support. Most important, the companies were offering a huge injection of cash. It was to be a new era of cooperation between the companies and the scientific community. Harvard accepted $2.8 million from the industry, the largest health-related grant tobacco had ever given a university, and the Tobacco and Health Research Program, known as the Harvard Project, got under way in the fall of 1972.

Huber's attitude toward tobacco had been instilled in him by his mentor at Harvard, Dr. Edward H. Kass, who ran the Channing Memorial Laboratory, where the Harvard Project began. Kass was a famous iconoclast who used to tell his doctors that if he ever heard them say they did something because Dr. Kass said they should, they were fired.

Examine every problem without preconceptions, that was the Kass motto. Kass liked to say that cigarette smoking was a high-frequency event with a low frequency of complications. Translated, that meant Kass believed that many people smoked a lot of cigarettes, but relatively few died from it. Huber idolized Kass and not only adopted his idea that most smokers never suffer consequences, but decided the entire case against smoking was largely fueled by anti-smoking zealots. The cigarette companies latched on to Huber for the simple reason that Huber was a born cigarette company scientist. He truly believed the link between cigarettes and disease was unproven. *Cause* was a sacred word, never to be taken lightly.

Huber wrote to the Tobacco Institute's Horace Kornegay in late 1971, while he and the industry were still getting to know each other, saying he hoped to "bring the tobacco controversy back into the realm of scientific objectivity."

"I am somewhat amazed, however, how our conventional funding establishments begin with the premise that tobacco is bad," he said.

Huber's previous research had shown that most animals develop an "adaptive tolerance" to a lung irritant and no longer suffer ill effects after a certain number of exposures. A few do not become tolerant, and get sick. Huber's key assumption in undertaking cigarette research was that it must be the same with human beings, given so many smokers and relatively few deaths. The long-term goal of the Harvard Project would be to identify the traits that put certain smokers at greater risk of illness.

Along with his naiveté about the cigarette companies, there was an arrogance to Huber. These things had been studied for more than twenty years, but not properly, that is, not by Huber and not at Harvard. Not enough quantification of results had been done. Too many of the studies were poorly designed. He was going to do it right and "resolve the tobacco problem," he wrote to the Tobacco Institute.

Doing it right meant mounting a massive assault on pulmonary disease involving thirty faculty members and sixty-three assistants across many specialties. State-of-the-art equipment and research techniques were used, such as an extremely precise way of analyzing tissue samples called stereology. Lorillard donated a sophisticated smoking machine, and another machine that could add nicotine or flavors to cigarettes. The project ran from 1972 until 1980, and generated some 239 medical publications, including 27 books, and 54 peer-reviewed scientific papers.

The Harvard Project first looked at emphysema, which is part of a group of diseases called chronic obstructive pulmonary disease that afflicts over 10 million people and is the fourth leading cause of death in the United States. Very little was known about emphysema, except that its victims were almost always cigarette smokers.

An irritant causes inflammation and stretching of the air sacs in the lungs, which ultimately collapse, leaving lungs that look like big, empty bags.

The companies were nervous about lawsuits from emphysema victims. They needed to look like they were searching for answers on chronic obstructive pulmonary disease just as they had pretended to seek them for cancer, and they hoped that given Huber's obvious sympathy with their position, the Harvard Project would yield studies helpful to their cause. Right from the beginning, the industry was planning to turn the Harvard Project into a major propaganda tool.

But how to handle it? Originally, the industry's liaison with Harvard was either Huebner or Horace Kornegay, president of the Tobacco Institute. There were periodic meetings in Washington at the Institute's offices at 1776 K Street, and at one of these, Huebner introduced Huber to a ruddy, Irish-looking gentleman with graying dark brown hair, impeccably dressed in a dark blue suit, a just-under-six-footer with an almost military carriage.

"Gary, meet Dave Hardy," said Huebner.

Hardy went into a long tirade that seemed to revolve around how important he was.

"We've got a product involved in litigation, and I run the litigation, so I need to get involved in the research," said Hardy. He should have been involved with Huber and Harvard from the first, he explained, because without him, the industry would soon be nibbled to death by plaintiff's lawyers.

Hardy lectured Huber on the Committee of Counsel, the Ad Hoc Committee, parts of an apparatus he not only claimed to run but to have designed. The others in the room had the air of people who had heard Hardy's speech before. Huber was bewildered—what did all this have to do with him?—but flew back to Boston impressed with Hardy's rapacious ego.

For his part, David Hardy knew what he had in Harvard and Huber and wanted to make sure the cowboys over at the Tobacco Institute didn't blow it. TI, he believed, was too hard line, too obviously and savagely partisan. Hardy's mission was to seed the universities with research money and grow an unassailable crop of advocates. The best place of all to seed was Harvard. To protect the industry's investment, he believed he needed to take over the operation from Huebner and Kornegay.

It took just one mistake for Dave Hardy to own the Harvard Project. The good Dr. Huebner, the Tobacco Institute's "medical director," had unfortunately taken to drinking heavily. He got drunk during one of his visits to Boston and made a fool of himself, groping at two young female technicians when they arrived to pick him up at his hotel. Huber was furious. Hardy found out and immediately flew to Boston, taking a room at the Harvard Faculty Club.

Over dinner there, Hardy apologized for the incident. Hardy had already gotten Huebner booted off the Harvard Project, and promised that nothing like that would ever happen again. Hardy would be the Project's new overseer and, from that moment on, Gary Huber's keeper. If Huber had a problem, he was to call Hardy. If he needed to speak to a cigarette company researcher, Hardy would make it happen.

Huber accepted the apology. Hardy seemed to relish sitting at the Harvard Faculty Club, a glass of whiskey in one hand, a Marlboro in the other, telling war stories about how he'd crushed plaintiff's lawyers like Melvin Belli.

"He's a blowhard," said Hardy. "Most of them are blowhards. Most of them collapse with just a little shove.

"I've beaten 'em all. Their best," he said.

He told Huber how he'd been a prosecutor in the army and never lost, then turned right around and defended a soldier and triumphed again; how, in the late fifties, he won one of the largest plaintiff's verdicts in Missouri history—$100,000 for a motorcycle accident, which attracted Philip Morris's attention; and how that led to his greatest victory—the *Ross* case, his transformation of a wheezing cripple, an object of pity, into a drunken ne'er-do-well who brawled in the street and had out-of-wedlock children with chorus girls in the great Sodom of Los Angeles.

"That's why they came to me," Hardy said. "I know how to win."

Over the next year, Huber saw more of Hardy and met almost all the power figures in tobacco. Indeed, once the project was up and running, they could not be kept away. There was an incessant parade of dignitaries through the labs, immortalized in publicity photos of the time. There was Arthur Stevens, counsel for Lorillard, squeezing Huber's hand and smiling majestically in front of bottles of frozen smoke samples. Standing off to one side in several frames was a little man with shiny dark hair—Ed Jacobs, lawyer and ringmaster at the Council for Tobacco Research.

Once every so often, the CEOs were brought in for a site visit. It was heady stuff for a boy from Spokane. Soon, Huber found himself being flown to Washington to be trotted out at a posh restaurant where someone from the Tobacco Institute would introduce him to Senator Henry Jackson or Israeli defense minister Moshe Dayan or Nixon cabinet member Melvin Laird as Tobacco Institute photographers fired away, capturing Huber, a giant in a tweed jacket and metal-rimmed glasses, bending slightly to shake hands with the celebrity of the moment. Mr. Secretary, this is Dr. Gary Huber. He's running our research program at *Harvard*.

Harvard! The peculiar industry could not believe its luck. These most notorious of companies were dining at the Harvard Faculty Club, passing carafes of wine and baskets of rolls down to their tablemates, who were the cream of the medical research community at the most prestigious university in the world. They ate at long tables covered with crimson tableclothes, surrounded by dark drapes and oak paneling according to a seating chart devised by David Hardy himself, who knew enough to sit Lorillard's Curtis Judge away from the Reynolds people, his former and now hated employers.

Huber enjoyed hosting the tobacco men, and became close to Hardy and Henry Roemer, the corporate counsel for Reynolds, a strong and early advocate of the Harvard Project. Roemer was a well-read, sophisticated man, son of an executive of International Telephone and Telegraph. Fine featured with coal-black hair and graceful manners, Jack Roemer had grown up in Paris, Cuba, all over the world, and was educated at Harvard. Roemer and Huber became good friends and together climbed much of the way up Annapurna, one of the highest Himalayan peaks.

There always seemed to be a strong mentor around Huber, from Dr. Kass to Roemer and Hardy. Huber tried hard to please, perhaps too hard. He was young and ambitious and the industry had a lot of practice cultivating the Gary Hubers of the world, while Huber had no experience with anything as Byzantine as the tobacco industry. He was moving in exalted circles, among senators and manufacturing kingpins and was thoroughly seduced. Especially by Hardy, who took him more and more into his confidence. His reaction was to become a sycophant. His letters to Hardy closed with, "My warmest personal regards and highest respect."

Hardy seemed like a bumpkin next to Roemer but was at least as sophisticated and the toughest of the lot. Like a latter-day Rasputin, Hardy came from the hinterlands to save tobacco from the lawsuit, the industry's inherited disease, and while some hated him, his magic worked. He was the price the dynasty paid for survival.

Dave Hardy and Huber were often together. They would meet for dinner in New York or Washington or Boston, and Huber always flew first class and stayed in the best hotels, all at industry expense. Yet Hardy lived in a modest two-story brick house in a middle-class section of Kansas City with his pleasant, self-effacing wife. Hardy's major vice seemed to be baseball, and he had four seats behind the visitors' dugout at Royals Stadium, where he took Huber more than once. Hardy would try to psyche out the opposing batters as they warmed up. His technique was a long, steady stare.

"They go up to the plate a little shaken up," he claimed. He gave Huber a Royals program, which he signed, "Dave Hardy, Official Scorekeeper." Huber framed it and hung it on the wall of his office in Boston.

Huber met the important people at Shook, Hardy & Bacon, and was once driven out to the firm's records storage area, located in natural limestone caves that ran deep into hills beyond the Kansas City limits. Outside the mouth of the cave was a guardhouse, and an armed man came out and opened the gate. The car drove right into the little mountain through an entrance wide enough to accommodate an eighteen-wheeler. Inside, among cold stone walls darkened by truck exhaust, sat thousands of boxes.

Hardy tried to edit certain troublesome terms out of Huber's letters, but Huber resisted, citing Harvard's strict rule against interference by funding agencies. Oh, no, Hardy said. We would never interfere.

One day, early in the Harvard Project, Hardy invited Huber for dinner at the Metropolitan Club, J. P. Morgan's hostel for plutocrats on Fifth Avenue in Manhattan. Huber walked through the atrium with its gilded Corinthian columns and up the staircase to the ballroom on the second floor, where he found Hardy and Jack Roemer. Huber didn't mind being wined and dined, not after growing up on a dirt floor in Spokane.

There was little conversation at dinner, and while Huber drank his usual quotient of wine, Hardy and Roemer drank almost nothing. Afterward Hardy and Roemer lit cigars. Hardy suggested a little walk.

Hardy opened a door at one end of the ballroom and behind it was a meeting room set up as a mock courtroom. Roemer sat in the audience section, puffing his cigar. The tone of the evening had suddenly turned a bit chilly.

"That's the witness stand," said Hardy, pointing to a folding chair. "Now you get up there."

Huber, who was tipsy, obeyed. Hardy pulled a folder from his briefcase. Roemer grinned.

Hardy read a sentence or two of one of Huber's letters.

"Aren't you saying, Dr. Huber, that smoking is known to be the major cause of emphysema?" Hardy asked.

"I am not saying that," Huber protested. "Emphysema is a complex, multi-factorial disease. We're still looking for mechanisms."

"But that's not what it says here, is it?" said Hardy. And he read a sentence out of context from one of Huber's letters to Roemer.

Huber tried to keep up, but he couldn't do it. No matter how adroitly he parried, Hardy's mind moved faster. Maybe it was the wine. He couldn't remember ever feeling so completely outclassed in sheer intellectual horsepower. It was like a chess match between a novice and a grandmaster.

Of course, it didn't take long for Huber to figure out that this was a rather brutal demonstration of why Hardy wanted Huber to edit certain terms from his letters.

When Huber stepped down an hour later, he felt like a horse's ass. Roemer came over and patted his shoulder.

"Don't feel too bad." He smiled. "You're in the hands of the master."

The mock cross-examination at the Metropolitan Club changed little. Huber still resisted being edited, and Hardy still sent letters back with comments scribbled in the margins.

What changed was Hardy. A series of small heart attacks in

1975 and 1976 left him weakened, although he was mortally afraid to show it. He believed his enemies would pounce on any sign he was faltering. He began to stay home some days to rest. Often he would call Huber, whom he had come to trust with intimate matters, to discuss his condition.

His old antagonist, Lyman Field, who had brought the *Ross* case, saw a pale and thin Hardy around Kansas City in the last year of his life and almost didn't recognize him. "The cigarette boys are working him to death," Field told someone in his office.

Even as his grip loosened, Hardy continued to generate streams of paper until he was hospitalized late in 1976 after still another heart attack. Hardy had smoked a pipe or cigarettes much of his adult life. He was fifty-nine years old and had now suffered at least four myocardial infarctions, each replacing his heart's muscle with more scar tissue so less and less blood could be pumped. David Hardy was dying.

Huber began to get phone calls from Hardy's hospital bed back in Missouri. Hardy was frightened. He would ask what certain pains meant and whether he was getting the right treatment. Sometimes he called well after midnight. Huber would explain and try to offer comfort, although he knew there was no hope.

"Thanks, Gary," Hardy would say as they hung up. Huber had the feeling that now he could sleep.

Hardy also talked about his life, his career, the work he had done for the tobacco companies, which he believed was his monumental achievement. Huber had somehow become Hardy's deathbed confessor. But it wasn't a confession. Even at the end, it was defiance.

"No matter what they've done, they deserve the best defense I can give them," Hardy said during a late-night call.

"Well, no one could have done a better job," said Huber.

"I bought 'em an extra twenty or thirty years," said Hardy.

Huber murmured something.

"But you know, it's temporary," Hardy said. "One of these days, we're going to have to pay up."

"Uh-huh," said Huber.

"You may live to see it," said Hardy. "I'm glad I won't."

A few days later, David Hardy was dead.

IN MID-1977, THE HARVARD PROJECT WAS RENEWED FOR three more years. Huber's findings had so far not threatened tobacco, partly because the research was years behind schedule owing to catastrophic problems with the physical facilities, such as marauding street rats who infected the research rats. Then Boston City Hospital evicted the program. The work became so disrupted that Huber sent back the industry's checks until stability returned.

Despite the problems, he believed his program was far superior to that of the Council for Tobacco Research, which he visited in New York.

"It's a third-rate operation," he told friends. CTR's smoking machines didn't work, he said, and its scientists were occupied chasing rabbits down holes.

What CTR did have, Huber discovered, was probably the world's largest database on smoking and health, called the Literature Retrieval Division, located on a floor restricted to those with special passes. The database was used by lawyers in product liability suits. During a trip to Louisville, a Brown & Williamson scientist showed it to Huber, a keyword-searchable index to over 180,000 scientific articles.

"We had an army working on this," said the scientist. "This cost a couple hundred million."

Later renamed L.S., Inc., the database was a potent secret weapon. It took over a hundred people to maintain. They read and coded 12,500 articles a year, translating those in foreign languages. Having the database made it practically impossible for a plaintiff to surprise the industry with some novel piece of research. Huber was impressed.

Although CTR seemed shoddy, Huber found several of the research and development shops at the companies to be top-notch, and the most impressive was Philip Morris. He made a number of trips to the ultra-modern research tower in Richmond, and was usually met by senior researcher Tom Osdene, who trotted Huber past a number of the labs and allowed him to glimpse others. The "non-tour," Huber called it.

Nevertheless it was apparent to Huber from meeting Philip Morris's research staff, especially Helmut Wakeham, the outgoing chief of R and D, that the company had the most advanced scientific capability in the industry. Wakeham, Huber believed, could have chaired a department at any Ivy League university, a first-class scientist. Philip Morris was smarter, more focused, and far more secretive than the other companies.

The level of curiosity was higher, too, and when it came to emphysema, it was insatiable. Wakeham would take Huber into his office and spend hours sucking out every bit of information he could get on the subject. And of course, everyone, not just the scientists, but the lawyers and executives as well, was curious what the Harvard team would tell the world about emphysema.

They found out in September 1977 when industry executives learned about a scholarly article Huber and his co-researchers had written, and it suddenly dawned on them that they were going to have a problem with Dr. Huber after all.

Alexander Holtzman at Philip Morris fired off a memo warning of "disturbing news" from the Harvard Project. Huber had told Shook, Hardy's William Shinn that "rats exposed to tobacco smoke for six months developed emphysema," or more precisely, "par enchymal alterations of the lung."

Worse, Huber would announce these findings in a few weeks at a meeting of the American College of Chest Physicians in Las Vegas, which could mean significant play in the media. Shinn had already made an emergency trip to Boston, Holtzman wrote, hoping to "lessen Huber's inclination to interpret the results as evidence of direct cause and effect.

"However, Shinn reported that he did not succeed," Holtzman noted.

Much to the industry's dismay, Huber, it turned out, though a contrarian and naïf, was a talented scientist, unlike many in tobacco's scientific stable. His experiments were flawlessly designed, and Huber had achieved a real breakthrough in the study of emphysema. He had discovered that exposure to smoke triggered the release in the lung of a key chemical mediator that first robbed the air sacs of their elasticity and function, and later destroyed them. He was now going to tell the world what he had learned, and since Huber wasn't being paid through "Special Projects" or under CTR contract, there wasn't a damned thing anyone could do about it.

Even though the public reaction, as it turned out, wasn't overwhelming, Huber's star started sinking fast, and from then on the Harvard Project was living on borrowed time. The industry was contractually bound to finish out its three-year commitment. But the love affair was over, and now Huber's requests for help from the cigarette makers were received with hostility. The companies, especially Philip Morris, had turned on him with a vengeance.

A few months after the emphysema report, Helmut Wakeham urged turning Huber down for money to rehabilitate his lab, saying Huber was "brazenly trying to 'milk' even more money from the industry. I think the longer we are in bed with him, the sorrier we will be that we ever jumped in."

With mordant sarcasm, Wakeham blamed the "Sanhedrin"—the supreme council of the Jews of antiquity but, in this context, the lawyers—for getting "us into this mess, now let them get us out with minimum damage.

"Better to bite the bullet now and amputate than to get gangrene later," he concluded.

The final straw for the industry was Huber's nicotine study, the last of the Harvard Project's three phases, the first two being emphysema and heart disease. The nicotine study used techniques that Huber and his colleagues had developed to precisely measure how the lungs work during the act of smoking. Magnetometers, which look like electrodes, were placed on the chest, abdomen, and back to measure the motion of the rib cage and diaphragm. Huber had determined in an earlier experiment that each person's depth and length of inhalation, along with other puff characteristics, were remarkably consistent over time.

In the nicotine experiment, Huber first obtained an "inhalation fingerprint" for sixty volunteers smoking high tar, regular nicotine cigarettes. He then measured their inhalation patterns smoking cigarettes of equivalent tar but much lower nicotine, doctoring the cigarettes with a machine designed by Lorillard Tobacco to add flavorants or nicotine.

What Huber discovered was that a majority of smokers radically changed their puff pattern when they smoked lower tar and nicotine cigarettes. They took more frequent puffs, inhaled three times more smoke, and held it twice as long. This meant the smoke penetrated farther into the lung, trapping particles of tar deep in its periphery.

Huber concluded two things from this study. One was that smokers who sucked harder or longer on low nicotine cigarettes were probably "titrating"—trying to maintain a certain nicotine level in their blood. In so doing, they were risking damage from adenocarcinoma, which develops in the outlying regions of the lung. Statistics were beginning to show a rise in this type of cancer as people switched to lower nicotine products. And adenocarcinoma was less treatable than other lung cancers.

The titration study was an even bigger blow to the industry than Huber's emphysema work. It was hard to challenge because Huber used mathematical measurements of puff patterns, which eliminated the weakness of earlier experiments where scientists relied on observation and verbal description.

The cigarette makers' marketing strategy for low tar and nicotine cigarettes was based on the public's belief that they were healthier than "high yield" smokes, even though the industry was careful never to explicitly claim this. Now Huber had proved "low yield" products were probably as deadly, and possibly worse.

But Huber's cardinal sin had been to perform some of his tests with commercially available True and Marlboro cigarettes, which made the results far more threatening than if he had stuck to the "Kentucky Reference" research cigarettes the industry used, which had no additives and few of the characteristics of a modern cigarette.

Huber's results were alarming enough that the National Institutes of Health decided to fund Huber to do an even bigger study, which further riled the tobacco companies. This was precisely the kind of research synergy they had succeeded in derailing for many years by keeping their own smoking and health experiments out of the public arena. Huber was turning into a very noisy fly in the ointment.

It so happened that the Project's latest three-year grant was about to expire. Huber wrote the companies, pleading for continued funding. In early 1980, the industry's top lawyers flew in to meet with Harvard administrators and Huber. Notably missing was Jack Roemer, who as general counsel for Reynolds, then the number one cigarette company, had been the Project's strongest booster since Hardy died.

The industry group made a great fuss over protocol, insisting on meeting the president of Harvard, who was unavailable. They claimed there was too much turmoil over finding quarters for the Project. Huber could see it all crumbling, just as his team was in a position to nail down how emphysema begins. The Harvard Project had been his life for seven years, keeping him in the lab from before dawn until after dark six days a week. He was devastated. After the meeting, he drove Alexander Holtzman, the Philip Morris lawyer, to the Hilton at Logan International Airport.

"Where's Jack? Did he call you?" said Holtzman, speaking of Roemer.

Huber said he had no idea where Roemer was. Holtzman seemed highly agitated.

It struck Huber that for the number one company in the industry not to be represented was certainly strange.

"This is Jack's project," said Holtzman. "I don't understand why Jack isn't here."

Huber thought he smelled a coup d'état in Roemer's disappearance, but at the moment he had other worries. At the Hilton, Holtzman and Huber walked into a double-sized guest room where they found Arthur Stevens, general counsel at Lorillard, Lee Stanford of Shook, Hardy & Bacon, and Ernest Pepples, counsel for Brown & Williamson. Holtzman gathered his things and left.

Stevens paced back and forth, and smoked. He wore a different face from the one he wore to the dinners at the Harvard Faculty Club.

"That nicotine titration study—that wasn't supposed to have even been done," said Stevens. "Nicotine was never part of your charter."

The Project was doomed. It was the emphysema experiment, too. The lawyers could never accept that it had happened. Huber felt a sense of menace in the room.

"You just got too close to things you weren't supposed to get into, Gary," said Stevens.

Huber drove back to Boston, feeling lower than he ever had.

In a few months, however, he got a miraculous second chance. The University of Kentucky ran a Tobacco and Health Research Institute funded by a state tax on cigarettes and overseen by a board on which sat Brown & Williamson's Ernest Pepples, who promised Huber could continue his Harvard work in Lexington. Other friends in the industry made noises about renewed funding at this new location, and Huber accepted a job as the institute's director.

A few weeks before moving his family to Kentucky in the summer of 1980, he was awakened around two A.M. by a phone call. It was Janet Brown, who had represented American Tobacco since the *Green* case, the lone woman lawyer in the top councils of the industry. She was a quick-witted, heavy-set woman, not someone Huber knew terribly well.

"Gary," she said. "Gary, this is Janet Brown."

"Janet," said Huber. "What a surprise. It's kind of late."

Brown sounded like she had been drinking.

"Yes," said Brown. "I've got to tell you something—very important. It's a trap."

"What's a trap?" said Huber.

"Kentucky. They're setting you up. To discredit you," said Brown. "Don't take it."

Huber thanked her for thinking of him.

"Just remember," Brown said. "It's a setup."

She hung up and Huber went back to sleep.

DOWN IN LEXINGTON, THINGS BEGAN TO GO WRONG IN a rather spectacular way. Huber found what he later described as a "mare's nest." Millions of dollars were unaccounted for at the Tobacco and Health Research Institute and its research was almost uniformly of the lowest caliber. The program's pride and joy was a study of smoking monkeys who were not actually inhaling smoke, leading to unusually healthy smoking monkeys. The program's "over six hundred scientific contributions" mentioned in PR materials actually consisted of about forty published papers on smoking and health. Huber terminated most of the institute's staff and almost all existing projects and demanded an audit.

Huber, in turn, was attacked, accused of manipulating scientific results, administrative incompetence, even sexual harassment. Then he was investigated by the university's legal department and the local district attorney while newspaper headlines screamed about grand juries and a potential indictment for theft. Someone poured sand in the gas tank of his car. Anonymous callers threatened his life and that of his teenage daughter, Melissa. To cheer her up, he bought Melissa a puppy, which bled to death while she was playing with him, apparently poisoned. An industry security consultant advised Huber to carry a handgun and to train Melissa to fire a shotgun. He felt like a hole had opened up in the ground and was swallowing him inch by inch. Within a year of moving to Lexington, he was fired from the Tobacco and Health Research Institute.

Huber kept his job as a teacher at the University of Kentucky medical school until 1985 so as not to disrupt his daughter's high school education, then moved to the University of Texas at Tyler. Although he was ultimately cleared, his reputation was permanently damaged. Those who knew him best said Huber was never the same after Kentucky. He seemed to have lost his air of authority and confidence. In any event, Gary Huber never did another smoking and health experiment.

At the University of Texas, Huber changed his specialty to nutrition. No longer the star scientist from Harvard, he had fallen into the ranks of hired guns paid to render opinions for tobacco in lawsuits and regulatory matters. Jones, Day, Reavis & Pogue, Reynolds's law firm, retained him to review articles linking lifestyle factors to pulmonary disease, thousands of studies shipped in from Cleveland that filled a room with filing cabinets. Working part-time, the Lifestyle Project took Huber seven years to finish. It may have been a coincidence, but it happened to tie him up at a time when a fresh crop of major lawsuits were proceeding in Texas, one a pioneering emphysema action.

Huber continued to socialize with a few tobacco men. When he remarried in 1987, Jack Roemer of Reynolds and Lee Stanford of Shook, Hardy were his best men. Roemer retired a few years after the Harvard fiasco, and never explained why he hadn't shown up that day in Boston. Huber always assumed Roemer took the blame for the Harvard Project running off the reservation.

Huber hadn't seen Roemer since the wedding when he traveled to Winston-Salem, North Carolina, in the mid-nineties to visit a nutrition center. Huber attended services at the Episcopal cathedral where the R. J. Reynolds executives worshiped, but Roemer wasn't among them. Curious, he decided to call him.

"Jack, I went to church this morning and you weren't there," said Huber.

Roemer said he was now a member of the Moravian Home

Church, a small, deeply devout Christian sect. When Huber stopped by the house he found Roemer wearing around his neck an enormous wooden cross. Roemer explained that the Moravians were not evangelical. They believed in a simple life, ran their own bakery, and kept apart from others. Roemer arose at four in the morning each day to pray, and play his bugle. He had already purchased his plot in the Moravian cemetery. Roemer seemed to Huber to be doing penance, but for what? He had never expressed qualms about the cigarette business. It was Huber's last visit.

Mary Huber, who met her husband in Texas, found the tobacco men remote. She could see they knew exactly which buttons to push to feed her husband's ego and keep him on the team. Then one day, much later, Huber dug up a videotape of a Philip Morris event from a box of junk. On the tape, research director Tom Osdene introduced Huber to the assembled officials.

"Ladies and gentlemen," said Osdene in Czech-flavored English. "I give you Gary Huber, one of the best friends the tobacco industry ever had."

There was prolonged applause and a vigorous dark-haired figure fairly bounded up to the podium and began speaking. Mary Huber was fascinated. Although the tape was not very old, the contrast to the hesitant silver-haired man sitting next to her was stark.

"My God, Gary," said Mary, shaking her head. "What happened to you?"

IT WAS NOT ONE GREAT THING, BUT A SERIES OF SMALL ones that finally turned Gary Huber against the industry that elevated and then destroyed him. Like every other whistle-blower, he watched the 1994 Waxman hearings in disbelief. When Lorillard's Alexander Spears—who provided the machine that added nicotine to the Harvard Project's cigarettes for the nicotine titration studies—declared that the industry did not and *could not* manipulate nicotine, Huber stormed out of the room.

"That lying asshole," he muttered.

Under pressure from the state of Texas, which had received a Freedom of Information Act request for Huber's work at Tyler from Ness, Motley, Huber ended his consulting arrangements with the tobacco law firms in 1996. Another turning point came when he re-

viewed data for R. J. Reynolds on Eclipse, a new "smokeless cigarette" similar to Premier. Huber pointed out that smokers were
likely to drag harder on the cigarette as they ran out of nicotine, exposing them to high carbon monoxide levels.

Then he realized that Reynolds almost *had* to know this already.
It was Reynolds that had shown Huber and his Harvard colleagues
tiny infrared probes that could be placed in a cigarette's filter to
monitor a smoker's puff patterns from a remote location. Incredible
technology. And that had been twenty years earlier.

"They can't seem to do anything honestly," he told Mary. He got
a little angry.

Then Wayne Reaud, the chubby Texas plaintiff's lawyer, began
showing up at Huber's Texas Nutrition Institute. Huber asked
Robert McDermott, a tobacco lawyer at Jones, Day, Reavis &
Pogue, if McDermott had heard of Reaud. McDermott had gotten
to know Huber well after seven years of being his chief "handler."
He told him Reaud was working on the attorney generals lawsuit
and to stay away from him.

When Motley's people began calling, Huber asked McDermott
about Motley.

"That son of a bitch is lower than whale shit," said McDermott.

The Shook, Hardy lawyers told Huber that Motley was a drunk,
that he chased teenage girls, used drugs. Don't be seduced by him,
they told him. Keep the faith.

And then Motley showed up at Huber's door in August, trudg-
ing up the stairs to Huber's very unglamorous warren of an office in
a partly vacant auxiliary building at Tyler Junior College, and of
course, Motley was surrounded by women, "all blond and all beautiful," as Huber said later.

Huber needed to believe and Motley could get people to believe. Motley was, after all, the lead warrior, by dint of accomplish-
ment, intelligence, and what happened in a room when he started
talking. After six or eight hours of telling Motley his story, Huber
was leaning toward the plaintiff's team. Still, before making any
commitment, Huber phoned a lawyer friend who told him Motley
was one of the great trial lawyers in the country. Huber was ready
for some kind of reckoning with the industry. Come nightfall,
Huber was just plain won over. He was in.

"Ann, he's the biggest conspiracy witness ever," Motley told Ann Ritter by cell phone as he drove back to the airport. Motley immediately deputized a top lawyer, Ed Westbrook, to deal full-time with the Huber matter.

The coming weeks began Huber's education in what had really been going on in the tobacco industry. Motley sent documents from the Merrell Williams collection, which fascinated Huber, as well as the industry's opening statement in a cigarette lawsuit that quoted Huber's pro-industry letters, which made him want to throw up.

In August, Motley called and told Huber he wanted him to come to Charleston.

"Doc, you've got to come down and look at these documents," Motley said. "I can't let them out of the office."

Huber protested that he was about to leave on an oft-postponed vacation to San Antonio with Mary and their three young children, and the trip couldn't be rerouted on such short notice.

Motley said he would take care of keeping Huber's family happy while Huber read through the files. And, he said, he could solve his transportation problem, too. Huber's children, John, Kathryn, and Michael, couldn't believe their eyes when they saw Motley's white jet waiting for them at the little airport in Tyler. Was this first class? John wanted to know.

"This is better than first class," said Huber.

In Charleston, Mary and the children were driven to the Kiawah Island house and went to the beach. Huber sat in Motley's Meeting Street office and read. It was not a pleasurable experience. Not all the documents were new, but they were new to Huber. A 1974 memo from Alexander Spears of Lorillard said industry-funded scientific programs like the Harvard Project "have not been selected against specific scientific goals, but rather for various purposes such as public relations, political relations, position for litigation, etc." Another Lorillard memo said of another project, "No PR value, à la Harvard."

But for Huber, the hardest thing to swallow was that the industry had already done, in secret, much of the Harvard Project research of which he had been so proud. They had produced emphysema in rabbits at the Mouse House at R. J. Reynolds ten years before he did and probably could have found the disease

mechanism. They knew smokers compensate for lower-nicotine cigarettes because they had done tons of puff pattern work. If they had
shared even a fraction of what they already knew during the Harvard
Project, truly significant breakthroughs might have been achieved.

"What we did was artifact. Pure artifact," he said in disgust.

And, of course, Dave Hardy was everywhere in the documents,
manipulating dozens of Gary Hubers at dozens of research institutes and universities, promising support, making them feel part of
something important. How eagerly they wrote back promising to be
"objective," just as Huber had. Huber was different only because he
was a better scientist at a better institution, which just made him a
more eye-catching puppet.

By the time Huber met Mary and the children for dinner, he felt
ill. He couldn't eat, and when he got back to the hotel he couldn't
sleep. He sat down on the bed and he began to cry.

In ten years, Mary had never seen her husband so unhappy. It
was the enormity of what he had helped to perpetrate, not only the
injury to public health but to science, which had pulled Huber from
the muck of Spokane. Science had been like a sparkling white
house in which he found everything he needed to live.

Over the ensuing days he read depositions by other scientists.
They, too, had been deceived, sent off to chase rabbits down holes,
just as Huber had been. One branch of the scientific tree had been
purposely denied nutrients, while another was artificially strengthened. How many years had this black magic set back the study of
lung disease? No one would ever know.

Huber called his best friend, Rob Pandina, a psychologist at
Rutgers University in New Jersey who had also done work for the
industry. Huber poured out his heart. How could he have been so
stupid? How could they have been so thoroughly suckered?

"Look," said Pandina. "It's a card game. We came to the table
honestly, played by the rules. They were playing a different game.
They knew all of the cards. They knew what they were going to feed
us. That's how they led us down those alleys."

Huber spent most of the next six days with Motley and Ed Westbrook being debriefed at Ness, Motley's Meeting Street headquarters. By the end of the week, he was on the plaintiff's team with a
vengeance. The day before he left Charleston, Motley and West-

brook sat with Huber and discussed his options. By now, Motley had subpoenaed Huber to give a deposition in the Texas attorney general's case.

"I am keeping you under wraps until we can get you under oath and preserve, shall I say, the *skeleton* of your story," Motley said.

Huber would be able to say, truthfully, that since his testimony was compelled by subpoena, he had not violated any agreement with the tobacco law firms.

Motley's tone changed.

"Hey, it'll be fun," he said. He reached across the table and squeezed Huber's shoulder.

Was he kidding? Huber couldn't really tell. And it didn't matter. The dice were cast. Everyone in the room knew that pain lay ahead for Gary Huber. His fate would be in the hands of judges who could decide, as they had with Jeff Wigand, to let the industry interrogate him for twenty days or so, more a prolonged civil flogging than a tool for generating information.

Then, in a quieter tone of voice, Motley described what he believed would happen next.

"You're going to get a phone call from one of them," said Motley. "And they'll offer to get a lawyer for you, and he'll call you and by the time he does, they've already got him on a million-dollar retainer.

"Now, we don't tell people what to do. That's not our style here," said Motley. "But I wouldn't trust who they come to you with."

"Don't get in the car," said Westbrook, looking down at the table, smiling.

"Because that guy is going to be their guy," said Motley.

"Wait a minute. What do you mean, 'Don't get in the car'?" demanded Huber.

It was a line from a Robert Redford film called *Three Days of the Condor*, said Westbrook. Huber had never seen it.

"I'll send it to you," said Westbrook.

Huber returned to Tyler and sure enough, the tobacco lawyers began calling about the subpoena.

This time when Robert McDermott called, Huber sounded quite different than in the past.

"Bob, I've been reading these documents and I'm really both-ered by them," said Huber. "They're from your company and some of them are from you."

McDermott sounded like he was going have a stroke.

"What documents?" he said. "Have you got the numbers on them?"

Huber described some of what he had looked at.

"Jesus, those aren't supposed to be out there," said McDermott. "I want you to give me an inventory of what you've seen."

McDermott had been in Huber's house many times. He had fished with Huber, shared dinner with Gary and Mary. Huber liked McDermott.

"I can't do that," said Huber.

"What the hell do you mean, you can't?" said McDermott.

"Bob, you don't look so good on those papers," said Huber.

"I'll tell you what," said McDermott. "Ron Motley and I are going to meet at the pearly gates, and one of us is going to go straight to hell. One of us can be condemned. We'll see who it is."

Huber had nothing to say to that, and after a few more minutes, they hung up.

Several of Huber's other lawyer-keepers weighed in with advice. One suggested that if he cleaned things from his files that were no longer necessary, that would be perfectly okay. Huber ignored that suggestion. McDermott called and asked if he appreciated that if he cooperated with Motley, the full weight of the Jones, Day law firm would fall on him. Huber ignored that as well, and other statements that sounded a bit like threats.

"I'd hate to see a repeat of Kentucky, Gary. Or, God forbid, something happen to your family," said Lee Stanford of Shook, Hardy.

An atmosphere of paranoia seems endemic to tobacco whistle-blowing, and though the law firms strenuously denied any wrong-doing—McDermott called Huber's allegations of pressure tactics "rot and nonsense"—the threats, real or imagined, terrified Mary. She lost weight. Sometimes she cried herself to sleep. Legal bills were mounting. Huber started recording his phone calls, and took out a life insurance policy on himself.

McDermott offered to arrange for a lawyer, but even before

Huber could make up his mind, the lawyer called and offered his services. Huber turned him down, and hired someone else, from a big firm in Dallas.

The night before Huber's deposition, a copy of *Three Days of the Condor* arrived by Federal Express. Gary and Mary sat down and watched it.

In the movie, a contract killer named Joubert, played by Max von Sydow, offers advice to "Condor," a CIA agent played by Robert Redford. Joubert tells Condor not to return to New York, implying that he will be killed.

"It would happen this way," he continued. "You may be walking. Maybe the first sunny day of the spring. And a car will slow down beside you. And the door will open, and someone you know, maybe even trust, will get out of the car. And he will smile, a becoming smile. But he will leave open the door of the car. And offer to give you a lift."

Westbrook's message couldn't have been plainer. There was no going back. Henceforth, the industry was Huber's mortal enemy.

"Well, that cheered me up," said Mary.

Huber reminded her of what Motley had said in Charleston, that by now, enough tobacco people had come forward that the industry couldn't punish them all.

"Yeah, right," said Mary.

After several postponements, the deposition finally took place on Saturday morning, September 20, 1997, before federal magistrate Wendell Radford in Beaumont.

Westbrook sidled up to Huber as they stood before the judge, waiting to begin.

"Remember," he whispered. "If a car pulls up—"

"Right, right, I know, yes," said Huber. They both laughed.

The judge took Huber into his chambers for several hours to untangle who would act as Huber's personal attorney. It turned out that Huber's current lawyer had somehow neglected to mention that until recently, he had shared a law practice with Dan Webb, lead tobacco lawyer in the Texas lawsuit. The judge gave Huber a new attorney, and directed the U.S. Marshals to investigate the alleged threats against Huber.

While this was going on, Motley, Westbrook, Reaud, and the rest of the Texas team were getting nervous, afraid Huber had developed cold feet. Motley was sucking on throat lozenges, tossing the wrappings around.

Finally the door opened and the judge emerged from chambers. Huber shook Motley's hand, which was ice cold, and they began the deposition. It was one-thirty P.M. Six hours later, they were done.

Afterward, Motley's black ostrich-skin boots clopped down the gray stone steps of the courthouse.

"Well, that clears one thing up," he said to Ed Westbrook.

"Which is?" said Westbrook.

"Now we know he's not an industry plant," said Motley.

SATYAGRAHA

DESPITE THE EXCITEMENT OVER THEIR STAR WITNESS, Motley found the atmosphere at the former Loony Bin at Pinewood little improved. Though the Five Firms were now working more effectively, the chain of command remained murky and the lawsuit was still not ready for trial. Many observers were convinced that despite their bluster, O'Quinn, Umphrey and company had always counted on settling. Sensing weakness, the tobacco lawyers, led by their capable chief trial counsel, Dan Webb, urged the companies to make a stand in Texas and let a Medicaid case go to a jury, rather than hurrying to the table as they had in Florida and Mississippi. Mock trials conducted in Texarkana by both sides revealed that the local population, as Motley suspected, believed in tobacco's freedom-of-choice argument.

"I don't know how the hell we're going to get this bunch of Branch Davidians up here to understand there's an industry conspiracy," he complained at dinner one night.

"Ron! *Please,*" shushed an assistant attorney general.

Also at the table were Keith Summa and Mark Curriden, a reporter for the *Dallas Morning News.* Motley was glad to see Summa and Curriden, who had been with him at so many other tobacco battles, especially Summa, whom he treated like a younger brother. When a publicist for the Texas team started making jokes sotto voce about "northern reporters," Motley cut him off.

"These people are my friends," he said quietly but audibly.

His spirits badly needed lifting. He had brought his little white bichons, Chase and Catch, down from Charleston and moved from the Holiday Inn to a condominium so he could play with them every morning before heading over to Pinewood. A few weeks after the Huber deposition, Catch, the female bichon, dashed into the road and was struck and killed by a car as Motley watched helplessly from the sidewalk. He sat in his room and cried.

Meanwhile, the outlook in Washington was forlorn. Joe Rice, Dickie Scruggs, Mike Moore, and the others had little progress to report on their global settlement bill in Congress.

"Introduce it in September, approve it in October" had been Moore's cocky prediction over the summer. But October came and there was still no consensus in Congress, while the White House refused to lead.

"My marching orders are to get ready for trial down here," Motley told a reporter who asked if he thought the companies would settle Texas to keep a trial and its attendant disclosures from hurting the global bill's chances in Congress.

Much as he hated the place, that meant spending a lot of time at Pinewood. One day as he walked past the "seclusion area," Motley noticed a strikingly beautiful black-haired woman, quite young. With her dark eyes, long hair, and long legs, she looked a bit like Catherine, his second wife.

He later found out she worked for the jury research company retained by the Five Firms. She was from a town called Ada in the foothills of the Wichita Mountains in south central Oklahoma. Her name was Elizabeth O'Neal.

Elizabeth had first noticed Motley at the Holiday Inn, where she was helping with a mock trial. She was in the Bridal Suite, where Motley lived, and brought him a chicken sandwich.

He peered under the bread. Stuck a finger into the fillet.

"This is cold," he complained.

What a jerk, she thought. Motley didn't even look at her.

Later that day, he did, and not long after that, and not by accident, met her.

He passed her a semi-legible note.

"Will you have dinner with me? I think you're beautiful," it said.

Elizabeth had a casual boyfriend. Being new to the trial lawyer world, she was ignorant of Motley's reputation and wealth. She was actually a bit taken aback by his interest. In fact, based on Motley's fondness for silk shirts in Caribbean colors and the way a gay lawyer at Pinewood kept staring at him, she had assumed that he was gay, too.

Then at the mock trial, in one of the Holiday Inn's conference rooms, he made his argument directly to her, looked at her the whole time. He was witty and funny and warm and she was mesmerized.

She let him dangle a few more days, but when he called and said he was flying to Dallas, where she lived, she met him for dinner. For quite a while, she spent weekends with him in Charleston or wherever in the United States they wound up, dutifully flying back to Dallas for work on Monday morning. He called every day to say good morning, and phoned most evenings, too. After a few months of this, she broke up with her boyfriend and moved to Charleston and into River House.

Motley's children, now in their twenties, were skeptical, especially Mark, who had seen girlfriends come and go. Jiffy had trouble adjusting to the fact that her dad was involved with a woman roughly her own age. But there was something new in the air, and whether it was Elizabeth or something else, she couldn't tell. Her father seemed happier. He called more, shared more. And gradually, the resentment faded a little.

Motley was moonstruck, but cautious.

"I'm taking this one slow," he said. "No quickie marriages."

As for Elizabeth, one day she was living in an apartment in Dallas and driving a Civic, the next she was being flown around in a private jet and chauffeured to Charleston Harbor, where she and Motley slept aboard his 108-foot yacht. Her parents visited one weekend and were speechless.

"I kind of forgot they hadn't seen how I'm living now," she said.

She had mixed feelings.

"You need to hold on to some sense of reality when you're inside all this," she said. Suddenly, her social life was Ness, Motley, which was like a medieval Japanese clan in a Kurosawa movie, full of gossip and plots, all revolving around Motley. She had a master's degree in psychology, and eventually returned to part-time jury consultant work to avoid getting swallowed up.

But though young, Elizabeth was strong and smart. She had a sense of humor. And she was already devoted to Motley.

"I love Ron," she told a friend. "This is it for me."

LUCKILY FOR THE STATE OF TEXAS, AFTER A COUPLE OF initial postponements, in mid-October, jury selection was put off indefinitely after federal District Judge David Folsom was diagnosed with prostate cancer. The cancer was treatable and the judge recovered, but the trial was rescheduled for mid-January, which was music to Motley's ears.

"Now we've got a chance," he said.

At pre-trial hearings, the defense contested every inch of ground. Shortly before Folsom took sick, they fought over admitting the Merrell Williams documents, though they had been on the Internet for two years.

"These documents were obtained by theft," said Brown & Williamson lawyer David Bernick, sounding a familiar theme.

Motley's strategy was to educate—and hopefully outrage— Judge Folsom by reading some of the riper passages from the Williams collection, like the "deadwood memo" about how troublesome documents should be removed from Brown & Williamson in Kentucky and secreted with the parent company, BAT, in England.

"Merrell Williams is no thief, he's a liberator," said Motley. "He's a public health hero."

Judge Folsom, spritely despite graying hair, seemed to be paying close attention, hands folded at his chin. Behind him were red curtains framing the marble fascia of a Greek temple, above which was a brightly painted federal seal.

The white stone courthouse is probably the most elegant thing in Texarkana. It sits smack in the middle of Stateline Avenue, which splits Texarkana in half, with the eastern side in Arkansas and the western side in Texas. This dividing line also cuts the courthouse into an Arkansas and a Texas half—the wall behind Judge Folsom's bench is the state line—staffed by two sets of marshals, two sets of clerks, and so on.

In the Texas clerk's office, stacks of boxes were stuffed into any spare nook, and every twenty minutes or so, a paralegal hand-trucked in some more. Two older women scanned documents into a computer all day long.

The industry had applied for dozens of "motions in limine," restrictions on the content of the case. They wanted to screen what the jury heard about destruction of evidence or child targeting. They wanted to make sure Texas Attorney General Dan Morales stuck to facts and didn't "compare defendants, for example, to murderers and criminals."

"But those *are* the facts," retorted Motley.

There in the clerk's office you could follow Gary Huber's deposition and Motley's efforts to drag the tobacco lawyers into the case. Motley tried to depose Robert McDermott, Huber's handler at Jones, Day. R. J. Reynolds moved to quash it. A few weeks later, Judge Folsom formally admitted McDermott to represent Reynolds in his court. That round had gone to Reynolds.

The trail ended abruptly, since Huber's deposition was under seal, the motions trying to get it unsealed were under seal, and the motions objecting to the motions to get it unsealed were under seal. Yet within weeks, the deposition itself was making the rounds of reporters, and newspaper stories were appearing. Huber was surprised and distressed to find himself described as a "whistle-blower."

As Huber's story became known, two theories about him circulated. The first was that Gary Huber was the most naive human being since Candide, but few subscribed to this. It was more plausible, many believed, that Huber said what he had to say to get the industry to give him money. In other words, a willing patsy. Some believed in his recent conversion. Many didn't.

Dick Daynard, the Northeastern University law professor, laughed at the conversion idea, and compared Huber to Louis, the police chief in the movie *Casablanca*, who pretends to be indignant over gambling he has long been bribed to ignore.

"Oh, yes, Dr. Huber is just shocked, *shocked*, that they lied to him," he said.

ABC's Keith Summa flew down and recorded more than six hours of videotape with Huber, but ABC never used it. Tobacco was fading from the radar of the media conglomerates. There was a residual interest in the Texas case because it could be the first AG lawsuit to go to trial, but the focus was on the floundering global settlement in Washington.

It seemed absurd to Motley. Dozens of reporters had covered every day of the puny little *Connor* trial in Jacksonville. Now, a few months later, the second most populous state in the country had sixty lawyers going for the jugular with $14 billion at stake and almost no one cared.

It was all the more frustrating because Motley felt he was getting close to the engine room of the conspiracy, to people who were very much alive and still at the control board.

Huber helped him see how David Hardy had designed that control board, and even helped build it out of switches and relays and copper wire, setting it running, thirty years earlier. It ran still, with updated circuitry.

It was really Hardy's plan Motley was fighting. In essence, he was fighting Hardy, a sort of phantom opponent who was detectable even when invisible, like dense air before a storm.

And so Motley tried to shoehorn as many hot lawyer documents as possible into the Texas case. No one had yet told the lawyers' story to a jury. Motley badly wanted to be first.

Gary Huber wanted a chance to tell his story, too. He wanted to do something for Motley's team, to prove himself.

"Do you think this stuff will ever come out?" he earnestly asked his lawyer friends. "I think it really needs to."

Huber took his role as star witness very seriously. Motley told him to keep a journal and write down whatever he remembered as it flooded back. He prepared narratives about the Harvard Project, the lawyers, the Tobacco Institute's Horace Kornegay, the Lifestyle Project. He reviewed and commented on hundreds of documents for Ness, Motley.

Settlement rumors began in September and October. They were denied. They persisted and intensified in early December. No one told Huber what was going on. He later learned the two sides had talked on and off through the fall. Joe Rice was brought in late in the game to close the deal after Meyer Koplow, leader of the tobacco team, called Rice and told him he had better get involved because Koplow believed Morales was making such a bad bargain, it would self-destruct when it became public. On January 16, the day jury selection was to begin, Huber saw on TV that a settlement had been announced at a press conference in Austin, a $15.3-billion deal, the biggest tobacco pact yet, more than a billion dollars higher than what was sought at trial.

Huber was at once relieved and frustrated, like he had screwed up his courage to take on the school bully, only to find he had left the playground and gone home.

"Why did we go through all this?" Mary Huber asked.

Motley was saying his testimony would be utilized, Huber told his wife. This wasn't the last chance.

Motley was disappointed. He had worked feverishly into the winter and the case had come a long way. But the prospects for a favorable jury were never good. And he was already looking forward to the next trial. That was where he'd get a chance, finally, to put on the One Big Tobacco Case he'd been assembling for five years. This would be the first secondhand smoke lung cancer case ever tried, with a missionary plaintiff who seemed to have stepped out of a Bing Crosby movie, a now-deceased nurse who worked at a smoky Veterans Administration hospital. The case was called *Wiley* v. *RJR Nabisco Holdings, et al.,* and it would go to trial in February. The place: Muncie, Indiana.

CLIFF DOUGLAS HAD BEEN WORKING TO DERAIL THE troubled global pact all winter. Two weeks after the Texas case ended, he sat in the audience for a hearing on the global settlement in the House of Representatives. The industry's CEOs, minus Bennett LeBow of Liggett, were appearing before the Committee on Commerce, Henry Waxman's committee, now chaired by Thomas Bliley of Richmond, Virginia, nicknamed "the congressman from Philip Morris" but whom Motley called "The Embalmer" because he owned funeral parlors.

The purpose of the hearing was to hear the tobacco men defend the global deal, and it reunited the coalition that forged it—Matt Myers, Rice, Scruggs, and Moore, as well as Wendell Gauthier, now fully recovered from his bout with cancer. The press was there in force.

Murray Bring and Steve Parrish backed up Geoff Bible. The Philip Morris group arrived first and took seats directly behind the witness table.

"Where's Goldstone?" Bring asked.

"It was too tough. He left," joked Bible.

Steven Goldstone of Reynolds showed up minutes later, attended by Arthur Golden. Lorillard, Brown & Williamson, and United States Tobacco, makers of the cherry-flavored Skoal Bandits chewing tobacco favored by rodeo-worshipping western children, were there, too.

Douglas had been in Washington for several days, doing his best to wreck Bliley's hearing, which many assumed would be a pro-global whitewash. He assembled the most embarrassing child-targeting documents he could find and fed them to Democrats, who distributed them to reporters and congressmen on the morning of the hearing. Then he sat in the audience and watched as member after member vented about how an industry that did such things didn't deserve the protection from lawsuits provided by the global settlement bills they were considering.

"'Today's teenager is tomorrow's regular customer,'" read Ohio's Sherrod Brown indignantly, from a Philip Morris document.

"'The base of our business is the high school student,'" he quoted from Lorillard.

Brown noted that the industry had no credible explanation for these documents.

"The response is, 'Just trust us,'" he said.

Even the white-haired Bliley, mournful looking in his spotted bow tie, felt obliged to join in.

"Frankly, I was shocked," he said.

The hearing was in Room 2123 at the Rayburn House Office Building, where the famous Waxman hearings of 1994 had taken place. But to Douglas, this repeat performance was pure farce. Bliley allowed only limited questioning, and aside from expressing remorse about the youth documents and assuring the committee that such things would never happen again, the CEOs stuck to the usual clichés about "a risky product" and "freedom of choice." None would admit flat out that nicotine was addictive or that smoking caused cancer. Despite all the fluff about a "new era," their position hadn't changed one iota from four years earlier.

The hearing lasted most of the day. When it was over, Bible ducked reporters who tried to cut through the debarking mob to question him.

"Sorry, mate," said Bible as he pushed past one of them, and then, gaining the hallway, literally broke into a run, dashing off into Rayburn's endless corridors. A moment later, Lorillard's Laurence Tisch, a bald little wizard, popped out of the hearing room and galloped for the closest exit.

Standing outside the committee room, Cliff Douglas shook his head in mock amazement.

"Was it something I said?" he grinned.

LIKE RON MOTLEY, MICHAEL CIRESI ALSO WANTED TO BE the first to tell the story of the tobacco lawyers. Whereas Motley had to lug around trailer loads of documents and alter his battle plan as he moved from Pascagoula to West Palm Beach to Texarkana, the Minnesota lawyer had one client, Attorney General Hubert Horatio Humphrey III. And Humphrey had so far refused to settle his case, for which the anti-tobacco Trotskyites loved him, just as they distrusted Mike Moore.

In January 1998, while Douglas sabotaged the Bliley hearings and Motley prepared for trial in Indiana, Ciresi began selecting a jury in state court in Minneapolis.

He had prepared an industry-style scorched-earth plaintiff's case, in essence using tobacco's tactics against them. Motley was voracious for every shred of information about his adversary, but once at trial, Motley wanted a simple story, illustrated by a few key pieces of paper. Motley's courtroom style was the dramatic revelation, the big, awful document, plus corporate insiders who could narrate what they had seen and put a human face on the story.

Ciresi was a merciless litigator, and his concept might be described as the Russian Front. The industry would slowly lose its élan vital and finally freeze to death while Ciresi methodically drubbed them through an endless Minnesota winter with the contents of his guarded warehouse of 33 million pages of tobacco documents.

Motley made fun of Ciresi's method. "He doesn't even know half of what he's got. We targeted our discovery. That idiot just asked for everything, and now he's stuck with it."

But Ciresi did break new ground. He sent his people to England to wander through "the BAT cave," which held some of British

American Tobacco's most secret and sensitive documents. Motley had beaten Ciresi to key Philip Morris scientists like Victor De-Noble and Bill Farone and extracted invaluable material, but Ciresi was building an offense in depth like no one had contemplated before. Document production in Minnesota dwarfed that of every other lawsuit because Ciresi, whose law firm was the size of a defense firm and did both plaintiff's and defense work, put the emphasis on documents. No one could match Ciresi for the sheer, numbing detail of his preparation.

So by the time his case went to trial in January, Minnesota had become *the big one* and everyone knew it. Ciresi had more resources than anyone else and fewer distractions. With Texas out of the picture, the stock analysts, the industry's own lawyers, all the smart money said that the prime chance to cripple the tobacco industry had now passed to Ciresi. And if any judge seemed predisposed to let him do it, it was Ramsey County District Court Judge Kenneth Fitzpatrick, who allowed Ciresi significant latitude at trial.

While Ciresi was intent on exposing the role of the tobacco law firms, his best documents were tied up by claims of privilege. This was the so-called Minnesota thirty-nine thousand, a subset of the six million that were sitting in the warehouse in Minneapolis. There was some overlap between Ciresi's thirty-nine thousand and other batches of lawyer-protected documents, but by and large, this was virgin territory. Because Minnesota had in place a protective order so rigid that virtually nothing became public before trial, and because Ciresi was so thorough and Fitzpatrick so helpful, the industry gave up material they never gave up anywhere else.

Motley and Ciresi played a sort of "discovery tag" for years. Motley pried out hitherto unseen lawyer documents about the Council for Tobacco Research and the Committee of Counsel. Ciresi turned up a hand-scribbled note from Philip Morris researcher Tom Osdene ordering that sensitive scientific documents be sent to his home.

"I will act on them + destroy," Osdene had scrawled.

Then Motley deposed Osdene, who took the Fifth several dozen times in two hours, citing the Justice Department's criminal investigation. Not long afterward, Ciresi deposed Osdene, with similar results. In Florida, Motley released the most important Liggett documents, the Liggett Eight. By the time of the Texas suit, Motley had fairly recent memoranda from Huber's handler Robert McDermott and was bringing the fight home to other lawyers who were still active in the industry's high councils. Steve Parrish's name had turned up on a lot of what Motley called secondhand-smoke disinformation documents. Those emerged first in Minnesota.

Ciresi actually put on most of his case. National press coverage was sparse. On May 8, after nearly four months of trial, Minnesota wheeled out an impressive settlement that brought $6.6 billion to the twentieth most populous state, the richest AG deal per capita.

But the attention of the media never strayed from Washington, where Dickie Scruggs and Mike Moore were for all intents and purposes living at the ANA Hotel, though even they had abandoned any real hope of enacting tobacco legislation. For almost a year, Scruggs and Moore preached the same message as the industry, that the June 20 agreement offered a historic opportunity that wouldn't come again. It was a message that quickly wore thin in Congress, where Scruggs and Moore came to be seen as monomaniacal pests.

The end result of the global process was a harsh bill by Arizona Senator John McCain that would have cost the industry $516 billion, up from $368 billion, and given it no real protection from lawsuits. Disgusted, the industry pulled out of the peace process in early April, then nuked the McCain bill with a blatantly distorted $40-million ad campaign. On June 17, just shy of a year after the global deal was announced, the Senate formally killed it. The ceasefire was over. However, by the time that happened, a demoralized Ron Motley was seriously considering getting out of tobacco litigation.

MUNCIE IS THE CAPITAL OF DELAWARE COUNTY, INDIANA, rolling, fertile land bounded on the north by the Mississinewa River. It sits on the eastern edge of the great plain that rolls west from Indianapolis into Illinois.

But driving from the corn and soybean fields of Delaware County into Muncie brings you out of the past into a forbidding present. Anyone suing a big company would be on fragile ground in Muncie, where plant closings had been in the headlines on an almost weekly basis leading up to the trial of the *Wiley* case. Among the fading storefronts of Walnut Street, thoughts of economic survival trumped all else.

Still, *Wiley* was a state-of-the-art tobacco lawsuit—the first secondhand smoke lung cancer suit ever tried and the first time P53 evidence, a technique that ties damage by smoke carcinogens to a specific gene, was used in an individual smoker's case. Within two weeks of the settlement in Texas, Ann Ritter had transferred enough staff from Texarkana to the Muncie Radisson to fill two floors. Motley's law firm, for the first time, pulled out all the stops to bring a cigarette case to verdict, spending $2 million. Elizabeth O'Neal came and worked with Theresa Zagnoli's jury research firm.

The arrival of these crack troops papered over some glaring weaknesses. The P53 analysis had been done by an expert named Cagle who frequently testified for asbestos companies. But Cagle's analysis was gutted in a deposition taken by Jeffrey Furr, a lawyer for R. J. Reynolds and an environmental tobacco smoke expert who had led the Reynolds lawyers at the 1994 OSHA hearings. It turned out Furr knew more about P53 than Cagle, and far more than the local Indiana lawyers who tried to defend their expert. Furr managed to knock the only physical evidence that cigarette smoke *caused* Mildred Wiley's lung cancer right out of the case. The P53 test fizzled.

So did the rest of the plaintiff's case when tested on the good people of Delaware County. Six consecutive focus groups voted for the defense after hearing the arguments for each side.

On opening day in early February, Motley took the floor against Shook, Hardy & Bacon's William Ohlemeyer, a seasoned veteran even though he had the fresh-faced look of a frat boy. The trial had been moved to the city's Horizon Convention Center for space reasons.

Motley argued that Mildred Wiley didn't indulge in coffee, much less liquor or cigarettes. No one could say she made a choice to inhale noxious fumes. Ohlemeyer countered that Wiley never filed a formal complaint about the blue haze that other nurses testified hung in the air at the Veterans Administration hospital in Marion, about sixty miles northeast of Indianapolis and thirty from Muncie.

Though Wiley had an enclosed office in her final years, she spent a good part of her working life in Building Sixteen, a largely unventilated structure from the 1920s where many of the dying lived out their final months, along with chronic psychiatric cases. During the seventies, access to cigarettes was considered a right for the hospital-bound veteran, as it had been on the battlefields of France, Korea, and Vietnam. Eighty percent smoked, many in an endless chain. Poor patients were furnished with "indigent cigarettes" at no charge. The nurses, Mildred Wiley included, had to "smoke the patient," meaning help a paralyzed veteran light and handle his cigarette. One blind, quadriplegic Vietnam veteran bit down so hard, nurses burned themselves trying to remove the butts. The hospital eventually purchased a dozen "smoking robots," cigarette holders attached to ashtrays with three-foot-long tubes through which smoke was inhaled.

But an industry expert named Roger Jenkins made some calculations that suggested Wiley didn't really inhale that much smoke at the Marion VA Hospital, though co-workers described nicotine stains so thick, normal cleaning fluids couldn't dissolve the residue, and despite testimony that in one four-year period, R. J. Reynolds alone sold over five million cigarettes—250,000 packs—to the hospital canteen. Jenkins also admitted that in her seventeen years at the Marion VA, Wiley was exposed to more smoke than airline stewardesses on smoking flights. Jenkins said none of that mattered, because his interviews with VA workers showed it wasn't that smoky.

Then Ness, Motley's Ed Westbrook started in on Jenkins, who had a habit of saying "to be honest with you," and adding quickly, "I'm always honest with you."

"I understand, Doctor," Westbrook would say patiently.

Westbrook led Jenkins through a seemingly endless list of lucrative industry contracts spread over more than a decade of tobacco work, the $20,000 he got for the *Wiley* case and the $150,000 an industry group paid for his book, his cultivation as a "Special Project" of CTR, his willingness to let tobacco lawyers preview his testimony at federal hearings, and it soon seemed rather doubtful that Roger Jenkins was quite the unbiased expert he claimed to be, and in fact Westbrook did such a good job at depicting Jenkins as an industry flunky, jurors started laughing.

"Doctor, who did you *think* was approving your funding from the industry?" asked Westbrook.

"I assumed it was somebody having to do with the Council for

Tobacco Research, their board of directors, and who else that they would—that was an assumption on my part. I really didn't know, to be honest with you," said Jenkins.

"And you've since learned that it was the Committee of Counsel who had to approve the work. Is that *right*?"

"Yeah," Jenkins said quietly.

Westbrook got Jenkins to agree that, at a conservative estimate, Mildred Wiley inhaled about 20,952,000 liters of air in her career at Marion. Motley had Jeff Wigand take the stand and sketch what was in the blue haze at the VA, a mixture of mainstream smoke, exhaled from the smoker's lungs, and sidestream smoke, which curls from the lit end of a cigarette. The lungs filter many of the toxins in mainstream, so it's not as dangerous as sidestream smoke, which is rich in tobacco-specific nitrosamines, extraordinarily carcinogenic compounds unique to tobacco smoke.

The industry had known all this for years, as Motley demonstrated with the deposition of Ray Morgan, the Philip Morris chemist who said he helped Jim Charles drop off the plywood box of tar at the guard shack at the research tower in Richmond.

In dramatic testimony hotly disputed by Philip Morris, Morgan told how he tested smoke in a stainless steel chamber the size of a restaurant's walk-in freezer. Inside was a thirty-port smoking machine. The sidestream rose through hoods mounted above each cigarette and bubbled through a liquid trap that left a residue of tar on a glass tube. When enough tubes of this goo had been collected, technicians concentrated it down to a few drops of purified tar, and brought Morgan a tiny vial which he analyzed. Morgan was not allowed to test "production" cigarettes, like Marlboros. If the need arose, a unit called "semiworks" could custom-blend a batch of cigarettes that would imitate Marlboros or Merits or whatever, always minus certain flavors and additives.

Morgan explained that the company's lab in Switzerland had a similar stainless steel room where they found that the amount of a nitrosamine called NNK *increased* as the sidestream smoke aged in the chamber. That was quite surprising and, for anyone breathing cigarette smoke in an enclosed space with poor air circulation, alarming.

Morgan then did similar "aged sidestream" tests in Richmond. It was decided to test the skinny hundred-millimeter cigarettes typical of some women's brands. To calibrate the equipment before beginning the actual tests, some long, skinny cigarettes that were more or less lying around were stuck into the smoking machine. Morgan dutifully measured the NNK level, and it was *ten times* higher than any cigarette they had ever tested.

He showed the results to Robin Kinser, his section leader down the hall, but since test cigarettes are identified only by a code number, neither of them knew what they were.

Kinser made a call. Those cigarettes that were lying around, the ones that had ten times the NNK of any others tested, were ordinary, production Virginia Slims.

Kinser left to talk to Cathy Ellis, her boss, the director of research for Philip Morris.

"She came back to me and told me that I was to destroy all the data," Morgan told Motley.

"What did you do?" Motley asked.

"I destroyed it," said Morgan.

"How did you destroy it?" said Motley

"I shredded it," Morgan replied.

"Where did you shred it?"

"In a shredding machine that was on the sixth floor of the tower," Morgan said. "It was the only copy."

"How do you know that?" asked Motley.

"Because I recorded the data and I knew that was it. I had the only copy," said Morgan.

MILDRED WILEY DIED AT AGE FIFTY-SIX, THREE WEEKS after the diagnosis of lung cancer. An autopsy discovered that Wiley's cancer had spread to her pancreas, and Philip Morris attorney Bill Ohlemeyer maintained her symptoms were characteristic of a cancer that started there, rather than the lung. In his summation, Ohlemeyer told a jury composed mostly of high school graduates that Wiley was such a strong personality, she surely would have asked to be transferred to a less smoky environment if it was that bad.

Motley hit back with his best documents.

"The date is December 1953," Motley said softly, leaning an elbow on the jury box, yellow pad in hand, regarding the jurors at close range.

"Folks, if you don't read anything else," he said, "just read this again. Cover to cover. Because if you want to know how it is that they got seventy-five thousand dollars to pay Dr. Smith to come in here, you just need to read this."

The document, its smudgy brown letters enlarged many times over, appeared on the TV set in front of the jury:

"'How are we going to free millions of Americans from the guilty fear that is going to arise deep in their biological depths regardless of any pooh-poohing logic every time they light a cigarette?'" he began to read.

The answer, of course, Motley said, was the Council for Tobacco Research, and later generations of scientific disinformationists, like Gary Huber, part of whose deposition had been played for the jury.

"'We can't overlook the fact that in this particular instance, the stakes for the public are even higher than for the tobacco manufacturers. For the public, an issue touching the deepest of human fears and instincts is involved: the issues of uncontrollable disease and death,'" the tobacco public relations man had written.

"'Hence cigarette companies might not readily be forgiven if their approach to the problem stemmed only from their eagerness'—to do what?" Motley said, interrupting himself excitedly.

"'*Protect their earnings*,'" he read triumphantly, "'and if they twist the research of medical science which seeks to save men.'"

At dinner that night, Motley felt he had connected.

"I had them today," Motley said. But the summations continued into a second day, and that, he felt, did not go as well.

AS HE TRIED VAINLY TO SLEEP THE NIGHT BEFORE THE verdict, the party roared on at the Radisson bar.

Elizabeth, who had given up trying to sleep next to the insomniac Motley, was perched on a barstool drinking white wine and sketching on a pad.

Joke awards were given out. Charles Patrick, a genial father figure for the Ness, Motley family on the road, was master of ceremonies. One award went to a paralegal who returned to her room at the Radisson one night and detected movement coming from her bathroom. She angrily swung open the bathroom door and found a young, dark-haired Shook, Hardy lawyer urinating into the toilet.

Then she realized she was in *his* bathroom on the fifth floor, a to-bacco floor, and she ran like hell.

Patrick gave another award to a local plaintiff's lawyer "for falling on his sword" for the cause.

"Fuck you, Charles," said the recipient.

"That's witty," the bartender observed.

Patrick gave himself one "for general wisdom."

"I'm only on this earth to do what Ron Motley wants me to do," Patrick said.

Who are you? Who ooh, who ooh.
Well, I really want to know . . .

By the time Motley and the rest of us who were jammed into the Suburban got to the steak restaurant on the other side of Muncie, the jury had been deliberating for nineteen hours. It was generally accepted they would reach a verdict that night because one of the jurors held tickets for a cruise and was to depart the follow ing day.

Once the cell phone call came announcing the jury's return, and once the nachos and beer had been gobbled down, the Suburban sped back across town to the courthouse. The courthouse was right across the street from the Radisson, a street now lined with TV satellite transmission trucks, including one for Keith Summa's ABC crew, ready to pump out news of the verdict, which many thought Motley and his saintly plaintiff could very well win.

When we arrived, the tobacco lawyers as well as Charles Patrick, Kim Vroon, and the rest of the Ness, Motley Tobacco Team were already waiting in the corridor outside the courtroom. So were the press, financial analysts, and Wiley's former co-workers. Philip Wiley, Mildred's husband, was escorted through the crowd inside a flying quadrangle made up of Motley's bodyguard, Larry, an Indiana lawyer, a Ness, Motley driver, and Wiley's son-in-law.

The jury was led in. The forewoman handed a red envelope to the bailiff. The bailiff pivoted, handed it up to the judge. The judge put on his glasses. He read it.

"'We, the jury, find in favor of all of the defendants and against all of the plaintiffs, on all claims,'" he said.

Men and women cried openly in the next room, which was Ness, Motley's prep room during the trial.

"That's it. I'm getting out of this town," said a local plaintiff's lawyer to his wife.

Motley ducked the press, striding out a side door from the Convention Center, then across the street and up to his suite.

Dan Donahue, R. J. Reynolds's deputy general counsel, was walking back to the Radisson, too. He gave a thumbs-up.

"Another one," he grinned.

Minutes later, up on the seventh floor, an exhausted, utterly despondent Motley sat on the sofa drinking orange juice and vodka, watching basketball with Elizabeth. In a chair right next to them was Larry.

"So?" I asked.

Motley stared straight ahead,

"I don't know what went wrong," Motley said. "You're asking the wrong fucking person."

The chocolate Labrador puppy, Okie, padded over and Motley rubbed his ears.

"I know one thing. I'm not going to do any more tobacco cases for a while," he said. "I don't know if I'm ever going to want to do another one."

I walked down the fire stairs to the fifth floor. The tobacco contingent, who not only had three floors of the Radisson but the basement of the courthouse building, were milling about the halls, talking and munching sandwiches. The next morning everyone packed and folded and wrapped. By the day after, the Radisson was mostly empty again, as it had been for many months before the trial, and the little litigation tornado that had descended on Muncie, Indiana, that winter was gone.

Two jurors later said the conspiracy evidence was convincing, but they had felt the need to quantify Mildred Wiley's smoke exposure—hearing from eight co-workers was evidently not enough. That left only the P53 test to tie secondhand smoke to Mildred Wiley's cancer. But unfortunately, the tobacco lawyers, who had spent years studying smoke chemistry and disease, knew more about P53 than did the plaintiff's scientist.

The *Wiley* jury was *not* allowed to hear one salient fact, because it would certainly have prejudiced them. More than two years before trial, in December 1995, an administrative law judge at the U.S. Department of Labor ruled that secondhand smoke at the Veterans Administration Hospital in Marion, Indiana, did indeed cause Mildred Wiley's lung cancer, and that her husband, Philip, would receive a death benefit of $21,500 a year, payable until his own demise. It was the first workman's compensation award ever made for a death due to environmental tobacco smoke.

MUNCIE TOOK THE FIGHT OUT OF MOTLEY FOR A WHILE.
"It's frustrating and it's really embarrassing," he told Jiffy on the phone the night of the verdict. "This was a real unusual lady. And, my God, we spent a fortune."

Jiffy usually found herself giving her father advice and listening to his problems rather than vice versa. "I swear my decisions are more rational than his," she would say. Now he sounded as low as she had heard him in a long while. There wasn't much she could offer except that they were all still proud of him. But the following month, she saw him in New York City, where he took her and her husband to see the musical *The Lion King* for her birthday, and he had begun to bounce back. Early that summer, he dived into preparations for the next case on his calendar, the Massachusetts AG's lawsuit.

By then, the McCain global settlement bill had collapsed, but Joe Rice was working on another strategy, known as the "states only" settlement, or "Plan B." Plan B had been floating around since 1997 as a fallback position in case no global bill could be coaxed through Congress. It meant settling all the attorney general lawsuits at one stroke, just the AGs and the industry, with no federal involvement or ramifications.

Joe Rice sat down with the industry in early June 1998, this time with a new group of attorneys general and without Dickie Scruggs, who wasn't even told of the meeting. Officially, Scruggs was excluded for fear he would leak to the press, but more probably on the suspicion he would torpedo a deal that was in fact little more than a cash lottery for the states. Moore, his own case settled, remained committed to a health-oriented federal resolution and Scruggs was closely identified with Moore's position.

"Plan B" was set into motion by Washington Attorney General Christine Gregoire, whose trial was to start in September. During the talks, Gregoire fought valiantly, but with little leverage, and as shrewd a negotiator as Rice proved to be, his job now was simply to get as much money as he could for the attorneys general. Without the promise of federal liability protection, which was out of the question without congressional involvement, the AGs had little to trade for health or marketing concessions.

Rice and Meyer Koplow, Herb Wachtell's partner, worked out the nuts and bolts, having already settled Mississippi, Florida, and Texas together. Philip Morris dominated the discussions, and Brown & Williamson and Reynolds pulled out in August, only to return near the end. Gregoire was flanked by states that filed very late in the game, and by Mike Easley, attorney general of North Carolina, which had never filed at all and wasn't likely to, that being the home state of R. J. Reynolds.

In July, Scruggs heard a rumor that Joe Rice was meeting with tobacco in New York, and called him. Rice gave Scruggs a cover story about being involved in some non-tobacco deal-making. Not long afterward, Scruggs read the truth in the *Wall Street Journal*.

"My friendship with Joe is over," Scruggs told Keith Summa. "We're going to have to work together, but we'll never be friends again."

Scruggs wouldn't talk to Rice for a month. There wasn't much doubt that forty-one states wouldn't have sued tobacco had it not been for him and Mike Moore flying all over America to sign them up. And Scruggs was always five moves ahead of the pack. He had foreseen the endgame. He knew way back in 1994 that in a hostile political climate, the industry would have to put up real money, and pushed the White House to keep the heat on.

Not only that, but Scruggs's firm shared the representation of most of the states Rice was negotiating for. But in the end it came down to muscle. Ness, Motley was six times bigger than Scruggs, Millette, Lawson, Bozeman & Dent and represented twenty-six AGs. There could be no negotiations without Rice. Scruggs's firm would never have been able to organize credible lawsuits on the grand scale of the attorney general cases, or to do it in three states in three months, as Ness, Motley had in the summer and fall of 1997.

Perhaps Ron Motley will be remembered for elevating the civil action to a form of mobile warfare so effective that a plaintiff could rapidly wreak havoc on a corporate opponent. Certainly by 1998, the plaintiff's lawyer had achieved unprecedented power. The big-business style of product suit pioneered by Motley, the joining together of huge masses of suing victims, had achieved what had once seemed impossible. It brought tobacco to the table, though not to its knees. Once at the top of the arc, the product liability lawyers found they had forced tobacco to pay money, but could do no more. Their grand alliance with law enforcement didn't fundamentally change the peculiar industry.

It was, on the surface, a *hell* of a lot of money, though. When Joe Rice's Master Settlement Agreement was unveiled on November 16, the industry had agreed to make payments of $8 billion per year in perpetuity, or $206 billion over twenty-five years, to the forty-six states that hadn't yet settled. Every state in the union, even those that hadn't sued, would get a share, according to Medicaid population and other factors.

There was also some very broad language in the Master Settlement Agreement ruling out similar lawsuits by other government entities or health organizations—forever. That led to court challenges that held up the flow of dollars, since the agreement needed court approval from states representing 80 percent or more of the payout, after which Ness, Motley's total fees, including its share from the individual settlements in Mississippi, Florida, and Texas, would be more than $1 billion over twenty-five years. Big business indeed.

The Master Settlement Agreement provided that the industry pay the plaintiff's lawyers' expenses and fees. The country then watched the unseemly spectacle of plaintiff's lawyers elbowing each other for a place at the trough, beginning with grotesque fee awards for the three states that reached individual settlements before the MSA was concluded. A fairly large group of Florida lawyers would divide $3.4 billion. Scruggs and his colleagues in Mississippi were awarded $1.43 billion. The Five Firms in Texas would each get a piece of $3.3 billion, probably the richest settlement per lawyer.

"Walter Umphrey can get another helicopter," a reporter said to Cliff Douglas when the awards were announced in December.

"He can buy the entire Air Cavalry," said a disgusted Douglas.

Exactly a week after the agreement was unveiled, the companies announced their largest price increase in history, almost 26 percent per pack, enough to generate the $10 billion the industry needed to make the first year's payment.

Such a price increase might lower smoking rates a little, but probably wasn't big enough to make a substantial dent in tens of millions of addicts. The industry had done such a good job of reversing a twenty-year decline in youth smoking—in Texas, almost half of public high school students were using tobacco in 1998—that the effect on the death rate would be minimal. And since higher prices would finance the deal, no company would go broke paying for it.

The pact abolished tobacco billboards, but its only other significant concession was to close the Council for Tobacco Research and stipulate that the industry "may not reconstitute CTR or its function in any form." It also extinguished the Committee of Counsel by doing away with the Tobacco Institute.

Late on the afternoon of Friday, November 20, 1998, when the last state faxed back its acceptance of the Master Settlement Agreement—the first step toward implementation, though the courts in each state still needed to approve it—Motley dashed from his office on the sixth floor down the stairs to the second-floor conference room at Meeting Street, where a champagne toast was under way. Though no trial lawyer could feel bad about forcing the tobacco warlords to pay the largest civil settlement in history, nor bemoan a billion-dollar fee, he had never won a verdict against tobacco, and it galled him.

He was toasted and cheered. He made a short speech, as did Joe Rice.

"This ain't the end," promised Motley. "It's just the end of the beginning."

Motley was a victim of his own success. Like nuclear weapons, the destructive potential of his attorney general suits was so great, neither camp could unleash them. However, the product lawyers had proven themselves a meaningful counterforce to tobacco, an enormous achievement after forty years of abject failure, during which, as Dickie Scruggs pointed out, "the right to sue tobacco was

really the right to lose." When Larry Hastings sued American Tobacco in the *Green* case, lawsuits were a bogeyman, feared but unknown. Now that bogeyman was flesh and it was rapping on the
boardroom door. In 1993, there were 48 smoking and health suits
pending against Philip Morris. In 1999, there were 800, including
attorney-general-style cases mounted by British Columbia, France,
Bolivia, Guatemala, Panama, Nicaragua, Venezuela, the state of Rio
de Janeiro, Brazil, and the Marshall Islands. Motley had had a lot
to do with that.

A few months later, Motley and Scruggs were given awards for
their contributions to tobacco control by the Campaign for
Tobacco-Free Kids, a lobbying and advocacy organization co-
founded by Matt Myers.

Both gave speeches at a large banquet in Washington. Motley
had his speech inside his jacket. As his name was called and he
started toward the stage, he passed Keith Summa.

"What do *you* think I ought to say, Brother Summa?" Motley
whispered.

"Talk about your mom," said Summa.

At the podium, Motley fumbled with his reading glasses, then
decided Summa was right.

"On March eleventh 1984, I took the longest walk of my life,"
he said.

"I walked down the corridors of a hospital in Charleston, South
Carolina. I entered a room and I saw a woman I didn't recognize. She
was balding. She was on a breathing machine. She was my mother."

His voice cracked.

"She died of emphysema. She smoked cigarettes, three packs a
day, all her life. Two days before that, the doctor called me in and
said, 'You've got to talk to your aunts. They're smuggling cigarettes
to your mother, disconnecting her oxygen and letting her smoke cigarettes until she gasps for air.'

"If you don't believe nicotine is addictive, you should have
walked with me down that hall that day and saw that stranger that
created you on earth," he said.

BUT THOUGH MOTLEY COULD SAY HE HAD WON A MEASURE
of justice for millions of victims, none was promised any of the bil-

lions from the Master Settlement Agreement. The MSA did not even compel the states to spend this windfall on tobacco control or health, and many were already planning to use it to lower property taxes, repair sidewalks, and build prisons.

In fact, it was of absolutely critical importance to the industry that the money *not* go to sick smokers, because remunerating the injured would signal plaintiff's lawyers that they could finally make money from the giant pool of dying addicts. And then the dam would truly burst.

Motley still had cigarette cases he wanted to pursue, but they would be done on a budget. The Tobacco Team was broken up, its lawyers reassigned. Jodi Flowers quit the firm to spend more time with her children though she returned a year later. Within a few months of the champagne toast, the partners at Ness, Motley were fighting like hyenas over shares of the profits, treating Motley as though he were just another senior lawyer. People had forgotten how timorously they followed their Ahab back in 1993.

Motley celebrated Christmas of 1998 at a marina in Fort Lauderdale on the *Themis,* his newest boat, named for the Greek goddess of justice. Tied next to the *Themis* for most of the week was Dickie Scruggs's craft, the *Emerald Cay.* They ate meals together and visited from boat to boat, Scruggs and his wife, Diane, and Ron and Elizabeth. Scruggs and Motley sat on the stern of the *Themis* and allowed themselves to reminisce a little over drinks. Scruggs was still miffed about having been left out of the denouement, but was again speaking to Joe Rice.

"We didn't do bad for a bunch of yahoos," said Scruggs. "Guys from Mississippi and South Carolina."

They remembered how they sat in Pascagoula talking about how bored they were with asbestos cases; how Mike Moore drew a line in the dusty carpet of his office, and the lawyers stepped over it. They talked about what people were doing now. Jeff Wigand was living alone in a small, sparsely furnished apartment in Charleston, giving talks about tobacco to youth groups, writing for scholarly journals, and pissing up the industry's leg at every opportunity. Woody Wilner was about to help try four tobacco cases that had been consolidated into a single trial, a first, in Memphis.

Scruggs had lost weight over the past two years and looked older. He admitted to being a bit burned out.

"I might take a sabbatical from practicing law," he said. He had just made a record gift of $25 million to his alma mater, Ole Miss law school. Maybe he'd teach there for a year.

Not Motley. By the time he returned to Charleston he was avidly studying lead paint cases.

"These guys essentially escaped liability for poisoning tens of thousands of young children. I'm going to try to do something about it," he told me. He was on his speakerphone, roaming the office. I could hear boxes being thrown around.

"Have you read *A Man in Full?* It's Tom Wolfe. He's explaining how southerners pronounce words. He spells it out phonetically. So the name of the lead institute would be the Lead Industry Association—LIA. It's pronounced in the South 'liah.' Two members of the LIA would be 'liahs.' I love it! It's a case about children versus liars!"

In succeeding calls, he was talking as earnestly about the "liahs" at the Lead Industry Association as he ever had about CTR, and soon he was sending his Babylonian scribble dashing across legal pads as he thought up catchphrases and angles to pursue and noted key personalities in the documents, as well as other documents he would now need to get, because every case is a story, with a beginning, a middle, and an end.

WHEN THE MASTER SETTLEMENT AGREEMENT WAS AN-nounced, Steve Parrish was already celebrating a remarkable summer and fall of 1998 atop the Philip Morris building in New York.

A North Carolina judge had ruled that the EPA inappropriately classified secondhand smoke as a carcinogen. A federal appeals court decided the FDA had no authority to regulate cigarettes, ne-cessitating an appeal by the government to the Supreme Court. And Woody Wilner, who had won another verdict against Brown & Williamson in June 1998, saw both that verdict and his original win in the *Carter* case overturned on appeal.

But perhaps most important for Parrish, he knew that with one deft stroke, the AGs' settlement had taken many of the biggest, most dangerous plaintiff's firms out of large-scale tobacco litiga-tion, probably forever.

However, that did not stop the smaller ones from continuing to sputter along, and in early February 1999, one struck gold when a jury in San Francisco returned a $50 million punitive damage award against Philip Morris in an individual smoker's case, on top of $1.5 million in compensatory damages.

That night, Keith Summa called Parrish at home for comment, but Parrish hadn't yet heard.

"Holy moly!" said Parrish. "Fifty million?"

"Fifty million," said Summa. "What do you think it means?"

"I don't have a clue," said Parrish. "I can't believe it. My beeper never even went off."

A jubilant Cliff Douglas sent a congratulatory bouquet of flowers to the victorious female attorney in San Francisco. And since he had recently happened upon e-mail addresses for Philip Morris lawyer Meyer Koplow and R. J. Reynolds counsel Dan Donahue, he sent each a note:

"Now it begins."

GARY HUBER COULDN'T HELP BUT THINK OF WHAT DAVID Hardy told him just before he died: "I bought 'em an extra twenty or thirty years." At century's end, the American companies were diversified global entities of enormous wealth, rich enough to pay $8 billion a year to be left alone and consider it a bargain. "That which doesn't kill me makes me stronger," wrote Nietzsche. Forty years of conflict had been a potent vaccination, with the rest of the world still to bustle in.

Huber was keenly disappointed that he would never have a chance to testify in one of the big state lawsuits, and hurt that Motley didn't stay in touch. Then, in January 1999, President Clinton dropped a surprise into his State of the Union by mentioning that the Justice Department was considering suing the tobacco companies for Medicare costs, just as the states had sued for Medicaid.

Almost immediately, the phone rang at Huber's house in Tyler, Texas. Huber thought it might be one of his plaintiff's attorney pals, maybe even Motley.

It was Frank Colby, the former head of research for R. J. Reynolds, who had once been a good friend of Huber's. They hadn't spoken since he became a witness in the Texas case.

"Bob McDermott suggested I could call you," said Colby. "How have you been?"

Colby turned on the charm. He wanted Huber to meet with him, a meeting that would undoubtedly be attended by McDermott, although Colby didn't say so. Huber was noncommittal.

Huber was convinced the call was related to the proposed federal lawsuit. The lawyers were having Colby sound Huber out. Maybe they could win him back.

He asked Mary what she thought he should do.

"I suppose it couldn't hurt to see Frank," he said.

Mary erupted.

"What is *wrong* with you?" she shouted. "Do I have to hit you over the head with a baseball bat? This is exactly what happened last year!"

You're right, said Huber. Bad idea.

MOTLEY WOULDN'T ADMIT IT, BUT HIS CLOSEST FRIENDS knew he was envious of the big verdict out in San Francisco, despite his own considerable achievement. The irony was that it was a group of industry documents gathered in the attorney general suits that outraged the San Francisco jurors into voting for punitives damages. And the losing attorney was none other than Bill Ohlemeyer.

Motley was preoccupied with more pressing matters. The day before the San Francisco verdict, Woody Motley, who had been in the hospital for weeks with circulatory problems and an infection that almost killed him, had his left leg amputated below the knee.

Ron was with him when he came out of the anesthesia. Woody said nothing, and looked up at his son.

Ron pulled up a chair next to his bed, and clasped his hand. Woody's eyes closed. He fell fast asleep.

Ron squeezed the hand, the big thick fingers.

"I'm going to be home more, Pop," he said. "I'll be right here with you."

Around the same time Woody got sick, Ron proposed to Elizabeth O'Neal and she accepted. They planned a wedding for the following fall.

But soon, bumps began appearing in the road.

"He doesn't talk to me," Elizabeth complained, noting in the next breath that he hated being alone, and how weary she was of having people around constantly. Ness, Motley people, witnesses, other lawyers, politicians, pilots, assistants. Where is *our* time? she wondered. Either Ron's life didn't belong to him, or Ron refused to admit it was his. It amounted to the same thing.

And there was his drinking, which turned him into someone else entirely.

They fought, and in May 1999, she walked out and got herself an apartment in Tulsa, Oklahoma. The engagement was off.

Then one day, Ron Motley collapsed.

In late May, he was having lunch with a lawyer involved in a lead-paint lawsuit at the Windsor Court Hotel in New Orleans when his pulse began racing. He felt nauseous, and had to excuse himself.

There had been a number of similar episodes, and in January, doctors had diagnosed an overproduction of adrenaline, triggered by stress. In plain language, panic attacks. The fee war at Ness, Motley, his troubles with Elizabeth, and Woody's illness had driven his normally high tension level over the breaking point and, working synergistically with his drinking, triggered the panic episodes, his doctor told him.

He was given a tranquilizer called Ativan for it, but it made him dopey, so he took it only when he felt an attack coming on.

But the attacks became more severe and more frequent.

After the incident at lunch, a New Orleans lawyer drove him to the airport, zigzagging through heavy traffic. Motley's heart began to palpitate. He broke into a sweat.

At the airport, he took Ativan. He tried walking around the tarmac to burn off the adrenaline, but his legs suddenly gave way and he collapsed against a chain-link fence, holding on, panting.

He was taken to the emergency room, but after two hours, the symptoms subsided and he flew home. Floating on the *Themis* in Charleston Harbor, he felt better, but suffered two more attacks on consecutive days while running.

The final straw came the day after the second one, when a panic surge felled him about nine o'clock at night as he stood near the stairs that ran between the *Themis*'s decks. He had the remarkable sensation of his body filling with electricity as his legs crumpled and he dropped like a sack of potatoes down the stairs, landing on his shoulder.

A by-now badly frightened Motley, who easily could have fallen into the dark water of Charleston harbor and drowned, was hospitalized at Medical University Hospital, on the same floor from which Woody had recently been discharged. Elizabeth flew immediately to Charleston after getting an emergency phone call from Larry Sanders, Motley's bodyguard and now Ness, Motley's director of security. She helped her former fiancé get settled into his hospital bed.

"Things've got to change, Ron," she said.

"I know," he said.

"You're fifty-four," she said.

"I know," said Motley.

Then Woody hobbled in on crutches.

He patted his son's shoulder.

"Somethin' wrong here. You supposed to be visiting *me*," he rumbled.

Motley's pulse swung wildly for a while, then settled down. Tests were run. After three days he was pronounced medically stable and released.

When Gary Huber heard about Motley's attacks, he thought it could be something called Wernicke's encephalopathy.

"It comes from a lifetime of drinking," he explained. "Alcohol at that level for that long becomes a neurotoxin. It's very classic. They lose their legs."

MOTLEY CAME BACK FROM THE HOSPITAL AND SAT WITH Elizabeth on the living room sofa. The *Themis* was large enough that it had as many rooms as most houses: dining room, living room, den, master bedroom, guest bedroom, game room. It was a very big boat.

Elizabeth had been after him, gently, about his drinking for some time. He drank enough on enough nights that sooner or later, it had to kill him.

"You have so much. And you've done so much," said Elizabeth. "You should be around to enjoy it a little. And I'd like to be able to enjoy it—and enjoy you."

"You're right," said Motley.

"And?" asked Elizabeth.

"And I'm gonna try," said Motley.

Four months later, on September 25, 1999, Ron Motley and Elizabeth O'Neal were married.

THERE ARE ALWAYS LOOSE ENDS. ONE EVENING MOTLEY was at his desk after everyone had gone home and found an envelope of photographs of Gary Huber and the Harvard Project. He knew Huber felt cut off, but from Motley's viewpoint there was little to say. He couldn't lead Huber on to some glowing moment of vindication. Not now.

Huber had turned over quite a number of photographs and other artifacts from his Harvard days. There was a picture of the young scientist at his desk in the hospital in Boston at which the Harvard Project was headquartered. Absorbed in some paperwork, he sat with his long arms folded in front of him. On the wall behind him was a portrait of David Hardy, which someone at Shook, Hardy & Bacon had given Huber after Hardy's death. The original still hangs in the lawyers' lounge in Kansas City. Another photo showed the painting close up. This is Hardy at the end of life, neatly cropped hair graying along the sides, holding a pipe. He gazes steadily from the frame, a trace of a smile above his broad chin. Under the portrait is a bronze plaque reading: "A man of utter simplicity and of the utmost sophistication; a fighter but also a lover; one who gave and at the same time received. A friend."

Motley held the picture carefully by one edge, regarding the face. Then he ripped it up and dropped the pieces into the wastebasket. He turned out the light. And he went home.

CLIFF DOUGLAS WENT TO THE RALLY IN WASHINGTON EVEN though he was not scheduled to speak and was fully occupied elsewhere, helping Miami lawyer Stanley Rosenblatt get ready for an all-Florida class-action suit, which was just weeks away from trial. Douglas was also polishing a legal analysis of why the federal government should sue the tobacco companies along the lines of the state AG suits, which would circulate in the Justice Department. It ultimately helped convince Justice that a medical cost recovery action suit was feasible, and a year later, the feds dropped their criminal investigation and filed a massive civil lawsuit.

He was working hard on the Florida case, and tried to get Victor DeNoble to testify. At first, DeNoble agreed. Some time later, Douglas and DeNoble spoke again, and this time DeNoble said his fee for being a witness was $10,000 a day, which Douglas considered ridiculous and far more than Rosenblatt could afford. Douglas persuaded DeNoble to take less. A few days later, Douglas got a voice mail message from DeNoble saying that he was sorry, but he would no longer be involved in tobacco litigation.

Douglas was disappointed. In contrast, former Philip Morris scientist William Farone, who had worked closely with Douglas for years, gave an affidavit in another case in which Douglas was involved and his "payment" was a painting of orchids, Farone being a dedicated gardener.

On the whole, it had been such a rotten summer for the anti-tobacco forces that Douglas thought this late-September gathering might be a morale booster, plus he would be accompanying a cancer survivors group with whom he frequently worked. But once there, the thing had a bad smell to it. Ten thousand people had been bused in from all over the country and gathered on a warm Friday evening at the Reflecting Pool by the Lincoln Memorial. It was a sort of ill-defined nineties feel-good event grouped around the theme of finding a cure for cancer, not very hard to support. It turned out that the rally was funded by big drug companies, not victims, so prevention was almost never mentioned.

Douglas couldn't help but notice that during the entire first day of the rally there was not a single reference to lung cancer, the biggest cancer killer in the world. His friends in the anti-cancer community called lung the "invisible cancer" because it receives little attention from the pharmaceutical industry, and this for the simple reason that the transition from lung cancer patient to corpse is so swift and certain, the victim is unlikely to soak up a lot of medication.

As the evening wore on, speaker after speaker took the stage to decry the perils of cancer and demand more funding, more research. Jesse Jackson spent an hour warning black folks to stay away from all that pork barbecue. Other celebrities, like Scott Hamilton, the figure skater, and Andrea Jaeger, tennis player, gave speeches. The evening was almost over and Douglas was becoming more and more incensed. After four solid years of escalating anti-tobacco warfare, here he was at the biggest goddamned cancer event he'd ever seen and the words *lung cancer,* much less *cigarette company,* had yet to be said.

Also infuriated was Douglas's friend and soul mate Susan Levine, who had heard Douglas speak the previous year to a group of cancer victims that included her now-deceased daughter Deena. Levine stood at a little distance from Douglas, toward the back of the throng.

Exchanging a knowing look, Douglas and Levine both started to walk from the back of the audience toward the stage, which was right in front of the Lincoln Memorial, and as Douglas threaded his way through the crowd, he saw there was really no security, just people wearing some kind of identification badges who were no more than parade marshals, standing by metal barriers.

As he reached the first barrier, he and Levine exchanged another glance and crept past it. They made it to the second barrier, right at the foot of the stage, where they were stopped by an official. By now, Douglas was ready to storm the barricades and seize the microphone, but Levine used her considerable powers of persuasion and talked her way around the official. Soon they were on the stairs that led up to the stage, where someone was handing out candles to a group of relatives of cancer victims or recovered victims, one of whom was Michael Milken, another of whom was Susan Levine, and a third of whom was, well, Cliff Douglas. Still on stage were Reverend Jackson, Hamilton, Jaeger, and the other celebrities.

So Douglas just walked onstage with the cancer survivors, even though he'd never had cancer, and was intent on giving a really different kind of message than the survivors were.

Each candle holder went to the microphone, made a short statement mentioning the loved one's name and the type of cancer, then stepped back into the group and lit his or her candle. And when Levine was the next to go up, Douglas turned to her and they shared this strange feeling of being about to talk to ten thousand people about something rather personal.

Their turn came and Douglas walked to the microphone with Levine and stood in the glare of the floodlights with his arm around her. Levine, a short-haired blond woman, cupped the mike and said:

"This is for my daughter, Deena, dead of lung cancer at age twenty-eight from cigarettes. Deena started smoking when she was fifteen."

Then Douglas leaned over and said:

"I am here with my friend Susan to say that it's shocking that not a single speaker has had the presence of mind or courage to talk about cigarette smoking, until now. Cigarette smoking is the leading cause of cancer in America. Lung cancer, most of which is caused by cigarette smoking, is the leading cause of cancer deaths in America, and now it's passed breast cancer as the leading cancer killer of women. Reverend Jackson mentioned diet. He should have mentioned cigarette smoking, too."

A good, solid cheer rose up from the crowd. As soon as Douglas got back to his spot and lit his candle, General Norman Schwarzkopf, the hero of the Persian Gulf War, went up, said a few prepared words, then very pointedly added, "And I also light my candle for my mother, dead of lung cancer from cigarette smoking," and looked over at Levine and Douglas. Levine ran up and hugged him.

At the march the following day, Graham Nash and David Crosby performed, and Nash urged the crowd to fight the tobacco industry and keep children away from cigarettes. And the Reverend Jesse Jackson gave a radically altered version of his sermon of the night before, skipping over all that stuff about staying away from the pork barbecue, and instead railing against the tobacco companies, which made for a much more fiery sermon, replacing pork barbecue with the devil.

Douglas went back to his motel room and called Martha and told her what he had done. Then a great wave of joy came over him, and he felt filled with Satyagraha, the Truth Force, or maybe more the feeling of having kicked the asses of some bad guys, which is not really Gandhi, but maybe not so very far from him either, and about as American as you can get. And Douglas jumped on the bed and punched the air in celebration.

ACKNOWLEDGMENTS

Much of this book is an eyewitness account, based on what I saw during six years covering the siege of this peculiar industry. None of the scenes in this book have been invented, but human recollections are imperfect, especially for events that may have happened decades ago, and to retell them, minor extrapolations are inevitable.

Nevertheless, with the exception of three names that have been changed—Diana Dollinger, Oscar, and Dr. Thuo—accuracy has been respected. Wherever possible, multiple sources have been interviewed to reconstruct what happened. Thousands of pages of industry documents liberated through the lawsuits have been consulted to buttress the narrative. More than three hundred interviews were conducted.

A number of those who spoke to me can't be thanked by name because they requested and received my assurance of confidentiality. Nothing worthwhile in journalism is done without people like them. So I am perhaps most indebted to those to whom I can never adequately express my appreciation.

I gratefully acknowledge several pioneering writers. Richard Kluger's *Ashes to Ashes* is both the *Encyclopaedia Britannica* and Gibbon of tobacco books, the one indispensable work. Philip Hilts's reporting for the *New York Times* and his book *Smokescreen*, were inspirational, as was the work of Alix Freedman in the *Wall Street Journal*, who, with Hilts and Walt Bogdanich, made contributions that radically changed the course of events reported here. I relied on Amy Singer, Myron Levin and Morton Mintz for their perceptive coverage of the *Horton* and *Cipollone* trials. I was fortunate also to have at my disposal Paul Brodeur's definitive volume on the asbestos wars, *Outrageous Misconduct: The Asbestos Industry on Trial,* which has lengthy, keenly observed sections on Ron Motley and Scott Baldwin, among others.

Web journalists and researchers like Gene Borio, Anne Landman, Jack Cannon, and Michael Tacelovsky have become a force to be reckoned with. These four have done the work of paid journalists, sometimes better, and always with the highest level of commitment, providing documents, legal papers, and, most important, news stories from around the world to anyone who signs on.

Above all, I owe an enormous debt of gratitude to Ron Motley, who opened his life to me as well as countless other doors that would otherwise never have opened. He is a man of great personal courage, and one of the warmest and most generous souls I have ever known. It has been my privilege to share some of his personal journey for the last six years, and I hope he is none the worse for it because of this book. I know I am much the better for being with him.

There are so many people who have helped. Keith Summa and Carrick Mollenkamp kept me in touch with the daily flow of events in a way I could not have done without them, and were terrific company on the road. Cliff Douglas trusted me with his life story, and was not only the source of some of the most important information this book contains, but a stalwart supporter of the project itself. Dr. Bruce Douglas, Frederica Douglas, Susan Levine, Joe Marx, Matthew Myers, Melanne Verveer and Martha Luckham, among others, contributed to my portrait of Douglas.

Woody Wilner and Ginny Steiger helped a month in Jacksonville pass by quite quickly. They fed me, took care of me, and diverted me by periodically putting me into airplanes and motorboats and driving around at high speed. Dana Raulerson, Stephanie Hartley, and Greg Maxwell were also indispensable during the *Connor* trial.

Walt Bogdanich granted multiple hours of interviews, reliving an experience that no one should have to go through even once, and James Neff's *Mobbed Up* and Thomas Maier's *Newhouse* provided additional background on Bogdanich's reporting career.

Jeff Wigand honored me with his confidence, his unparalleled knowledge, and his hospitality. Victor DeNoble gave many hours of his time and patiently explained the science of nicotine reinforcement, as did Paul Mele. Ann Ritter helped me understand the legal issues in countless phone calls, and provided innumerable details and materials that enriched the narrative. Jack McConnell and Charles Patrick dug out correspondence and documents and explained key events. Fred Baker helped a layman understand judicial decisions and documents. Merrell Williams hosted two visits to Ocean Springs and led me through his analysis of the tobacco wars. Dr. Gary Huber shared his personal archives and many extraordinary anecdotes, and he and his wife, Mary, had me to their home. Wendell Gauthier and Dickie Scruggs were the indispensable statesmen of their sometimes opposing legal camps and both were extremely gracious. Don Barrett always kept the faith, and has a contagious enthusiasm for this subject. Joe Rice, who almost never came home for three years, faithfully found time for me whenever I needed him. Dr. Larry Hastings took me to a memorable dinner at the Metropolitan Club, which usually won't even let people like me in, and Neil Rutledge provided details of the *Green* trial, while Caesar Belli, Kerry Alexander and Richard Gerry helped with other early tobacco cases. The late Lyman Field and his partner James Benjamin spoke to me about *Ross,* as did jurors Robert Ostermeyer and Alan Carpenter.

William Farone, Ian Uydess, Mitch Zeller, and I spoke frequently over a period of years and their insights were invaluable, as were those of Professor Richard Daynard.

I had the assistance of the following in piecing together Ron Motley's life and career: Solomon Blatt, Jr., William T. Jones, Lively Wilson, Henry Weinstein, Thomas Taft, Theresa Zagnoli, Ruby Neff, Sam Pryor, Jr., Joan Cusick, Steve Davis, Sandra Cone, Jennifer Motley, Mark Motley, Woody Motley, Dan Moore, and Patrick Alderson.

I have many friends at Ness, Motley who were simply indispensable during this project. Cheryl Glenn was unstintingly helpful in the waning days of the research, as was Laura Norris. Crucial assistance over a period of years came from Carolyn James, Sandra Burley, Tammy Cauley, Kim Vroon, Jodi Flowers, Stacy Shimek, Sally Roy, Christa Winn, Kim Atkinson, Alex Wagner, Ed Westbrook, Susan Nial, Larry Sanders, Karen Woods, Terry Richardson,

Andy Berly, and Jason Hamm. Elizabeth Motley, nee O'Neal, made me feel right at home whenever I was with her and Ron.

Attorney General Mike Moore shared some of his very precious free time with me and Attorneys General Christine Gregoire, Dick Blumenthal, and Grant Woods granted multiple interviews, as did Steve Berman, Tom Green and Congressmen Martin Meehan, Henry Waxman, and their staffs.

Other lawyers who made substantial contributions include Christopher Placitella, who first introduced me to Ron Motley, and Gary Galiher, who shared some wonderful stories, as did Scott Baldwin, one of the greatest trial lawyers of all time, and Cindy Langston. W. C. Gentry and Wayne Hogan were class acts among the Florida lawyers. Stanley and Susan Rosenblatt entered the tobacco battle long before most, and are still in it.

A number of people in the tobacco industry and its law firms were extremely helpful. First and foremost was Philip Morris's Steven Parrish, who provided extraordinary insight into the decision-making at the top of the industry. Aaron Marks, of Kasowitz, Benson, Torres & Friedman, spoke to me at length, along with Bennett LeBow and his spokesman, Paul Caminiti. Dan Donahue, at R. J. Reynolds, and Don Hoel, William Ohlemeyer, Gary Long, and Dale Chaffin at Shook, Hardy & Bacon also granted interviews.

Others who extended valuable assistance—or upon whose written works I relied for background—include: in Mississippi, Michael Lewis, James Carroll, Thomas Rhoden, Steve Bozeman, Charles Mikhail, Ava Butler, Jimmy Sherriel Clark, Roe Frazer, Shane Langston, Tom Wixon; in Florida, Patricia McEvoy, Kim Tucker, Robert Butterworth, Mike Maher; from the *Castano* trial, John Coale, Russ Herman, Suzy Foulds, Elizabeth Cabraser, Julie Beiser, Joe Bruno, Walter Leger, Richard Heimann; among plaintiff's lawyers, J. D. Lee, Jim Early, Marc Edell, Alan Darnell, Patrick Coughlin, Frank Janacek, Kenneth McClain, Greg Leyh, Graham Esdale, Rhett Klok, Evan Yegelwel; in Washington, Ralph Nader, Joseph Belluck, Sander Lurie, Allison Zieve, Alan Morrison, John Banzhaf, Jack Mitchell; for scientific and technical assistance, Dietrich Hoffmann, Dr. Michael Baden, Bogdan Prokopczyk, William Rosen, Dr. Lowell Bush, Dr. John Pauly, Jack Henningfield, Dr. Neal Benowitz, Dr. John Slade; on advertising and youth targeting, Dr. Joseph DiFranza, Dr. Paul Fischer, Dr. John Pierce, Dr. Adam Goldstein,

Richard Pollay; in Texas, Dan Wess, Grant Kaiser, Harold Nix, John Eddie Williams, Walter Umphrey, Wayne Reaud, John O'Quinn, Tom Banning, Harry Potter, Ward Tisdale, and Ron Dusek; in Muncie, Will Riley, Joe Young, and Greg Cross; on CTR, John Kreisher, Vincent Lisanti, and Kurt Enslein; among the press, Peter Jennings, Mark Curriden, Michelle Nicholasen, Marrie Campbell, David Fanning, Joe Menn, Chip Jones, Bob Kur, Kate Berry; for help with legal questions, Robert Blakey, Michael Rustad, Donald Garner, Gary Schwartz; in Minnesota, Michael Ciresi, Roberta Walburn, Corey Gordon, and Eric Johnson; among plaintiffs, Dianne Castano, Susan Haines, and Grady Carter.

I had research assistance from Eric Epstein, Annie Ruderman, and Heather Murray. At the very top of the list is researcher Jennifer Borkowski, who refused to leave this project, despite pitiful pay, until the bitter end. She brought intelligence and energy to everything she did.

This book grew out of two articles in the *Nation* that were shaped and nurtured by its savvy editor, Katrina vanden Heuvel. An editor at Harcourt Brace, Yoji Yamaguchi, showed the initial interest that got me to bring this story to a publisher sooner rather than never. Steven Schechter began as lawyer and adviser to a neophyte author, but became a true friend.

My editor at Delacorte, Tom Spain, understood what this project was all about from the moment he saw my rather murky proposal, and gave it the strongest backing and most generous encouragement at every stage, while putting up with numerous delays. He took a chance on an unknown author with an unconventional bent and I will never forget it. His assistants Mitch Hoffman, Andrea Nicolay, and Theresa Pulle helped with dozens of questions about the publishing process, always cheerfully and professionally.

My mother, Patricia Sargent Zegart, is the original—and still the best—writer in the family, and she and my sister Caroline, a talented artist, have supported my career despite its many culs-de-sac.

My former reporting colleague and indispensable friend Peter Page kept me going through every phase of this project with warm, unconditional encouragement. Another friend, Kent Olson, pinpointed legal and biographical details, and critiqued the manuscript.

Laura Zegart's name deserves to stand apart. A talented photojournalist, she worked six-day weeks to support me financially while

I did this project, yet mustered the will to keep up my spirits. If the book has a heart, it is hers.

And last, I would never have written anything without the example of my father, Arthur, a documentary filmmaker who saw the golden age of television news turn bronze, or maybe something cheaper. He was a brilliant reporter, with an affinity for what lay beneath the surface. Above all, he was a dreamer: of better times, of better worlds, and someday perhaps, of better men.

ABOUT THE AUTHOR

DAN ZEGART is a seasoned journalist whose articles have appeared in newspapers and magazines throughout the country, including Ms., Penthouse, and The Nation. he lives with his wife, Laura, in Titusville, New Jersey.

INDEX